Imperialism, Sovereignty and the Making of International Law

This book examines the relationship between imperialism and international law. It argues that colonial confrontation was central to the formation of international law and, in particular, its founding concept, sovereignty. Traditional histories of the discipline present colonialism and non-European peoples as peripheral concerns. By contrast, Anghie argues that international law has always been animated by the 'civilizing mission' – the project of governing non-European peoples. Racial discrimination, cultural subordination and economic exploitation are constitutively significant for the discipline, rather than aberrations that have been overcome by modern international law. In developing these arguments, the book examines different phases of the colonial encounter, ranging from the sixteenth century to the League of Nations period and the current 'war against terror'. Anghie provides a new approach to the history of international law, illuminating the imperial character of the discipline and its enduring significance for peoples of the Third World.

ANTONY ANGHIE is Professor of Law at the S. J. Quinney School of Law, University of Utah. He received his LLB (Hons.) and BA (Hons.) degrees from Monash University, Melbourne, Australia, and his SJD degree from Harvard Law School. He practised law for several years in Melbourne, and now teaches Contracts and various subjects in the International Law curriculum, including International Business Transactions and International Environmental Law. He has served as a tutor at Monash and Melbourne Universities, where he has taught Development Politics and International Relations; and as a Teaching Fellow at Harvard College where he has taught International Relations. He also served as Senior Fellow at Harvard Law School and a Visiting Professor at the University of Tokyo. He is a member of the Third World Approaches to International Law network of scholars.

CAMBRIDGE STUDIES IN INTERNATIONAL AND COMPARATIVE LAW

Established in 1946, this series produces high-quality scholarship in the fields of public and private international law and comparative law. Although these are distinct legal subdisciplines, developments since 1946 confirm their interrelation.

Comparative law is increasingly used as a tool in the making of law at national, regional and international levels. Private international law is now often affected by international conventions, and the issues faced by classical conflicts rules are frequently dealt with by substantive harmonisation of law under international auspices. Mixed international arbitrations, especially those involving state economic activity, raise mixed questions of public and private international law, while in many fields (such as the protection of human rights and democratic standards, investment guarantees and international criminal law) international and national systems interact. National constitutional arrangements relating to 'foreign affairs', and to the implementation of international norms, are a focus of attention.

The Board welcomes works of a theoretical or interdisciplinary character, and those focusing on the new approaches to international or comparative law or conflicts of law. Studies of particular institutions or problems are equally welcome, as are translations of the best work published in other languages.

Imperialism, Sovereignty and the Making of International Law

Antony Anghie

S. J. Quinney School of Law, University of Utah

CAMBRIDGE
UNIVERSITY PRESS

PUBLISHED BY THE PRESS SYNDICATE OF THE UNIVERSITY OF CAMBRIDGE
The Pitt Building, Trumpington Street, Cambridge, United Kingdom

CAMBRIDGE UNIVERSITY PRESS
The Edinburgh Building, Cambridge, CB2 2RU, UK
40 West 20th Street, New York, NY 10011–4211, USA
477 Williamstown Road, Port Melbourne, VIC 3207, Australia
Ruiz de Alarcón 13, 28014 Madrid, Spain
Dock House, The Waterfront, Cape Town 8001, South Africa

http://www.cambridge.org

First published 2005

Printed in the United Kingdom at the University Press, Cambridge

Typeface Swift 10/13 pt.   *System* LATEX 2$_\varepsilon$ [TB]

A catalogue record for this book is available from the British Library

Library of Congress Cataloguing in Publication data
Anghie, Antony.
Imperialism, sovereignty, and the making of international law/Antony Anghie.
   p. cm. – (Cambridge studies in international and comparative law; 37)
Includes bibliographical references and index.
ISBN 0 521 82892 9
1. International law. 2. Imperialism. 3. Sovereignty. 4. Indigenous peoples – Legal
status, laws, etc. I. Title. II. Cambridge studies in international and comparative law
(Cambridge, England : 1996); 37.
KZ3410.A54 2004
341 – dc22   2004049732

ISBN 0 521 82892 9 hardback

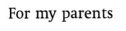

For my parents

Contents

Foreword

In this challenging book, Dr. Anghie examines a series of episodes in the legal history of the relations between the West and non-Western polities. He argues that they possess common features, reproducing at different epochs and in different ways an underlying pattern of domination and subordination – and doing so despite continued professions of idealism and universal values by the (Western) lawyers and leaders who have been dominantly engaged.

The first of these episodes dates from the earliest phase of international law. Of the five studied, it is the least institutional. Rather it is an episode of justification and apology – Vitoria's attempt to deal with the rights of the Amerindians faced with Spanish colonization. Of course, Vitoria was dealing with this problem after the event and he was teaching (a generation after Columbus) in the Catholic tradition of moral–religious theory and not as a self-perceived international lawyer. But his work, Anghie argues, inaugurated our subject. From the beginning, international law was not exclusively concerned with the relations between states but, and more importantly, with the relations between civilizations and peoples. Moreover these were relations of *domination*. Colonization and Empire were present at the creation, and the apologetic use of universalist ideals has never been abandoned, whatever new forms it may have taken.

The second episode is that of the 1884–5 Congress of Berlin and the final stages of colonial expansion. It was as a result of this process – or, as with Japan and Siam, of the pre-emptive adoption of Western techniques (including international law) by the few entities that managed to survive it without losing their independence – that international law became global. The ancient ideal of universality was realized as a result of and in the course of the substantial (and historically rather recent) suppression of the non-Western world. In the process the concept of 'civilization' was used as a form of the *exclusion* of non-Western values, of non-Western identity and even of legal personality. This process can be traced through writers such as Westlake just as much as through statesmen such as Bismarck or events such as the Maori wars.

The third episode is that of the Mandate System under the League of Nations, the beginning of the reversal of colonization that was effectively completed under the United Nations. Under the guise of a 'sacred trust of civilization', Western powers (and Japan) under nominal international tutelage applied the concept of the sacred trust to effect the reality of exploitation. The 1992 *Nauru* Case is an illustration, even if it is one for which a modicum of compensation was, uniquely, obtained after the event.[1]

And when, after a long process, independence was achieved (for all but one of the mandated territories[2]) and extended beyond the original list of mandates to all colonial territories, the independence that was granted turned out to be less than it seemed. The newly independent states (this is the fourth episode) fought to develop new rules, even a new international economic order. But in the event the Bretton Woods Institutions triumphed, imposing their own view of development and a certain set of structures of governance on half the world's population and a majority of its governments. The outcome has been, on the whole, increased indebtedness and new forms of dependence.

Finally (for the time being) we have the war on terrorism, a new form of branding of a significant fraction of the world, in particular the Muslim world, as barbarian and as enemies. In Dr Anghie's words, 'law . . . in the name of security, reproduces a new form of imperialism.' Moreover it is a new imperialism in which neo-conservatism vies with neo-liberalism in the assertion of control.

International lawyers have always assumed that their subject existed BC (before colonization), just as they have tended to assume its florescence, as yet open and undetermined, in our time of AD (after decolonization). Anghie's thesis is that we live still in a common era of Continued Empire (CE), albeit under new forms. Not everyone will agree with his argument, or that each of his chosen instances necessarily exemplifies it. Evidently there is a measure of generalization and simplification. There

---

[1] *Certain Phosphate Lands in Nauru (Nauru v. Australia)*, ICJ Reports 1989 p. 15. Following the decision the claim was settled by Australia, with subsequent contributions from the two partner governments.

[2] Palestine is still the exception.

are many differences among 'Third World' states, and we should resist equating 'Third World' with 'the countries that lack governance' or those in which 'development has failed'; otherwise debates about governance and development will become viciously circular.

It must be admitted that the general theme of the work – that '[t]he colonial history of international law is concealed even when it is reproduced' – is sobering. The book is not, however, unrelievedly pessimistic. In Anghie's view 'the Third World cannot abandon international law because law now plays such a vital role in the public realm in the interpretation of virtually all international events'. It may be doubted whether 'it is possible to create an international law that is not imperial', and faith in the future is hardly balanced by our recorded history of good works. But the fact remains that, although not under circumstances of their own choosing, people and communities do nevertheless make their own history; indeed they are condemned to do so. An understanding of those circumstances, we may hope, may help prevent their endless repetition under new forms. In this way, we can read Anghie as challenging us to think of ways of creating a non-imperial international law.

James Crawford

Lauterpacht Research Centre for International Law
University of Cambridge

Acknowledgements

I have acquired many debts over the years it has taken me to write this book. My profound thanks are due to Nathaniel Berman, Abram Chayes, B. S. Chimni, Robert Chu, Karen Engle, James Thuo Gathii, Daniel Greenwood, Qadri Ismail, Susil Jayaratne, Karen Knop, Martti Koskenniemi, Mitchel Lasser, Karin Mickelson, Herbert Morais, Vasuki Nesiah, Celestine Nyamu, Liliana Obregon, Obiora Okafor, Onuma Yasuaki, Ileana Porras, Balakrishnan Rajagopal, Rhee Zha Hyoung, Annelise Riles, Kerry Rittich, Henry Steiner, Detlev Vagts and Robert Wai, who all contributed in different ways to my thinking on the issues I explore in this book. I owe a special debt to my colleagues in the Third World Approaches to International Law network of scholars who persuaded me that the lines of inquiry undertaken here were worth pursuing. This book originated as a SJD thesis which I completed at Harvard Law School, and I am grateful to K. Anthony Appiah and Duncan Kennedy, who were on my thesis committee, for their valuable guidance. Thomas Franck, one of my examiners, provided me with extremely acute, detailed and illuminating comments, the true significance of which, in some cases, I realised only years later. I have the great good fortune of being the student of two extraordinary teachers. Christopher Weeramantry inspired me by his example to take up the study of international law and he has been unstinting in his support and concern ever since I was his student. His vision of international justice, his integrity, his erudition and wisdom establish the standards to which I will always aspire but never attain. David Kennedy supervised my thesis, and his brilliance, support, encouragement and provocation were indispensable to the writing of this work. It was only gradually, as I embarked on my own teaching career, that I better appreciated the magnitude of the generosity, insight and understanding that he extended to me, and that made this work, for better or worse, possible. His vision and dedication created a remarkable SJD programme at Harvard Law School, which supported not only my own scholarship, but that of many other younger scholars whose important and innovative work was uniquely appreciated and encouraged. I am indebted to two institutions in particular. My colleagues at the S. J. Quinney School of Law, at the University of Utah, through their kindness and support, provided an ideal environment in which I could pursue my work, as did the Graduate Programme at Harvard Law School and all the people associated with it during the five years I spent there. Mike Truman and Aaron Jordan provided both superb research assistance and much-needed organization. John Bevan and Laura Ngai of the S. J. Quinney law library were indefatigable in locating and providing me with the most obscure and elusive materials. The University of Utah provided me with a Faculty Fellowship and sabbatical leave that made my research possible during the last stages of the writing of this work. The S. J. Quinney School of Law provided me with financial support through the Summer Stipend Program. My thanks to the University of Tokyo and Onuma Yasuaki for enabling me to spend three valuable months at the University of Tokyo. I am also very grateful to James Crawford who was kind enough to write the Foreword to this book, and who also made several valuable suggestions and corrections. At Cambridge University Press, many thanks to Finola O'Sullivan, Jane O'Regan, Mary Leighton and Barbara Docherty for their patience and professionalism. This book was completed in February 2004.

Parts of this book have been previously published, in somewhat different form, as 'Francisco de Vitoria and the Colonial Origins of International Law', 5(3) *Social and Legal Studies*, 321–336 (1996); 'Francisco de Vitoria and the Colonial Origins of International Law', in *Laws of the Postcolonial*, edited by Eve Darian-Smith and Peter Fitzpatrick, University of Michigan Press (1999), pp. 89–109; 'Finding the Peripheries: Sovereignty and Colonialism in Nineteenth Century International Law', 40(1) *Harvard International Law Journal* (Winter 1999), 1–80; 'Colonialism and the Birth of International Institutions: Sovereignty, Economy and the Mandate System of the League of Nations', 34(3) *New York University Journal of International Law and Politics* (Spring 2002), 513–633. *Omnia pro deo.*

Table of cases

Table of treaties

Introduction

The empires of our time were short lived, but they have altered the world forever; their passing away is their least significant feature.[1]

The colonizer constructs himself as he constructs the colony. The relationship is intimate, an open secret that cannot be part of official knowledge.[2]

The themes and concerns that animate this book emerged from my experiences as a research assistant working for C. G. Weeramantry who was then Chief Commissioner of an Inquiry established by the Government of Nauru to examine the history of the phosphate mining that took place on the island. The League of Nations placed Nauru under a mandate and appointed three partner governments, Australia, New Zealand and the United Kingdom to be the mandatory powers. In effect, however, Nauru was administered by Australia, acting on behalf of the partner governments, first as a mandate territory under the League and then, as a trusteeship territory under the United Nations. Nauru was rich in phosphates and the Australian administration commenced mining the phosphates very shortly after assuming control over Nauru. The mining operations, which was very destructive to the territory, had been opposed by the people of Nauru, who asserted that they held the three partner governments responsible for the damage caused. Upon becoming an independent state, Nauru continued to maintain this claim, which was consistently denied by the partner governments. Finally in 1986, Nauru established a Commission of Inquiry and gave it the task of examining the legal, historical and scientific aspects of the phosphate industry, and the feasibility of rehabilitating the worked-out phosphate lands. Acting

[1] V. S. Naipaul, *The Mimic Men* (Harmondsworth: Penguin Books, 1980), p. 32.
[2] Gayatri Chakravorty Spivak, *A Critique of Postcolonial Reason: Toward a History of the Vanishing Present* (Cambridge, MA: Harvard University Press, 1999), p. 203.

1

upon the conclusions of that Inquiry, the government of Nauru sought
compensation from the partner governments for the exploitation of the
phosphates and for the massive environmental damage that had been
caused to the territory of Nauru as a result of the mining.

It is surely the fantasy of every student who has ever participated
in the Jessup international law mooting competition to research a dispute that could eventually be presented to the International Court of
Justice; and the central issue involved in this case could hardly have
been more compelling to me: was it possible for a formerly dependent territory to bring a claim in international law for what in essence
was colonial exploitation? Professors Ian Brownlie, Barry Connell, James
Crawford, V. S. Mani and C. G. Weeramantry were all involved in
analysing and advising on this matter, and my fellow research assistant,
Deborah Cass and I were in the extraordinarily fortunate position of wit-
nessing how these expert international lawyers approached the issues
and constructed the case that was later argued before the International
Court of Justice.

While the needs and demands of the Inquiry consumed my immediate attention, what I found both curious and disturbing, as I researched
the questions arising from the dispute – and this involved examining
many aspects of the relationship between colonialism and international
law – was the fact that international law had not only legitimized colonial exploitation, a fact well established by many Third World scholars but, in addition, it appeared to me, had developed many mechanisms to prevent any claims for colonial reparations. The acquisition of
sovereignty by the Third World was an extraordinarily significant event;
and yet, various limitations and disadvantages appeared to be somehow peculiarly connected with that sovereignty. In any event, 'Third
World' sovereignty appeared quite distinctive as compared with the
defining Western sovereignty. What, then, were the links, the nature
of the relationships connecting sovereignty, colonialism and international law? This was the question I took with me to my graduate
studies, and it gave specific form to a more general question that distinguished Third World scholars had asked for many years and that
had begun to preoccupy my own work: how is it possible to construct an international law that is responsive to the needs and aspirations of the peoples of the Third World? When I wrote about the
case when it was finally argued before the International Court of Justice, I tentatively formulated the arguments that colonialism was central to the development of international law, and that sovereignty

doctrine emerged out of the colonial encounter. This book further explores and elaborates on the basic themes presented in that initial article.[3]

These are the beginnings of this book, which examines the historical relationship between international law and the 'Third World'[4] – the contemporary term for those non-European societies and territories which were colonized from the sixteenth century onwards by the European Empires, and which acquired political independence since the 1940s. My broad argument is that colonialism was central to the constitution of international law in that many of the basic doctrines of international law – including, most importantly, sovereignty doctrine – were forged out of the attempt to create a legal system that could account for relations between the European and non-European worlds in the colonial confrontation. In making this argument, I focus on the colonial origins of international law; I attempt, furthermore, to show how these origins create a set of structures that continually repeat themselves at various stages in the history of international law. In so doing I seek to challenge conventional histories of the discipline which present colonialism as peripheral, an unfortunate episode that has long since been overcome by the heroic initiatives of decolonization that resulted in the emergence of colonial societies as independent, sovereign states.

I examine the relationship between international law and colonialism by focusing on the civilizing mission, the grand project that has justified colonialism as a means of redeeming the backward, aberrant, violent, oppressed, undeveloped people of the non-European world by incorporating them into the universal civilization of Europe. I argue that in the field of international law, the civilizing mission was animated by what I crudely term the question of 'cultural difference'. The imperial idea that fundamental cultural differences divided the European and non-European worlds was profoundly important to the civilizing mission in

---

[3] Antony Anghie, 'The Heart of my Home: Colonialism, Environmental Damage, and the Nauru Case', (1993) 34 *Harvard International Law Journal* 445–506.

[4] The term 'Third World' might be anachronistic and misleading, but I will use it nevertheless. For some recent works which point in very different ways to the usefulness of the term, see B. S. Chimni, 'Third World Approaches to International Law: A Manifesto', in Antony Anghie, Bhupinder Chimni, Karin Mickelson and Obiora Okafor (eds.), *The Third World and International Order: Law, Politics and Globalization* (Leiden: Brill Academic Publishers, Martinus Nijhoff, 2003), pp. 47–75 at pp. 48–51; Karin Mickelson, 'Rhetoric and Rage: Third World Voices in International Legal Discourse', (1998) 16(2) *Wisconsin International Law Journal* 353–419; Balakrishnan Rajagopal, 'International Law and Third World Resistance: A Theoretical Inquiry' in Anghie, Chimni, Mickelson and Okafor, *The Third World*, pp. 145–172.

a number of ways: for example, the characterization of non-European societies as backward and primitive legitimized European conquest of these societies and justified the measures colonial powers used to control and transform them. Equally, however, the assertion of this dichotomy between the two worlds, the civilized and the uncivilized, posed several novel problems for the European jurists who sought to account for the colonial project in legal terms. How could it be claimed the European civilization, in all its avowed specificity, was somehow universal and binding on non-European states?

International lawyers over the centuries maintained this basic dichotomy between the civilized and the uncivilized, even while refining and elaborating their understanding of each of these terms. Having established this dichotomy, furthermore, jurists continually developed techniques for overcoming it by formulating legal doctrines directed towards civilizing the uncivilized world. I use the term 'dynamic of difference' to denote, broadly, the endless process of creating a gap between two cultures, demarcating one as 'universal' and civilized and the other as 'particular' and uncivilized, and seeking to bridge the gap by developing techniques to normalize the aberrant society. My argument is that this dynamic animated the development of many of the central doctrines of international law – most particularly, sovereignty doctrine. The dynamic is self-sustaining and indeed, as I shall argue, endless; each act of arrival reveals further horizons, each act of bridging further differences that international law must seek to overcome. It is in this way that international law extends itself horizontally, to encompass the entire globe and, once this is achieved, vertically, within each society, to ensure the emergence of civilized states.

Despite what I claim to be the centrality of colonialism for the generation of international law, the relationship between international law and the colonial encounter has not been seen in this way. Rather, many international lawyers, from both the First and the Third world[5] write as if international law came to the colonies fully formed and ready for application, as if the colonial project simply entailed assimilating these aberrant societies into an existing, stable, 'Eurocentric' system – as if, in

---

[5] Mohammed Bedjaoui, one of the foremost Third World jurists, appears to subscribe to this view when stating that 'The New World was to be Europeanized and evangelized, which meant that the system of European international law did not change fundamentally as a result of its geographic extension to continents other than Europe'. Mohammed Bedjaoui, 'General Introduction', in Mohammed Bedjaoui, *International Law: Achievements and Prospects* (Boston: Martinus Nijhoff, 1991), p. 7.

short, the doctrines of international law solved the problem of difference by preceding it.

This understanding of the colonial encounter is characteristic of the traditional approach to international law, which understands the discipline in terms of the fundamental question of how order is created among sovereign states. For the traditionalists, international law may be broadly explained as an attempt to resolve this primordial problem, which acquired an especially threatening character when seized upon by the nineteenth-century positivist John Austin to make his famous argument that international law was not law properly so called because it did not emanate from a single, global sovereign. The attempts to resolve this problem, and the critiques of these attempts have, on the whole, constituted the central theoretical debate of the discipline.[6] The defining character of this problem to the whole discipline of international law is further reflected by the structure of many of the major textbooks of international law, which introduce the subject by outlining the problem and offering some sort of solution to it by suggesting the different ways in which international law could be regarded as law.[7]

European states were sovereign and equal. The colonial confrontation, however, particularly since the nineteenth century when colonialism reached its apogee, was not a confrontation between two sovereign states, but rather between a sovereign European state and a non-European society that was deemed by jurists to be lacking in sovereignty – or else, at best only partially sovereign. My argument, then, is that what passes now as the defining dilemma of the discipline, the problem of order among states, is a problem which, from the time of its origins, has been peculiar to the specificities of European history. And, further, that the extension and universalization of this European experience, which is achieved by transmuting it into the major theoretical problem of the discipline, has the effect of suppressing and subordinating other histories of international law and the peoples to whom it has applied. Within the axiomatic framework which decrees that European states are sovereign while non-European states are not, there is only one means of relating the history of the non-European world: it is a history

---

[6] The works of John Austin, and the response of nineteenth-century jurists to this charge, are examined in chapter 2.

[7] This is usually done under the rubric of something like: 'Is International Law Really Law?' See Louis Henkin, Richard C. Pugh, Oscar Schachter and Hans Smit, *International Law* (3rd edn., St Paul, MN: West Publishing Co., 1993).

of the incorporation of the peoples of Africa, Asia, the Americas and the Pacific into an international law which is explicitly European, and yet, universal. This task having been accomplished, the Third World having been granted all the powers of sovereignty, imperialism becomes only a matter of historical interest. This is the history I examine, not with a view to furthering it, but in an attempt to illuminate the tragedies and violence inherent[8] in the project of the civilizing mission, and its continuing operation in international law. My broad argument is that the very mechanisms by which the civilizing mission is furthered prevent its fulfilment, and that, further, the process of incorporation that is conventionally understood to be empowering and liberating for the Third World is, in significant ways, debilitating and excluding.

My approach to the colonial encounter differs from the traditional approach on a number of counts. First, I focus on the civilizing mission and the problem of cultural difference, and not on the issue of order among sovereign states. A focus on the problem of order among sovereign states cannot illuminate the prior question of how certain states were excluded from the realm of sovereignty in the first place. Secondly, I argue that the application of sovereignty doctrine to the colonies cannot be properly understood as the simple extension of sovereignty, as it developed in Europe, into the peripheral colonies. According to this version of the conventional history, the European model of sovereignty, established by the defining event of the Peace of Westphalia, was gradually extended to the non-European peripheries.[9] My argument, by contrast, is that sovereignty was improvised out of the colonial encounter, and adopted unique forms which differed from and destabilized given notions of European sovereignty. As a consequence, Third World sovereignty is distinctive, and rendered uniquely vulnerable and dependent by international law. Thirdly, I adopt a historical approach to sovereignty doctrine, seeking to show how the colonial encounter shaped the underlying structures of the doctrine. My broad argument, then, is that doctrinal and institutional developments in international law cannot be understood simply and always as logical elaborations of a stable, philosophically conceived sovereignty doctrine, as an outcome of the continuing attempt to create order among sovereign states. Rather, we might see

---

[8] Dipesh Chakrabarty, 'Postcoloniality and the Artifice of History: Who Speaks for "Indian" Pasts', in Ranajit Guha (ed.), *A Subaltern Studies Reader, 1986–1995* (Minneapolis, MN, University of Minnesota Press, 1997), p. 263.

[9] See Nathaniel Berman, 'In the Wake of Empire', (1999) 14 *American University International Law Review* 1521–1554 at 1523.

these doctrines and institutions as being generated by problems relating to colonial order.

Broadly, then, this approach enables an exploration of the problems and politics of who was sovereign and why, the relationship between ideas of culture and sovereignty and the ways in which sovereignty became identified with a specific set of cultural practices to the exclusion of others. What does it mean to say that 'international law governs sovereign states' when certain societies were denied sovereign status? What are the processes by which this denial was justified and enforced? What continuing effects follow from this exclusion? How does an understanding of these processes of denial offer a means of reinterpreting contemporary understandings of sovereignty doctrine? The practices of racial discrimination, economic exploitation, territorial dispossession and cultural subordination were all central to the imperial project, and it is by raising these broad questions of the relationship between colonialism and international law that I seek to explore their enduring significance for the discipline. The traditional approach tends to disregard the historical dimension of sovereignty, focusing instead on the powers and competences of the sovereign in attempting to adjudicate between competing sovereignties. The inequalities that were inherent in the colonial encounter are a thing of the past.

My account of the relationship between colonialism and international law also differs in certain respects from the extraordinarily important work done by pioneering Third World scholars such as, R. P. Anand, Mohammed Bedjaoui and T. O. Elias who have closely scrutinized the relationship between colonialism and international law.[10] Each of these figures, representatives of the 'New States', worked on articulating Third World perspectives and formulating a new international law by which the Third World could advance its own interests. At least two strategies characterized these efforts. First, many Third World jurists attempted to demonstrate that some of the fundamental principles of international law – relating, for example, to treaties and to equity – were also to be found in African or Eastern systems of thinking and statecraft and indeed, originated not in the West, but the colonial world itself.[11] In

---

[10] See chapter 4.

[11] This effort was provoked by comments of the sort made by J. H. W. Verzijl, 'the actual body of international law, as it stands today, is not only the product of the conscious activity of the European mind, but has also drawn its vital essence from a common source of European beliefs, and in both these aspects is mainly of Western European origin'. Cited in Bedjaoui, 'General Introduction', p. 9.

adopting this approach, these writers stressed the existence of certain universal principles regarding the character and exercise of authority. Secondly, many of these writers denounced classical international law as being the product of imperialism and a means by which European interests were promoted and maintained.[12] The law regulating the nationalization of alien property was classically cited as an example of this imperialist international law.[13] The project, then, was to excise these colonial aspects of international law from the system of international law and to recreate a new, open and non-colonial international law.

It is now hardly disputable that classical international law was complicit in the imperial project and the exploitation which accompanied it. If, however, the colonial encounter, with all its exclusions and subordinations, shaped the very foundations of international law, then grave questions must arise as to whether and how it is possible for the postcolonial world to construct a new international law that is liberated from these colonial origins. The question is an old one: can the postcolonial world deploy for its own purposes the law which had enabled its suppression in the first place? It is approached here from the different perspective offered by focusing on the impact of the colonial encounter on the underlying structures of international law.

It is by adopting this approach that I attempt to question conventional histories of international law, in an effort to understand why peoples living in Third World societies continue to be, on the whole, the most disadvantaged and marginalized. The study of history is in many respects a practical exercise, a means of facilitating and furthering the reconstructive project which a number of scholars, working within the traditions of Critical Race Theory, Feminism, Lat-Crit theory or Third World Approaches to International Law, have in common, the project of creating an international law that is responsive to the needs of variously disadvantaged peoples.

As against conventional histories, then, what may be required is the telling of alternative histories – histories of resistance to colonial power, history from the vantage point of the peoples who were subjected to international law and which are sensitive to the tendencies within such conventional histories to assimilate the specific, unique histories of non-European peoples within the broader concepts and controlling structures of such conventional histories. My work is indebted to the pioneering efforts of post-colonial scholars, working within a number of

---

[12] *Ibid.*, pp. 5–11.   [13] See chapter 4.

disciplines, who have attempted the task of interrogating conventional histories of imperialism.[14]

In sketching a history of the relationship between colonialism and international law, I have focused principally on the period from, roughly, 1870 to 2003. However, chapter 1 examines the writing of Francisco de Vitoria, the sixteenth-century Spanish jurist whose work, *De Indis Noviter Inventis* (hereafter, *De Indis*), is widely regarded as the first international law text.[15] My argument is that we can see in the works of Vitoria some of the crucial themes and issues that continue to preoccupy the discipline. Vitoria addresses the problem of accounting for the Spanish conquest of the Indies by using the doctrinal and jurisprudential resources of natural law. Vitoria first characterizes the Indian as primitive and therefore lacking in full legal personality, and then proceeds to outline a series of legal principles, based on natural law, which justify Spanish intervention in the Indies for the purposes of civilizing the Indians. Vitoria's work exemplifies, I argue, the formulation and operation of the dynamic of difference, and this at the very beginning of the discipline international law. The dynamic precedes, indeed generates, the concepts and dichotomies – for example, between private and public, between sovereign and non-sovereign – which are traditionally seen as the foundations of the international legal order. Despite Vitoria's significance as the first international legal jurist, the importance of his work has not been generally recognized as outlining, in clear and stark terms, the colonial origins of international law. My purpose in studying Vitoria is to establish my analytic framework, my methodology as it were, and to use some of the themes and concepts evident in his work to study subsequent periods.

Chapter 2 deals with the late nineteenth century, the apogee of colonial expansion. The international lawyers of the period, such as John Westlake and Thomas Lawrence, characterized themselves as positivists, as radically different from their naturalist predecessors. Nevertheless, the positivists used their new vocabulary of sovereign consent and recognition to exclude the non-European world as backward and

---

[14] My approach is indebted to the pioneering work of post-colonial scholars, including Edward Said, *Orientalism* (New York: Pantheon Books, 1978); Edward Said, *Culture and Imperialism* (New York: Knopf, 1993); Spivak, *A Critique of Postcolonial Reason*; Homi Bhabha, *The Location of Culture* (London: Routledge, 1994); David Scott, *Refashioning Futures: Criticism After Postcoloniality* (Princeton: Princeton University Press, 1999); Chakrabarty, 'Postcoloniality and the Artifice of History'. For a good overview, see Bart Moore-Gilbert, *Postcolonial Theory: Contexts, Practices, Politics* (New York: Verso, 1997).

[15] See the discussion in chapter 1.

uncivilized and to elaborate a legal framework that justified colonization as a means of accomplishing the civilizing mission. The dynamic
was reconstructed in this way in the positivist era.

Chapter 3 focuses on the jurisprudence of the inter-war period (1919–
39) and traces in general terms the shift from positivism to the new
jurisprudence of pragmatism that was related to the emergence of the
first major international institution, the League of Nations. My particular focus is on the Mandate System of the League of Nations that provided the international system with a new means of managing colonial relations through the technologies developed by international institutions. The Mandate System commences the task of promoting self-
government among colonized peoples, and consequently can be seen as
the beginning of the great project of decolonization that was taken up
and completed by the United Nations. I focus on how colonial problems,
as they were understood in the League period, shaped the character and
identity of these institutions and, correspondingly, how these institutions shaped the governance of the non-European societies to which they
applied. I argue that a study of this history illuminates the operations
of contemporary international institutions such as the World Bank and
the International Monetary Fund (IMF) which exercise an extraordinary
influence on Third World states and peoples.

Chapters 4–6 basically trace developments since the emergence of the
United Nations, and might be simply summarized in terms of the key,
governing themes of each, which deals with a particular period: decolonization, globalization and terror. The colonial confrontation was characterized by resistance and rebellion by the non-European states that
were colonized by the great Empires. However, it was only in the United
Nations period that the independent societies of the Third World were
able to use the newly acquired resources of sovereignty to develop their
own internal polities, on the one hand, and to advance their interests
in the international system on the other. Chapter 4 examines both the
internal and external dimensions of the newly emergent post-colonial
state. In the internal sphere, the state sought to control and assimilate
minorities in order to create a coherent nation-state. Here, I argue, the
civilizing mission is reproduced by the post-colonial state itself in its
application to minorities. In the international sphere, I examine the
attempts of the new post-colonial states, acting together as the Third
World, to advance their interests by exercising their recently acquired
sovereignty to create a 'New International Economic Order' (NIEO).
Having traced the way in which the colonial encounter affected the

formulation of sovereignty doctrine, I explore the ways in which this doctrine operates, in contemporary international law, to retard Third World attempts to reverse the effects of colonialism. Sovereignty doctrine, because created out of the colonial encounter, works to prevent legal attempts to re-open the colonial past, as I argue in my exploration of the New International Economic Order.

Chapter 5 examines the related phenomena of 'governance and globalization', the effects of globalization on Third World sovereignty, and the development of the concept of 'governance', through the use of international human rights doctrines, to manage Third World peoples and sovereignties. Chapter 6 makes some tentative connections between the themes I have developed previously and the current 'war against terror' (WAT). My simple argument here is that the 'war against terror', while proclaimed to address a novel and unprecedented situation, promises to create a new form of imperialism that relies for its furtherance on a structure of ideas and doctrines that may be traced back to far earlier times.

The periods I examine here correspond roughly with different paradigms of international jurisprudence: Vitoria and the sixteenth century represent naturalism, the nineteenth century positivism and the twentieth century pragmatism. I seek, then, to examine the civilizing mission first, over a period of time, and secondly, in relation to jurisprudential paradigms regarded as radically different.

'Colonialism' refers, generally to the practice of settling territories, while 'imperialism' refers to the practices of an empire. As Michael Doyle puts it, empire is

a relationship, formal or informal, in which one state controls the effective political sovereignty of another political society. It can be achieved by force, by political collaboration, by economic, social or cultural dependence. Imperialism is simply the process or policy of maintaining an empire.[16]

I have generally used the terms 'colonialism' and 'imperialism' interchangeably because of their close relationship to each other. The British Empire of the nineteenth century engaged in both colonial and imperial practices. But, as I shall attempt to argue, imperialism (which has also been called neo-colonialism by some Third World leaders and statesmen) is a broader and more accurate term with which to describe the practices of powerful Western states in the period following the establishment of

[16] Michael W. Doyle, *Empires* (Ithaca, NY: Cornell University Press, 1986), p. 45.

the United Nations. This period witnessed the end of formal colonialism, but the continuation, consolidation and elaboration of imperialism. This is the period in which we now live, and my interest lies in part in understanding the recent revival of imperial relations in terms of the themes I have previously explored.

My subject, the relationship between colonialism and international law over many decades and with respect to many different areas of international law of which I lack specialized knowledge, is a large one, and I have doubtless committed many errors. Colonialism manifested itself in different ways in different non-European societies. Different non-European societies fought against colonialism in different ways, British colonialism differed from French colonialism and, compounding matters, we have the case of a country such as Sri Lanka, colonized in succession by the Portuguese, the Dutch and the English – which is why both *Donoghue* v. *Stevenson* and the writings of an expert on the Roman–Dutch law of contracts, Hugo Grotius, have become a part of the living jurisprudence of that country. And why, further, the colonial mores of cricket ('Umpire's word is law' we chanted in our prep school days in attempting to quell any dissent against a controversial decision) have had such a resilient impact on that society. Further, of course, my attempts to sketch an alternative and more inclusive history of international law confronts the inevitable paradox that it effects its own exclusions. In adopting a particular the method and framework I disregard the many other histories and themes that could have been explored. For all these reasons, I request your indulgence.

My hope, however, is that the sketch of this large subject that I have offered here might suggest new lines of research and make some contribution towards the writing of alternative histories of the discipline: histories of resistance to colonial power, history from the vantage point of the peoples who were, in many ways, the victims of international law. Further, if we understand how colonialism has shaped the fundamental structures of international law, then it might become possible, having recognized this fact, for us to rethink a system of international law that might in some way make good on its promise to further international justice.

1   Francisco de Vitoria and the colonial origins of international law

Sir, As I know you will be pleased at the great victory with which Our Lord has crowned my voyage, I write this to you, from which you will learn how in thirty-three days, I passed from the Canary Islands to the Indies with the fleet which the most illustrious king and queen, our sovereigns, gave to me. And there I found many islands filled with people innumerable, and of them all I have taken possession for their highnesses, by proclamation made and with royal standard unfurled and no opposition was offered to me.[1]

AMAZING LETTER

Introduction

While Hugo Grotius is generally regarded as the principal forerunner of modern international law, historians of the discipline trace its primitive origins[2] to the works of Francisco de Vitoria, a sixteenth-century Spanish theologian and jurist.[3] Consequently, it is entirely appropriate that the Carnegie endowment commenced its renowned series of *Classics of International Law* with Vitoria's two famous lectures, *De Indis Noviter Inventis* and *De Jure Bellis Hispanorum in Barbaros*.[4] Traditional approaches to

---

[1] Christopher Columbus, 'Letter of Columbus on the First Voyage', in Cecil Jane (ed. and trans.), *The Four Voyages of Columbus* (New York: Dover, 1988), I, p. 1.

[2] David Kennedy, 'Primitive Legal Scholarship', (1986) 27(1) *Harvard International Law Journal* 1–98.

[3] For accounts of Vitoria's place in the discipline of international law, and his relationship to Grotius, see James Brown Scott, *The Spanish Origin of International Law* (Oxford: Clarendon Press, 1934); Arthur Nussbaum, *A Concise History of the Law of Nations* (rev. edn., New York: Macmillan, 1954).

[4] The titles of the two lectures may be translated as 'On the Indians Lately Discovered' and 'On the Law of War Made by the Spaniards on the Barbarians'. The two lectures are collected together in one volume, Franciscus de Victoria, *De Indis et de Ivre Belli Relectiones* (Ernest Nys ed., John Pawley Bate trans., Washington, DC: Carnegie Institution of Washington, 1917), p. 116. This is the first work in the series *The Classics of*

Vitoria's work and his place within the discipline pointed, among other things, to Grotius' indebtedness to the teachings of Vitoria,[5] to Vitoria's identification of certain fundamental theoretical issues confronting the discipline and to the enduring significance of Vitoria's thinking on the law of war and on the rights of dependent peoples.[6]

Vitoria's two lectures, as their titles suggest, are essentially concerned with relations between the Spanish and the Indians. Colonialism is the central theme of these two works designated as the founding texts of international law. It is hardly possible to ignore the fact that Vitoria is preoccupied with a colonial relationship.[7] While traditional approaches to Vitoria duly acknowledge this fact, they fail to appreciate the extent to which Vitoria's jurisprudence is constructed around his attempts to resolve the unique legal problems arising from the discovery of the Indians. Instead, these traditional approaches essentially characterize Vitoria as extending and applying existing juridical doctrines developed in Europe to determine the legal status of the Indians. Thus, for example, Kooijmans argues that

the dealings of the Spaniards with the Indians were subject to the rules that apply to intercourse between states. Vitoria introduced an essentially new element in relentlessly drawing the consequences from the theories which until then had remained outside the European horizon . . . [T]he rules that apply to European inter-state intercourse also apply to the intercourse with the American-Indian political communities, because there is no intrinsic difference. The small Indian states are legal persons, they enjoy the same rights as European states.[8]

International Law published by the Carnegie Institution of Washington. 'Victoria' is more commonly referred to in the literature as 'Vitoria' and I have accordingly adopted the latter version.

[5] Scott, The Spanish Origin, pp. 3–4.

[6] For examples of his influence on the rights of dependent peoples, see Quincy Wright, Mandates Under the League of Nations (Chicago: University of Chicago Press, 1930); and Christopher G. Weeramantry, Nauru: Environmental Damage Under International Trusteeship (New York: Oxford University Press, 1992), p. 78.

[7] For a brilliant analysis of Vitoria's justification of colonial relations, see Robert A. Williams, Jr., The American Indian in Western Legal Thought: The Discourse of Conquest (New York: Oxford University Press, 1990).

[8] (Pieter Hendrik Kooijmans, The Doctrine of the Legal Equality of States: An Inquiry into the Foundations of International Law, Leyden, A. W. Sijthoff, 1964, p. 57). Kooijmans does make it clear, however, that for Vitoria, the Indians would acquire the rights of states once 'these communities correspond to the requirements laid down by him for the state'. Ibid.

My argument, in contrast, is that while Vitoria's jurisprudence relies in many respects on existing doctrines, he reconceptualizes these doctrines, or else invents new ones, in order to deal with the novel problem of the Indians. The essential point is that international law, such as it existed in Vitoria's time, did not *precede* and thereby effortlessly resolve the problem of Spanish–Indian relations; rather, international law was created out of the unique issues generated by the encounter between the Spanish and the Indians. It is in this context that the question arises: what is the relationship between the origins of international law and the colonial encounter in these, the first teachings on international law? Further, what does an examination of these origins suggest about the relationship between colonialism and international law as a whole, the relationship that is a central concern of this book?

The classical problem confronting the discipline of international law is the problem of how order is created among sovereign states. The identification of this problem as the defining dilemma of the discipline has encouraged scholars seeking to clarify Vitoria's place within the discipline to explore his work in terms of his understanding and treatment of this problem.[9] My argument is that Vitoria does not interpret the problem of Spanish–Indian relations as a problem of creating order among sovereign states. Vitoria's analysis does not proceed on the basis that both the Indians and Spaniards are sovereign, that sovereigns possess certain powers and that the interaction between the two parties is therefore regulated by the rules managing and limiting the exercise of such powers which he, the jurist, identifies, examines and applies. Rather, Vitoria's work addresses a prior set of questions. Who is sovereign? What are the powers of a sovereign? Are the Indians sovereign? What are the rights and duties of the Indians and the Spaniards? How are the respective rights and duties of the Spanish and the Indians to be decided?

In dealing with these issues, Vitoria focuses on the social and cultural practices of the two parties, the Spanish and the Indians. He assesses and formulates the rights and duties of the Indians, for example, by examining their rituals, customs and ways of life. The problem confronting

---

[9] For example, see Kooijmans, *The Doctrine of the Legal Equality*. Kennedy discusses this point at some length. As he notes: 'Most historians who treat primitive texts do so in a way which both presupposes and proves the continuity of the discipline of international law – reaffirming in the process that the project for international law scholars is and always was to construct a social order among autonomous sovereigns.' Kennedy, 'Primitive Legal Scholarship', 11.

Vitoria, then, was not the problem of order among sovereign states, but the problem of creating a system of law to account for relations between societies which he understood to belong to two very different cultural orders, each with its own ideas of propriety and governance.

This problem is suggested in Columbus' account of his 'taking possession' of the New World: what meaning could his legal ceremonies have for the people who were ostensibly to be bound by them; whose presence is acknowledged, if only through their silence, who offered no opposition to Columbus? In any event, what can hardly be disputed is the central significance of law to the whole colonial enterprise. Columbus' first sentence succinctly sketches the background to his voyage, due prominence being given to God and his sovereigns; his second sentence begins by relating his discovery of various undefined islands and peoples which are no sooner described than taken possession of by means of a legal ceremony that may or may not take cognizance of those peoples. Would it have legally mattered if the people had offered opposition? Or was the ceremony complete in itself, opposition indicating only the hostility of the natives? The passage raises several enduring issues concerning the connection between law and imperialism.[10]

Sovereignty doctrine – by which I broadly refer to the complex of rules deciding what entities are sovereign, and the powers and limits of sovereignty – was not already formulated and then simply applied by Vitoria to resolve the problem of creating order between different societies. Rather, for Vitoria, sovereignty doctrine emerges through his attempts to address the problem of cultural difference.

I explore the relationship between colonialism and international law, cultural difference and sovereignty doctrine, by focusing on four broad issues. First, I focus on Vitoria's repudiation of traditional techniques of accounting for relations between the Spanish and the Indians. Having dismissed the old medieval jurisprudence based on the notion that the Pope exercised universal authority, Vitoria clears the way for his own version of secular international law. Secondly, I focus on the techniques by which Vitoria creates a universally binding system of law by evoking a notion of natural law; this system resolves Vitoria's problem of creating a common framework binding both Spanish and Indian alike. Thirdly, I consider the rules and norms prescribed by this system, and the effect

---

[10] See Stephen Greenblatt, *Marvelous Possessions: The Wonder of the New World* (Chicago: University of Chicago Press, 1991), p. 54; for the more elaborate protocol of conquest later developed by Spain, see Patricia Seed, *Ceremonies of Possession in Europe's Conquest of the New World, 1492–1640* (New York, Cambridge University Press, 1995), p. 69.

of their application to Spanish–Indian relations. Finally, I examine the question of enforcement and the sanctions applied once the norms prescribed by natural law have been violated. In examining each of these areas, I attempt to delineate how Vitoria's understanding of cultural difference and the identity of the Indian shapes his jurisprudence, and how in turn this jurisprudence determines the Indians' legal status.

Vitoria and the problem of universal law

The issue of accounting for Spanish title over the Indies was conventionally decided by applying the jurisprudence developed by the Church to deal with the Saracens to the Indies. Within this framework, the Indians could be characterized as Saracens, as heathens, and their rights and duties determined accordingly. Vitoria criticises this traditional framework, which had emerged out of the several centuries of interaction and confrontation between the Christian and heathen worlds, and replaces it with his own. The traditional framework relied basically on two premises. First, it was asserted that human relations were governed by divine law. As Vitoria's jurisprudence suggests, the medieval Western world relied on three different types of law; divine law, human law and natural law.[11] Of these, divine law was asserted to be primary by many scholars and theologians of the fifteenth century. Secondly, it was argued that the Pope exercised universal jurisdiction by virtue of his divine mission to spread Christianity. Consequently, sovereigns, the rulers of Europe, relied upon the Pope's authority to legitimize their invasions of heathen territory; in expanding the Christian world by military conquest, these rulers were making real the jurisdiction which the Pope possessed in theory.[12] Pope Alexander VI's Papal Bull, which divided the world into Spanish and Portuguese spheres, exemplified the application of this set of doctrines: the rule of the sovereign was legitimate only if sanctioned by religious authority.[13]

Vitoria vehemently denies each of these assertions, and in the course of refuting the conventional basis for Spanish title creates a new system of international law which essentially displaces divine law and its administrator, the Pope, and replaces it with natural law administered

---

[11] Alfred P. Rubin, 'International Law in the Age of Columbus' (1992) XXXIX *Netherlands International Law Review* 5–35 at 11–14.

[12] See Rubin, 'International Law' and Anthony Pagden, *Lords of All The World, Ideologies of Empire in Spain, Britain and France c. 1500–c.1800* (New Haven: Yale University Press, 1995).

[13] Pagden, *Lords of All The World*, p. 32.

by a secular sovereign. Thus, the emergence of a secular natural law –
the natural law which was proclaimed to be the basis of the new international law – is coeval with his resolution of the problem of the legal
status of the Indian, for it is this problem which initiates Vitoria's
inquiry.

Vitoria commences his construction of a new jurisprudence by posing
the question of whether 'the aborigines in question were true owners
in both private and public law before the arrival of the Spaniards'.[14]
Could the Indians, the unbelievers, own property? Rather than adopt
the traditional approach of dismissing the Indians as lacking in rights
merely because of their status as unbelievers, Vitoria reformulates the
relationship between divine, natural and human law. Having examined
numerous theological authorities and incidents in the Bible, he concludes that whatever the punishments awaiting them in their after-life,
unbelievers such as the Indians were not deprived of their property in
the mundane realm merely by virtue of that status. Vitoria concludes:

Unbelief does not destroy either natural law or human law; but ownership and
dominion are based either on natural law or human law; therefore they are not
destroyed by want of faith.[15]

Crucially, then, Vitoria places questions of ownership and property in
the sphere of natural or human law, rather than divine law. As a consequence of the inapplicability of divine law to questions of ownership,
the Indians cannot be deprived of their lands merely by virtue of their
status as unbelievers or heretics.[16] Vitoria's argument that vital issues
of property and title are decided by secular systems of law – whether
natural or human – inevitably diminishes the power of the Pope, for
these secular systems of law are administered by the sovereign rather
than the Pope.

Vitoria further undermines the position of the Church by refuting
another justification for Spanish conquest of the Indies: the argument
that 'the Emperor is lord of the whole world and therefore of these
barbarians also'.[17] Vitoria's emphasis here shifts to the Christian emperors of Europe whose authority was related in various complex ways to

[14] Vitoria, De Indis, p. 120.   [15] Ibid., p. 123.
[16] 'From all this the conclusion follows that the barbarians in question cannot be barred
from being true owners, alike in public and private law, by reason of the sin of
unbelief or any other mortal sin, nor does such sin entitle Christians to seize their
goods and land.' Vitoria, De Indis, p. 125, note x.
[17] Vitoria, De Indis, p. 130.

the authority of the Church.[18] Vitoria denies that the sovereign, the Emperor, could have acquired universal temporal authority through the universal spiritual authority of Christ and the Pope. He questions whether divine law could provide the basis for temporal authority, methodically denies a number of assertions of Papal authority and concludes that 'The Pope is not civil or temporal lord of the whole world in the proper sense of the words "lordship" and "civil power"'[19] and goes even further to assert that even in the spiritual realm, the Pope lacks jurisdiction over the unbelievers.[20] The Pope's authority is partial, limited to the spiritual dimension of the Christian world.

Vitoria's rejection of the argument that the Pope exercised universal authority which empowered sovereigns to pursue military action against heathens and infidels such as the Indians results in a novel problem:

Now, in point of human law, it is manifest that the Emperor is not lord of the world, because either this would be by the sole authority of some law, and there is none such; or if there were, it would be void of effect, inasmuch as law presupposes jurisdiction. If, then, the Emperor had no jurisdiction over the world before the law, the law could not bind someone who was not previously subject to it.[21]

The Spanish and the Indians are not bound by a universal, overarching system; instead, they belong to two different orders, and Vitoria interprets the gap between them in terms of the juridical problem of jurisdiction. The resolution of this problem is crucial both for Vitoria's new jurisprudence and his construction of a common legal framework which would enable him to resolve the problem of the Indians' status. The two techniques by which Vitoria addresses the issue of jurisdiction comprise essentially two related parts: first, his complex characterization of the personality of the Indians and, second, his elaboration of a novel system of universal natural law.

Vitoria first focuses on the issue of Indian personality. As his own work suggests, the writers of the period appear to have characterized the Indians as being, among other things, slaves, sinners, heathens, barbarians, minors, lunatics and animals. Vitoria repudiated these claims, humanely asserting instead that

---

[18] Vitoria was writing during the reign of Charles V of Spain, who was designated the Holy Roman Emperor. This was a time of massive Spanish imperial expansion. See Pagden, *Lords of All the World*, p. 32.
[19] Vitoria, *De Indis*, p. 153.   [20] *Ibid.*, p. 136.   [21] *Ibid.*, p. 134.

the true state of the case is that they are not of unsound mind, but have, according to their kind, the use of reason. This is clear, because there is a certain method in their affairs, for they have polities which are orderly arranged and they have definite marriage and magistrates, overlords, laws and workshops, and a system of exchange, all of which call for the use of reason; they also have a kind of religion. Further, they make no error in matters which are self-evident to others; this is witness to their use of reason.[22]

It is precisely because of his insistence that the Indians are human beings that Vitoria is lauded as a protector of native peoples against colonial exploitation. For Vitoria, then, the Indians established their own versions of many of the institutions found in Vitoria's world, in Europe itself.[23] They are governed by a political system which has its own coherence, and possess the reason necessary, not only to create institutions, but to determine moral questions which are 'self-evident' to others.

Vitoria's characterization of the Indians as human and possessing reason is crucial to his resolution of the problem of jurisdiction. He argues that 'What natural reason has established among all nations is called *jus gentium*'.[24] The universal system of divine law administered by the Pope is replaced by the universal natural law system of *jus gentium* whose rules may be ascertained by the use of reason. As a result, it is precisely *because* the Indians possess reason that they are bound by *jus gentium*. Vitoria hardly mentions the concept of *jus gentium* in his earlier discussion. Nevertheless, the problem of jurisdiction is resolved by his simple enunciation of this concept which he elaborates primarily by demonstrating how it creates doctrines which govern Spanish–Indian relations. Natural law administered by sovereigns rather than divine law articulated by the Pope becomes the source of international law governing Spanish–Indian relations.

The character of this natural law is illuminated in Vitoria's argument that the Spanish have a right under *jus gentium* to travel and sojourn in the land of the Indians; and that providing the Spanish do not harm the Indians, 'the natives may not prevent them'. Vitoria argues that:

it was permissible from the beginning of the world (when everything was in common) for any one to set forth and travel wheresoever he would. Now this was not to be taken away by the division of property, for it was never the intention of peoples to destroy by that division the reciprocity and common user which prevailed among men, and indeed, in the days of Noah, it would have been inhuman to do so.[25]

---

[22] *Ibid.*, p. 127.   [23] Pagden, *Lords of All the World*.
[24] Vitoria, *De Indis*, p. 151.   [25] *Ibid.*, p. 151.

The natural law which solves the problem of jurisdiction is based on something akin to a secular state of nature existing at 'the beginning of the world'. As this passage suggests, *jus gentium*, naturalizes and legitimates a system of commerce and Spanish penetration. Spanish forms of economic and political life are all-encompassing because ostensibly supported by doctrines prescribed by Vitoria's system of universal law. The gap between the two cultures now ceases to exist in that a common framework by which both Spanish and Indian behaviour may be assessed is established. Equally importantly, an idealised version of the particular cultural practices of the Spanish assume the guise of universality as a result of appearing to derive from the sphere of natural law.

The Indians seem to participate in this system as equals. The Spanish trade with the Indians 'by importing thither wares which the natives lack and by exporting thence either gold or silver or other wares of which the natives have abundance'.[26] The exchange seems to occur between equals entering knowledgeably into these transactions, each meeting the other's material lack and possessing, implicitly, the autonomy to decide what is of value to them. The Indian who enters the universal realm of commerce has all the acumen and independence of market man, as opposed to the timid, ignorant child-like creatures Vitoria presents earlier. The fairness of the system and the equal status of the Indians are further suggested by Vitoria's argument that the Indians are subject to the same limitations imposed on Christian nations themselves: 'it is certain that the aborigines can no more keep off the Spaniards from trade than Christians can keep off other Christians'.[27] Reciprocity, it seems, would permit the Indians to trade in Spain.

While appearing to promote notions of equality and reciprocity between the Indians and the Spanish, Vitoria's scheme must be understood in the context of the realities of the Spanish presence in the Indies. Seen in this way, Vitoria's scheme finally endorses and legitimizes endless Spanish incursions into Indian society. Vitoria's apparently innocuous enunciation of a right to 'travel' and 'sojourn' extends finally to the creation of a comprehensive, indeed inescapable system of norms which are inevitably violated by the Indians. For example, Vitoria asserts that 'to keep certain people out of the city or province as being enemies, or to expel them when already there, are acts of war'.[28] Thus any Indian attempt to resist Spanish penetration would amount to

---

[26] *Ibid.*, p. 152.   [27] *Ibid.*, p. 153.   [28] *Ibid.*, p. 151.

an act of war, which would justify Spanish retaliation. Each encounter between the Spanish and the Indians therefore entitles the Spanish to 'defend' themselves against Indian aggression and, in so doing, continuously expand Spanish territory, as discussed below.

Vitoria further endorses the imposition of Spanish rule on the Indians by another argument, which relies explicitly on the *cultural differences* between the Spanish and the Indians. In establishing his system of *jus gentium*, Vitoria characterizes the Indians as having the same ontological character as the Spanish. This is a crucial prerequisite for his elaboration of a system of norms which he presents as neutral, and founded upon qualities possessed by all people. According to Vitoria, Indian personality has two characteristics. First, the Indians belong to the universal realm like the Spanish and all other human beings because, Vitoria asserts, they have the facility of reason and hence a means of ascertaining *jus gentium* which is universally binding. Secondly, however, the Indian is very different from the Spaniard because the Indian's specific social and cultural practices are at variance from the practices required by the universal norms – which in effect are Spanish practices – and which are applicable to both Indian and Spaniard. Thus the Indian is schizophrenic, both alike and unlike the Spaniard. The gap between the Indian and the Spaniard – a gap that Vitoria describes primarily in cultural terms by detailed references to the different social practices of the Spanish and the Indians – is now internalized; the ideal, universal Indian possesses the capacity of reason and therefore the potential to achieve perfection. This potential can only be realized, however, by the adoption or the imposition of the universally applicable practices of the Spanish. The discrepancy between the ontologically 'universal' Indian and the socially, historically, 'particular' Indian must be remedied by the imposition of sanctions which effect the necessary transformation. Indian will regarding the desirability of such a transformation is irrelevant: the universal norms Vitoria enunciates regulate behaviour, not merely between the Spanish and the Indians, but among the Indians themselves; thus the Spanish acquire an extraordinarily powerful right of intervention and may act on behalf of the people seen as victims of Indian rituals: 'it is immaterial that all the Indians assent to rules and sacrifices of this kind and do not wish the Spaniards to champion them.'[29] Thus Spanish identity or, more broadly, an idealised Western

---

[29] Vitoria, *De Indis*, p. 159. Indeed, for Vitoria, it would suffice for these purposes if the Spaniards were obstructed in their attempts to convert the Indians. This affected the

identity, is projected as universal in two different but connected dimensions of Vitoria's system; Spanish identity is both externalized, in that it acts as the basis for the norms of *jus gentium*, and internalized in that it represents the authentic identity of the Indian.

War, sovereignty and the transformation of the Indian

War, the central theme of Vitoria's second lecture, is vitally important to an understanding of his jurisprudence – first because the transformation of the Indian is to be achieved by the waging of war and secondly because Vitoria's concept of sovereignty is developed primarily in terms of the sovereign's right to wage war.

War is the means by which Indians and their territory are converted into Spaniards and Spanish territory, the agency by which the Indians thus achieve their full human potential. Vitoria, I have argued, displaces the realm of divine law and thereby diminishes the power of the Pope. Nevertheless, once Vitoria outlines and consolidates the authority of a secular *jus gentium*, which is administered by the sovereign, he reintroduces Christian norms within this secular system; proselytising is authorised now, not by divine law, but the law of nations, and may be likened now to the secular activities of travelling and trading. Vitoria elegantly presents the crucial transition:

ambassadors are by the law of nations inviolable and the Spaniards are the ambassadors of the Christian peoples. Therefore, the native Indians are bound to give them, at least, a friendly hearing and not to repel them.[30]

Thus all the Christian practices which Vitoria dismissed earlier as being religiously based, as limited in their scope to the Christian world and therefore inapplicable to the Indians, are now reintroduced into his system as universal rules. This astonishing metamorphosis of rules, condemned by Vitoria himself as particular and relevant only to Christian peoples, into universal rules endorsed by *jus gentium* is achieved simply by recharacterizing these rules as originating in the realm of the universal *jus gentium*. Now, Indian resistance to conversion is a cause for war, not because it violates divine law, but the *jus gentium* administered by the sovereign.

'welfare of the Indians themselves', in which event the Spanish might intervene 'in favor of those who are oppressed and suffer wrong' (*ibid.*, p. 157).
[30] *Ibid.*, p. 156.

Vitoria elaborates on the many situations in which war is now justified:

If after the Spaniards have used all diligence, both in deed and in word, to show that nothing will come from them to interfere with the peace and well-being of the aborigines, the latter nevertheless persist in their hostility and do their best to destroy the Spaniards, they can make war on the Indians, no longer as on innocent folk, but as against forsworn enemies and may enforce against them all the rights of war, despoiling them of their goods, reducing them to captivity, deposing their former lords and setting up new ones, yet withal with observance of proportion as regards the nature of the circumstances and of the wrongs done to them.[31]

Given that any Indian resistance to Spanish presence is a violation of the law of nations, which would justify sanctions, Spanish war against the Indians is inevitable and endless. The Indian is ascribed with membership within an overarching system of *jus gentium*, with intention and volition; as a consequence of this, violence originates within Vitoria's system through the Indians' deviance.

Vitoria's exploration of the law of war raises many of the traditional questions which still occupy international lawyers: Who may wage war?, When can war be waged?, What limits must be observed in the waging of war?, What constitutes a just war?, and so forth. Furthermore, war is a special phenomenon, because it is the ultimate prerogative of the sovereign. Vitoria's most sustained and explicit exploration of sovereignty doctrine thus occurs in the context of his examination of the law of war.

Vitoria understands sovereignty, in part, as a *relationship* – the sovereign has a duty towards his people and the state and has certain prerogatives – the right to wage war and to acquire title being among the most prominent. The sovereign, the prince, is the instrumentality of the state, posited almost as the metaphysical embodiment of the people.[32]

---

[31] *Ibid.*, p. 155.

[32] The prince is the entity in whom all power is vested:

for the prince only holds his position by the election of the State. Therefore he is its representative and wields its authority; aye, and where there are already lawful princes in a State, all authority is in their hands and without them nothing of a public nature can be done either in war or in peace.

(Vitoria, *De Indis*, p. 169)

Vitoria later concludes: 'Such a state, then, or the prince thereof, has authority to declare war and no one else.' *Ibid.*, p. 169.

The prince expands the state, as the successful waging of war brings people outside the state within its scope.[33]

While Vitoria thus defined the powers of the sovereign, he had greater difficulty in identifying the sovereign himself. 'Now the whole difficulty is in the questions: What is a State and who can properly be called a sovereign prince?'[34] Sovereigns cannot be defined independently of states. The state, claims Vitoria, 'is properly called a perfect community'.[35] But then 'the essence of the difficulty is in saying what a perfect community is'.[36] Vitoria's answer is tautologous: 'By way of solution be it noted that a thing is called perfect when it is completed whole, for that is imperfect in which there is something wanting, and, on the other hand, that is perfect from which nothing is wanting.'[37] Neither does it help to define the sovereign as the ultimate authority within the community, for even this proposition is subject to complex qualifications; the complicated hierarchies of the time defy Vitoria and he acknowledges that a doubt may well arise whether, when a number of states of this kind or a number of princes have one common lord or prince they can make war of themselves without the authorization of their superior lord.[38] Amid this confusion, Vitoria finally resorts to empiricism, citing as examples of sovereignty the kingdoms of Castile and Aragon, communities, which have their own laws and councils.

The foregoing suggests that the power of the state has not been consolidated in any significant way. Authority is too dispersed and hierarchies, while established theoretically, are too confusing and uncertain for Vitoria to use them convincingly as a means of structuring sovereignty doctrine. Vitoria's discussion of sovereignty is at its most detailed, however, in his analysis of the laws of war, as a consequence of the fact that it is the sovereign who declares war and exercises all the rights of war. Just war doctrine is a crucial aspect of the whole complex of issues relating to the law of war. Even if the sovereign authority can be properly identified, does the sovereign's subjective belief in the justice of the war ensure that the war is indeed 'just'?[39]

---

[33] 'It is, therefore, certain that princes can punish enemies who have done a wrong to their State and that after a war has been duly and justly undertaken the enemy are just as much within the jurisdiction of the prince who undertakes it as if he were their proper judge.' Vitoria, De Indis, p. 172.
[34] Vitoria, De Indis, p. 169.   [35] Ibid., p. 169.   [36] Ibid., p. 169.
[37] Ibid., p. 169.   [38] Ibid., p. 169.   [39] Vitoria, De Indis, p. 173.

Vitoria rejects the argument that subjective belief in the 'justness' of a war would suffice to render it truly just because 'were it otherwise, even Turks and Saracens might wage just wars against Christians, for they think they are thus rendering God service'.[40] Instead of examining the issues of subjective belief and just war doctrine and then deciding whether or not they applied to the Saracens, Vitoria arrives at his conclusion by first establishing the proposition, the fundamental premise of his argument, that *the Saracens are inherently incapable of waging a just war.* The initial exclusion of the Saracens – and, in this case, by extension, the Indians – then, is fundamental to Vitoria's argument. In essence, only the Christians may engage in a just war; and, given Vitoria's argument that the power to wage war is the prerogative of sovereigns, it follows that the Saracens can never be truly sovereign, that they are at best, partially sovereign because denied the ability to engage in war.

Earlier, in his first lecture, Vitoria had argued that the Indians too possess their own form of rulership, that they 'have polities which are orderly arranged and they have definite marriage and magistrates, overlords, laws and workshops'.[41] Such a passage may suggest that Indian communities are governed by sovereigns; but Vitoria's insistence, in his analysis on just war, that only Christian subjectivity is recognized by the laws of war, ensures that the Indians are excluded from the realm of sovereignty and exist only as the objects against which Christian sovereignty may exercise its power to wage war.

The task of identifying sovereign authority and defining the powers wielded by such an authority, in the complex political systems of Renaissance Europe, proved extraordinarily difficult, and the techniques and conceptual distinctions used by Vitoria for this purpose were problematic and ambiguous. The distinction between the Indians and the Spanish, however, was emphatic and well developed. Indeed, in the final analysis, the most unequivocal proposition Vitoria advances as to the character of the sovereign is that the sovereign, the entity empowered to wage a just war, cannot, by definition, be an Indian.

Since the Indians are by definition incapable of waging a just war, they exist within the Vitorian framework only as violators of the law. The normal principles of just war, which would prohibit the enslaving of women and children, do not apply in the case of the pagan Indians:

---

[40] *Ibid.*, p. 173.   [41] *Ibid.*, p. 127.

And so when the war is at that pass that the indiscriminate spoliation of all enemy-subjects alike and the seizure of all their goods are justifiable, then it is also justifiable to carry all enemy-subjects off into captivity, whether they be guilty or guiltless. And inasmuch as war with pagans is of this type, seeing that it is perpetual and that they can never make amends for the wrongs and damages they have wrought, it is indubitably lawful to carry off both the children and women of the Saracens into captivity and slavery.[42]

Once fault is established, as the above passage suggests, the war waged against the Indian is, in Vitoria's phraseology, 'perpetual'. Similarly, in his discussion of whether it is lawful and expedient to kill all the guilty, Vitoria suggests that this may be necessary because of the unique case of the unredeemable Indian:

and this is especially the case against the unbeliever, from whom it is useless ever to hope for a just peace on any terms. And as the only remedy is to destroy all of them who can bear arms against us, provided they have already been in fault.[43]

A certain respect is extended to sovereignty in the case of wars between European powers as the 'overthrow of the enemy's sovereignty and the deposition of lawful and natural princes' are 'utterly savage and inhu-mane measures'.[44] In the case of the Indians, however, such a deposi-tion of sovereigns is not merely permitted but necessary in order to save the Indians from themselves. These conclusions stand in curious juxtaposition to other parts of Vitoria's work, where he emphasizes the humanity of the Indians. Simply, war waged against the Indians acquires a meta-legal status.[45] Many of the legal doctrines of consent, limits and proportion that Vitoria outlines earlier, cease to apply to the Indian once the all-encompassing and inescapable obligations of *jus gentium* are breached.

In summary, then, there are two essential ways in which sovereignty relates to the Indian: in the first place, the Indian is excluded from the sphere of sovereignty; in the second place, it is the Indian who acts as the object against which the powers of sovereignty may be exercised in

<hr>

[42] *Ibid.*, p. 181. It is notable that Vitoria refused to characterize the Indians as slaves in his first lectures. Now, however, with respect to war and the new scheme of natural law he outlines, he achieves much the same result: the enslavement of the whole Indian population, including women and children.
[43] Vitoria, *De Indis*, p. 183.   [44] *Ibid.*, p. 186.
[45] Onuma Yasuaki, *A Normative Approach to War: Peace, War, and Justice in Hugo Grotius* (Oxford, Clarendon Press, 1993), pp. 383–384.

the most extreme ways. Perhaps even more profoundly, it is through its application to the Indian that new aspects, powers and techniques of sovereignty can be discovered, as few limits are imposed on sovereignty when it is applied to the Indian. The most characteristic and unique powers of the sovereign, the powers to wage war and acquire title over territory and over alien peoples are defined in their fullest form by their application to the non-sovereign Indian.

Conclusion

Vitoria is an extremely complex figure. A brave champion of the rights of the Indians in his time,[46] his work could also be read as a particularly insidious justification of their conquest precisely because it is presented in the language of liberality and even equality. Vitoria continuously alludes to the theme of the novelty of the discovery of the Indians: thus his work addresses the controversy generated by 'the aborigines of the New World, commonly called the Indians, who came forty years ago into the power of the Spaniards, not having been previously known to our world'.[47] Later he argues 'at the time of the Spaniards' first voyages to America they took with them no right to occupy the lands of the indigenous population'. In these different ways, Vitoria seizes upon the discovery of the Indians to claim that traditional understandings of law were inadequate to deal with such a novel situation; in so doing, Vitoria clears the way for his own elaboration of a new, secular, international law.

My argument, then, is that Vitoria is concerned not so much with the problem of order among sovereign states but the problem of order among societies belonging to two different cultural systems. Vitoria resolves this problem by focusing on the cultural practices of each society and assessing them in terms of the universal law of *jus gentium*. Once this framework is established, he demonstrates that the Indians are in violation of universal natural law.

The problem of cultural difference plays a crucial role in structuring Vitoria's work – his notions of personality, *jus gentium* and, indeed, sovereignty itself. Vitoria's jurisprudence can be seen to consist of three primary elements connected with this problem. First, a difference is

---

[46] Georg Cavallar, *The Rights of Strangers: Theories of International Hospitality, the Global Community and Political Justice Since Vitoria* (Aldershot: Ashgate, 2002), pp. 75–121.
[47] Vitoria, *De Indis*, p. 116.

postulated between the Indians and the Spanish, a difference which is rendered primarily in terms of the different social practices and customs of each society. Secondly, Vitoria formulates a means of bridging this difference, through his system of *jus gentium* and his characterization of the Indian as possessing universal reason and therefore capable of comprehending and being bound by the universal law of *jus gentium*. Thirdly, the Indian – possessing universal reason and yet backward, barbaric, uncivilized – is subject to sanctions because of his failure to comply with universal standards. It is precisely whatever denotes the Indian to be different – his customs, practices, rituals – which justify the disciplinary measures of war, which is directed towards effacing Indian identity and replacing it with the universal identity of the Spanish. These sanctions are administered by the sovereign Spanish to the non-sovereign Indians.

Cultural difference is also crucial to Vitoria's version of sovereignty doctrine. Vitoria's attempts to outline a coherent vision of sovereignty doctrine in the shifting political conditions of Renaissance Europe encountered a number of difficulties which he tried to resolve by proposing various distinctions – between, for example, the public and the private, the municipal and international spheres. Each of these attempts fails,[48] however, and ultimately, the one distinction which Vitoria insists upon and which he elaborates in considerable detail is the distinction between the sovereign Spanish and the non-sovereign Indians. Vitoria bases his conclusions that the Indians are not sovereign on the simple assertion that they are pagans. In so doing he resorts to exactly the same crude reasoning which he had previously refuted when denying the validity of the Church's claim that the Indians lack rights under divine law because they are heathens. Despite this apparent contradiction, Vitoria's overall scheme is nevertheless consistent: the Indians who inevitably and invariably violate *jus gentium* are denied the status of the all-powerful sovereign who administers this law.

Clearly, then, Vitoria's work suggests that the conventional view that sovereignty doctrine was developed in the West and then transferred to the non-European world is, in important respects, misleading. Sovereignty doctrine acquired its character through the colonial encounter. This is the darker history of sovereignty which cannot be

---

[48] In the final analysis, as Kennedy argues, Vitoria 'does not locate the sovereign between a distinct municipal and international legal order, nor does he distinguish internal and external or private and public sovereign identities'. Kennedy, 'Primitive Legal Scholarship', 35.

explored or understood by any account of sovereignty doctrine assuming the existence of sovereign states.

My argument, then, is that Vitoria is indeed a seminal figure in the history of international law on account of his intimation of certain fundamental problems of the discipline and his attempt to resolve them. The problem Vitoria identifies and explores is the problem of legally accounting for relations between two radically different societies. In addressing this issue, Vitoria develops a number of concepts and relationships – regarding divine and natural law, sovereignty and culture, particularism and universalism – which are then constituted into a jurisprudence which executes a formidable series of manoeuvres by which an idealised form of particular Spanish practices become universally binding, Indians are excluded from the realm of sovereignty, and Indian resistance to Spanish incursions becomes aggression which justifies the waging of a limitless war by a sovereign Spain against non-sovereign Indians. The colonial encounter is central to the formulation of Vitoria's jurisprudence whose significance extends to our own times.

The classic question of how order is created among sovereign states and the framework of inquiry it suggests lends itself to a peculiarly imperialist version of the discipline as it prevents any searching examination of the history of the colonial world which was explicitly excluded from the realm of sovereignty. The interactions Vitoria examines occur not between sovereign states, but between the sovereign Spanish and non-sovereign Indians. The crucial issue, then, is how it was decided that the Indians were not sovereign in the first place.

Once the initial determination had been made and accepted that the colonial world was not sovereign, the discipline could then create for itself, and present as inevitable and natural, the grand redeeming project of bringing the marginalized into the realm of sovereignty, civilizing the uncivilized, and developing the juridical techniques and institutions necessary for this great mission. Within this framework, the history of the colonial world would comprise simply the history of the civilizing mission.

Vitoria's account of the inaugural colonial encounter suggests that an alternative history of the colonial world may be written by adopting a different framework and posing a different set of questions. How was it determined that the colonial world was non-sovereign in the first place? How were the ideas of universality and particularity used for this purpose? How did a limited set of ideas which originated in Europe present themselves as universally applicable? How, armed with these concepts, did European empires proceed to conquer and dominate non-European territories? How does resistance to colonialism – for a close reading of Vitoria does suggest, however subtly, the powerful presence of Indian resistance – become a further justification for imperialism? Furthermore, if sovereignty is so intimately connected with the problem of cultural difference, and if it is shaped in such a manner as to authorize certain cultures while suppressing others, vital questions must arise as to whether and how sovereignty may be utilised by these suppressed cultures for their own purposes.

In raising these issues, we may better understand the difficulties colonized peoples have encountered in entering the realm of sovereignty, the compromises they have made for the purposes of doing so and the limitations from which they suffer in attempting to pursue their interests and aspirations through a 'universal' language of international law which, arguably, was devised specifically to ensure their disempowerment and disenfranchisement. In examining these issues it may finally become possible to write a different history of the relationship between colonialism and international law and, thereby, of international law itself.

2   Finding the peripheries: colonialism in nineteenth-century international law

By the simple exercise of our will we can exert a power for good practically unbounded.[1]

Introduction

International law is universal. It is a body of law which applies to all states regardless of their specific and distinctive cultures, belief systems and political organizations. It is a common set of doctrines which all states, whether from Europe or Latin America, Africa or Asia use to regulate relations with each other. The association between international law and universality is so ingrained that pointing to this connection appears tautologous; it is today hard to conceive of an international law which is not universal. And yet, the universality of international law is a relatively recent development. It was not until the end of the nineteenth century that a set of doctrines was established as applicable to all states, whether these were in Asia, Africa or Europe.

The universalization of international law was principally a consequence of the imperial expansion which took place towards the end of the 'long nineteenth century'.[2] The conquest of non-European peoples for economic and political advantage was the most prominent feature of this period termed, by one eminent historian, the 'Age of Empire'. By

[1] Joseph Conrad, 'Heart of Darkness', in Morton Dauwen Zabel (ed.), *The Portable Conrad* (rev. edn., New York: Penguin Books, 1976), p. 561.
[2] Historians of the period tend to see the nineteenth century as extending up to 1914; it is the commencement of the First World War that marks the end of the century. See Eric Hobsbawm, *The Age of Empire, 1875–1914* (New York: Pantheon Books, 1987).

1914, after numerous colonial wars, virtually all the territories of Asia, Africa and the Pacific were controlled by the major European states and this resulted in the assimilation of all these non-European peoples into a system of law which was fundamentally European in that it derived from European thought and experience. The late nineteenth century was also the period in which positivism decisively replaced naturalism as the principal jurisprudential technique of the discipline of international law. The sovereign is the foundation of positivist jurisprudence, and nineteenth-century jurists sought to reconstruct the entire system of international law as a creation of sovereign will. Positivism was the new analytic apparatus used by the jurists of the time to account for the events which resulted in this dramatic development, the universalization of international law and the formulation of a body of principles which was understood to apply globally as a result of the annexation of 'unoccupied' territories such as the continent of Australia, the conquest of large parts of Asia and the partitioning of Africa.

This chapter focuses on the relationship between positivism and colonialism. My interest lies in examining the way in which positivism managed the colonial confrontation: what were the techniques, the doctrines, the legal methodologies developed to account for the expansion of European Empires and the various peoples and societies they dispossessed? In studying this relationship I seek not only to outline an architecture of the legal framework, but to question extant understandings of the relationship between colonialism and positivism, and the significance of the nineteenth-century colonial encounter for the discipline as a whole. This task requires an understanding of two bodies of scholarship, that relating to positivism and that relating to the application of positivism to the colonial encounter.

Positivist jurisprudence is based on the notion of the primacy of the state; and, despite subsequent attempts to reformulate the foundations of international law, the basic positivist position, that states are the principal actors of international law and they are bound only by that to which they have consented, continues to operate as the basic premise of the international legal system. Positivism, furthermore, has generated the problem which has governed the major theoretical inquiries into the discipline. That problem is: how can legal order be created among sovereign states? As I have previously suggested, the attempts to resolve this problem, and the critiques of these attempts, have, on the whole, constituted the central theoretical debate of the discipline over the twentieth century.[3] Indeed, it was in the nineteenth century that this problem took on the particularly challenging form that has marked the discipline ever since, this as a consequence of the emergence of positivism, and John Austin's famous criticism, explored in more detail below, of international law as failing to meet the requirements of international law properly so called. Colonialism features only very incidentally within this scheme. This appears inevitable, as the colonial confrontation was not a confrontation between two sovereign states, but between a sovereign European state and a non-European state which, according to the positivist jurisprudence of the time, was lacking in sovereignty. Such a confrontation poses no conceptual difficulties for the positivist jurist who basically resolves the issue by arguing that the sovereign state can do as it wishes with regard to the non-sovereign entity which lacks the legal personality to assert any legal opposition. This resolution was profoundly important from a political point of view as its operation resulted in the universalization of international law. However, it poses no theoretical difficulties; hence, the colonial world is relegated to both the geographical and theoretical peripheries of the discipline. This is the history I am examining; not with a view to furthering it but in an attempt to question its assumptions and its exclusions, and to point to the 'ambivalences, contradictions, the use of force, and the tragedies and ironies that attend it'.[4]

Certainly, colonies were often exasperatingly troublesome, in terms of both their governance and international jurisprudence; but for the international lawyers, colonial problems constituted a separate and distinct set of issues which were principally of a political character – how

---

[3] I am indebted to a number of important recent works which examine the importance of the nineteenth century to international law, as seen within this framework. These include Anthony Carty, *The Decay of International Law?: A Reappraisal of the Limits of Legal Imagination in International Affairs* (Manchester: Manchester University Press, 1986); David Kennedy, 'International Law and the Nineteenth Century: History of an Illusion', (1997) 17 *Quinnipiac Law Review* 99; Martti Koskenniemi, *From Apology to Utopia: The Structure of International Legal Argument* (Helsinki: Finnish Lawyers' Publishing Co., 1989); Martti Koskenniemi, 'Lauterpacht: The Victorian Tradition in International Law', (1997) 2 *European Journal of International Law* 215. I am also indebted to major works which deal with the entry of colonial states into the international system: James Crawford, *The Creation of States in International Law* (New York: Oxford University Press, 1979); Gerrit Gong, *The Standard of 'Civilization' in International Society* (New York: Oxford University Press, 1984).

[4] Dipesh Chakrabarty, 'Postcoloniality and the Artifice of History: Who Speaks for "Indian" Pasts?', (1992) 37 *Representations* 1, extracted in Bill Aschcroft, Gareth Griffiths and Helen Tiffin (eds.), *The Post-Colonial Studies Reader* (London: Routledge, 1995), p. 386.

COLONIALISM IN NINETEENTH-CENTURY INTERNATIONAL LAW

should the people be governed, what role should international law play in decolonization – issues which did not generally impinge in any significant way on the core theoretical concerns of the discipline.

Even when the colonies were perceived to challenge some of the fundamental assumptions of the discipline, as in the case of the doctrine of self-determination which was used in the 1960s and 1970s for the purpose of effecting the emergence of colonial territories into sovereign states, these challenges were perceived as threatening to disrupt a stable and established system of international law which was essentially and ineluctably European and which was now faced with the problem of accommodating these outsiders. The conceptualization of the problem in this way suggested again that the non-European world was completely peripheral to the discipline proper; and it was only the disconcerting prospect of Africans and Asians acquiring sovereignty in the 1950s and 1960s that alerted international lawyers to the existence of a world which was suddenly discovered to be multicultural.[5]

Scholars focusing on the colonial world naturally adopted a very different approach to the issue. The principal concern of these scholars was to show how positivist international law disenfranchised and subordinated non-European peoples. The naturalist international law which had applied in the sixteenth and seventeenth centuries asserted that a universal international law deriving from human reason applied to all peoples, whether European or non-European. By contrast, positivist international law distinguished between civilized states and non-civilized states and asserted further that international law applied only to the sovereign states which comprised the civilized 'family of nations'.

---

[5] For an examination of this period see, for example, Adda B. Bozeman, *The Future of Law in a Multicultural World* (Princeton: Princeton University Press, 1971); Réné-Jean Dupuy (ed.), *The Future of International Law in a Multicultural World: Workshop, The Hague, 17–19 November 1983* (London: Martinus Nijhoff, 1984). The axiomatically European character of international law has been often proclaimed. In his monumental work on the history of the discipline, Verzijl, for example, states:

> Now there is one truth that is not open to denial or even to doubt, namely that the actual body of international law, as it stands today, not only is the product of the conscious activity of the European mind, but has also drawn its vital essence from a common source of beliefs, and in both of these aspects it is mainly of Western European origin.
>
> (J. H. W. Verzijl, *International Law in Historical Perspective*, 10 vols., Leyden: A. W. Sijthoff, 1968, I, pp. 435–436)

It is not entirely surprising, then, that colonialism features only very incidentally even in much more recent works; see, for example, Jens Bartelson, *A Genealogy of Sovereignty* (New York: Cambridge University Press, 1995).

The important work of these scholars focused, then, on the complicity between positivism and colonialism.[6] Although the traditional view of the discipline downplays the importance of the colonial confrontation for an understanding of the subject as a whole, it is clear that much of the international law of the nineteenth century was preoccupied with colonial problems. It is explicitly recognised that special doctrines and norms had to be devised for the purpose of defining, identifying and placing the uncivilized, and this was what the jurists of the period proceeded to do when listing among the modes of acquiring territory, 'conquest' and 'cession by treaty'. While analysing and critiquing these doctrines and their effects, however, distinguished scholars such as Alexandrowicz tend implicitly to treat the colonial encounter as marginal to the discipline by studying it in terms of the effects of positivism on the colonial state.

My approach both borrows from and differs from these two broad approaches to the relationship between international law and the colonial confrontation. My argument is that the colonial confrontation is central to an understanding of the character and nature of international law, but that the extent of this centrality cannot be appreciated by a framework which adopts as the commencing point of its inquiry the problem of how order is created among sovereign states. In attempting to demonstrate this centrality I have focused not on the problem of how order is created among sovereign states, but on an alternative problem,

---

[6] The most notable scholar of this area is C. H. Alexandrowicz, whose extensive and pioneering body of work includes *An Introduction to the History of the Law of Nations in the East Indies* (Oxford: Clarendon Press, 1967) and *The European–African Confrontation: A Study in Treaty Making* (Leiden: A. W. Sijthoff, 1973). Many Third World scholars have examined the effect of the nineteenth century in their broader treatment of the relationship between colonialism and international law, e.g., R. P. Anand, *New States and International Law* (New Delhi: Vikas Publishing House, 1972), Taslim O. Elias, *Africa and the Development of International Law* (Leiden: A. W. Sijthoff, 1972) and Mohammed Bedjaoui, *Towards a New International Economic Order* (New York: Holmes & Meier, 1979). These works were written at a time when the newly independent states of Africa and Asia were assessing the history of the international system of which they were now full members. Other recent important works which deal with the issue of the significance of nineteenth-century colonialism to international law include Georges Abi-Saab, 'International Law and the International Community: The Long Road to Universality', in Ronald St John Macdonald (ed.), *Essays in Honor of Wang Tieya* (Dordrecht: Martinus Nijhoff, 1994), p. 31; Annelise Riles, 'Aspiration and Control: International Legal Rhetoric and the Essentialization of Culture', (1993) 106 *Harvard Law Review* 723; Siba N'zatioula Grovogui, *Sovereigns, Quasi Sovereigns and Africans: Race and Self-Determination in International Law* (Minneapolis, MN: University of Minnesota Press, 1996); Martti Koskenniemi, *The Gentle Civilizer of Nations: The Rise and Fall of International Law 1870–1960* (Cambridge: Cambridge University Press, 2002).

that of how order is created among entities characterized as belonging to entirely different cultural systems, the framework I sketched in chapter 1. I suggest, then, that the manoeuvres engaged in by positivist jurists with respect to colonialism may be best understood in terms of what might be termed the 'dynamic of difference': jurists using the conceptual tools of positivism postulated a gap, understood principally in terms of cultural differences, between the civilized European and uncivilized non-European world; having established this gap they then proceeded to devise a series of techniques for bridging this gap, of civilizing the uncivilized.

Such an approach enables an exploration of the relationship between ideas of culture and sovereignty, and the ways in which sovereignty became identified with a specific set of cultural practices to the exclusion of others. By adopting this framework I hope to inquire into a series of related problems: what does it mean to say that international law consists of rules to which sovereigns have acquiesced when certain societies were denied sovereign status? What are the processes by which this denial was justified and enforced? How does an understanding of these processes of denial offer a means of reinterpreting contemporary understandings of sovereignty doctrine and of positivism itself?

My broader and further goal is to contest the received and traditional understandings of positivism and of sovereignty doctrine which treat each of these ideas as independently and completely constituted within European thought and history. Within this framework, the relationship between positivism and colonialism is understood principally in terms of the disempowering effect that an already established positivism had on non-European peoples. Similarly, sovereignty doctrine is understood as a stable and comprehensive set of ideas which extended inexorably and imperiously with Empire into darkest Africa, the inscrutable Orient and the far reaches of the Pacific, acquiring control over these territories and peoples and transforming them into European possessions. The effects of the operation of these doctrines is no insignificant thing. My interest lies, however, not only in the important point that positivism legitimized conquest and dispossession, but in the reverse relationship, in identifying how positivism itself, sovereignty itself, were shaped by the encounter. In contrast to the view that the colonial confrontation illuminates a minor and negligible aspect of sovereignty doctrine, my argument is that no adequate account of sovereignty can be given without analyzing the constitutive effect of colonialism on sovereignty.

Colonialism was not an example of the application of sovereignty; rather, sovereignty was constituted through colonialism.[7]

In attempting to sketch this alternative history, I depart from the tendency, even among writers such as Alexandrowicz who are sympathetic to the injustices of colonialism, to focus on positivism's triumphant suppression of the non-European world. The violence of positivist language in relation to colonialism is hard to overlook. Positivists developed an elaborate vocabulary for denigrating non-European people, presenting them as suitable objects for conquest, and legitimizing the most extreme violence against them, all in the furtherance of the civilizing mission, the discharge of the white man's burden.[8] Despite this, it is incorrect to see the colonial encounter as a series of problems that were effortlessly resolved by the simple application of the formidable intellectual resources of positivism. Rather, I argue, positivists were engaged in an ongoing struggle to define, subordinate and exclude the native; my argument, further is that colonial problems posed a significant and, in the end, insuperable set of challenges to positivism and its pretensions to develop a set of doctrines which could coherently account for native personality, a task which was crucial to the positivist self-image. The brutal realities of conquest and dispossession can hardly be ameliorated by the assertion that the legal framework which legitimized this dispossession was contradictory and incoherent. But it is perhaps by pointing to these inconsistencies and ambiguities, by interrogating how it was that sovereignty became the exclusive preserve of Europe, by questioning this framework, even while describing how it came into being, that it might be possible to open the way not only towards a different history of the discipline, but to a different understanding of the workings and effects of colonialism itself.[9] This in turn is part of a larger project which has been the preoccupation of many jurists of the non-European

---

[7] This is to follow, with a little adaptation, Edward Said's concern to 'regard imperial concerns as constitutively significant to the culture of the modern West'. See Edward Said, *Culture and Imperialism* (New York: Knopf, 1993), p. 66.

[8] This corresponds exactly with Said's notion of Orientalism: 'Orientalism can be discussed and analysed as the corporate institution for dealing with Orient – dealing with it by making statements about it, authorizing views of it, describing it, by teaching it, settling it, ruling over it: in short, Orientalism as a Western style for dominating, restructuring, and having authority over the Orient.' Edward Said, *Orientalism* (New York: Pantheon Books, 1978), p. 3.

[9] The broad attempt, then, is to begin in some way the problematic task, which Dipesh Chakrabarty has formulated, of 'provincializing Europe'. 'Who Speaks for "Indian" Pasts?', p. 383. To attempt this project is paradoxical given that what I am examining is the process by which European international law became universal; as Chakrabarty

world: to understand the relationship between international law and colonialism in order to better formulate the potential of the discipline to transform the enduring inequities and imbalances which resulted from the colonial confrontation.

This inquiry is conducted through an analysis of the works of prominent jurists of the nineteenth century;[10] these include James Lorimer,[11] W. E. Hall,[12] John Westlake,[13] Thomas Lawrence,[14] and Henry Wheaton.[15] I have also considered the works of later jurists such as Lassa Oppenheim[16] and M. F. Lindley,[17] who wrote in the 1920s, but whose work adopts and elaborates the nineteenth-century framework.[18]

notes, 'The project of provincializing "Europe" refers to a history which does not yet exist'. *Ibid.*, p. 385.

[10] For a searching exploration of how European international lawyers as a community responded to issues of colonialism, see Koskenniemi, *The Gentle Civilizer of Nations*.

[11] James Lorimer, *The Institutes of the Law of Nations: A Treatise of the Jural Relations of Separate Political Communities* (Edinburgh: Blackwood & Sons, 1883).

[12] W. E. Hall, *A Treatise on International Law* (2nd edn., Oxford: Clarendon Press, 1884), the first edition of which was published in 1880 and which was revised on numerous occasions, was the major English treatise on the subject prior to the appearance of Oppenheim's *International Law* in 1905.

[13] Westlake was Whewell Professor of International Law in the University of Cambridge in 1894, at the time of the publication of his work, *Chapters on the Principles of International Law* (Cambridge: Cambridge University Press, 1894). It is notable that, for a work which purports to be general in scope, three of the eleven chapters deal quite explicitly with issues regarding the status and treatment of colonies and natives.

[14] Thomas Lawrence, *The Principles of International Law* (Boston: D.C. Heath, 1895).

[15] Henry Wheaton, *Elements of International Law* (Boston: Little, Brown & Co., 1866). Wheaton's work, which passed through several editions, was widely respected and used at this time.

[16] The first edition of Lassa Oppenheim's magisterial *International Law* was published in 1905. The work could be regarded as a superb embodiment of positivist jurisprudence. The analysis of this chapter is based on *International Law: A Treatise* (2nd edn., London: Longmans, Green & Co., 1912). This is perhaps the last great international law text of the long nineteenth century. Subsequent editions have been edited by a series of extremely eminent international lawyers, and Oppenheim's *International Law* continues to be, in all likelihood, the most authoritative and distinguished treatise on international law in the English language.

[17] M. F. Lindley, *The Acquisition and Government of Backward Territory in International Law: Being A Treatise on the Law and Practice Relating to Colonial Expansion* (New York: Negro Universities Press, 1969).

[18] For comprehensive accounts of the broader political contexts in which these judicial developments occurred, see Gong, *The Standard of 'Civilization'*; Hedley Bull and Adam Watson (eds.), *The Expansion of International Society* (New York: Oxford University Press, 1984); Adam Watson, *The Evolution of International Society: A Comparative Approach* (London: Routledge, 1992). For other useful but shorter works dealing with the same themes, see David Strang, 'Contested Sovereignty: The Social Construction of Colonial Imperialism', in Thomas J. Biersteker and Cynthia Weber (eds.), *State Sovereignty as Social Construct* (Cambridge: Cambridge University Press, 1996), pp. 22–50.

The second section of this chapter focuses on the basic elements of positivism, the analytical tools, methods and ambitions of positivist jurists, this in order to examine how issues of race and culture were always central to the very conceptualization and project of positivism, rather than a set of issues for which an established positivism developed an ancillary vocabulary. Furthermore, in studying the ambitions and methods of positivists, it becomes possible to appreciate the importance that these jurists placed on establishing the intellectual coherence and rigour of their discipline and, thereby, the significance of positivist attempts to coherently account for the colonial confrontation. The third section of this chapter explores the first step in the dynamic of difference, the process by which a gap is postulated between European and non-European peoples; it examines how cultural distinctions became the basis for establishing a legal status, and how sovereignty doctrine is constituted by the elaboration of these distinctions in such a way as to exclude non-European peoples from the realm of sovereignty.

The next section examines the process by which the gap is bridged and the non-European world is brought into the realm of international law. It focuses, first, on the techniques of assimilation and secondly, on the Berlin Africa Conference of 1885 which provides an example of the broader diplomatic and political contexts in which these doctrines were applied. The final section offers a reinterpretation of the significance of the nineteenth century to the discipline in the context of the previous analysis.[19]

Elements of positivist jurisprudence

Introduction

Positivists such as Westlake, Lawrence and Oppenheim, using a familiar technique, begin their works by providing a brief history of international law up to the time of their writing, this in order to better demonstrate how they differed from naturalists. These jurists distanced themselves from the inadequacies of naturalism by elaborating a positivism which, they asserted, was scientific, precise, comprehensive and capable of

---

[19] The language of the period is replete with racial aspersions to the 'uncivilized', 'natives', 'backward' and so forth, but I have refrained from placing these terms in quotations as I hope it is understood that the appearance of these terms in this work does not reflect my acceptance of them.

providing clear and coherent answers to any legal dispute it had to resolve. To these positivists, law was an abstract set of principles which was in important respects autonomous.

The philosophy of positivism provided the primary jurisprudential resource for the jurists of the late nineteenth century. In the naturalist scheme, the sovereign administered a system of natural law by which it was bound. Positivism, by way of contrast, asserts, not only that the sovereign administers and enforces the law, but that law itself is the creation of sovereign will. The sovereign is the foundation of positivist jurisprudence; and nineteenth-century positivist jurists essentially sought to reconstruct the entire system of international law based on their new version of sovereignty doctrine. Two additional factors are important to an understanding of the positivist project. Positivist international lawyers were heavily influenced by the English jurist, John Austin, who questioned whether international law could be regarded as law at all. International lawyers thus attempted to develop a jurisprudence which could address these objections. Finally, positivists sought to present their discipline as 'scientific' in character. Each of these factors was an important aspect of the positivist self-image, and played an important role in the development of positivist jurisprudence. Not only did positivism establish the legal framework that dealt with international disputes but, more broadly, it established the vocabulary, the set of constraints and considerations, which both shaped and were shaped by sovereignty doctrine.

Positivism and the shift from natural law

Positivist jurists generally commenced their campaign of articulating their new, distinctive versions of international law by employing the very traditional technique of sketching the histories of their discipline up to their own time, this as a means of distinguishing themselves from their naturalist predecessors. As discussed previously, even early jurists such as Francisco de Vitoria made a distinction between 'natural law' and 'human law'. In broad terms, natural law consisted of a set of transcendental principles which could be identified through the use of reason. Human law, on the other hand, as the term suggests, was created by secular political authorities, and positivism was an extended elaboration of this framework. Natural law was strongly identified with principles of justice, with the notion that all human activity was bound by an overarching morality. Thus within the naturalist framework, sovereign states were bound by the principles of natural law.[20]

The techniques of naturalist jurists are illustrated by jurists such as Grotius who argued that reason revealed a set of rules which governed relations between nations. Nineteenth-century writers such as Wheaton understood Grotius's science[21] to have been,

First, to lay down those rules of justice which would be binding on men living in a social state, independently on any positive laws of human institution; or, as is commonly expressed, living together in a state of nature; and,

Secondly, to apply those rules, under the name of Natural Law, to the mutual relations of separate communities living in a similar state with respect to each other.[22]

Naturalists did not completely ignore the importance of man-made laws, 'the positive laws of human institution' which were manifested in forms such as state practice, the customs observed among nations and the treaties into which they entered. Essentially, however, custom was still approached through the naturalist framework which examined and assessed the validity of state behaviour with reference to the transcendental principles originating from the 'state of nature', the model society whose laws could be identified and elaborated by reason and which, ideally, governed state behaviour. A gradual shift in this approach is evident from the mid-seventeenth century onwards. Vattel, whose major work, The Law of Nations,[23] first appeared in 1758, is a pivotal figure in this shift towards positivism; while Vattel retained many aspects of naturalist thinking, he emphasized the power and authority of the sovereign to an extent which raised doubts as to whether international law could ever bind the sovereign.[24] Jurists in the late eighteenth century and early nineteenth century combined positivism and naturalism in various

---

[20] However, as Richard Tuck has shown, naturalist techniques could be used to provide the sovereign with extensive powers. See Richard Tuck, The Rights of War and Peace: Political Thought and the International Order From Grotius to Kant (New York: Oxford University Press, 1999).

[21] The discussion here of naturalist jurisprudence is based on nineteenth-century understandings of this jurisprudence, rather than on my own analysis of the original works of jurists such as Grotius.

[22] Wheaton, Elements of International Law, chapter 1.1.

[23] Emer de Vattel, The Law of Nations or Principles of Natural Law Applied to the Conduct and to the Affairs of Nations and of Sovereigns (Charles G. Fenwick trans., Washington, DC: Carnegie Institution of Washington, 1916).

[24] See Koskenniemi, From Apology, pp. 85–98; Carty, The Decay of International Law, pp. 71–74; for a short and general treatment of Vattel, see Arthur Nussbaum, A Concise History of the Law of Nations (rev. edn., New York: Macmillan, 1954), pp. 156–158.

ways, arguing, for example, that while a certain universal natural law applied to all nations without distinction between civilized and non-civilized, a considerable body of positive law specific to Europe was also emerging.

Positivist law consisted of those rules which had been agreed upon by sovereign states, either explicitly or implicitly, as regulating relations between them.[25] Several late eighteenth-century jurists such as von Ompteda, Moser, Surland and Martens, noting the powerful emergence of positivist law, attempted to reconcile positivism and naturalism into an overall scheme of international law.[26] Traces of this reconciliatory approach may be found in some nineteenth-century jurists such as Lorimer who accepted that the law of nations comprised treaties and customs, but who argued that the overall purpose of the law of nations, derived from the law of nature,[27] was that of securing and furthering liberty.[28] Overall, however, the most influential late nineteenth-century positivists such as Westlake and Hall were emphatically and exclusively positivist. This trend was such that by 1908, Oppenheim, probably the most eminent scholar of his time, emphasized that 'we are no longer justified in teaching a law of nature and a "natural" law of nations'.[29]

For positivists, the sovereign state was the foundation of the entire legal system, and their broad project was to reconstitute the entire framework of international law based on this premise. Thus positivists rejected completely the naturalist notions that sovereign states were bound by an overarching natural law or that state action had to be guided by a higher morality. The sovereign was the highest authority, and could be bound only to that which it had agreed. Thus for positivists, the rules of international law were to be discovered not by speculative inquiries into the nature of justice or teleology, but by a careful study of the actual behaviour of states and the institutions and laws which they created.

Thus Westlake, for example, outlines his own approach in criticizing Pufendorff's argument that the rules relating to the immunities of ambassadors may be sought in natural law; Pufendorff.

---

[25] See C. H. Alexandrowicz, 'Doctrinal Aspects of the Universality of the Law of Nations', (1961) 37 British Yearbook of International Law 506–515 at 506.

[26] See ibid.

[27] Lorimer insisted on 'the exceptional dependence of the law of nations on the law of nature'. Lorimer, The Institutes of the Law of Nations, p. 23.

[28] See ibid., pp. 19–27.

[29] Lassa Oppenheim, 'The Science of International Law: Its Task and Method', (1908) 2 The American Journal of International Law   pp. 313, 328.

while insisting much on the social nature of man as the source of his duties . . .
missed the essential facts that, if society is to exist, it must establish rules free
from such undefinable elements as the principal purpose of an ambassador's
residence, and those rules must be acquiesced in by the members of the society.[30]

The teleological basis of Pufendorff's rule was unacceptable to positivists, for whom treaties and custom had replaced natural law as the
exclusive and primary source of international law. Treaties were an
expression of sovereign will. Furthermore, positivists argued, the practice of states was also a manifestation of sovereign will and could suggest
consent – either expressly or impliedly – to a set of customary laws. Thus,
for positivists, treaties and the developing body of custom was the best
guide to the proper rules of international behaviour.

In focusing on the sovereign as the exclusive and ultimate source of
law, positivist international jurists were following a long tradition which
had been notably developed by eminent political philosophers such as
Thomas Hobbes and Jean Bodin. The English jurists of the late nineteenth century, however, were most influenced by John Austin, the foremost spokesman for positivism at the time, who asserted famously that
'Laws properly so called are a species of commands. But, being a command, every law properly so called flows from a determinate source.'[31]
The source is, for Austin, as for international jurists, a sovereign.

International law could conform in many respects to Austin's notion
of law: international lawyers based their legal framework on sovereign
behaviour and, like Austin, insisted on the distinction between law and
morality or justice.[32] However, the international system lacked the global
sovereign crucial to Austin's scheme. Given his premise that all authority
derived from a determinate source and the acknowledged absence in
international relations of an overarching international sovereign, Austin
argued that 'the law obtaining between nations is not positive law: for
every positive law is set by a given sovereign to a person or person in a
state of subjection to its author'.[33]

Positivist international lawyers prided themselves on having rid the
discipline of insupportable arguments regarding 'natural law' and
its associated idea of a higher morality. Austin, however, intent on

---

[30] Westlake, *Chapters on the Principles of International Law*, p. 63.
[31] John Austin, *The Province of Jurisprudence Determined* (New York: Noonday Press, 1954),
p. 133.
[32] While Austin critiqued international law, in other respects, of course, Austin and
positivist international law were in close agreement.
[33] Austin, *The Province of Jurisprudence*, pp. 133, 201.

defining law in such a manner as to establish a sound basis for a science of jurisprudence, and rescuing it from the muddy speculations of naturalists, threatened such pretensions by his categorical assertion that international law itself was nothing more than morality.

Austin's challenge was taken up, not only by the international lawyers of succeeding generations, but by his contemporaries. Westlake,[34] Lawrence,[35] Oppenheim[36] and Walker,[37] for example, commence their works with attempts to refute or qualify Austin. In effect, these responses present a modified and more specific version of what law and positivism meant to international lawyers who set about establishing why international law was law despite its failure to meet Austinian criteria.

International jurists used both analytical and historical arguments,[38] often in combination, to refute Austin. The analytical argument questioned the adequacy of Austin's definition of law itself. Lawrence, for example, meets Austin's objection by arguing that his definition of law is not authoritative, and that alternative definitions should also be taken into account. Thus Lawrence argues 'If we follow Austin and hold that all laws are commands of superiors, International Law is improperly so called. If we follow Hooker and hold that whatever precepts regulate conduct are laws, International Law is properly so called.'[39] Lawrence seems to argue, in effect, that law can be said to exist as long as states observe a set of norms; it is irrelevant whether or not these norms are enunciated by some supreme, sovereign authority. Oppenheim similarly argued that Austin failed to take into account the reality of unwritten or customary law.[40] This law did not originate from a sovereign and hence failed to meet Austin's definition, and yet, even within national systems, such customary laws were recognised and administered by municipal courts.[41]

---

[34] See generally Westlake, *Chapters on the Principles of International Law*, preface and chapter 1.

[35] See generally Lawrence, *The Principles of International Law*, chapters 1, 2.

[36] See generally Oppenheim, *International Law*, p. 5.

[37] Thomas Alfred Walker, *A History of the Law of Nations: From the Earliest Times to the Peace of Westphalia* (Cambridge: Cambridge University Press, 1899).

[38] Analytical arguments focused on the consistency and adequacy of definitions; historical arguments drew on what had been revealed by historical researches into other societies. For an outline of what the two approaches constituted for international jurists, see Westlake, *Chapters on the Principles of International Law*, pp. vii–ix.

[39] Lawrence, *The Principles of International Law*, p. 25.

[40] See Oppenheim, *International Law*, p. 5.

[41] See *ibid*.

The reality and efficacy of customary law was further illustrated by the historical work of writers such as Sir Henry Maine. Maine adopted a distinctive approach to the relationships between law and society.[42] He had been a consistent critic of Austin and his fellow positivist Jeremy Bentham, and his works such as *Ancient Law* suggested powerfully that Austin's view of law was very limited and that societies had generally been governed by conceptions of law which differed markedly from those defined by Austin.[43] International jurists such as Walker[44] and Lawrence[45] seized upon Maine's researches, the 'hard facts of History'[46] to point to the inadequacy of Austin's definition. International jurists, furthermore, had a particular interest in stressing the importance of customary law, as customary law was one of the principal, if not the principal, sources of international law.

Austin had anticipated such criticisms by explicitly arguing that custom was not a proper source of law. Referring to the existence of custom in a domestic setting, Austin argued:

At its origin, a custom is a rule of conduct which the governed observe spontaneously, or not in pursuance of a law set by a political superior. The custom is transmuted into positive law, when it is adopted as such by the courts of justice, and when the judicial decisions fashioned upon it are enforced by the power of the state. But before it is adopted by the courts and clothed with the legal sanction, it is merely a rule of positive morality: a rule generally observed by the citizens or subjects but deriving the only force, which it can be said to possess, from the general disapprobation falling on those who transgress it.[47]

This passage illustrates not only the indispensability of a sovereign to Austin's scheme, but the extent to which his whole concept of law is based on a very specific idea of society and political arrangements. The debate remained – and remains – unresolved. But to the extent that international jurists could make a case, it depended largely on establishing that a functioning system of rules governed the behaviour of states, as exemplified by the operation of customary international law.

---

[42] Carl Landauer, 'From Status to Treaty: Henry Sumner Maine's International Law', (2002) XV(2) *Canadian Journal of Law and Jurisprudence* 219–254.

[43] Sir Henry Sumner Maine, *Ancient Law: Its Connection with the Early History of Society and Its Relation to Modern Ideas* (1st American edn., New York: C. Scribner, 1864), p. 6.

[44] Walker, *A History of the Law of Nations*, pp. 8–19.

[45] For a discussion of Lawrence's use of Maine, see Riles, 'Aspiration and Control', 723.

[46] Walker, *A History of the Law of Nations*, p. 8.

[47] Austin, *The Province of Jurisprudence*, p. 31.

This raised a further question for the jurist: in what circumstances, among which actors, could custom be said to arise in the dispersed international context? Custom, to international jurists, presupposed the existence of society. And 'society' is the metaphor, the central concept used elsewhere by Lawrence and by virtually all international lawyers of this period in their efforts to credibly suggest the existence of rules which are observed even in the absence of a supreme authority. 'International law', proclaims Westlake, 'is the body of rules prevailing between states'.[48] He proceeds to explain this to mean that

states form a society, the members of which claim from each other the observance of certain lines of conduct, capable of being expressed in general terms as rules and hold themselves justified in mutually compelling such observance, by force if necessary; also that in such society the lines of conduct in question are observed with more or less regularity, either as the result of compulsion or in accordance with the sentiments which would support compulsion in case of need.[49]

Within this scheme, sovereignty is important, inasmuch as society is constituted by sovereign states. Equally, however, it is because these states exist in society that international law can claim to be law. The interaction of the members of this society gives rise to rules which are regularly observed and which are enforced by sanctions. Consequently, society constituted law and law constituted society. It is through a complicated inter-play between law and society that the result is circularly achieved, that international order is maintained and international law created:

Without society no law, without law no society. When we assert that there is such a thing as international law, we assert that there is a society of states: when we recognize that there is a society of states, we recognize that there is international law.[50]

When focusing on the idea of law, Westlake writes that

perhaps no better account can be given of what is commonly understood by law than that it is a body of rules expressing the claims which, in a given society, are held to be enforceable and are more or less commonly observed.[51]

Westlake unsurprisingly deviates here from the Austinian approach of looking to the source of these laws in order to locate the single

[48] Westlake, *Chapters on the Principles of International Law*, p. 1.
[49] *Ibid.*, p. 2.   [50] *Ibid.*, p. 3.   [51] *Ibid.*, p. 2.

authority, the sovereign, from whom they should all properly emanate. Law is not imposed from above by a sovereign but agreed upon by the relevant entities. Law exists where there is a regularity in dealings, when the members of the society regard themselves as bound by the rules, and where sanctions of some sort would follow a breach. The notion of a 'community', 'society' or a 'family'[52] becomes fundamental to the definition of law, as illustrated by Oppenheim's argument that 'law is a body of rules for human conduct within a community which by common consent of this community shall be enforced by external law'.[53]

Thus, society, rather than sovereignty, is the central concept used to construct the system of international law. Despite the positivist claims that the sovereign was the exclusive basis for the international system, it was only if society was introduced into the system that positivists could approximate the idea of 'law' to which they urged adherence. Society, then, provides the matrix of ideas, the analytical resources which, allied with sovereignty, could establish a positivist international legal order. This is an important shift: for implicit in the idea of society is membership; only those states accepted into society and which agree upon principles regulating their behaviour can be regarded as belonging to society. The concepts of society, furthermore, enabled the formulation and elaboration of the various cultural distinctions that were crucial to the constitution of sovereignty doctrine.

International law as science

The decisively important status accorded to natural sciences such as physics and biology profoundly influenced both domestic and international law. The epistemological validity of the scientific method was demonstrated, not only by the triumph of Darwin's ideas[54] on natural selection, but the massive success of the industrial revolution which had been made possible by scientific discoveries.[55] While jurists understood

---

[52] The terms 'family of nations' or 'community of nations' are used quite interchangeably by positivist jurists.

[53] Oppenheim, *International Law*, p. 8. For Oppenheim's general discussion on 'community', see *ibid.*, pp. 8–9. 'Innumerable are the interests which knit all the individualised civilized States together and which create constant intercourse between these States as well as between their subjects.' *Ibid.*, p. 10. (The creation of unity among European states.)

[54] On the importance of Darwin for validating the new 'scientific method', see J. M. Roberts, *A History of Europe* (Oxford: Helicon, 1996), pp. 342–344.

[55] On the place of science in society at the end of the nineteenth century, see generally Hobsbawm, *The Age of Empire*, chapters 10–11.

that jurisprudence could not achieve the same results as the natural sciences, it was important for them to be engaged in a 'scientific inquiry'; this involved redefining their disciplines in ways which appeared compatible with the scientific framework in an attempt to elevate not only their discipline, but their profession.[56] The human sciences, of which international law was a part, could not, of course be studied in the same way as natural sciences: but while asserting that international law is not a natural science, Westlake nevertheless introduces his work as considering 'the place of international law among the sciences',[57] and international lawyers of the period invariably refer to the 'science' of international law.[58] The positivist self-image of being engaged in a scientific inquiry – and all that suggested in terms of rigour, consistency and precision – played an important role in the method, elaboration and application of nineteenth-century jurisprudence. The positivists sought to develop a scientific methodology to identify and interpret relevant forms of state behaviour in the midst of the general flux and confusion of international relations. Thus Lawrence writes of the great international lawyers of the nineteenth century as producing 'order from chaos, and made International Law into a science, instead of a shapeless mass of undigested and sometimes inconsistent rules'.[59]

[handwritten margin note: THIS WAS ALL ABOUT SELF-IMAGE AND STATUS]

The term 'science' was used in very varied and complex ways by different international lawyers, but some of the core ideas as to the science of international law are illustrated by Lawrence, who

regards International Law, not as an instrument for the discovery and interpretation of a transcendental rule of right binding upon states as moral beings whether they observe it or not in practice, but as a science whose chief business it is to find out by observation the rules actually followed by states in their mutual intercourse, and to classify and arrange these rules by referring them to certain fundamental principles on which they are based.[60]

---

[56] This issue is explored by David Sugarman, '"A Hatred of Disorder": Legal Science, Liberalism and Imperialism', in Peter Fitzpatrick (ed.), *Dangerous Supplements* (Durham, NC: Duke University Press, 1991), p. 47. As Koskenniemi notes: 'By [the] early 19th century, international law has become a science, an academic discipline taught separately from, on the one hand, theology, philosophy and natural law and, on the other, civil law.' Koskenniemi, *From Apology*, p. 98 (footnotes omitted).

[57] Westlake, *Chapters on the Principles of International Law*, p. vi.

[58] Thus Oppenheim's notable attempt to define the project of international law is titled *The Science of International Law: Its Task and Method*, see Oppenheim, *The Science of International Law*.

[59] Lawrence, *The Principles of International Law*, p. 94.   [60] *Ibid.*, p. 1.

Order could be established through classification, of both the legal phenomena of state behaviour and of the rules of international law itself. Law is concerned, according to Westlake, with the 'classification of institutions or facts';[61] furthermore, it is 'with law as an institution or fact that the legal student has to deal.[62] Facts having been classified and the rules of international law having been identified, the further and broader task was to 'classify and arrange these rules' in an effort to develop a coherent and overarching international law.

This endeavour pointed to a further tension in positivist jurisprudence. On the one hand, as its reliance on custom demonstrated, this jurisprudence encompassed the idea of flux and development. As the needs of states changed, so too would the treaties they entered into and the practices they engaged in. The positivist differed from the naturalist precisely in asserting that there were no immutable, transcendent laws. At the same time, however, positivists argued that whatever the changes in international law, all the rules emerging from such developments referred back to certain 'fundamental principles', to use Lawrence's terminology. Thus, whatever the haphazardness, flux and uncertainty of state practice, it was ordered and understood by a fixed set of principles which classified and processed the raw material of practice and reconstituted it into a coherent and complete legal framework.

The origins and character of the ordering mechanism which performed these vital tasks, however, assumed a transcendental quality which seemed beyond history and beyond inquiry. Indeed, to adopt any approach which denied the fixed quality of these principles could undermine the entire system of law. For many jurists, it was only by adopting an historical approach that international law could overcome Austinian objections. Nevertheless, once established as a discipline, international law repudiated the historical approach which had the potential to challenge the implicit assumption that the principles used by jurists to order

---

[61] Westlake, *Chapters on the Principles of International Law*, p. 12. Horwitz's comments on the American jurisprudence of the period apply no less accurately to the international jurists of the time:

> Nineteenth-century legal thought was overwhelmingly dominated by categorical thinking – by clear, distinct, bright-line classifications of legal phenomena. Late nineteenth-century legal reasoning brought categorical modes of thought to their highest fulfilment.
>
> (Morton J. Horwitz, *The Transformation of American Law 1870–1960: The Crisis of Legal Orthodoxy*, New York: Oxford University Press, 1992, p. 17)

[62] Westlake, *Chapters on the Principles of International Law*, p. 12.

the world of legal phenomena were in some way eternal, beyond history. The danger of adopting such an approach was evident even to lawyers in the domestic sphere. Adoption of the historical or literary approach would result in a debilitating awareness of flux and contingency, warned Frederick Harrison, Professor of Jurisprudence at the Inns of Court in 1879:

It would lead to the utmost confusion of thought . . . if we come to regard historical explanations as the substantial or independent part of jurisprudence. From history we always get ideas of . . . constant development, of instability. But in law, at any rate for the purposes of the practical lawyer, what we need are ideas of fixity, of uniformity. It is so great a strain upon the mind to build up and retrace the conception of a great body of titles reducible to abstract and symmetrical classification, and capable of statement as a set of consistent principles – and this is what I take jurisprudence to be – that we are perpetually in danger of giving to law a literary instead of a scientific character, and in slipping in our thoughts from what the law is into speculating upon the coincidences which make it what it once was.[63]

This scientific methodology favoured, then, a movement towards abstraction – a propensity, to rely upon a formulation of categories and their systematic exposition as a means of preserving order and arriving at the correct 'solution' to any particular problem. Legal science in the latter half of the nineteenth century was conceived of, even in the municipal sphere, as a struggle against chaos which could be won only by ensuring the autonomy of law, and establishing and maintaining the taxonomies and principles which existed in fixed relations to each other. What Harrison warns against is any attempt to examine the manner in which a particular mode of classification or system of law came into being; it is precisely this inquiry, however, that the 'historical approach' which he condemns would advocate.[64] Thus, within the

---

[63] Cited in Sugarman, '"A Hatred of Disorder"', p. 51.

[64] It must be noted that other nineteenth-century writers such as Lawrence espoused the historical approach. See Lawrence, *The Principles of International Law*, p. 16, where he raises the issue of whether the inquiry into international law should be based on an *a priori* or historical method. As Lawrence himself makes clear, however, he uses these terms to signify the distinction between 'what the rules of international intercourse ought to be, or an historical investigation of what they are'. *Ibid*. There is no inconsistency between Lawrence and Harrison, then, as they use the term 'historical' in different respects. The larger historical challenge was presented by writers such as Sir Henry Maine, who pointedly criticized Austin's attempt to outline a system of law based on logic rather than history. Maine himself elaborated the Historical approach in his own famous work *Ancient Law* (1864).

analytic approach, the myth of the state of nature is replaced, in positivist jurisprudence, with the myth of a fixed set of principles and a scheme of classifications which reveals itself to the scrutiny of the expert jurist who uses this scheme to establish and develop international law.

While thus outlining a sophisticated scientific technique, however, the question remained as to how these positivist jurists related these techniques – this emphasis on taxonomy, on the juridical character of state behaviour – with the idea of 'society' which was indispensable to any claim that international law possessed any sort of status as law, and which was the basis of the defence presented by Westlake and Lawrence against Austin's charges. In order for the reconstructed system of positivism with all its claims to being a science to work, international lawyers had to develop something like a sociological vision, an understanding of various attributes of societies and their customs and the way in which they functioned, both internally and externally, in relation to each other. Society and history were the subject of positivist scrutiny. For positivists, the concepts and classifications they employed could be used to order history and society, but these same concepts and classifications were outside and beyond history. This was one means by which positivism presented itself as universal and eternal, existing in a realm beyond the reach of historical scrutiny. Positivism, in this way sought to suppress its own past. How could the positivist insistence on the primacy of concepts and on the autonomy of law accommodate, encompass, this sociological aspect upon which it was so curiously and ambivalently dependent for its functioning?

The tensions and ambivalences generated by positivist attempts to articulate a new and scientific jurisprudence were as important a part of that body of thought as its self-consciously proclaimed modernity and rigour.

Defining and excluding the uncivilized

Positivism, society and the uncivilized

A further central feature of positivism was the distinction it made between civilized and uncivilized states. The naturalist notion that a single, universally applicable law governed a naturally constituted society of nations was completely repudiated by jurists of the mid-nineteenth century.[65] Instead, nineteenth-century writers such as Wheaton claimed that international law was the exclusive province of civilized societies. Wheaton's brief discussion of earlier jurists such as Grotius suggests a trend which culminated in Wheaton's own stance; Grotius states that law (*jus gentium*) 'acquires its obligatory force from the positive consent of all nations, or at least of several'.[66] While this emphasis on the consent of nations foreshadows a central characteristic of positivism, Wheaton notes that Grotius makes no further distinction between different types of nations; nor does he suggest, while acknowledging these differences, that some nations should be granted priority as opposed to others, that some nations participate in the law of nations while others do not.[67] No distinction is made between the civilized and the uncivilized.

Within Wheaton's scheme, the relative cosmopolitanism of Grotius contrasts with the narrower approaches of jurists such as Bynkershoek, who argued that only the practice of civilized states acquires legal currency. He states that 'the law of nations is that which is observed, in accordance with the light of reason, between nations, if not among all, *at least certainly among the greater part, and those the most civilized*' (emphasis in the original).[68]

Despite this trend towards excluding the uncivilized states, non-European states were recognised as part of the law of nations even in the early part of the nineteenth century. In a decision handed down in 1825, *The Antelope*, the Supreme Court of the United States confronted the issue of whether slavery was an acceptable practice according to the law of nations. Chief Justice Marshall, in examining this issue, asserted that:

---

[65] Hence Wheaton's critique of Wolf, who argued that the law of nations was something to which all nations had consented, basing this theory on 'the fiction of a great commonwealth of nations (*civitate gentium maxima*) instituted by nature herself, and of which all the nations of the world are members'. Wheaton, *Elements of International Law*, p. 10 (footnote omitted).

[66] Wheaton, *Elements of International Law*, p. 10.   [67] *Ibid.*

[68] Wheaton, *Elements of International Law*, p. 10. Montesquieu offers a further variation on these themes; even while dismissing the practices of non-European peoples, he suggests that all nations have some sort of 'international law', which governs their relations with their neighbours: thus 'even the Iroquois, who eat their prisoners, have one. They send and receive ambassadors; they know the laws of war and peace; the evil is, that their law of nations is not founded upon true principles.' *Ibid.*

The parties to the modern law of nations do not propagate their principles by force; and Africa has not yet adopted them [the modern principles relating to the abolition of slavery]. Throughout the whole of that immense continent, so far as we know its history, it is still the law of nations that prisoners are slaves.[69]

The passage is notable for its gesture towards including Africa within the law of nations and suggesting that European states, indeed America itself, had to respect the law of nations as practised within Africa – although, ironically, it is African law which ostensibly supports slavery.

By the latter part of the nineteenth century, however, whatever the systems of law existent on that 'immense continent', they are made irrelevant; the custom which counts as law is that which is practised only among the 'civilized countries'. By 1866, Wheaton by contrast argued:

Is there a uniform law of nations? There certainly is not the same one for all the nations and states of the world. The public law, with slight exceptions, has always been, and still is, limited to the civilized and Christian people of Europe or to those of European origin.[70]

As I have argued, naturalists such as Vitoria recognised the existence of important cultural differences between, for example, the Spanish and the Indians of the Americas. Nevertheless, they asserted that all societies were bound by a universal natural law. The gap between the European and non-European worlds was as evident to Wheaton as it was to Vitoria. For Wheaton and the jurists who succeeded him, however, this gap was to be bridged not by a universal natural law but by the explicit imposition of European international law over the uncivilized non-Europeans. It is simply and massively asserted that only the practice of European states was decisive and could create international law. Only European law counted as law. Non-European states were excluded from the realm of law, now identified as being the exclusive preserve of European states, as a result of which the former were deprived of membership and the ability to assert any rights cognizable as legal. In its most extreme form, positivist reasoning suggested that relations and transactions between the European and non-European states occurred entirely outside the realm of law.[71]

Thus the state of nature that naturalists used as a basis for the formulation of rules of international law was unsatisfactory, not only

[69] *The Antelope*, 23 U.S. (10 Wheaton) 5 at 66 (1825).
[70] Wheaton, *Elements of International Law*, p. 15.
[71] Gong, *The Standard of 'Civilization'*, pp. 53–57.

because it was subjective, imprecise and based on transcendental principles rather than the realities of state behaviour, but because it failed to make the distinction between the civilized and uncivilized. Westlake writes:

No theorist on law who is pleased to imagine a state of nature independent of human institutions can introduce into his picture a difference between civilized and uncivilized man, because it is just in the presence or absence of certain institutions or in their greater or less perfection, that that difference consists for the lawyer.[72]

The existence of a distinction between the civilized and the uncivilized was so vehemently presupposed by positivist jurists, that the state of nature – and therefore naturalism – becomes epistemologically incoherent because it lacks this central distinction. Quite apart from the notorious failure of naturalism to focus exclusively on state will, then, it was rejected by the positivists for this second reason. Positivist jurisprudence was so insistent on this distinction that any system of law which failed to acknowledge it was unacceptable. In crude terms, in the naturalist world, law was given; in the positivist world, law was created by human societies and institutions. Once the connection between 'law' and 'institutions' had been established, it followed from this premise that jurists could focus on the character of institutions, a shift which facilitated the racialization of law by delimiting the notion of law to very specific European institutions.

As for the political implications following adherence to this distinction, Westlake himself immediately suggests how it could be deployed by justifying his claim that 'the occupation by uncivilized tribes of a tract, of which according to our habits a small part ought to have sufficed for them, was not felt to interpose a serious obstacle to the right of the first civilized occupant'.[73] Once the distinction is made, then, completely different standards could be applied to the two categories of people. Whatever the practices of the 'uncivilized tribes', in a situation where these practices conflict with the assessment made by the civilized as to the 'real needs' of the uncivilized in relation to land, it is the latter which prevails. Broadly, once non-European states were excluded from the realm of sovereignty, they were precluded from making any sort of legal claim in the realm of international law because only sovereign states were able to participate as full members with all the attendant rights and powers.

[72] Westlake, *Chapters on the Principles of International Law*, p. 137.   [73] *Ibid.*

In summary, the distinction between the civilized and uncivilized was a fundamental tenet of positivist epistemology and thus profoundly shaped the concepts constituting the positivist framework. The racialization of positivist law followed inevitably from these premises – as demonstrated, for example, by the argument that law was the creation of unique, civilized and social institutions and that only states possessing such institutions could be members of 'international society'. In distinguishing between the civilized and uncivilized at all these different levels, positivist jurisprudence created the first element of what I have termed the 'dynamic of difference', the postulation of a gap between the European and non-European worlds which had to be bridged by positivist international law.

The uncivilized and defining sovereignty

The task of defining sovereignty was fundamental to positivist jurisprudence – and not merely because definition was such an integral part of positivist reasoning and methodology. The positivist insistence that sovereignty was the founding concept of the international system led naturally to a careful scrutiny of what entities could be regarded as 'sovereign'. This was an important theoretical and practical issue, given the positivist argument that the sovereign had supreme authority. Such a project of definition was not so fundamental to the naturalist framework as that jurisprudence outlined a system of law which applied to all human activity, whether of an individual or a sovereign. By contrast, the jurisprudence of 'personality', which dealt with the question of defining the proper subjects of international law, was one of the central issues explored by positivist jurists.[74] Given that the civilized–non-civilized distinction expelled the non-European world from the realm of law and society, the question arose: could non-European societies be regarded as sovereign? It was simple enough to assert that the civilized possessed sovereignty while the uncivilized did not. But positivist jurisprudence had to plausibly establish that cultural difference translated into legal difference. Positivists were equipped with a number of analytical tools to

---

[74] Thus the major treatises of the period, such as Hall and Oppenheim, discussed the 'law of persons' in either the first or second chapter of their works. Hall begins his work with a chapter titled 'Persons in International Law, and Communities Possessing A Character Analogous to Them'. See generally Hall, *A Treatise on International Law*, chapter 1, while Oppenheim provides a theory and history of international law in his introductory chapter and titles the next part of his work 'The Subjects of the Law of Nations'. Oppenheim, *International Law*, Table of contents.

arrive at such a conclusion but, given the positivist preoccupation with consistency and coherence, it had to do so in a manner consistent with the broad complex of ideas and systems of thinking which constituted sovereignty doctrine and positivist jurisprudence.

The task of identifying the 'sovereign' and defining 'sovereignty' were inter-related tasks which posed a number of complex problems for jurists. The task involved distinguishing sovereigns proper from other entities – such as pirates, non-European states and nomads – which also seemed to possess the attributes of sovereignty. How could it be claimed within this jurisprudence that the barbarian nations, 'a wandering tribe with no fixed territory to call its own', a 'race of savages' and a 'band of pirates'[75] were not sovereign? This question posed a dilemma to nineteenth-century jurists, whose understanding of positivism was ineluctably affected by Austin: simply, these entities satisfied the essential Austinian criteria of sovereignty. As Lawrence acknowledges, even the wandering tribe might 'obey implicitly a chief who took no commands from other rulers';[76] pirates, similarly, 'might be temporarily under the sway of a chief with unrestricted power'.[77]

The general answer was that <u>sovereignty implied control over territory.</u> For positivists, sovereignty could be most clearly defined as control over territory. Thus Lawrence states:

International Law regards states as political units possessed of proprietary rights over definite portions of the earth's surface. So entirely is its conception of a state bound up with the notion of territorial possession that it would be impossible for a nomadic tribe, even if highly organised and civilized, to come under its provisions.[78]

Whatever the extent to which an entity may have satisfied the other criteria of statehood, then, a failure to occupy territory would preclude that entity from being treated as sovereign. The primacy of territory is again emphasized by Lawrence when considering two possible bases for the exercise of jurisdiction by a state, and deciding finally that juris-diction over territory takes precedence over jurisdiction over citizens. Thus Lawrence argues that 'Modern International law, being permeated throughout by the doctrine of territorial sovereignty, has adopted the latter principle as fundamental.'[79]

<u>Territorial control is thus fundamental to sovereignty,</u> whatever the exceptions established to this rule – in the form of the principle, for

---

[75] Lawrence, *The Principles of International Law*, p. 58.   [76] *Ibid.*   [77] *Ibid.*
[78] *Ibid.*, p. 136.   [79] Lawrence, *The Principles of International Law*, p. 190.

example, that foreign sovereigns and diplomats are not completely subjected to a state's jurisdiction although they may be present within the
territory of that state.[80] Thus wandering tribes could not be sovereign
because they failed the territorial requirement; they were not in sole
occupation of a particular area of land. But the problem then confronting the jurists was that many of the uncivilized Asiatic and African
states easily met both the Austinian definition of sovereignty and the
requirement of control over territory; they thus posed a great problem
to positivist attempts to distinguish civilized and uncivilized societies.
Further, the historical reality, as Alexandrowicz points out regarding the
Indies, for example, was that:

> All the major communities in India as well as elsewhere in the East Indies were
> politically organised; they were governed by their Sovereigns, they had their
> legal systems and lived according to centuries-old cultural traditions.[81]

In Africa, as scholars such as Elias have argued, the kingdoms of Benin,
Ethiopia and Mali, for instance, were sophisticated and powerful polit-
ical entities which were accorded the respect due to sovereigns by the
European states with which they established diplomatic relations.[82]

Positivist jurists could hardly disregard these facts, given especially
that European powers had entered into treaties with such communities.
The works of eighteenth-century jurists, for instance, gave accounts of
diplomatic usages in countries such as Persia, Siam, Turkey and China,
analysed the negotiations which led to the making of various treaties,
and included these treaties within larger collections of international
treaties.[83] Confronted with this dilemma, positivists resorted once more
to the concept of society. The broad response was that Asiatic states,
for example, could be formally 'sovereign'; but unless they satisfied the
criteria of membership in civilized international society, they lacked the
comprehensive range of powers enjoyed by the European sovereigns who
constituted international society.[84]

---

[80] Ibid., p. 221.   [81] Alexandrowicz, An Introduction, p. 14.

[82] See Elias, Africa, pp. 6–15. For a detailed study of the early history of treaty making
between African and European states, see Alexandrowicz, The European–African
Confrontation.

[83] See Alexandrowicz, 'Doctrinal Aspects'; see also Jeremy Thomas, 'History and
International Law in Asia: A Time for Review?', in Ronald St John Macdonald (ed.),
Essays in Honor of Wang Tieya (Dordrecht: Martinus Nijhoff, 1994).

[84] On the problems of categorizing these entities, see Oppenheim: 'No other explanation
of these and similar facts [the fact that these non-entities engaged in sovereign
behaviour] can be given except that these not-full Sovereign States are in some way or

The creation and maintenance of the division between the civilized and uncivilized was crucial to the intellectual and political validity of positivist jurisprudence. The distinction between the civilized and uncivilized was to be made, then, not in the realm of sovereignty, but of society. Society and the constellation of ideas associated with it promised to enable the jurist to link a legal status to a cultural distinction. Thus positivists argued that sovereignty and society posed two different tests, and the decisive issue was whether or not a particular entity – even a sovereign – was a full member of international society. Lawrence makes this point when considering the legal status of a wandering tribe:

> yet none of these communities would be subject to International Law, because they would want various characteristics, which, though not essential to sovereignty, are essential to the membership of the family of nations.[85]

The tribes remain outside the realm of international law, not so much because they lack sovereignty, but because they are wanting in the other characteristics essential to membership of international society. It follows then, despite positivist preoccupations with sovereignty doctrine, that 'society' and the 'family of nations', is the essential foundation of positivist jurisprudence and of the vision of sovereignty it supports. In the final analysis, non-European states are lacking in sovereignty because they are excluded from the family of nations. The novel manoeuvre of focusing on society enabled positivist jurists to overcome the historical fact that non-European states had previously been regarded as sovereign, that, by and large, they enjoyed all the rights accompanying this status, and that their behaviour constituted a form of practice and precedent that gave rise to rules and doctrines of international law.

The concept of society enabled positivists to develop a number of strategies for explaining why the non-European world was excluded from international law. One such strategy consisted of asserting that no law existed in certain non-European, barbaric regions. According to this argument, the distinction between the civilized and uncivilized was too obvious to require elaboration. Thus Lawrence, for example, states 'It would, for instance, be absurd to expect the king of Dahomey to establish a Prize Court, or to require the dwarfs of the central African

---

another International Persons and subjects of International Law.' Oppenheim, *International Law*, p. 110. See *ibid.*, pp. 154–156.

[85] Lawrence, *The Principles of International Law*, p. 58.

forest to receive a permanent diplomatic mission'.[86] Such powerful evo-
cations of the backward and barbaric confirmed the incongruity and
unthinkability of any correspondence between Europe and these societies. Law did no more than maintain an essential and self-evident
distinction.

And yet, closer examination of primitive societies suggested disconcerting parallels. Westlake describes the inquiries of the 'historical
school' into societies 'remote from our own':

> We learn from them how the different peoples whom we study usually con-
> ducted themselves with regard to family, property, or any other matter which
> in our actual England is regulated by law; by what beliefs and motives and by
> what commands or compulsion if any, their conduct was kept to its usual lines.
> And by accumulating a number of such investigations we learn how what we
> now know as the law of a country has arisen. But the analytical school are cer-
> tainly right in maintaining that, if we give the name of law to anything which
> we so discover in a remote state of society before we have fixed in our minds
> what we mean by that name, we beg the question, and have no security that
> our language has any consistent and therefore useful sense.[87]

The passage reflects many of the techniques of positivism analysed
earlier. The 'analytical school' establishes a definition, adheres to it and
applies it rigorously and unyieldingly. Any conflict between the realities disclosed by the historical researchers and the definition must
be resolved in favour of the definition, in order to maintain its 'consistent and therefore useful sense'. Language, it would seem, cannot
yield to acknowledged empirical reality where this could lead to destabilizing the concepts and categories on which the system is based. In
the final analysis, it would seem, the matter is decided by the simple
assertion that whatever the commonalities between European and non-
European societies, European societies are civilized and sovereign while
non-European societies are not. Thus Westlake, even while acknowledging the fact that 'different peoples' can possess a system which

---

[86] *Ibid.* For an insightful study of this rhetoric, see Riles, 'Aspiration and Control', 723. As
Riles points out in her important study, 'Lawrence's polemic participated on a number
of levels in the creation of an essentialised and coherent European community
defined in dichotomous opposition to non-European "savages".' *Ibid.*, 736. As Riles
further elaborates: 'This essentialised European identity depended however, upon an
opposition of Europe to non-Europe that articulated in symbolic terms inequalities of
power between Europeans and their colonial subjects.' Riles, 'Aspiration and Control',
737.

[87] Westlake, *Chapters on the Principles of International Law*, p. viii.

disconcertingly parallels that of England, quickly proceeds to affirm that 'our actual England is regulated by law'.[88]

Law, then, is the preserve of England; and while other remote societies may appear to have their own laws, any tendency to affirm this similarity must be immediately repulsed as it could result in the collapse of the language of sovereignty and therefore of international law itself. Simply and summarily then, within nineteenth-century jurisprudence, law cannot be defined in such a way as to encompass the practices which historical research demonstrates as serving the same function as 'law' in Western society.

The methodology of the analytical school was thus important, not merely in terms of the broad theoretical debate it was engaged in with the historical school, but because it was through the suppression of implications arising from the historical school that the analytical school could make the distinction between the civilized and non-civilized which was central to positivist attempts to preserve the coherence of their jurisprudence in the face of the problems posed by the non-European world.

A second strategy used to distinguish the civilized from the uncivilized consisted of asserting that while certain societies may have had their own systems of law these were of such an alien character that no proper legal relations could develop between European and non-European states. Positivist jurists such as Westlake, then, made further distinctions between the Asiatic states, for example, which were characterized as being in certain respects civilized but 'different'[89] and the 'tribal peoples' who were more severely denounced as completely backward.[90]

In this way, positivists formulated different classifications for the non-Europeans, and distinctions were made for certain purposes between the societies of Asia, Africa and the Pacific.[91] Basically, however, these classifications were irrelevant in terms of the broad issue of the central

---

[88] The word 'actual' is used in a curious fashion, almost as though to add reassurance, to suppress the suggestion – which Westlake himself provokes – that there could be some other England which compares with the savage societies which Westlake is intent on separating from England.

[89] Westlake, *Chapters on the Principles of International Law*, p. 102. For Westlake, government is the test of civilization; Asiatic states satisfy this test as they comprise populations 'leading complex lives of their own' with their own systems of family relations, criminal law and administration. *Ibid.*, pp. 141–142.

[90] See Westlake, *Chapters on the Principles of International Law*, pp. 142–155.

[91] See discussion on pp. 84–86.

distinction between the civilized and uncivilized. All non-European societies, regardless of whether they were regarded as completely primitive or relatively advanced, were outside the sphere of law, and European society provided the model which all societies had to follow if they were to progress.

The positivist attempt to distinguish between the civilized and uncivilized was fraught with unresolvable complications. Westlake's analytic approach sought to extinguish any suggestion of correspondence between advanced European and primitive non-European peoples; but seen from a broader perspective, there was a complete irony in this insistence that only one form of law could accurately be given the term 'law'. After all, it was precisely by relativizing and contesting Austin's rigid definition of law, a strategy used by members of both the analytical and historical schools, that international law could claim to be law at all.[92] If states could be regarded as governed by 'law' they were governed by law in the same way that the primitive societies described by Maine were governed by law, notwithstanding the lack of a determinate sovereign who issues laws enforced by controls.[93] Seen from this perspective, there is an identity between primitive societies and international law; and it is by asserting the validity of primitive societies governed by custom, the principal source of international law, that international law is established as a scientific discipline. Having been so established, however, international law then emphatically disassociates from the primitive by becoming the authoritative, master discipline which identifies, places and expels the primitive. The implications of the disconcerting identity between the international and the primitive is not explored. For if the uncivilized non-European societies were to be expelled from the field of international society because they were barbaric and primitive, it followed that international law occupied a similar status with respect

---

[92] The analytic approach relativised Austin by arguing that his definition was only one definition of law. This is the approach taken by Westlake, *Chapters on the Principles of International Law*, pp. viii–ix. Walker went further and argued that Austin's definition was philologically inaccurate. See Walker, *A History of the Law of Nations*, pp. 14–17. The historical approach suggested that Austin's definition of law appplied only to modern European society. Others, such as Bryce, went further and argued that Austin's definition did not apply accurately to *any* societies. See Wilfrid E. Rumble, 'Introduction', in John Austin, *The Province of Jurisprudence Determined* (Wilfrid E. Rumble, ed., New York: Cambridge University Press, 1995), p. xxii. In essence, both the analytic and historical schools, in attempting to rescue the discipline of international law, were attacking Austin for privileging one very specific meaning of the word 'law'.
[93] For a discussion of Maine's work in this context, see Walker, *A History of the Law of Nations*, p. 12.

to domestic law, law properly so called. If this was so then international law was an inferior discipline just as non-European peoples were inferior peoples; correspondingly, rather than possessing any integrity and coherence of its own, international law bore only a faint and subordinate relationship with domestic law, and could hope to evolve only by imperfectly mimicking the definitive institutions and practices of domestic law. Conformity with the master model of Europe, after all, was the path to progress prescribed by positivist international lawyers for the non-European peoples. These implications are not addressed by the positivist jurists intent both on establishing their discipline and demonstrating its usefulness.

Even at the theoretical, jurisprudential level, then, alien societies are a primary threat to the integrity of the overall structure. Consequently, the international law of the period can be read, not simply as the confident expansion of intellectual imperialism, but as a far more anxiety-driven process of naming the unfamiliar, asserting its alien nature, and attempting to reduce and subordinate it.

Within the positivist universe, then, the non-European world is excluded from the realms of sovereignty, society, law; each of these concepts which acted as founding concepts to the framework of the positivist system was precisely defined, correspondingly, in ways which maintain and police the boundary between the civilized and uncivilized. The whole edifice of positivist jurisprudence is based on this initial exclusion, this determination that certain societies are beyond the pale of civilization. Furthermore, it is clear that, notwithstanding positivist assertions of the primacy of sovereignty, the concept of society is at least equally central to the whole system.

Quite apart from the fact that the concept of society was crucial to any refutation of Austin's criticism, it was only by recourse to this concept that jurists could divide the civilized from the uncivilized and thereby demarcate in legal terms the exclusive sphere occupied by European states. This distinction having been established, it was possible for jurists to draw upon disciplines such as anthropology to elaborate on the characteristics of the uncivilized. Finally, the constitution of sovereignty doctrine itself was based on this fundamental distinction because positivist definitions of sovereignty relies on the premise that civilized states were sovereign and uncivilized states were not.

Afflicted by all the insecurities generated by Austin, positivist jurists nevertheless attempted to present international law as a coherent and autonomous scientific discipline which could play an important role in the management of international relations. For an international law anxious to establish itself and make good its claims to be both scientific and practical, colonialism could be seen as an ideal subject. This was not merely because 'colonial problems' had become a central preoccupation of European powers to whom the acquisition of colonies had become fundamental to their prestige, and whose consequent competition for colonies threatened to lead to the first great European war since the defeat of Napoleon. It was also because the colonial problem appeared, at least initially, to be free of many of the central complications raised by Austin. Both the analytical and historical schools pointed to the deficiencies of Austinian thinking, but the real power of his critique of international law emerged whenever a dispute developed between two sovereign states. How was such a dispute to be resolved in the absence of an overarching sovereign to articulate the appropriate law, adjudicate the dispute and enforce the verdict? The absence of any such system was made explicit by the efforts made at the end of the nineteenth and early twentieth centuries to institute a system of international arbitration and to codify international law, which could be seen as attempts to address exactly these problems.[94] By contrast, the colonial encounter did not directly pose such problems: it was an encounter, not between two sovereign states, but between a sovereign European state and an amorphous uncivilized entity; and enforcement posed no real difficulties because of massively superior European military strength. Having stripped the non-European world of sovereignty, then, the positivists in effect constructed the colonial encounter as an arena in which the sovereign made, interpreted and enforced the law. In this way, the colonial arena promised international jurists a chance to develop a jurisprudence which demonstrated the efficacy, coherence and utility of international law free of the ubiquitous and unanswerable Austinian objections.[95] In short, the colonies offered international law the same opportunity they traditionally extended to the lower classes – and the dissolute members of the aristocracy – of the imperial centre:

---

[94] On these efforts and the importance attached to them, see Oppenheim, 'The Science of International Law', 313; Koskenniemi, *From Apology*, pp. 123–129.

[95] As Riles notes jurists such as Lawrence 'diverted attention from the positivist vision of law as *force*, and reorganised international law around the theme of *order* to reassure the reader of viability of the discipline's project'. Riles, 'Aspiration and Control', 726 (footnotes omitted, italics in original). Further, it was particularly in the colonial context that the idiom of order could acquire an especially compelling significance. *Ibid.*, p. 727.

the opportunity to make something of yourself, to prove and rehabilitate yourself.

The division between the civilized and the uncivilized was central to this project: however, efforts to effect this crucial distinction were disrupted by the complication that the uncivilized resembled the civilized in very important respects, while the discipline of international law itself bore disconcerting connections with the primitive. The primitive was not so much outside international law awaiting its ordering ministrations, but within the very heart of the discipline, and the subsequent efforts of the international jurist to define and manage the primitive served to conceal this fundamental connection.

Native personality and managing the colonial encounter

Introduction

Whatever the positivist assertions as to the legal absence of non-European societies, however, contact between European Empires and the societies of Asia, Africa and the Pacific was intensifying at precisely this period, the latter half of the nineteenth century. The exparsion of colonial Empires was one of the defining features of the international relations of the period. Jurisprudentially, the task confronting the positivists was that of formulating the doctrines which could legally account for this expansion of Europe. The interaction between European and non-European societies, which had by this time been taking place for more than four centuries, had generated a significant and complex body of treaties.[96]

Despite this, the positivists purported to expel the non-European world from the realm of legality by insisting on the distinction between civilized and non-civilized states and then proceeding to effect the re-admission of non-European states into 'international society' by the use of the modern and distinctive analytic tools of positivism. Basically, then, just as positivists sought to reconstitute the discipline according to prevailing ideas of modernity and science, so too they endeavoured to recast entirely the legal basis of relations between the civilized and uncivilized by framing the project as though the colonial encounter

---

[96] See Alexandrowicz, An Introduction and The European–African Confrontation; Ian Brownlie, 'The Expansion of International Society: The Consequences for the Law of Nations', in Hedley Bull and Adam Watson (eds.), The Expansion of International Society (New York: Oxford University Press, 1984), pp. 357–369 at pp. 358–361.

was about to occur, as opposed to having already taken place. This was accomplished by basing the inquiry on the premise that the uncivilized were outside the law, and the positivist task was to define the terms and methods by which they were to be assimilated into the framework of law. Positivist jurists made little attempt to acknowledge, much less engage with, the naturalist past and the techniques used by the naturalists to account for the preceding centuries of contact between European and non-European peoples. The principal importance of this manoeuvre was that the re-entry of non-European societies into the sphere of law could now take place on terms which completely subordinated and disempowered those societies. This was achieved by deploying the new, racialised scientific lexicon of positivism which, it was asserted, represented a higher and decisive truth. The language of positivism was only one part of a far larger and massively elaborate vocabulary of conquest that had been developing in many of the disciplines of the late nineteenth century. Anthropology, science, economics and philology, while purporting in various ways to expand impartial knowledge, participated crucially in the colonial project.[97] International law relied upon, reinforced and reflected this larger body of thought, from which it could borrow when required to further its own project.

This section explores this positivist project by focusing on three closely related and intersecting concerns. First, I examine how the positivist method, with its ambitions to be scientific and coherent, effected the assimilation of the non-European world into international society, and the different doctrines and techniques it developed for this purpose. Second, I focus particularly on the concept of sovereignty and the variations of sovereignty that are embodied in the doctrines of assimilation and, in particular, the notion of 'quasi-sovereignty' that positivists developed in order to remedy problematic aspects of their theory of assimilation. This was only one example of sovereignty doctrine mutating in the confusions arising from the colonial encounter. Thirdly, I examine how positivists characterized the different peoples of Asia, Africa and the Pacific, and the effects and function of these characterizations within the overall positivist framework. Finally, I seek to place these jurisprudential developments within a broader context, as diplomatic, political and ideological considerations inevitably

---

[97] This is one of the central themes of Said's work. See Said, *Orientalism*, pp. 12–13.

affected the development and application of these doctrines. For these purposes, I focus on the Berlin Africa Conference of 1884–5, which sought to deal with the problems attendant upon the partitioning of Africa.

Doctrines of assimilation

In somewhat simplistic terms, non-European peoples could be brought within the realm of international law through four basic and often inter-related techniques. First, treaty making constituted the basic technique for regulating relations between European and non-European peoples. Treaties could provide for a broad set of arrangements, ranging from agreements governing trading relations between the two entities to treaties by which the non-European entity ostensibly ceded complete sovereignty to the European entity. Secondly, non-European peoples were colonized and thus subjected to the control of European sovereignty. Colonization took place by a number of methods including by a treaty of cession, by annexation, or by conquest. Thirdly, independent non-European states such as Japan and Siam (as it then was) could be accepted into international society by meeting the requirements of the standard of civilization of, and being officially recognised by, European states, as proper members of the family of nations. Fourthly, European states, particularly in the latter part of the nineteenth century, often acquired control over Asian and African societies by a special type of treaty, protectorate agreements. While these four categories are crudely distinct, they are nevertheless far from mutually exclusive: protec-torates were established through treaties, for example, and protectorates sometimes became colonies.

Treaty relations between Europeans and non-Europeans

The juridical problems that positivists faced in developing a jurispru-dence that would account for colonialism were attributable not only to the analytic limitations of positivism but to the particular character of the colonial expansion as it occurred in the latter part of the nineteenth century.

It is hardly controversial that one of the primary driving forces of nineteenth-century colonial expansion was trade. The right to enter other territories to trade, the freedom of commerce asserted so pow-erfully and inevitably even in Vitoria's time, was a principal rule of nineteenth-century legal and diplomatic relations. Historically, much of the early trade had been conducted by trading companies such as the British East India Company and the Dutch East India Company.[98] The characteristics and functions of such companies had been clearly summarized by M. F. Lindley:

Formed in most cases, at all events from the point of view of the shareholders, for the purpose of earning dividends, these corporations have proved to be the instruments by which enormous areas have been brought under the dominion of the States under whose auspices they were created, and in this way they have been utilised by all the important colonizing Powers. The special field of their operation has been territory which the State creating them was not at the time prepared to administer directly, but which offered good prospects from the point of view of trade or industrial exploitation.[99]

All these factors inevitably affected the international law of the period. Doctrines were developed to give trading companies some measure of legal personality by characterizing them as extensions of the Crown by virtue of royal charter.[100] Trading companies were thus capable of asserting sovereign rights over non-European peoples who were deprived of any sort of sovereignty by this same law.[101] Company charters allowed them not merely to trade in particular areas, but to make peace and war with natives, and the power to coin money.[102] The control of territories by companies established for the explicit purpose of making money meant, inevitably, that the territories were administered simply for profit.[103] Unsurprisingly, governance driven by such imperatives resulted in excesses which led to wars between the companies and the African and Asian peoples they purported to govern, as a consequence

---

[98] See generally D. K. Fieldhouse, *The Colonial Empires: A Comparative Survey from the Eighteenth Century* (London: Weidenfeld & Nicolson, 1966).

[99] Lindley, *The Acquisition and Government*, p. 91.

[100] For a discussion of the powers and status of the British East India Company, *see Nabob of Arcot v. The East India Company*, 3 Bro.C.C. 292; 29 Eng. Rep. 544 (1791), reprinted in (1967) 6 *British International Law Cases* 281.

[101] Thus, as Lindley notes of the British East India Company, 'what was at first a mere trading Corporation came in the course of time to exercise sovereign rights over an immense area which afterwards passed under the direct administration of the British Crown'. Lindley, *The Acquisition and Government*, p. 94.

[102] *Ibid.*

[103] See Lawrence, *The Principles of International Law*, pp. 174–175. As Fieldhouse points out, these trading companies changed their modes of operation very significantly over the years. From being intent simply on trading in the sixteenth and seventeenth centuries, these companies increasingly engaged in acquiring and governing territories in order to protect their interest in the eighteenth and nineteenth centuries. See Fieldhouse on the East India Company and England's colonization of India. Fieldhouse, *The Colonial Empires*, pp. 149–152, 161–173.

of which these companies often embroiled their chartering sovereigns in complex foreign wars.

By the end of the nineteenth century, European states were directly assuming responsibility for colonial territories. Direct rule by the European sovereign itself often followed. Thus, The East Indian Company was dissolved and the British Crown took direct control over India in 1858.[104] The direct involvement of European states in the whole process of governing resulted in a shift from the vulgar language of profit to that of order, proper governance and humanitarianism. This new synthesis was articulated at the Berlin Conference in 1884–5, where humanitarianism and profit-seeking were presented in proper and judicious balance as the European Powers carved up Africa. The Berlin Conference marked a new phase in the colonial enterprise, not only because it formulated a new ideological basis for the expansion of European Empires but because it attempted to establish a firm and clear framework for the management of the colonial scramble which otherwise threatened to exacerbate inter-European rivalries.[105]

The direct involvement of European states in the scramble for colonies led to a number of complications. Legal niceties were hardly a concern of European states powerfully intent on imperial expansion. The positivists insisted on the supreme power of the sovereign state; but if everything a state did was 'legal', then law had no place at all in the scheme of international relations. Thus, in order to assert the existence and relevance of the discipline, positivism had to balance its emphasis on sovereign power with the formulation of a clear set of rules which were observed and obeyed by sovereign states. This familiar problem, of the relationship between law and politics in positivist international law, manifested itself uniquely in the colonial encounter. State behaviour was the basis of positivist jurisprudence; but it was difficult to detect any consistent and principled behaviour in the flux, confusion and self-interest of the colonial encounter. Consequently, there was every danger that law would degenerate into expediency.

A further problem was posed by the fact that although positivists asserted that non-European societies were officially excluded from the

---

[104] Pursuant to the Government of India Act of 1858. Lindley, *The Acquisition and Government*, p. 95.

[105] The Berlin Conference, however, hardly succeeded in eliminating such rivalries. Britain and France nearly went to war over the 1898 'Fashoda incident', for example. See generally David Levering Lewis, *The Race to Fashoda: European Colonialism and African Resistance in the Scramble for Africa* (New York: Weidenfeld & Nicolson, 1987).

realm of international law, numerous treaties had been entered into between these supposedly non-existent societies and European states and trading companies in the period from the fifteenth century onwards. Furthermore, these treaties, and the state practice which followed, suggested that both the European and non-European parties understood themselves to be entering into legal relations. Many doctrines of international law, accepted even by the nineteenth-century jurists, had been produced by this intercourse. As Alexandrowicz's comprehensive account of the relations between the European and East Indian states prior to the nineteenth century points out, for example

the details of mutually agreed principles of inter-State dealings can be ascertained from the texts of treaties and documents relating to diplomatic negotiations which took place before and after their conclusion.[106]

The status of these treaties became problematic as a result of the emergence of positivism. Indeed, several jurists of the eighteenth century had anticipated the problem which now confronted the nineteenth-century positivists. Noting that positive law – the custom and treaty law developing among European states – was becoming increasingly significant, these jurists raised the problem of the implications of these developments for the 'universal' international law which applied to all states and which regulated centuries of interaction between Europe and Asia.[107]

This history of treaty making posed a challenge to the positivist framework as the fundamental premises of positivism, when extended to their logical conclusion, implicitly suggested that treaties with non-Europeans were impossible. After all, the treaty is a legal instrument; it presupposes, at least, a sense of mutual obligations and an overarching system of law which would both recognize the treaty as a legal instrument and would be resorted to in the event of disputes as to the meaning of the treaty. The existence of a treaty, in this way, presupposed a legal universe to which both parties adhered.[108] This presupposition, however, contradicted the powerful positivist claim that non-Europeans were uncivilized, that they were lacking in any understanding of law at all – or else,

---

[106] Alexandrowicz, *An Introduction*, p. 2.

[107] See Alexandrowicz, 'Doctrinal Aspects'. Alexandrowicz's general argument, presented in this article and in his book on the Asian–European encounter, is that treaties in the period from the fifteenth to the eighteenth centuries were generally more equal than the imposed, unequal treaties of the nineteenth century.

[108] Further, as Carty notes, 'treaty making capacity was a vital mark of sovereignty and independence'. Carty, *The Decay of International Law*, p. 65.

that their understanding of law was so fundamentally different from that of the Europeans that the two parties existed in incommensurable universes.

Despite this, the positivists were compelled to apply their science to a legal institution, the treaty, whose existence seemed an aberration within the positivist conceptual universe. Positivists prided themselves on their empiricism, on their focus on state practice as opposed to the subjective metaphysical speculations of the naturalists. The nineteenth-century European states, demonstrating a lamentable disregard for the positivist assertion so systematically established and elaborated, that non-European peoples were outside the scope of law, relied very heavily on treaties with non-European societies in expanding their empires.

For example, European states intent on creating empires in Africa claimed very often to derive their title from treaties with African chiefs. Positivists had thus to formulate a way of incorporating the inescapable phenomenon of treaty relations between these entities within their system. Furthermore, it was not merely unrealistic but also dangerous to ignore the many detailed treaties between European and non-European states. Many states had conducted themselves on the basis that these treaties were valid. International stability would have been severely undermined if it suddenly became possible for states to question the arrangements, titles and interests which had been ostensibly established by these treaties.[109] It was precisely the fear of disputes over title to colonial territories among European powers that inspired the Conference of Berlin of 1884–5.[110] Consequently, the non-European world had to be located in the positivist system, not merely for purposes of control and suppression, but to prevent its ambiguous status from undermining European solidarity.

Treaties between European and non-European states thus became the objects of positivist scrutiny. But the methodology used by positivists to examine these treaties had the paradoxical effect of erasing the non-European side of the treaty even when claiming to identify and give effect to the intentions of that party. This was a consequence of the

---

[109] European and non-European states had entered into many such treaties. See C. H. Alexandrowicz, 'The Theory of Recognition in Fieri', (1958) 34 British Yearbook of International Law 176–198.

[110] For a discussion of this, see Westlake, Chapters on the Principles of International Law, pp. 137–140. The Berlin Conference, apart from dividing up Africa among the European powers, sought to establish a system by which European powers making claims to African territories had to notify the conference of their claims; it was then open to other members to make objections. Ibid.

positivist practice of focusing on the words of the treaty, to the complete exclusion of the circumstances in which the treaty had been arrived at. In this way, the positivist ignored the massive violence inflicted on non-European peoples, and the resistance of these peoples to that violence.

Anti-colonial resistance took a number of complex and singular forms; the rulers of Ethiopia used both diplomatic and military techniques to maintain Ethiopian independence;[111] the Kings of Thailand played off rival European powers one against another;[112] the Chinese authorities relied on translations of Vattel and Wheaton to try and protect their interests against European states.[113] Almost invariably, however, African and Asian states resorted to war in an attempt to stem colonial expansion. Defeat was inevitable given the superior military power of the European states, and it was principally by using force or threatening to use force that European states compelled non-European states to enter into 'treaties' which basically entitled the European powers to do whatever they pleased. Coercion and military superiority combined to create ostensibly legal instruments. Under the positivist system, it was legal to use coercion to compel parties to enter into treaties which were then legally binding.[114]

The resulting 'unequal treaties' – unequal not only because they were the product of unequal power, but because they embodied unequal obligations – were humiliating to the non-European states, which sought to terminate such treaties at the earliest opportunity.[115] Rights to trade were an important part of such treaties. Thus the Treaty of Nanking[116] required the Emperor of China, among other things, to

---

[111] See K. V. Ram, 'The Survival of Ethiopian Independence', in Gregory Maddux (ed.), *Conquest and Resistance to Colonialism in Africa* (New York: Garland, 1993).

[112] See Gong, *The Standard of 'Civilization'*, pp. 210–211, for an account of King Mongkut's dealings with the British.

[113] See Wang Tieya, 'International Law in China: Historical and Contemporary Perspectives', (1990-II) 221 *Académie du Droit International, Recueil De Cours* 195, 232–237.

[114] See Gong, *The Standard of 'Civilization'*, p. 43.

[115] On the origins of capitulations, see Gong, *The Standard of 'Civilization'*, pp. 64–65.

[116] The Treaty was in effect imposed on the Emperor of China after the Chinese defeat in the Opium Wars of 1839–42. The war broke out as a result of Chinese attempts to stamp out the trade in opium which had been a source of immense wealth to European traders in China. See generally Jonathan D. Spence, *The Search for Modern China* (New York: Norton, 1991), pp. 147–164. For details about legal aspects of trading with China in the era preceding the opium wars, see Randle Edwards, 'The Old Canton System of Foreign Trade', in Victor H. Li (ed.), *Law and Politics in China's Foreign Trade* (Seattle: University of Washington Press, 1977), p. 362. As the works of Spence and Edwards make clear, the metaphor of barbarity was used by both sides of the

cede Hong Kong to Great Britain,[117] to open five Chinese ports for trade[118] and to establish a 'fair and regular' tariff for British goods[119] – in addition to which the Emperor was required to pay some 21 million dollars to the British for various losses suffered by the British government and citizens as a result of the Opium War which had occurred because the Chinese Emperor sought to prevent British traders from selling opium in China. As a consequence of these developments, non-European peoples were governed not by general principles of international law, but the regimes created by these unequal treaties.[120]

The history of violence and military conquest which led to the formation of these treaties plays no part in the positivist's approach to the treaty.[121] Moreover, the positivists, on the whole, accepted the treaties as expressing clearly and unproblematically the actual intentions of the non-European party. Thus positivists regarded as perfectly authentic and completely natural treaties such as those in which the Wyanasa Chiefs of Nyasaland apparently stated:

We . . . most earnestly beseech Her Most Gracious Majesty the Queen of Great Britain and Ireland, Empress of India, Defender of the Faith, &c., to take our country, ourselves and our people, to observe the following conditions:–
    I. That we give over all our country within the above described limits, all sovereign rights, and all and every other claim absolutely, and without any reservation whatever, to Her Most Gracious Majesty . . . and heirs and successors, for all time coming.[122]

interaction. Many of the legal complications that early European traders confronted in China were attributable to the Chinese view that the traders were barbarians and that no direct communication was to occur between the traders and the Emperor. See Edwards, 'The Old Canton System', pp. 364–365.

[117] Treaty of Nanking, Treaty of Peace, Friendship, and Commerce Between Her Majesty the Queen of Great Britain and Ireland and the Emperor of China, 29 August 1842, G.B.-Ir.-P.R.C., art. III, 93 Consol. T.S. 467.

[118] This allowed British merchants and their families to reside in these cities for purposes of trade. See Article II of the Treaty of Nanking.

[119] See Article X of the Treaty of Nanking.

[120] Wang Tieya describes the collapse of the traditional Chinese view after the attack of the European powers: 'It was not replaced by the modern international order of the system of foreign States, but a new order of unequal treaties. In China's foreign relations, what applied were not principles and rules of international law, but unequal treaties.' Tieya, 'International Law in China', p. 251.

[121] Although a treaty obtained by coercion would be invalid under contemporary international law, it is difficult to find an example of any of the unequal colonial treaties being set aside on the basis that it was obtained by force.

[122] Cited in Lindley, The Acquisition and Government, p. 186.

Lindley cites this, apparently without any irony, as an example of a treaty of cession. The parties most knowledgeable about treaty making had no illusions about the legal status of these treaties, recognizing them to be simple manifestations of military superiority. Lord Lugard, doyen of colonial administrators,[123] who had actually been involved in the whole treaty making process, made short shrift of the hypocrisy surrounding the issue:

The frank assertion of the inexorable law of progress, based on the power to enforce it if need be, was termed 'filibustering'. It shocked the moral sense of a civilisation content to accept the naked deception of 'treaty-making,' or to shut its ears and thank God for the results.[124]

Lugard himself thought it far more preferable for the European powers to 'found their title to intervention on force', rather than in treaties 'which were either not understood, or which the ruler had no power to make, and which rarely provided an adequate legal sanction for the powers assumed'.[125]

Jurists had some perception of the fraudulence of such treaties; however, they made no contribution to revealing the deceptions of treaty making, instead treating them with the utmost seriousness, and as valid legal instruments; they applied all their considerable scholarship, insight and learning towards identifying the proper import of such treaties and giving them effect. The acceptance of Lugard's argument, after all, would simply confirm the absence of any coherent or effective international legal system and the irrelevance of international lawyers to the great project of Empire.

Rather than confront this possibility the positivist turned to the judicial arena: the broad question here was if the non-European world did not exist for the purposes of international law until properly incorporated into international society, what was to be made of the

---

[123] Lugard's extraordinary life was inextricably interwoven with Empire; born in India in 1858, the year after the Mutiny, he was the son of a chaplain of the East India Company; he trained for soldiering at Sandhurst, and was employed for several years in the Imperial British East African Company. In that capacity he 'annexed' large parts of Uganda and explored the Niger in an attempt to fend off French competition. His appointment as High Commissioner of Northern Nigeria led to the experiences which resulted in his classic work on colonial administration, *The Dual Mandate*. Recognised internationally as the foremost colonial expert of his time, he served on the Permanent Mandates Commission of the League of Nations; he died in 1945. See Margery Perham, 'Introduction', in Lord Frederick Lugard, *The Dual Mandate in British Tropical Africa* (5th edn., London: Frank Cass, 1965).
[124] *Ibid.*, p. 17.   [125] *Ibid.*

many treaties between European and non-European states, supposedly non-existent entities?[126] Although evading this larger issue, Westlake confronts a part of the problem when writing of Europeans entering alien territories:

We find that one of their first proceedings is to conclude treaties with such chiefs or other authorities as they can discover: and very properly, for no men are so savage as to be incapable of coming to some understanding with other men, and whatever contact has been established between men, some understanding, however incomplete it may be, is a better basis for their mutual relations than force. But what is the scope which it is reasonably possible to give to treaties in such a case, and what effect which may be reasonably attributed to them?[127]

In attempting to resolve this difficulty, positivists resorted to concepts of recognition and quasi-sovereignty.

Recognition doctrine was one technique for accounting for the meta-morphosis of a non-European society into a legal entity. In broad terms, the doctrine stipulated that a new state came into being when its existence was recognised by established states.[128] The fact that a non-European society may have constituted a state was not in itself sufficient, because of the civilized–non-civilized distinction, to belong to the realm of international law.[129] In its particular application to uncivilized states, recognition takes place when 'a state is brought by increasing civilisation within the realm of law'.[130] But until this stage was reached, non-Europeans were excluded from the proper application of the doctrine as it operated in the European realm.[131]

Westlake and other positivists attempted to resolve the problem of whether or not the native states were part of international law by

[126] This problem would not have arisen, in the natural law universe, where these treaties would have been interpreted as the understanding between different societies governed by universal natural law. This is the problem posed by authorities on the nineteenth century such as Gong:

> How could treaty relations with these 'backward', non-European countries be made consistent with the fact that such relations might be construed of as recognition of legal personality?   (Gong, Standard of 'Civilization', p. 60)

[127] Westlake, Chapters on the Principles of International Law, p. 144.

[128] See Hall, A Treatise on International Law, pp. 82–83. See also Oppenheim, International Law, p. 116. 'For every State that is not already but wants to be, a member, recognition is therefore necessary. A State is and becomes an International Person through recognition, only and exclusively.'

[129] 'As the basis of the Law of Nations is the common consent of the civilized States, statehood alone does not include membership in the family of nations.' Oppenheim, International Law, p. 116.

[130] Hall, A Treatise on International Law, p. 83.

[131] As Lorimer asserts:

arguing that such states, although not proper, sovereign members of international society, were nevertheless partial members[132]: hence, Westlake proposed that 'Our international society exercises the right of admitting outside states to parts of its international law without necessarily admitting them to the whole of it'.[133] The non-European states thus existed in a sort of twilight world; lacking personality, they were nevertheless capable of entering into certain treaties and were to that extent members of international law.[134]

But how was the determination made as to who had been admitted into international society, to what extent and for what purposes? The answers to these questions were extremely vital as it was common for European states to challenge the claims made by rival states that they had acquired property rights or even sovereignty over territory by way of treaty with, for example, an African chief. A European state attacking a rival claim to sovereignty over territory would argue that the chief who had entered into the treaty had no authority to do so, that he was not properly a chief, that the land covered by the treaty was not within the chief's authority to transfer and so forth. It was important, then, to devise rules that could resolve all these disputes and that would fix and stabilise the personality of non-European entities; failure to achieve this would lead to an exacerbation of inter-European tensions. Moreover, positivists regarded the successful resolution of such problems as a test of the coherence and value of positivist international law. Indeed, it was precisely this accomplishment which distinguished the positivist from his less able naturalist predecessor. Thus Lawrence dismissed the law of the Middle Ages, when the European expansion

> The right of undeveloped races, like the right of undeveloped individuals, is a right not to recognition as to what they are not, but to guardianship – that is, to guidance – in becoming that to which they are capable, in realising their special ideals.   (Lorimer, *The Institutes of the Law of Nations*, p. 157)

Thus it was only through 'guardianship' that the non-Europeans could achieve any status.

[132] As Lorimer put it: 'He [the international jurist] is not bound to apply the positive law of nations to savages, or even to barbarians, as such; but he is bound to ascertain the points at which, and the directions in which, barbarians or savages come within the scope of partial recognition.' Lorimer, *The Institutes of the Law of Nations*, p. 102.

[133] Westlake, *Chapters on the Principles of International Law*, p. 82. Westlake presents this flexibility as an advantage offered by the system: 'This is an instance of the way in which all institutions, being free and not mechanical products, shade off from one to another.' *Ibid.*

[134] Oppenheim, too, developed a similar doctrine; see Oppenheim, *International Law*, p. 155. See also the opinion of arbitrator Max Huber in the Island of Palmas Case (*U.S. v. Netherlands*), 2 R.I.A.A. 829, 852 (1928).

COLONIALISM IN NINETEENTH-CENTURY INTERNATIONAL LAW

commenced, as 'it was powerless to decide what acts were necessary in order to obtain dominion over newly discovered territory, or how great an extent of country could be acquired by one act of discovery or colonisation'.[135]

The basic method of resolving the problem of personality comprised a complex process of determining the status of the non-European entity through the doctrine of recognition, and then examining whether the right the European state claimed with respect to that entity was consistent with its legal status.[136] For example, if the entity was recognised as having a personality which enabled it to alienate its lands, then European states which had entered into a treaty with that entity regarding rights to the land could claim to possess valid title. But the use of recognition for these purposes raised further tensions. On the one hand, recognition was bestowed by a state according to its own discretion; on the other, positivists argued that recognition could take place only within certain confines which were juridically established.[137] Positivists such as Westlake argued that the legal capacity of the entity was pre-determined by the degree of civilization it had attained. Thus African tribes, according to Westlake, could not transfer sovereignty because they were incapable of understanding the concept;[138] whereas Asian states possessed this capacity, being of a higher level of civilization.[139] Within this scheme, the jurist's task was to develop a system of classification, of taxonomy, which could properly categorise every entity encountered in the course of colonial expansion. The implication is that the individual, and often self-interested, recognition bestowed by a European state could not operate in such a way as to change the inherent

---

[135] Lawrence, *The Principles of International Law*, p. 52. Lawrence then characterizes Grotius as being engaged in the task of solving this problem by an application of the Roman law of property. It was from this prism, then, that doctrines of sovereignty were formulated.

[136] It was vital for these purposes that some agreement be established between international lawyers from different backgrounds. Hence Westlake is at pains to point out that his views on some of these issues correspond with those of Portuguese jurists. See Westlake, *Chapters on the Principles of International Law*, p. 146.

[137] This is a familiar problem with respect to recognition doctrine as a whole.

[138] Thus for Westlake, sovereignty was acquired by other procedures some of which had been formalised at the Berlin Conference. While natives could alienate property, sovereignty was obtained, 'not in treaties with natives, but in the nature of the case and compliance with conditions recognized by the civilized world'. Westlake, *Chapters on the Principles of International Law*, p. 145. Westlake's argument was completely contrary to actual state practice; see Alexandrowicz, *The European–African Confrontation*, pp. 48–50.

[139] Oppenheim, *International Law*, p. 286.

capacities of the entity in question, capacities which were objectively established by the entity's position on the scale of civilization. In short, international law had established rules defining the capacities of native peoples and individual states had to exercise their discretion within the boundaries of such rules.

Each of these elements of the positivist framework intended to establish objective legal standards whose application could resolve international disputes faced insuperable problems. The project of classification, for example, faced a formidable challenge. Essentially, positivist jurisprudence sought to combine anthropological insight with taxonomic precision: each entity was to be studied, its degree of civilization ascertained and its legal status allocated accordingly. This was the system used to account for a proliferation of entities ranging from 'Amerindian and African kings and chiefs, Muslim sultans, khans and emirs, Hindu princes and the empires of China and Japan'.[140] Given the range of societies and practices it had to deal with, however, it is hardly surprising that positivist jurists themselves finally acknowledged the limitations of their own methods. Lawrence asserts, in discussing the question of whether or not an entity should be admitted into international membership, that 'a certain degree of civilization is necessary, although it is difficult to define the exact amount'.[141] The willingness of a non-European to be bound by international law would not in itself suffice to ensure membership; but beyond this, Lawrence suggests that 'In matters of this kind, no general rule can be laid down'.[142]

Nor did state practice reveal a consistent set of principles as to questions of admittance and capacity. Recognition was granted by states not in accordance with any international principle, but according to the powerful and unpredictable expediencies of competition for colonies. Certainly, there were occasions on which unanimity prevailed among European states, as when Turkey was ceremoniously admitted into the circle of European nations.[143] In such a case, the collective act of recognition established the existence of an entity whose capacity was

---

[140] Hedley Bull, 'The Emergence of a Universal International Society', in Hedley Bull and Adam Watson (eds.), *The Expansion of International Society* (New York: Oxford University Press, 1984), pp. 117–141 at p. 117.

[141] Lawrence, *The Principles of International Law*, p. 58.   [142] *Ibid.*, p. 59.

[143] Lawrence, *The Principles of International Law*, p. 84. On this occasion, by the Treaty of Paris of 1856, Turkey was 'admitted to participate in the advantages of the public law and system of Europe'.

accepted and agreed upon by European states. This, however, was a relatively rare occurrence. Colonial expansion was achieved by a haphazard and chaotic series of encounters between rival European states, trading companies and Asian and African societies. European states adopted different views of native personality, depending on their own interests. The problem was that native personality was fluid, as it was created through the encounter with a European state which would inevitably 'recognise' the capacity of the non-European entity according to its own needs.[144] A European state which had been granted particular treaty rights by an African chief would insist on the validity of the treaty and on the capacity of the chief to enter into such an agreement.[145] But acceptance of this approach meant that whatever an individual state did created law: this, as Lorimer points out 'deprives international law of permanent basis in nature and fails to bring it within the sphere of jurisprudence'.[146] The cost of accepting this solution was to dispense with the idea of law altogether at the expense of sovereignty. Recognition doctrine was based on the premise that each state could make its own decision; having gone this far, international law failed to establish any boundaries to this discretion, as a consequence of which the subjective and self-interested views of the state appeared to prevail.[147]

In an attempt to establish standards independent of arbitrary state will, Westlake was prepared, ironically,[148] to base the capacity of non-European peoples on the degree of understanding of the non-European party entering into a treaty: 'We have here a clear apprehension of the principle that an uncivilized tribe can grant by treaty such rights as it understand and exercises, but nothing more.'[149] He continues that

---

[144] Oppenheim seems to accept this when noting 'when they [Christian states] enter into treaty obligations with them [non-Christian states], they indirectly declare that they are ready to recognize them for these parts as International Persons and the subjects of the Law of Nations', Oppenheim, *International Law*, p. 155.

[145] It was a common tactic among states disputing each other's claims to argue, for example, that the chieftain who entered into a treaty ceding the disputed territory was not the proper chief. See generally S. E. Crowe, *The Berlin West African Conference 1884–1885* (Westport, CN: Negro Universities Press, 1970), pp. 158–159.

[146] Lorimer, *The Institutes of the Law of Nations*, p. 104.

[147] As Gong notes: 'The subjective nature of the recognition process and the political element within the standard of "civilization" put the European powers in the always powerful and sometimes awkward position of having to be judge in their own cases.' Gong, *Standard of 'Civilization'*, p. 61.

[148] Ironic because of the basic positivist premise that natives are entirely outside the law.

[149] Westlake, *Chapters on the Principles of International Law*, p. 149.

cession of this sort 'may confer a moral title to such property or power as they understand while they cede it, but that no form of cession by them can confer title to what they do not understand'.[150] As a consequence, 'it is possible that a right of property may be derived from natives, and this even before European sovereignty has existed over the spot'.[151]

If native understanding was the test, the question then naturally arose: how was a jurist to ascertain what these natives were capable of understanding? Westlake addresses this problem in his examination of two treaties which were the subject of disputes between Portugal and England, each claiming rights over the same territory. Westlake is finally compelled to resort to his conjecture as to native understanding in order to decide this issue. He dismisses one treaty as 'mixed with a farrago which must have been mere jargon to him [the Chief]'. As opposed to another where 'there is nothing beyond the comprehension of the Makololo chiefs'.[152] Having initially asserted that non-Europeans were absent from the legal universe, Westlake now resorts to constructing the Makololo chiefs and divining their consciousness in order to give his scheme some semblance of coherence. Fundamentally, then, the positivist attempt to obliterate the non-European from their scheme having failed, it then resorted to acknowledging the presence of the non-European and accounting for it in a manner consistent with positivist notions of international law, objectivity and precision. Even this more compromised endeavour, however, was far from successful; no clear, objective standards were established for deciding whether a particular African chief could cede only property rather than sovereignty.

It is almost superfluous to note that while European powers claimed to derive rights from treaties they entered into with non-European states, they refused to accept the obligations arising from them. Thus Hall, noting the tendency on 'the part of such [non-European] states to expect that European countries shall behave in conformity with the standards which they themselves have set up', concludes that treaties create only obligations of 'honour' on the part of the European states.[153]

---

[150] Ibid., p. 145.

[151] Ibid. In asserting this proposition, Westlake also cited Chief Justice Marshall's views in Johnson v. McIntosh 121 U.S. 18 Wheat. 1543 (1823), in Westlake, International Law, p. 148.

[152] Ibid., p. 153.

[153] See W. E. Hall, A Treatise on International Law, cited in Gong, Standard of 'Civilization', p. 61. See also Crawford's summary of statehood doctrine in the nineteenth century in Crawford, The Creation of States, pp. 12–15.

Oppenheim, similarly, argued that European states interacted with non-European states on the basis of 'discretion, and not International Law'.[154]

Positivism claimed to provide, through a precise examination of state behaviour, and the employment of a comprehensive and carefully articulated system of classification, a precise answer to any legal problem with which it was confronted. Once the actualities of the application of positivism to resolving problems of native title are examined, however, it becomes evident that such claims were hardly well founded. The matter is resolved not in accordance with these detailed and elaborate principles, but on an almost completely ad hoc basis, by a process which is finally reduced to attempting to reconstruct what Makololo chiefs imagine themselves to be agreeing to. The randomness of this process is acknowledged by the jurists themselves. Thus Lawrence acknowledges that 'Each case must be judged on its own merits by the powers who deal with it'.[155] All this is quite apart from the fact that jurists simply could not account for the ambiguous position occupied by the non-European world, simultaneously capable of entering into treaty relations, and yet lacking in any cognizable international personality. Positivists grandiosely claimed that while their system was based on empirical science, it nevertheless remained autonomous from the messy world of politics, society and history that it imperiously and decisively ordered. The complex realities of late-nineteenth-century politics and the ambiguous character of the native overwhelmed the positivist system; its failure to coherently place and incorporate the non-European entity into its overall scheme, negated its much-vaunted claims of being comprehensive, systematic and consistent. The ambivalent status of the non-European entity, outside the scope of law and yet within it, lacking in international personality and yet necessarily possessing it if any sense was to be made of the many treaties which European states relied on, was never satisfactorily defined or resolved, as Oppenheim acknowledges:

No other explanation of these and similar facts [the fact that these non-sovereign entities engaged in sovereign behaviour] can be given except that these not-full

---

[154] Oppenheim, *International Law*, pp. 34–35. See also Westlake: 'The moral rights of all outside the international society against the several members of that society remain intact, though they have not and can scarcely could have been converted into legal rights.' Westlake, *Chapters on the Principles of International Law*, p. 140.
[155] Lawrence, *The Principles of International Law*, p. 85.

Sovereign States are in some way or another International Persons and subjects of International Law.[156]

Colonization

The problem of the legal personality of non-European peoples could be most simply resolved by the actual act of colonization which effectively extinguished this personality. Once colonization took place, the colonizing power assumed sovereignty over the non-European territory, and any European state having business with respect to the territory would deal with the colonial power; in this way, legal relations would take place, once more, between two European powers. Whatever the continuing frictions and tensions between these powers – as to access to the markets and resources of the colony, for example – they were in many respects less jurisprudentially complicated than relations between European and non-European entities.

Once again, however, questions of native personality played an important role in determining whether colonization had properly taken place in the first instance. The jurisprudence concerning the issue of how sovereignty was acquired over non-European peoples was controversial and unsettled because, once again, states took very different views on this matter depending on their own interests.[157] Broadly, however, discovery,[158] occupation, conquest,[159] and cession[160] were some of the doctrines historically devised to deal with this issue. The conceptual framework offered by private law, and in particular property law, played an influential role in the jurisprudence regarding the acquisition of territory.[161] Positivist analysis focused on questions such as what acts

---

[156] Oppenheim, *International Law*, p. 110.   [157] See *ibid.*, p. 283.

[158] The basic idea underlying discovery was that the mere 'discovery' of a territory sufficed to provide title; discovery was used as a basis for title in the fifteenth and sixteenth centuries, but was generally discredited by international lawyers as a valid basis for establishing title because it was so prone to abuse. See Lindley, *The Acquisition and Government*, pp. 128–138.

[159] See Hall, *A Treatise on International Law*, pp. 522–529, 'Conquest consists in the appropriation of the property in, and of the sovereignty over, a part or the whole of the territory of a state, and when definitively accomplished, vests the whole rights of property and sovereignty over such territory in the conquering state.'

[160] In 1912, an authority such as Oppenheim listed five modes of acquiring territory: cession, occupation, accretion, subjugation and prescription. See Oppenheim, *International Law*, p. 284.

[161] See generally Carty, *The Decay of International Law*, for a study of the complex ways in which these analogies were made.

were sufficient to show that the European state had acquired control over the territory, or that occupation had been 'effective' in order to prevent a state from claiming that it had acquired valid title over an entire territory simply by landing there.

Conquest generally involved militarily defeating an opponent and thus acquiring sovereignty over the defeated party's territory.[162] Conquest was one of the most ancient ways of acquiring title and, within the nineteenth-century framework, it was a completely legal and valid way of expanding territory. Recognition of such a right of conquest is completely contrary to the very concept of law, as it legitimizes outcomes dictated by power rather than legal principle. Nevertheless, conquest received legal sanction. Given the military weakness of the non-European states, and the absence of any legal limitations on a state's ability to commence a war, it was inevitable that European Empires would expand by the conquest of large parts of Asia and Africa.[163] Furthermore, as Korman notes, European states quite openly relied on the doctrine of conquest as a basis for their title.[164]

The emphasis on the concept of property, and the positivist view that uncivilized peoples were not legal entities, also contributed towards doctrines such as 'occupation', erasing the existence of many non-European peoples:

Only such territory can be the object of occupation as is no State's land, whether entirely uninhabited, as e.g. an island, or inhabited by natives whose community is not to be considered as a State. Even civilized individuals may live and have private property on a territory without any union by them into a State proper which exercises sovereignty over such territory. And natives may live on a territory under a tribal organization which need not be considered a State proper.[165]

This meant that the territory of 'tribal' peoples could be appropriated simply through occupation by the European state on the basis that tribal organization did not correspond with a 'State'. Thus British title to the Australian continent was based on occupation of uninhabited territory,

[162] For a comprehensive and detailed study of conquest, see Sharon Korman, *The Right of Conquest: The Acquisition of Territory by Force in International Law and Practice* (New York: Oxford University Press, 1996).
[163] For an outline of conquest see Oppenheim, *International Law*, pp. 302–307. Conquest seems to have been officially outlawed in contemporary international law as a means of acquiring title to territory.
[164] See Korman, *The Right of Conquest*, p. 66.   [165] Oppenheim, *International Law*, p. 292.

territorium nullius; it was irrelevant that Aboriginal peoples had occupied the continent for many thousands of years.[166]

Each of these doctrines relied upon different notions of native personality, as the particular means of asserting title depended on the positivist assessment of the degree of civilization of the peoples occupying the land. Using this scale, the positivists asserted, for example, that in the case of merely tribal peoples occupation itself would suffice. If the natives belonged to what positivists regarded as an uncivilized and yet organised polity, however, European powers would have to assert title through some other means such as conquest or cession.[167] The issue of cession raised the problems discussed earlier as to treaty relations between European and non-European peoples. The legitimacy of conquest as a mode of acquiring control, together with the positivist argument that resort to force was a valid expression of sovereign will, meant that few restrictions were imposed on imperial expansion.

Complying with the standard of civilization

Certain states, such as Japan and Siam, succeeded in retaining their nominal independence. For such states, acceptance into the family of nations could occur only if they met the 'standard of civilization' which amounted, essentially, to idealized European standards in both their external and, more significantly, internal relations.

These standards pre-supposed and legitimized colonial intrusion, in that a non-European state was deemed to be civilized if it could provide an individual, a European foreigner, with the same treatment that the individual would expect to receive in Europe.[168] The development of this framework appears to correspond with the changing nature of European penetration of the non-European world and the legal regimes which had been devised to accommodate this. As discussed earlier, the first phase of contact took place through trading companies which confined their activities principally to trade; as they gradually adopted a more intrusive role in the governance of the non-European state in order to further their trading interests, more demands were made on non-European states,

---

[166] See Lindley, *The Acquisition and Government*, pp. 40–41.

[167] For discussion of the various ways in which title could be obtained over territories occupied by primitive peoples, see Westlake, *Chapters on the Principles of International Law*, pp. 155–166. British acquisition of title over India presented a different set of problems by virtue of the existence of what was posited as a complex political system there. See *ibid.*, p. 191.

[168] See Westlake, *Chapters on the Principles of International Law*, pp. 102–103, 141–142.

which were compelled under threat of military action to make increasing concessions to the interests of the traders. Apart from demonstrating some of the characteristics of an unequal treaty, the Treaty of Nanking (1842) suggests how different European practices and policies were gradually introduced into non-European societies and then expanded. Once it had been established by way of treaty that Europeans had a right to reside and trade in a particular state, it was not altogether surprising that international jurists would use this as a measure of whether a country was civilized or not. Westlake presents the basic test:

When people of European race come into contact with American or African tribes, the prime necessity is a government under the protection of which the former may carry on the complex life to which they have been accustomed in their homes.[169]

Westlake argued that the 'Asiatic Empires' were capable of meeting this standard, provided that the Europeans were subject to the jurisdiction of a European consul rather than subject to the local laws; but even so, this meant only that European international law had to merely 'take account' of such Asiatic societies rather than accept them as members of the family of nations.[170] For the European states, the local systems of justice were completely inadequate, and there was no question of submitting one of their citizens to these systems. Non-European states were thus forced to sign treaties of capitulation which gave European powers extra-territorial jurisdiction over the activities of their own citizens in these non-European states.[171] This derogation from the sovereignty of the non-European state was naturally regarded as a massive humiliation by that state, which sought to terminate all capitulations at the earliest opportunity.[172] Capitulations were a part of the unequal treaty regime imposed on these states and generally comprised one part of a treaty which usually granted rights to trade and rights to establish residences,

---

[169] Ibid., p. 141.   [170] See ibid., p. 142.

[171] See Oppenheim, International Law, p. 395; this jurisdiction was exercised by European consuls in the non-European states; these competence of these consuls comprised 'the whole civil and criminal jurisdiction, the power of protection of the privileges, the life, and property of their countrymen'. Ibid., p. 497.

[172] See Anand, New States, pp. 21–23; Tieya, 'International Law in China', p. 195. Alexandrowicz argues that originally, capitulations were voluntarily undertaken by Asian states who were sympathetic to the problems faced by traders in a foreign culture, and who sought to facilitate trade by means of the capitulation which, in the early stage of the colonial encounter, took place on equal terms. Capitulations at that stage did not signify inequality or inferiority; that occurred by the nineteenth century. See Alexandrowicz, An Introduction, p. 97.

for example.[173] Once these treaties allowed for a trading presence, it was almost inevitable that the scope of the rights demanded by the European powers to enable them effectively to carry on their trade expanded.

Both external and internal reform had to be carried out by a state seeking entry into the family of nations. In the external sphere, the state had to be capable of meeting international obligations and maintaining the diplomatic missions and channels necessary to enable and preserve relations with European states. In the internal sphere, the state was required to reform radically its legal and political systems to the extent that they reflected European standards as a whole. Put another way, this test in effect suggested that the project of meeting the standard of civilization consisted of generalizing the standards embodied in the capitulation system which was specific to aliens, to the entire country.[174] In the domestic sphere, then, the non-European state was required to guarantee basic rights – relating to dignity, property, freedom of travel, commerce and religion, and it had to possess a court system which comprised codes, published laws and legal guarantees.[175] All these rules compelling domestic reform essentially required profound transformations of non-European societies in ways that negated the principle of territorial sovereignty. Oppenheim states the principle in its fullest form:

In consequence of its internal independence and territorial supremacy, a State can adopt any Constitution it likes, arrange its administration in a way it thinks fit, make use of legislature as it pleases, organise its forces on land and sea, build and pull down fortresses, adopt any commercial policy it likes and so on.[176]

While positivist jurisprudence insisted that states were formally equal and that they possessed extensive powers over their own territory, a different set of principles applied in the case of non-European states, which significantly compromised their internal sovereignty and their cultural distinctiveness in order to be accepted as legal subjects of the system. It was not open for non-European states to exercise the far-ranging freedoms over their internal affairs suggested by Oppenheim, principally

[173] See Gong, *Standard of 'Civilization'*, p. 211, citing the Treaty of Friendship and Commerce Between Her Majesty and the Kings of Siam, 18 April 1855 (the Bowring Treaty).
[174] Thus it was only after Japan had extensively revised its civil and criminal codes that it was admitted to the family of nations. See Gong, *Standard of 'Civilization'*, p. 29.
[175] See *ibid.*, pp. 14–15. Gong provides a clear and useful summary, taken from various texts, of what the standard of civilization required.
[176] Oppenheim, *International Law*, p. 178.

because it was only if the non-European states had adopted Western forms of political organization that they were accepted into the system. Basically, then, the actions non-European states had to take to enter into the system negated the rights which they were supposed formally to enjoy upon admittance.

Protectorates

Towards the latter part of the nineteenth century, protectorates were a common technique by which European states exercised extensive control over non-European states while not officially assuming sovereignty over those states.[177] Although used to regulate relations within Europe itself, the protectorate device was modified by European states and used in unique ways to further their colonial empires. The protectorate was ostensibly a means of protecting vulnerable states from 'great power politics' by entrusting those very same great powers with the task of looking after the interests of these vulnerable states.[178] Thus the 'protectorate' was essentially a treaty by which uncivilized states placed themselves under the 'protection' of European states. Under this regime, the European state would acquire complete control over the external affairs of the non-European state, and this meant that the non-European state could not communicate with any other European state without the permission of its 'protector'.[179] In theory, then, the non-European states retained their sovereignty over internal affairs. Indeed, a number of disputes heard by the British courts, for example, established and affirmed this proposition.[180]

The distinction between internal and external sovereignty, that protectorates technically established was, however, porous. As Westlake remarks, for example, 'the institution of protectorates over uncivilized nations has given greater freedom to the initial steps towards their

[177] On protectorates in general, see Lindley, *The Acquisition and Government*, pp. 180–206; Oppenheim, *International Law*, pp. 296–298.

[178] See Alexandrowicz, *The European–African Confrontation*, p. 62.

[179] See *ibid.*, pp. 62–83. Alexandrowicz defines a protectorate in the following terms:
> The Protectorate means a split of sovereignty and its purpose is to vest in the Protector rights of external sovereignty while leaving rights of internal sovereignty in the protected entity. In this way the Protector shelters another entity against the external hazards of power politics.
>   (Alexandrowicz, *The European–African Confrontation*, p. 62)
See also Crawford, *The Creation of States*, pp. 187–188.

[180] For example, *Duff Development Co. v. Kelentan Govt.* [1924] A.C. 797. See Lindley, *The Acquisition and Government*, pp. 194–200 for a discussion of the status of Malay and Indian protectorates.

acquisition'.[181] This was legally justified by protectorate provisions which enabled the protecting power to assume control over internal affairs because this was explicitly provided for in the agreement,[182] or else because the native ruler was incapable, for example, of maintaining 'good government' within the protectorate.[183] The artificiality of the supposed distinction between external and internal sovereignty is suggested by the fact that even questions of succession, which were the very core of native sovereignty, were often to be approved of by the protecting power.[184] As Maine points out, regimes such as the protectorate were a complete aberration from Austin's idea of sovereignty:

> It is necessary to the Austinian theory that the all-powerful portion of the community which make laws should not be divisible, that it should not share its power with anybody else, and Austin himself speaks with some contempt of the semi-sovereign or demi-sovereign states which are recognised by the classical writers of International Law. But this indivisibility of Sovereignty, though it belongs to Austin's system, does not belong to International Law. The powers of sovereigns are a bundle or collection of powers and they may be separated one from another.[185]

Significantly, then, the protectorate mechanism enabled European states to exercise control over a state with respect to both its internal and external affairs, even while asserting that sovereignty was properly located in the native ruler. As Lindley notes,

> By such an arrangement, one state could acquire complete control over another, so far as third nations were concerned, without necessarily assuming the burden

---

[181] Westlake, *Chapters on the Principles of International Law*, p. 184. Lindley goes further in saying: 'The more modern protectorates [i.e. protectorates established with respect to non-European states] . . . have been usually intended or destined to result in the incorporation of the protected region into the Dominions of the protecting Power, or, at all events, in an increasing control by that Power over the internal affairs of the protected country.' Lindley, *The Acquisition and Government*, p. 182.

[182] See *ibid.*, p. 184, discussing the Warsangali Treaty between chiefs of the Warsangali – near the Somali coast – and Britain, whereby the Warsangali agreed to act upon the advice of British Officers 'in matters relating to the administration of justice, the development of the resources of the country, the interests of commerce, or in any other matter in relation to peace, order and good government and the general progress of civilization'.

[183] See Lindley, *The Acquisition and Government*, p. 196.

[184] See *ibid.*, p. 200.

[185] Henry Sumner Maine, *International Law: A Series of Lectures Delivered Before the University of Cambridge, 1887* (London: John Murray, 1888), p. 58.

of its administration, and it was this feature of the protectorate which favoured its extensive adoption by European Powers in the spread of their dominion.[186]

The protectorate was a wonderfully flexible legal instrument because it could be used for a number of different purposes. It could, as Lindley suggests, be used to exclude competing European powers. Equally, it could be used to acquire control over the interior realm of the native state when that was considered desirable. The existence of a protectorate enabled European states to regulate the degree of sovereignty of a local ruler, depending on the circumstances. Thus in terms of some issues, the local ruler could be characterized as having capacity to transfer property to the protecting power, for example. In other cases, where the protecting power wished to assert its own power, it could declare that the matter in question was within the protecting power's sphere of authority.[187] In analysing British practice as a protecting state with respect to Indian princely kingdoms, it is asserted that

There *is* paramount power in the British Crown, of which the extent is wisely left undefined. There *is* a subordination in the native states, which is understood but not explained. The paramount power intervenes only on grounds of general policy, where interests of the Indian people or the safety of the British power are at stake.[188]

What is notable is that, at a time when sovereignty was generally regarded as fixed, stable and monolithic,[189] colonial jurists self-consciously grasped the usefulness of keeping sovereignty undefined in order that it could be extended or withdrawn according to the requirements of British interests. It is also notable in this passage that Britain had by now assumed responsibility for the well being of the natives and used this, too, as a basis for intervention. In the final analysis, then, the distinction between protectorates and colonies was gradually eroded; the protectorate was a vehicle by which the European power controlled both the internal and external relations of the native

---

[186] *Ibid.,* p. 182.
[187] For the complications which could arise in the context of which rights attributable to sovereignty were being exercised, see *R.* v. *Crewe,* 2 Eng. Rep. 576 (K.B. 1910).
[188] Westlake, *Chapters on the Principles of International Law,* p. 207 (1894), citing William Lee-Warner, *The Protected Princes of India* (London: Macmillan & Co., 1894), pp. 37–40.
[189] For an analysis of this image of nineteenth-century sovereignty see Kennedy, 'International Law', p. 119: 'By century's end, international law would countenance but one form of political authority, absolute within its territory and equal in its relations with other sovereigns.'

state.[190] As in the case of Vitorian jurisprudence, intervention was endorsed by a number of techniques, by the powerful invocation of disorder and lawlessness which necessitated the imposition of order which could take place only through conquest posited as unwillingly undertaken. The protectorate, then, demonstrated yet another variation on sovereignty as it developed in the colonial encounter. The use of the protectorate as a flexible instrument of control corresponded with a growing appreciation of the uses of 'informal Empire' and the realization that an important distinction could be made between economic and political control.[191] While it was desirable to exploit the raw materials of Asian and African countries and develop new markets there, this was achieved, where possible, without assuming political control over the territory and with it all the costs and problems of managing a colony. Seen from this perspective, the ideal situation was one in which economic control could be exercised over a non-European state which was nominally, at least, 'sovereign'. As a legal instrument, the protectorate arrangement was ideally suited for the implementation of such a policy.[152]

The Berlin Conference of 1884–1885

Introduction

Given the conceptual inadequacies of the positivist framework for dealing with the colonial encounter, the positivist validation of the use of force, and the intense competition among European states for colonies, it was hardly surprising that international law contributed very little towards the effective management of the colonial scramble. The tensions arising from the scramble were such that the European powers held the Berlin Conference of 1884–5 to try and resolve matters. Here, diplomacy and the traditional balance of power politics combined with

---

[190] Lindley asserts that the protectorate was intended to lead to 'an increasing control by that [protecting] Power over the internal affairs of the protected country. The sovereignty is to be acquired piecemeal, the external sovereignty first.' Lindley, The Acquisition and Government, p. 182.

[191] See John Gallagher and Ronald Robinson, 'The Imperialism of Free Trade' (1953) 6 The Economic History Review 1–15. For a discussion of the role of informal empire in the broad context of the imperial project see Michael W. Doyle, Empires (Ithaca, NY: Cornell University Press, 1986).

[192] In the final analysis, however, the British, for example, found it necessary to assume political control over most of the territories which they initially treated as protectorates; it was only in this way that they could create the political conditions and stability which enabled economic expansion.

international law, as the imperial powers of Europe attempted to create a legal and political framework, to ensure that colonial expansion in the Congo Basin took place in an orderly way which minimised tensions among the three most powerful European states at the time, England, France and Germany. This part of the chapter focuses on the legal attempts to define and domesticate the native and place him securely within the authoritative framework of positivist jurisprudence, together with the related theme of the complex ways in which law and politics intersected in the grand project of colonial management.

African peoples played no part at all in these deliberations. As U. O. Umozurike points out, 'The most irrelevant factor in deciding the fate of the continent was the Africans themselves who were neither consulted nor apprised of the conference',[193] a conference which determined in important ways the future of the continent and which continues to have a profound influence on the politics of contemporary Africa.[194] This exclusion was reiterated and intensified in a more complex way by the positivist argument that African tribes were too primitive to understand the concept of sovereignty to cede it by treaty: as a consequence, any claims to sovereignty based on such treaties were invalid.[195] This proposition may have been advanced not only for reasons of theoretical consistency, but in order to preclude the rampant abuse by European adventurers of the treaty mechanism by which they claimed to acquire sovereignty. Nevertheless, its effect was to transform Africa into a conceptual *terra nullius*; as such, only dealings between European states with respect to those territories could have decisive legal effect.[196] The Berlin Conference[197] was a unique event, furthermore, as it was the first occasion on which European states[198] sought as a body to address the

---

[193] U. O. Umozurike, *International Law and Colonialism in Africa* (Enugu, Nigeria: Nwamife Publishers, 1979), p. 26. See also Elias, *Africa*, pp. 18–34.

[194] See Makau wa Mutua, 'Why Redraw the Map of Africa?: A Moral and Legal Inquiry', (1995) 16 *Michigan Journal of International Law* 1113–1176.

[195] See Oppenheim, *International Law*, pp. 285–286 for the general proposition that cessions of territory by native tribes made to States fall outside the Law of Nations; for the application of the doctrine to Africa specifically, see Westlake, *Chapters on the Principles of International Law*, pp. 149–155.

[196] See Westlake, *Chapters on the Principles of International Law*, p. 154.

[197] See Crowe, *The Berlin West African Conference*, pp. 158–159; Mutua, 'Why Redraw the Map', pp. 1126–1134.

[198] The instrument which emerged from the Conference was the General Act of the Conference of Berlin Concerning the Congo, Signed at Berlin, 26, 1885, Official Documents, *American Journal of International Law 7*. France and Germany first developed the idea of holding the Conference; invitations were issued in three stages,

'colonial problem'. Although concerned with the division of Africa, the conference's deliberations illuminated many aspects of the broader question of colonialism as a whole. The management of the division of Africa by systematizing the colonial scramble and the articulation of a new ideology of colonialism were two of the conference's major projects.

Partitioning and managing Africa

Trade was the central preoccupation of the conference, which focused on issues of free trade in the Congo basin,[199] and free navigation of the Congo and Niger Rivers.[200] In discussing these issues, the implicit failure of international law to devise a coherent framework for regulating the European–African encounter became evident. As the previous discussion on treaties suggests, the modes of acquiring trading rights and control over non-European territory were easily open to abuse, as European trading companies or even adventurers such as Henry Morton Stanley[201] could enter into 'treaties' which, they claimed, provided them with rights, if not actual sovereignty, over vast areas of land. The Berlin Conference, in addition to focusing on trade issues, thus sought to create a unified system by which claims could be asserted and recognised.

The underlying and crucial issue in this debate was the issue of the legal personality of African tribes. Despite the objections of jurists such as Westlake,[202] treaties with African tribes were the basis on which claims were made to African territory. This raised the familiar and by now apparently insurmountable problem of deciding the capacity of the African entity and the status of that entity within the overall political structure of the tribe.

first to Great Britain, Belgium, the Netherlands, Portugal, Spain and the United States; later, to Austria, Russia, Italy, Denmark, Sweden and Norway; and finally to Turkey. See Crowe, *The Berlin West African Conference*, pp. 220–221.

[199] See *ibid.*, pp. 105–118.   [200] See Article 3 of the General Act.

[201] Stanley, acting on behalf of the International Association of the Congo headed by King Leopold II, King of the Belgians, made hundreds of treaties with native 'sovereigns' in the region and thus gained control over large portions of the Congo basin which eventually formed the Congo Free State; Leopold was the personal sovereign over the state whose existence was recognized by the powers at the Berlin Conference. See Lindley, *The Acquisition and Government*, p. 112; Crowe, *The Berlin West African Conference*, pp. 158–160.

[202] Westlake argued that African tribes were too simple to understand the concept of sovereignty and hence were incapable of transferring it by treaty. See Westlake, *Chapters on the Principles of International Law*, pp. 144–146.

An alternative proposal was made by the American representative to the Berlin Conference, Mr Kasson, who argued that:

Modern international law follows closely a line which leads to the recognition of the right of native tribes to dispose freely of themselves and of their hereditary title. In conformity with this principle my government would gladly adhere to a more extended rule, to be based on a principle which should aim at the voluntary consent of the natives whose country is taken possession of, in all cases where they had not provoked the aggression.[203]

Kasson's proposal was greeted cautiously, and the conference 'hesitated to express an opinion' on such a delicate matter;[204] scholarly opinion was divided as to whether Kasson's proposal, even though not officially accepted, nevertheless reflected the practice of states.[205] On the one hand, Kasson's proposal would have severely and unacceptably curtailed colonial powers if indeed the principle had been implemented in such a way as to require scrupulous evidence of proper consent.[206] On the other hand, absent such an inquiry into the validity of the ostensible consent, the proposal simply offered a justification for entering into more treaties with African states, claiming that such treaties conformed with the scheme outlined by Kasson.

Several jurists such as Westlake pointed out that Kasson's scheme was impractical and dangerous. Its proper implementation raised questions to which there were no clear answers:

Is any territorial cession permitted by the ideas of the tribe? What is the authority – chief, elders, body of fighting men – if there is one, which those ideas point out as empowered to make the cession? With what formalities do they require it to be made, if they allow it to be made at all?[207]

There is more than a suggestion in Westlake, furthermore, that the individuals characterized as 'African chiefs' in these treaties exploited all these confusions for their own purposes.[208]

Overall, therefore, no clear procedure for acquiring valid title was laid down by the conference. This same vagueness afflicted the conference's attempt to clarify the issue of 'effective occupation'. The conference

---

[203] Cited in Westlake, *Chapters on the Principles of International Law*, p. 138. On Kasson's contribution to the Conference see Crowe, *The Berlin West African Conference*, pp. 97–98.
[204] See Westlake, *Chapters on the Principles of International Law*, p. 138.
[205] See Crawford, *The Creation of States*, p. 179.
[206] See Westlake, *Chapters on the Principles of International Law*, p. 139.
[207] *Ibid.*, pp. 139–140.
[208] See Westlake, *Chapters on the Principles of International Law*, pp. 139–140.

basically stipulated that any party taking possession of a tract of land in Africa was required to notify all other members of this possession[209] and, further, was required to exercise its authority in its possessions in such a way as to protect existing rights within the territory.[210] This was intended to prevent countries from making claims to territory based only on the most tenuous connections with that territory, and to ensure that control was accompanied by international responsibility. The conference was only partially successful in achieving these ambitions, as Britain, which had the largest interests in Africa, opposed all efforts to impose greater responsibility on the colonizing powers.[211] These attempts to formulate rules for effective occupation acknowledged the lack of any precise, accepted and workable principles regulating the colonial encounter. The best that could be achieved was to proceduralise the matter by requiring states acquiring territorial interests to notify other signatories of their claims, to enable these states to lodge any objections.[212] No clarity existed as to how such claims were to be resolved, or in what forum.

This unsatisfactory resolution represented a fundamental irony for positivist jurisprudence. Positivists had sought at numerous levels of their jurisprudence to erase the problematic native from their scheme; the native was expelled from the realm of the family of nations and excised from history by positivist disregard for the four preceding centuries of diplomatic relations, and excluded from the process of treaty making. Native resistance and opposition were silenced by the positivist practice of reading a treaty with no regard to the violence and coercion which led to its formation. Despite all such attempts to exclude the African from the conference, however, the identity of the African native became the central preoccupation of its deliberations over the question of systematizing territory. And despite positivist attempts to assume complete control over the identity of the native, the native remained unknowable in a way which threatened the stability and unity of Europe. Conventional histories of the conference make the powerful point that Africans were excluded from its deliberations. The story of

---

[209] See Chapter VI, Article 34 of the General Act. For discussion as to the problem of effective occupation see Crowe, *The Berlin West African Conference*, pp. 176–191.

[210] Article 35 of the General Act.

[211] See Crowe, *The Berlin West African Conference*, pp. 176–191. In particular, Britain sought to restrict the application of these principles to the coastal states in Africa; and, further, prevented these principles from applying to protectorates.

[212] The term used in the Act is 'reclamations' rather than protest. Article 34 of the General Act.

the conference may also be written, however, from another perspective which focuses on the complex way in which the identity of the African was an enduring and irresolvable problem that haunted the conference's proceedings.

The existence of unassimilability, and the problems of native identity and their effect in bringing to crisis the colonial will to power, may well be worth identifying and celebrating; but such a celebration must be tempered with the knowledge that whatever the disruptions inflicted on the logic of colonial narratives, these did little to ameliorate the real and violent consequences which followed for African societies.

Although Kasson's approach was attacked and criticized, subsequent practice suggests that to that extent that *any* remotely legal explanation could be given to the partition of Africa, it was based on his proposal.[213] Seen in this perspective, which accepted the possibility of treaties between Africans and Europeans, consent, as ostensibly granted by Africans, became a complete reversal of what it was supposed to mean. Consent, rather than an expression of the will of the relevant party, was instead created in accordance with the exigencies of the situation. What resulted, in effect, was a system of treaty making in which ideas of 'consent' acquired a peculiar and completely distorted form. Consent, of course, was the basis of positivist jurisprudence, and the science of jurisprudence, authorities such as Oppenheim argued, consisted precisely in determining whether such consent had led to the formation of certain rules, which would then be binding on the state which had so consented. A rich and complex set of ideas – which are still an integral aspect of contemporary international legal jurisprudence – developed out of this set of considerations. However, with regard to native consent, a very different set of issues arose. Here, consent was created by the jurist; agency was created by the writer, as African chiefs, Indian princes and Chinese Emperors, were ascribed powers to consent to various measures which benefited the European powers. They were excluded from personality; when granted personality, this was in order to enable the formulation of a consistent jurisprudential system or else to transfer the entitlement which the Europeans sought. Having articulated a legal framework for acquiring sovereignty over African territory which was radically disconnected from the actual practice[214] on which they purported to base their system, positivists,

---

[213] See Crawford, *The Creation of States*, pp. 178–179 and sources cited therein, which include Lugard.

[214] See Crawford, *The Creation of States*.

in a now familiar reversal, discarded several important elements of their jurisprudence; whereas previously they insisted that treaties could not be the basis for acquiring sovereignty over African territory, they now applied their science to the interpretation and application of treaties.

Justifying colonialism: trade, humanitarianism and the civilizing mission[215]

The Berlin Conference was perhaps the first occasion on which Europe as a body went some way towards articulating a philosophy of colonialism which was appropriate for the late nineteenth century, a time in which the colonial project entered a new phase because of the direct involvement of states in the furtherance of colonialism, and because of the systematic economic exploitation of the colonies which led not only to intense inter-state rivalries but the increasing importance of the colonies for the metropolitan economy. The idea of the civilizing mission, of extending Empire for the higher purpose of educating and rescuing the barbarian, had a very ancient lineage.[216] Versions of the civilizing mission were used by all the actors who participated in imperial expansion. New challenges were posed to the way in which imperial states conceived of themselves and their colonies once, for example, the United Kingdom dissolved the East India Company and assumed direct responsibility towards its Indian subjects.[217]

The humanitarian treatment of inferior and subject peoples was thus one of the issues addressed by the conference. Over the previous century or so, the slave trade had been gradually abolished by international law. The conference, however, while reiterating the necessity to stamp out

---

[215] 'The conquest of the earth, which mostly means the taking it away from those who have a different complexion or slightly flatter noses than ourselves, is not a pretty thing when you look at it too much. What redeems it is the idea only. An idea at the back of it.' Joseph Conrad, *Heart of Darkness* (Edinburgh: W. Blackwood & Sons, 1902).

[216] See Pagden's study of how the modern European Empires modelled themselves on the Roman Empire, and the Roman idea of what may be termed the 'civilizing mission'. Anthony Pagden, *Lords of All the World: Ideologies of Empire in Spain, Britain and France c. 1500–c.1800* (New Haven: Yale University Press, 1995). See especially his discussion of Cicero's version of the 'civilizing mission', *ibid.*, pp. 22–23.

[217] This led Queen Victoria to declare that the Crown was as responsible towards its native Indian subjects as it was to all its other subjects. See Quincy Wright, *Mandates Under the League of Nations* (Chicago: University of Chicago Press, 1930), p. 11, n. 18.

COLONIALISM IN NINETEENTH-CENTURY INTERNATIONAL LAW

the trade, went further. In his opening speech at the conference, Prince Bismarck noted that 'all the Governments invited share the wish to bring the natives of Africa within the pale of civilization by opening up the interior of the continent to commerce'.[218] The British representative made similar remarks, warning of the dangers of completely unregulated trade and arguing for that type of trade which would 'confer the advantages of civilization on the natives'.[219] The conference concluded that it had properly embodied these concerns in Article 6, which read in part:

> All the Powers exercising sovereign rights or influence in the aforesaid territories [the conventional Basin of the Congo] bind themselves to watch over the preservation of the native tribes, and to care for the improvement of the conditions of their moral and material well-being, and to help in suppressing slavery and especially the Slave Trade.[220]

These vaguely expressed concerns were only sporadically implemented;[221] indeed, the most notable achievement of the conference was the creation of the Congo Free State, which was subsequently recognised as belonging to the personal sovereignty of King Leopold II of the Belgians and which was the scene of mass atrocities.[222] Nevertheless, the humanitarian rhetoric of the conference was extremely important because it refined the justification for the colonial project. Trade was not what it had been earlier, a means of simply maximizing profit and increasing national power. Rather, trade was an indispensable part of the civilizing mission itself; the expansion of commerce was the means by which the backward natives could be civilized. 'Moral and material' well being were the twin pillars of the programme. This gave the whole rhetoric of trade a new and important impetus. Implicit within it was a new world view: it was not simply the case that independent communities would trade with each other. Now, because trade was the mechanism for advancement and progress, it was essential that trade be extended as far as possible into the interior of all these societies.

---

[218] Quoted in Lindley, *The Acquisition and Government*, p. 332.
[219] *Ibid.*   [220] Article 6 of the General Act.
[221] Crowe, for example, asserts quite forcefully that humanitarian issues played only a very small role in the Conference. See Crowe, *The Berlin West African Conference*, pp. 3, 103–04.
[222] See Lindley, *The Acquisition and Government*, pp. 112–113. Adam Hochschild, *King Leopold's Ghost: A Story of Greed, Terror, and Heroism in Colonial Africa* (Boston: Houghton, Mifflin, 1999).

Recognition and the reconstruction of positivism

I have stressed and reiterated the importance of the concept of society because its significance for the whole edifice of positivist jurisprudence has not been adequately appreciated. Although a fundamental part of the nineteenth-century positivist vocabulary, 'society' has ceased to be a legal concept of any importance in contemporary discussions of international law. This is because recognition doctrine serves to obscure the role and function of 'society' by presenting it as a creation of sovereignty. In terms of my overall argument, this manoeuvre is crucial for the purposes of obscuring the understanding of society's operational role as a mechanism by which cultural assessments can be transformed into a legal status. Furthermore, presenting society as a creation of sovereignty suggests another way in which international law suppresses the colonial past at the doctrinal level. Recognition doctrine was fundamental, not only to the task of assimilating the non-European world, but to the very structure of the positivist legal system. Lorimer points to this in arguing that 'Recognition, in its various phases, constitutes the premise of the positive law of nations when stated as a logical system'.[223] The link between positivism and recognition may be traced both historically[224] and logically. In logical terms, Lorimer's assertion appears correct, in that the positivist emphasis on the sovereign as being the fundamental basis of international law suggests that it is only the phenomena which the sovereign recognize that become part of the legal universe. Recognition doctrine is implicitly based on the assumption of the existence of a properly constituted sovereign. Only those principles which are created and accepted by sovereigns constitute law, only those entities which are granted legal personality by the sovereign exists within the legal universe. Once established, the sovereign becomes the prism, the gaze, which reconstitutes the legal universe. What this view of recognition doctrine conceals, however, is the complex process by which the sovereign is constituted in the first place.

---

[223] Lorimer, *The Institutes of the Law of Nations*, p. 3. Indeed, Lorimer commences his work by stating that the Law of Nations is divided into three leading doctrines: (1) The doctrine of recognition; (2) The doctrine of normal relations that result from the doctrine of recognition; (3) The doctrine of the abnormal relations that result from the doctrine of recognition. *Ibid.*

[224] For an account of the beginnings of the doctrine of recognition in the eighteenth and early nineteenth centuries and how this corresponded with the emergence of positivism, see Alexandrowicz, 'The Theory of Recognition', p. 176.

The origins of sovereignty have always constituted a major problem for the discipline, as suggested by contemporary debates about the right of self-determination, for example. Within the framework of the colonial encounter, however, it is possible to trace how a very self-conscious effort was made to constitute sovereignty in ways that were explicitly racialised. Austin argued that law was the command of the sovereign. Positivists focused on sovereignty, but at least with respect to the European–non-European distinction, the powerful and defining idea that sovereignty was the exclusive preserve of Europe was enabled by an elaboration of the concept of 'society'. Law properly prevailed only among the members of society. Consequently, for the positivists, the concept of law was intimately connected with the concept of society, rather than that of sovereignty as outlined by Austin.[225] The concept of society is crucial to the positivist scheme because it enables a distinction to be made between different types of states; the effect of the distinction is to exclude non-European states from the family of nations and hence from the realm of sovereignty itself.[226] Seen in this way. the constitution of sovereignty depended on the elaborations which 'society doctrine' alone could develop. This reliance on the concept of society to establish sovereignty seems somewhat at odds with the claim that sovereignty is the core and essential principle of international law, and that everything within the system derives from sovereignty.

The sovereign European state was established through reliance on the concept of society. Once constituted, however, the sovereign asserts supremacy by presenting itself as the means by which society operates and comes into being. It is through recognition doctrine that sovereignty doctrine is reconstructed and presents itself as self-contained, coherent, comprehensive and all-encompassing. A structure of power and decision making is implicit in the doctrine because the power to 'recognise' new

---

[225] See Hall, *A Treatise on International Law*, p. 40. 'It is scarcely necessary to point out that as international law is a product of the special civilisation of modern Europe, and forms a highly artificial system of which the principles cannot be supposed to be understood or recognized by countries differently civilized, such states can only be presumed to be subject to it as inheritors of that civilisation. They have lived, and are living, under law, and a positive act of withdrawal would be required to free them from its restraints.'

[226] Crawford summarizes the situation in the nineteenth century as: 'States as such were not therefore necessarily members of the Society of Nations. Recognition, express or implied, solely created their membership and bound them to obey international law.' Crawford, *The Creation of States*, p. 13.

states is vested in the states that are already sovereign. The doctrine is premised on the existence of a sovereign state whose will establishes law and whose actions may be subject to lawyers' inquiry.

Once the existence of the state may be presumed, positivist jurisprudence acquires some semblance of consistency. Once a particular group of states wins the title of 'sovereign', an authoritative interpretive framework, employing clearly established categories of 'backward' and 'advanced' is established, and used to determine the status of other, excluded states. Simple acceptance of this framework precludes an inquiry into how this distinction was made and why one set of states becomes sovereign while the other does not, even though anthropological and historical research subversively suggests various disconcerting parallels between these apparently disparate societies.

My argument is that recognition doctrine was not merely, or even primarily, about ascertaining or establishing the legal status of the entity under scrutiny; rather, it was about affirming the power of the European states to claim sovereignty, to reinforce their authority to make such determinations and, consequently, to make sovereignty a possession that they could then proceed to dispense, deny, create or partially grant. The history of sovereignty doctrine in the nineteenth century, then, is a history of the processes by which European states, by developing a complex vocabulary of cultural and racial discrimination, set about establishing and presiding over a system of authority by which they could develop the powers to determine who is and is not sovereign. Recognition does not so much resolve the problem of determining the status of unknown entities as obscure the history of the process by which this decision making framework comes into being.

Sovereignty is explicitly identified with particular cultural characteristics and a particular cultural process: that of Europe. The history of sovereignty then becomes the coming into being of European civilization and, at the same time, the conventional history of how international law becomes universal.

Reconceptualizing sovereignty

Colonialism and the racialization of sovereignty

An examination of the foundations of positivist views of sovereignty and their complex relationship with colonialism suggests new ways of approaching traditional understandings of sovereignty doctrine and the character of sovereignty as it was inherited by the non-European world.

COLONIALISM IN NINETEENTH-CENTURY INTERNATIONAL LAW

In attempting to formulate a new, scientific international law, the jurists of the nineteenth century articulated a formalist model of sovereignty; sovereignty as an absolute set of powers which was bound by no higher authority and which was properly detached from all the imprecise claims of morality and justice. This model of sovereignty has been the subject of a considerable and important critique. The fundamental problem with this model, the problem which was evident from the time it was first articulated, was the problem of how order could be created among sovereign states in the absence of an overarching sovereign authoritatively to articulate and enforce the relevant law. The conundrum presented by this image of sovereignty has been, in one way or another, the central preoccupation of the discipline, and scholars have generated an enormous amount of important work that seeks to address the basic question of why sovereign states obey, or should obey, international law.

A major concern of this chapter is to identify what this framework excludes. Although this framework plays a significant role in international legal thinking, the relationship between sovereignty and the non-European world cannot be properly understood within it. The interaction between European and non-European societies in the colonial encounter was not an interaction between equal sovereign states but between sovereign European states and non-European states denied sovereignty. The conventional way of accounting for this relationship is by recourse to recognition doctrine,[227] and to the story of the 'expansion of international society' – an ambiguous, euphemistic and somewhat misleading term when it is understood that this refers not to an open process by which the autonomy and integrity of non-European states were accepted, but to the colonial process by which Asian and African societies were made to accept European standards as the price of membership.

The paradigm of 'order among sovereign states' excludes from critical inquiry the processes which I have attempted to trace here; the process by which non-European states are deemed to be lacking in sovereignty and hence excluded from the family of nations and of law; and the racialization of the vocabulary of the period, in terms not only of the explicit distinctions between civilized and uncivilized, advanced and barbaric, but in terms of the integration of these distinctions into the very

---

[227] See the discussion above on the way in which recognition doctrine restores the integrity of the positivist framework.

foundations of the discipline, the ostensibly neutral concepts of 'law', 'society' and 'sovereignty'. The 'order' paradigm, then, cannot give any account of the role of race and culture, not only in the application of these concepts but in their very formation. I argue, by contrast, that sovereignty can be understood only in terms of its complex relationship with the colonial encounter and the constellation of racial and cultural distinctions it generated and elaborated. At the simplest level, the connection between sovereignty and culture was embodied by the fundamental positivist proposition that only European states could be sovereign. This complete identification of Europe with sovereignty is maintained, reiterated and reinforced at a number of different levels. Not only was the non-European excluded from the realm of sovereignty but European culture and society were naturalized. Hence, Lawrence argues that European states had belonged to the family of nations 'since time immemorial'. Lawrence continues:

Many of them existed before the great majority of its rules came into being. There was no need for them to be formally received among its subjects. Anything like a ceremony of initiation would have been wholly inapplicable to their case.[228]

The naturalist notion of a mythic state of nature is replaced by a positivist notion of a mythic age when European states constituted a self-evident family of nations. Lawrence emphatically argues that the origins of European supremacy are beyond history and inquiry, and incapable of identification. The appeal to 'time immemorial' precludes inquiry into how European states were deemed sovereign in the first place.[229]

In effect, Europe is the subject of sovereignty and non-Europe the object of sovereignty. Acceptance of these premises – the primacy of sovereignty and the identification of Europe as exclusively sovereign – creates a conceptual framework within which the only history of the non-European world which may be written by the discipline is the history of its absorption into the European world in order to progress towards the ultimate point of acquiring sovereignty. Two different dimensions of sovereignty can be seen when studied from this point of view: since sovereignty in a European context is a given, the European issue is how conflicts between sovereign states may be resolved in the absence of an overarching sovereign; the problem for the non-European

---

[228] Lawrence, *The Principles of International Law*, p. 84.
[229] Writers such as Westlake were insistent that the origins of sovereignty could not be inquired into. See Westlake, *Chapters on the Principles of International Law*, pp. 134–136.

world, by contrast, is its acquisition of sovereignty. This framework creates, in effect, something like a linear, evolutionary scheme in which the non-European world is the past and the European world the future. Thus, while the non-European world may illuminate aspects of the past of the European world that may otherwise remain hidden, the complex work of the future lies in the elaboration of established sovereignty, an elaboration which occurs through an examination of the conceptual problems arising from the interaction of sovereign European states.

Sovereignty manifested itself quite differently in the non-European world as compared with the European world. First, since the non-European world was not 'sovereign', virtually no legal restrictions were imposed on the actions of European states with respect to non-European peoples. European states could inflict massive violence on non-European peoples, invariably justified as necessary to pacify the natives, and follow this with the project of reshaping those societies in accordance with the European vision of the world. Sovereignty was therefore aligned with European ideas of social order, political organization, progress and development. This points to a second and implicit difference between sovereignty in Europe and sovereignty in the non-European world. In Europe, nineteenth-century positivism created a situation in which sovereignty was supreme and a sovereign's actions within its own territory were beyond scrutiny. In contrast, lacking sovereignty, non-European states exercised no rights recognizable by international law over their own territory. Any restrictions on the actions of European states towards non-European states resulted from conflicts between European states regarding the same territory, not from the rights of the non-European states. This was evident in the partition of Africa, which was determined in accordance with the needs of the major European states.

An understanding of the role of race and culture in the formation of basic international law doctrines such as sovereignty is crucial to an understanding of the singular relationship between sovereignty and the non-European world. It is singular in that sovereignty manifested itself in very different ways and with very different effect in the non-European world in contrast with the European world.

The positivist intent to erase the non-European world from any subjectivity or personality pervades positivism at virtually every level of its jurisprudence: in the distinction between civilized and non-civilized states, in the doctrine of *terra nullius*, in the attempted suppression of the long history of treaty practice between European and non-European peoples and inevitably, as Westlake points out, in the European acquisition of sovereignty itself:

The form which has been given to the question, namely what facts are necessary and sufficient in order that an uncivilized region may be internationally appropriated in sovereignty to a particular state? implies that it is only the recognition of such sovereignty by the members of the international society which concerns us, that of the uncivilized natives international law takes no account.[230]

As a consequence of the positivist conception of sovereignty, the character of sovereignty in the non-European world is profoundly different from its character in the European world. Within the nineteenth-century positivist framework, sovereignty was paramount. Sovereignty represents, then, at the most basic level, an assertion of power and authority, a means by which a people may preserve and assert their distinctive culture. For the non-European world, sovereignty was the complete negation of power, authority and authenticity. This was not only because European sovereignty was used as a mechanism of suppression and management, but because the acquisition of sovereignty was the acquisition of European civilization. In effect, then, for the non-European society, personhood was achieved precisely at that point of time when it ceased to have an independent existence; when it was absorbed into European Empires or when it profoundly altered its own cultural practices and political organizations. This paradox and irony is nicely if unselfconsciously suggested by Oppenheim when discussing the transfer of sovereignty by cession:

cession of territory made to a member of the family of nations by a State as yet outside that family is real cession and a concern of the Law of Nations, since such State becomes through the treaty of cession in some respects a member of that family.[231]

The sovereignty acquired by the non-European state, then, was only tenuously connected with its own identity;[232] rather, it was artificially created in accordance with the interests and world view of Europe; it emerged and was inextricably linked with a complex of practices which were explicitly directed towards the exploitation and domination of non-European peoples.

---

[230] Ibid., p. 136.   [231] Oppenheim, International Law, p. 86.

[232] For a powerful argument as to the continuing effects of this artificiality for African states, see Mutua, 'Why Redraw the Map'. The problem, of course, remains as to whether it is possible or desirable to return to some 'natural' identity.

GOOD
QUESTION

SEE P. 272

Sovereignty for the non-European world is alienation and subordination rather than empowerment. This point emerges powerfully from a study of positivist approaches to treaty making when it is clear that the only occasion when native 'sovereignty' or 'personality' is bestowed or recognised is in a context where that personality enables the native to transfer title, to grant rights – whether trading, to territory, or to sovereignty itself.[233] The basic point is that the development of the idea of sovereignty in relation to the non-European world occurs in terms of dispossession, its ability to alienate its lands and rights. As in the case of Vitorian jurisprudence, the native is granted personality in order to be bound. This is a radical contrast with the elaboration of sovereignty in the European world where the question is: are there any limits at all which can be persuasively applied to the Leviathan of state sovereignty? Sovereignty in the European and non-European worlds are characterized, then, in two conceptual frameworks which, though related in the fact that they are inverses of each other, are mutually exclusive.

The peculiar character of sovereignty in the non-European context is further evident in protectorate arrangements. On the one hand, it may appear that such arrangements recognised and embodied native sovereignty. It is clear, however, that native sovereignty is accommodated largely to the extent that this is compatible with the interests of colonial powers. In cases where vital issues were at stake, European states simply assumed sovereignty over the issues. Native sovereignty could be calibrated, then, in terms of the interests of the European powers which clearly recognised the advantages of sometimes *not* assuming sovereignty over the territories they controlled, as such sovereignty could be accompanied by responsibilities – such as the responsibility to protect other Europeans within that territory. The protectorate arrangement was a legal embodiment of a very contemporary phenomenon: the self-conscious exercise of control over a territory without the accompanying burden of assuming official sovereignty over that territory. Similar arguments may be made with regard to consent: consent was the very bedrock of the positivist system, and the whole science of positivism was dedicated to identifying whether in fact a state had consented to be bound by a particular principle; in the case of the non-European world, Kasson's apparently well-meaning attempt to make native consent an integral part of the scheme facilitated the construction of the pretence that natives had in fact consented to their own dispossession. Consent

---

[233] See the discussion above.

was not so much an expression of an independent will, then, as constructed according to the dictates of the colonial scramble; rather than being the stable foundation of the international legal system, in the non-European context it was a variable entity which could be ascribed the content which gave the system some semblance of coherence.

These inversions of sovereignty were a manifestation of a more profound change in the jurists' understanding of sovereignty resulting from the colonial encounter. On the one hand, European society becomes naturalized as sovereignty and placed beyond scrutiny and inquiry. Thus it was principally through the operations of sovereignty in the non-European world that European states acquired a new, self-conscious understanding of the origins of sovereignty and its potential operations. Some sense of this is conveyed by Westlake in his discussion of how title over territory may be acquired over backward peoples who inhabit the new countries:

Thus, the title to territorial sovereignty in old countries not being capable of discussion apart from the several dealings, as cession or conquest, which transfer it, we must turn to new countries.[234]

Once again, as in evolutionary theory, it is by examining the primitive that the modern acquires a better, clearer sense of itself. The history of the origins of sovereignty can now be written through an examination of its operations in the non-European world. And with the peculiar thrill which accompanies the magnification and universalization of the self, the history which emerges from this structure confirms that the history of sovereignty is the coming into being and expansion of European civilization, and that progress suggests an inevitable evolution towards that highest point.

Furthermore, Westlake suggests that the colonies played an important role in the discipline of international law, not simply because they offered an arena in which sovereignty, uninhibited by constraint, could exercise itself in new ways which were denied to it in Europe, but because it was through an examination of the process of sovereignty coming into being – whether through protectorates, annexation or meeting the standard of civilization – that jurists could self-consciously grasp sovereignty as a mechanism, an artifact, a technology whose characteristics could be both theoretically understood and practically developed precisely through its operation in the 'new countries' of the

---

[234] Westlake, *Chapters on the Principles of International Law*, p. 134.

non-European world. <u>Sovereignty, in the case of non-European societies</u> <u>does not arise 'naturally'; rather, it has to be bestowed.</u> Law was the creation of 'positive institutions', international law is a 'highly artificial system', Hall argues.[235] The nineteenth century is the age of science, the application of industry for the betterment and progress of human society. We see here, then, the suggestion of the idea that international law is not merely a science but a technology.[236] As a technology it could lend itself to the project of making real the Victorian ideals of progress, optimism and liberalism[237] which, when applied specifically to the non-European world, meant the civilizing of the benighted native peoples.

In summary, then, there are two distinctive models of sovereignty that developed in the nineteenth century: one model, the explicit model, generated the problem of order among sovereign states; the other, which I have attempted to develop here, focuses on the problem of cultural difference. My argument is that it is a fundamental mistake to see the second model as being in some way subsumed by the first; this chapter has attempted to elaborate the uniqueness of the second model. Nor can the first model account in any satisfactory way for the process by which European sovereignty became 'universalised'. However, these two models cannot be seen in isolation; rather, they are inextricably inter-related by virtue of the fact that they emerged at the same period out of the same philosophical matrix of positivism, and any attempt to outline a comprehensive theory of sovereignty surely must take this inter-dependence into account and resist the prevailing tendency to assimilate the unique history of the non-European world into the conventional model.

The legacy of the nineteenth century

The jurisprudence of the nineteenth century has had profound and enduring consequences for the non-European world. Basically, it presented non-European societies with the <u>fundamental contradiction</u> of <u>having to comply with authoritative European standards in order to win</u> <u>recognition and assert themselves.</u> The implications of this situation are powerfully summarized by Fanon:

---

[235] Hall, *A Treatise on International Law*, p. 40.

[236] But it is a technology of legal norms; the major advance with pragmatism is the understanding that the technology could be elaborated by using legal norms to create institutions which had a far greater range and flexibility.

[237] For a searching study of the 'Victorian tradition', see Koskenniemi, 'Lauterpacht', pp. 215–263.

Man is human only to the extent to which he tries to impose his existence on another man in order to be recognised by him. As long as he has not been effectively recognised by the other, that other will remain the theme of his actions. It is on that other being, on recognition by that other being, that his own human worth and reality depend. It is in that other being in whom the meaning of his life is condensed.[238]

Achieving the European ideal becomes the goal of the non-European states. Consequently, for the non-European world, the achievement of sovereignty was a profoundly ambiguous development, as it involved alienation rather than empowerment, the submission to alien standards rather than the affirmation of authentic identity.

Furthermore, as R. P. Anand has argued, 'having lost their international personality, the Asian states could not play any active role in the development of international law during the most creative period of its history'.[239] Many of the rules of international law that Anand refers to, such as the rules of state responsibility, were explicitly devised to facilitate the economic exploitation of non-European territories.

The question of the enduring effects for non-European societies of the history of exclusion is related to the issue of the legacy of the nineteenth century for the discipline as a whole. Lawrence's definition of international law reflects both the view prevalent at the time and the fundamental nexus between race and law: 'International law may be defined as *The rules which determine the conduct of the general body of civilized states in their dealings with one another*'.[240] A century later, international law is defined by Henkin and his colleagues in their major textbook on the subject as 'the law of the international community of states'.[241] The notion of 'community' is retained, but no distinctions are made between civilized and non-civilized states. The international community of the late twentieth century appeared open, cosmopolitan, accommodating, neutral; sovereignty is a set of powers and competences which can be enjoyed by all states regardless of their particular cultural identities.

Profound changes have occurred in the discipline in the intervening years, and the nineteenth century is something of an embarrassment to international law, for a number of reasons. Its monolithic view of sovereignty, its formalism and rigidity, were important causes of the First

---

[238] Frantz Fanon, *Black Skin, White Masks* (Charles Lam Markham trans., New York: Grove Press, 1967), pp. 216–217.

[239] Anand, *New States*, p. 21.   [240] Lawrence, *The Principles of International Law*, p. 1.

[241] See Henkin, Pugh, Schachter and Smit, *International Law*, p. xvii.

World War in the view of a number of distinguished inter-war jurists such as Lauterpacht and Alvarez, who set about the task of reconstructing a New International Law.[242] Its complete complicity with the colonial project has led to its denunciation as an international law of imperialism. Subsequent generations of international lawyers have strenuously attempted to distance the discipline from that period, in much the same way that positivists distanced themselves from naturalists. And as with that previous attempt at distancing, the results are ambiguous.

My argument has been that the discipline operates very much within the framework it has inherited from the nineteenth century. The problem of how order may be established in the absence of an overarching sovereign to articulate and enforce the law is a problem which arises with the articulation of the positivist framework. Since its articulation, it has been, and continues to be, the problem which has preoccupied both mainstream and critical theorizing about the discipline. In making this point I am not in any way seeking to diminish the extraordinary or defining importance of this body of work. Rather, I am arguing that an exclusive focus on this framework cannot provide an understanding of the history of the relationship between international law and the non-European world. The non-European world, relegated to the geographical periphery, is also relegated to the margins of theory. The specific historical experience of European states is generalised and universalised by its metamorphosis into the defining theoretical preoccupation of the discipline.[243]

Nor does it appear sufficient to me to claim that the racism of the nineteenth century has been transcended by the achievement of sovereign statehood by the non-European world. The argument that the nineteenth century has now been transcended by the discipline may be supported by the extent to which international law is now open and cosmopolitan and by the efforts made by international law to dismantle rather than promote the colonialism it had previously facilitated so exuberantly; international law, after all, promoted the process of decolonization by formulating doctrines of self-determination where once it formulated doctrines of annexation and *terra nullius*. This movement towards

---

[242] See Kennedy, 'International Law'.
[243] Underlying the conventional approach to the universalization of international law is the tendency to simply treat it as an accomplished historical reality which is of no larger theoretical significance; thus there appears to be in operation a further dichotomy whereby Europe is 'theory' and what occurs in the non-European world is simply secondary.

the decolonization of international law was by no means universally acclaimed; in the 1960s, when it was clear that the emergence of the Third World would radically change the character of the international system, a number of eminent international lawyers voiced concern about the dilution, because of these new states, of an international law which was, in the final analysis, European.[244]

The question which remained was the possibility and effectiveness of reversing the consequences of colonialism. The optimistic international lawyers of the 1960s, even those notable Third World scholars who were the most trenchant critics of the Eurocentric character of international law, were hopeful that the acquisition of sovereignty and the participation of the Third World in international legal forums, would result in the creation of a truly universal, just and equal international system.[245] Guha-Roy, while pointing to the obvious inequities of the doctrines of state responsibility, thus argued that the Third World was intent not on repudiating the whole of international law, but those rules which facilitated colonialism. The civilized–non-civilized distinction which had featured in the doctrines and treaties of the nineteenth century was generally expunged from the vocabulary of international law.[246] Nevertheless, as I shall argue in more detail in chapter 4, the legacies of the nineteenth century presented Third World attempts to reform international law and create a system that reflected the needs of Third World peoples with formidable obstacles.

---

[244] See Anand, *New States*, pp. 6–11; the scholars discussed include J. H. W. Verzijl, Josef Kunz and Julius Stone. The implicit view was that international law should continue to be European despite the repressive effects of such a policy. Equally, a number of Western-based lawyers, such as Richard Falk, were consistently and forcefully sympathetic to the cause of decolonization. See Richard Falk, 'The New States and International Legal Order', (1966-II) 118 *Académie du Droit International, Recueil de Cours* 1–102.

[245] I rely here on the distinction developed by James Gathii between weak and strong forms of anti-colonial scholarship. Gathii elaborates:

> The *weak* form of anti-colonial scholarship is basically integrationist: meaning that it is largely complimentary of the liberatory claims of principles such as self-determination as uncompromising tenets of world peace and indicators of the rejection of the colonial experience and specifically as an expression of the value these principles uphold against the unacceptable repression of non-European humanity under colonialism, slavery and other forms of discrimination and repression of the non-European personality.
>
> (James Thuo Gathii, 'International Law and Eurocentricity', (1998) 9 *European Journal of International Law* 189)

[246] Some vestiges are still evident, as in Article 38(1)(c) of the Statute of the International Court of Justice.

The alternative position, then, is that the nineteenth century is very much an integral part of contemporary international law. At a material level, the systems of economic and political inequality which were created by colonialism under the auspices of nineteenth-century international law continue to operate despite the ostensible change of legal regime.[247] It is doubtful whether a discipline whose fundamental concepts, 'sovereignty' and 'law' had been so explicitly and clearly formulated in ways which embodied within them the distinctions and discriminations which furthered colonialism could be readily reformed by the simple expedient of excising or reformulating the offending terminology.[248] Thus, for example, while the International Court of Justice (ICJ) may theoretically draw upon 'the general principles of law recognised by civilized nations' in a context where 'civilized' must now be understood as all nations, an examination of the recent jurisprudence of the Court suggests that little effort has been made to draw upon the legal traditions and systems of non-Western peoples in the administration of international justice.[249] International law remains emphatically European in this respect, regardless of its supposed receptivity to other legal thinking.

The nineteenth century remains within the system in even more fundamental ways: despite recognizing that the treaties were unequal and often extracted by force, these treaties continue to be given binding legal quality. The doctrine of *terra nullius* is recognised as a fiction, and yet it was this doctrine which was accepted until very recently as the official legal basis for the annexation of Australia by the British Crown. These doctrines are not so much confronted as evaded through

---

[247] See Gathii, 'International Law', 184.

[248] I have tried to argue this point at greater length in the context of an actual international dispute and the manner in which the use of the supposedly empowering language of 'self-determination' and 'permanent sovereignty over natural resources' limit the character of the claims that can be made. See Antony Anghie, 'The Heart of my Home: Colonialism, Environmental Damage, and the Nauru Case', (1993) 34 *Harvard International law Journal* 445. Critical race theory provides a very perceptive and powerful analysis of the continuation of racist and discriminatory practices through the application of a legal vocabulary which has been ostensibly sanitised. See particularly Kimberle Crenshaw, 'Race Reform and Retrenchment: Transformation and Legitimation in Anti-Discrimination Law', (1988) 101 *Harvard Law Review* 1331–1387; Patricia Williams, *The Alchemy of Race and Rights* (Cambridge, MA: Harvard University Press, 1991).

[249] Certain notable exceptions to this are evident. Judge Weeramantry's decisions, in particular, have made far-reaching attempts to incorporate other legal traditions into the jurisprudence of the Court.

reinterpretation of the relevant facts; the argument is made that – for example – more recent anthropological evidence suggests that the Aboriginal peoples of Australia did have a form of 'political organization', as a consequence of which the doctrine could not be said to apply to Australia. While the effects of the application of the doctrine are negated, then, the doctrine itself is rarely dismissed as outmoded or simply racist.[250] Similarly, in the 1975 *Western Sahara* Case, the judges of the ICJ asserted that the Western Sahara could not have been *terra nullius* because the peoples who lived there did in fact have a form of political organization.[251] Thus the doctrines consolidated by nineteenth-century jurists continue to establish the framework within which indigenous peoples struggle to assert their rights. Jurists and courts attempting to reverse the effects of these laws must do so within the established frameworks of these doctrines.

The question, then, is not so much whether the nineteenth century has been transcended, but how its continuing effects within the contemporary legal system may be obscured. Any tendency to treat the nineteenth century as being only of historical interest must be treated cautiously precisely because, as I have attempted to argue, there appears to be an inherent reflex within international law which conceals the colonial past on which its entire structure is based. My overall argument is an attempt to demonstrate this by attempting to recover that past; but, more specifically, the same reflex may be seen, for example, in the way that the construction of 'law' depends on a notion of 'society' which, once it has served its purpose, is re-presented, in a reconstructed jurisprudence in which 'society' has been successfully constituted as a function of law. On a larger scale, as discussed earlier, positivists themselves vehemently set out to detach themselves from their naturalist past. The process of distancing and suppressing the past is a common feature of the discipline, a ritual enacted whenever it attempts to renew and revive itself.

Positivism and the nineteenth century are an integral part of the contemporary discipline. Simplifying considerably, the nineteenth century could be said to embody a particular set of attitudes and methods. It posits an essentialist dichotomy between the non-European and the European; it characterizes relations between these entities to be

---

[250] For discussion see, for example, Anthony Mason, 'The Rights of Indigenous Peoples in Lands Once Part of the Old Dominions of the Crown', (1997) 46 *International and Comparative Law Quarterly* 813.

[251] *Western Sahara*, Advisory Opinion, ICJ Reports 1975, p. 12.

inherently antagonistic; it establishes a hierarchy between these entities, suggesting that one is advanced, just and authoritative while the
other is backward, violent and barbaric; it asserts that the only history
which may be written of the backward is in terms of its progress towards
the advanced; it silences the backward and denies it any subjectivity or
autonomy; it assumes and promotes the centrality of the civilized; and it
contemplates no other approaches to the problems of society than those
which have been formulated by the civilized. Many of these elements
are evident in the work of prominent international relations scholars
from Samuel Huntington's influential argument regarding the 'clash of
civilizations', to Francis Fukuyama's assertions as to the 'end of history'.
There is a real danger, furthermore, that the important work being done
on the distinction between liberal and non-liberal states could embody
and reproduce many of the elements and attitudes of the nineteenth
century.

The nineteenth century may be with us not merely because of conceptual affinities, but because of historical coincidence. Powerful arguments
have been made since the collapse of communism that we have arrived
at the 'end of history' – that a particular set of ideas, basically those
of Western liberalism, provide an authoritative answer to the question
of what political and economic arrangements are best for mankind. It
would appear that the supremacy of Western ideas has been established
more powerfully and emphatically now than at any other time since the
late nineteenth century. And, as in the late nineteenth century, adoption
of the Western systems of democracy and economic liberalization appear
to offer the only feasible alternative to states around the globe, whether
in Asia, Africa or Eastern Europe. Whatever the differences in legal status and international law since then and now, the present resembles
the late nineteenth century in that basic respect.

More generally, the nineteenth century offers us an example of a far
broader theme: the importance of the existence of the 'other' for the
progress and development of the discipline itself. Seen from this perspective, the nineteenth century is both distinctive and conventional. Its
method, its focus and its techniques are in many respects unique. But
in another respect, the nineteenth century is simply one example of the
nexus between international law and the civilizing mission. The same
civilizing mission was implemented by the vocabulary of naturalism in
sixteenth-century international law. Arguably, furthermore, the succeeding paradigm of international law developed in the inter-war period, the
paradigm of pragmatism, was similarly preoccupied with furthering the

civilizing mission even as it condemned nineteenth-century positivism for being formalist and colonial. Thus the only thing unique about the nineteenth century is that it explicitly adopted the civilizing mission and reflected its goals in its very vocabulary. The more alarming and likely possibility is that the civilizing mission is inherent in one form or another in the principal concepts and categories which govern our existence: ideas of modernity, progress, development, emancipation and rights.

I have argued that because sovereignty was shaped by the colonial encounter, its exercise often reproduces the inequalities inherent in that encounter. But the further and broader point is that sovereignty is a flexible instrument which readily lends itself to the powerful imperatives of the civilizing mission, in part because it is through engagement with that mission that sovereignty extends and expands its reach and scope. This is why the essential structure of the civilizing mission may be reconstructed in the very contemporary vocabulary of human rights, governance and economic liberalization. In this larger sense, then, the nineteenth century is both a very distinctive, and yet entirely familiar, part of international law.

3 Colonialism and the birth of international institutions: the Mandate System of the League of Nations

What is wanted here is law, good faith, order, security. Anyone can declaim about these things, but I pin my faith to material interests. Only let the material interests once get a firm footing, and they are bound to impose the conditions on which alone they can continue to exist. That's how your money making here is justified here in the face of lawlessness and disorder. It is justified because the security it demands must be shared with an oppressed people. A better justice will come afterwards.[1]

Introduction

The expansion of European Empires ensured that the entire globe was encompassed by one, European system of international law by the conclusion of the nineteenth century. The great project of dismantling these Empires, of facilitating the transformation of colonial territories into sovereign, independent states, was to become one of the central preoccupations of the United Nations from the 1950s onwards.

The first efforts to begin this radical project of transforming colonial territories into sovereign states commenced, however, immediately after the First World War. It occurred at the same time that another monumental change was taking place in international law, the emergence of international institutions in the form of the League of Nations. Up to the beginning of the twentieth century, sovereign states were the only actors recognized by international law. With the creation of the League, however, the international institution emerged as a new actor in the international system, providing international law with a new range of ambitions and techniques for the management of international relations.

[1] Joseph Conrad, *Nostromo: A Tale of the Seaboard* (New York: Penguin Books, 1990), p. 100 (first published 1904).

115

This chapter seeks to explore the relationship between these two developments: the relationship between the project of transforming colonial territories into independent sovereign states, and the international institution which was supposed to implement this project – the Mandate System of the League of Nations.[2] The Mandate System was an international regime created for the purpose of governing the territories – stretching from the Middle East and Africa to the Pacific – that had been annexed or colonized by Germany and the Ottoman Empire, two of the great powers defeated in the First World War. Rather than distribute these territories among the victorious powers as the spoils of war, the international community resolved to place them under a system of international tutelage. In this sense, the Mandate System represented a dramatically different approach to what broadly might be termed 'colonial problems': the complex problems generated by Western governance of colonized peoples. Whereas the positivist international law of the nineteenth century endorsed the conquest and exploitation of non-European peoples, the Mandate System, by contrast, sought to ensure their protection. Whereas positivism sought to exclude non-European peoples from the family of nations, the Mandate System was created to achieve precisely the reverse: it attempted to do nothing less than to promote self-government and, in certain cases, to integrate previously colonized and dependent peoples into the international system as sovereign, independent nation-states.

At the most immediate level, then, I examine the legal structure of the system, the political context in which it was created, the goals it sought to advance and the manner and effects of its operation. The task confronting the Mandate System was both unprecedented and formidable.

---

[2] The Mandate System has generated an enormous body of literature. See, e.g., Quincy Wright, *Mandates Under the League of Nations* (Chicago: University of Chicago Press, 1930); Norman Bentwich, *The Mandates System* (London: Longmans, Green, 1930); R. N. Chowdhuri, *International Mandates and Trusteeship Systems: A Comparative Study* (The Hague: Martinus Nijhoff, 1955); H. Duncan Hall, *Mandates, Dependencies and Trusteeship* (Washington, DC: Carnegie Endowment for International Peace, 1948); Hersch Lauterpacht, 'The Mandate Under International Law in the Covenant of the League of Nations', in Hersch Lauterpacht, Elihu Lauterpacht (ed.), *International Law* (4 vols., Cambridge: Cambridge University Press, 1970), III, pp. 29–84. For a later assessment of the system, see James C. Hales, 'The Reform and Extension of the Mandate System', (1940) 26 *Transactions of the Grotius Society* 153. For accounts of specific Mandates, see Christopher G. Weeramantry, *Nauru: Environmental Damage Under International Trusteeship* (New York: Oxford University Press, 1992), pp. 41–122; and see generally Isaak I. Dore, *The International Mandate System and Namibia* (Boulder, CO: Westview Press, 1985). I have relied heavily on Wright's masterly work, cited above. Although it is one of the earliest, it is in many ways the most comprehensive, penetrating and prescient.

It involved far more than simply bestowing a juridical status on dependent people; rather, it contemplated nothing less than the creation of the social, political, and economic conditions thought necessary to support a functioning nation-state. This project required international law and institutions to produce a new set of technologies, and my interest lies in examining the character of these technologies and their actual use in, and development through, the mandate territories. At a more general level, my claim is that an examination of the Mandate System reveals issues of enduring theoretical and practical significance about sovereignty, international institutions and the management of relations between European and non-European peoples. My argument is that colonialism profoundly shaped the character of international institutions at their formative stage, and that by examining the history of how this occurred we might illuminate the operations and character of contemporary international institutions.

My exploration of the Mandate System is informed by the same themes and concerns that are outlined in my earlier analysis of Vitoria and the nineteenth century. That is, I attempt to demonstrate how the dynamic of difference was constructed by the jurisprudence of the League period, and the role it played in the operations of the Mandate System. Further, I seek to identify the distinctive character of non-European sovereignty by exploring the manner in which the League conceptualised self-government and sovereignty and then attempted to achieve these ends. I then attempt to point to some of the larger consequences and implications of the Mandate System for Third World peoples and, indeed, for the international institutions that play such a prominent role in the lives of these peoples.

I have argued that international law consistently attempts to obscure its colonial origins, its connections with the inequalities and exploitation inherent in the colonial encounter. This theme is central to an understanding of the Mandate System, which was in many ways established in opposition to the type of colonialism practised in the nineteenth century. The transformation of colonial territories into sovereign states is central to the claim that international law is now truly universal because all societies, whether European or non-European, participate as equal and sovereign states in the international system. International institutions, further, have played a major role in this process. If my argument has any validity, however, if an understanding of the distinctive character of non-European sovereignty can support a claim that all states are not equally sovereign and that this is because of international law and institutions rather than despite international law and institutions, then it may become important to reassess the relationship between international law and Third World sovereignty. All these issues are of importance to Third World states that have to confront the disempowering effects of neocolonialism – the enduring character of what in essence are colonial relations even after Third World states acquired independence.[3] Third World statesmen and international lawyers have long recognized this phenomenon. My endeavour here is to examine the role that international law and institutions have played in furthering neo-colonialism by studying the origins of the whole process of decolonization as it emerged in the Mandate System.

These are the broad themes and concerns I seek to explore in this chapter. In order to help place the distinctive problems of sovereignty as they emerged in the Mandate System within the broader context of interwar discussions about sovereignty, international law and international institutions, I sketch some of the debates relating to sovereignty that took place immediately after the First World War. My interest here lies in the challenge that the new international law of pragmatism posed to the formalist and to the now-discredited theory of positivist international law of the nineteenth century. The pragmatist challenge was based in important ways on the insights and proposals of American jurists, and I attempt to show how the Mandate System embodied many of the insights of pragmatism in its operations. The conceptualization and operation of the Mandate System was inevitably shaped by the politics of the period, and I examine how colonial problems were perceived at the end of the war. The distinctive character of non-European sovereignty is illuminated by an analysis of the problems and puzzles that the Mandate System generated in relation to conventional understandings of sovereignty doctrine, and the specific, if not unique, technologies adopted by the League to address these problems. In this context, I proceed to examine the actual policies formulated by the League to promote self-government and sovereignty in the mandate territories. In particular, I examine the importance given to economic development in the formulation of these policies, and the ways in which the discourse of economics shaped policy choices and resolved various policy

---

[3] The Ghanaian leader Kwame Nkrumah provides a good definition of neo-colonialism: 'The essence of neocolonialism is that the State which is subject to it is, in theory, independent and has all the outward trappings of international sovereignty. In reality its economic system and thus political policy is directed from outside.' Cited in Robert J. C. Young, *Postcolonialism: An Historical Introduction* (Oxford: Blackwell, 2001), p. 46.

problems. I then discuss what I claim are the unique characteristics of sovereignty doctrine as it manifested itself in the non-European world. I focus on the novel techniques of power and discipline that are created by the Mandate System and used to manage relations between European and non-European peoples. In particular, I argue that the contemporary discipline of development originated with the Mandate System in important ways. The concluding part of this chapter attempts to outline the legacy of the Mandate System and the enduring significance of this great experiment in international management at both the practical level and at the theoretical level for contemporary international law and institutions.

The creation of the Mandate System

Introduction

The Mandate System was devised in order to provide internationally supervised protection for the peoples of the Middle East, Africa and the Pacific who previously had been under the control of Germany or the Ottoman Empire. Initially, however, General Smuts of South Africa, who originally proposed the creation of the Mandate System, envisaged its application to European territories that had been left behind by the collapse of the Russian, Ottoman and Austro-Hungarian Empires. These territories were inhabited by peoples who were characterized as 'incapable of or deficient in power of self-government', 'destitute', and requiring 'nursing towards political and economic independence'.[4] The Mandate System was to play the role of the 'reversionary' of the defeated Empires.[5]

President Woodrow Wilson of the United States supported the basic framework of Smuts' plan, but argued for its application not to the European territories – many of which were to become the subject of the minority treaty regimes – but to the Ottoman territories in the Middle East and to the German colonies in Africa and the Pacific. Wilson vehemently argued against annexation of these non-European territories by the victorious powers, as such actions would have been contrary to the principles of freedom and democracy for which the war ostensibly had

[4] The outlines of Smuts' views can be found in his proposal. J. C. Smuts, 'The League of Nations: A Practical Suggestion', reprinted in David Hunter Miller, *The Drafting of the Covenant* (2 vols., New York: G. P. Putnam's Sons, 1971, 1928), II, p. 26.

[5] Smuts stated that 'Europe is being liquidated, and the League of Nations must be heir to this great estate.' *Ibid.*

been fought.[6] Wilson instead proposed the application of the Mandate System to these non-European peoples and territories. The essential purpose of the system was to protect the interests of backward people, to promote their welfare and development and to guide them toward self-government and, in certain cases, independence.[7] This was to be achieved by appointing certain states, officially designated as mandatories, as administrators of these territories on behalf of the League, and subjecting these mandatories to the League's supervision.[8]

The legal structure of the Mandate System

The Mandate System embodied two broad sets of obligations: first, the substantive obligations according to which the mandatory undertook to protect the natives and advance their welfare and, second, the procedural obligations relating to the system of supervision designed to ensure that the mandatory power was properly administering the mandate territory.

The primary and substantive obligation undertaken by the mandatory power is stated in Article 22 of the League Covenant, which enunciates the concept of a 'sacred trust of civilization':

To those colonies and territories which as a consequence of the late war have ceased to be under the sovereignty of the States which formerly governed them and which are inhabited by peoples not yet able to stand by themselves under the strenuous conditions of the modern world, there should be applied the principle that the well-being and development of such peoples form a sacred trust of civilization and that securities for the performance of this trust should be embodied in this Covenant.

The best method of giving practical effect to this principle is that the tutelage of such peoples should be entrusted to advanced nations who, by reason of their resources, their experience or their geographical position, can best undertake

---

[6] Wilson declared at the Peace Conference: 'We are done with the annexations of helpless peoples meant by some Powers to be used merely for exploitation.' Ruth Cranston, *The Story of Woodrow Wilson: Twenty-Eighth President of the United States, Pioneer of World Democracy* (New York: Simon & Schuster, 1945), p. 318.

[7] The question of how law should administer territories for the purpose of developing them was the subject of much scholarly work at that time. See, e.g., M. F. Lindley, *The Acquisition and Government of Backward Territory in International Law* (London: Longmans, Green & Co., 1926); Alpheus H. Snow, *The Question of Aborigines in the Law and Practice of Nations* (New York: Putnam, 1921); Charles G. Fenwick, *Wardship in International Law* (Washington, DC: Government Printing Office, 1919).

[8] The idea that certain territories should be internationally administered was not new. For example, such a system had been proposed at the Congress of Berlin for the administration of the Congo. See Wright, *Mandates*, pp. 18–20.

this responsibility and who are willing to accept it, and that this tutelage should be exercised by them as Mandatories on behalf of the League.[9]

The broad, primary goal of the Mandate System was to prevent the exploitation of the native peoples; its secondary goal was to promote their well being and development.[10] The term 'not yet able to stand by themselves' suggested that the system was a temporary arrangement until such time as the peoples were capable of becoming independent. As a result, Article 22 was described as meaning 'trusteeship with independence as the goal of the trust'.[11] While it was provided explicitly that the Middle Eastern mandates were to become sovereign states, the status of the mandate peoples in Africa and the Pacific was more uncertain. This was largely because the Dominion powers – South Africa, Australia and New Zealand, who were intent on annexing the former German territories and were placated only partially by being appointed mandatories over those territories – were unwilling to accept any provisions suggesting that such territories might become independent.[12] Article 22 was generally interpreted as requiring mandatories to promote 'self-government' – a term capacious enough to suggest progress toward full sovereign statehood, while not explicitly making this the ultimate and inevitable goal. Thus, Hall asserts that '[s]elf-government is the central positive conception set out in Article 22 of the League Covenant'.[13]

Article 22 provided essentially for a three-tiered system of administration, as mandate territories were classified according to their degree of advancement.[14] The non-European territories of the former Turkish Empire were classified as A mandates whose 'existence as independent nations can be provisionally recognized'.[15] German territories in Central Africa were placed within the B regime; South-West Africa and the Pacific

---

[9] League of Nations Covenant, Article 22, paras. 1–2.

[10] For a detailed and illuminating analysis of these provisions, see Lauterpacht, 'The Mandate Under International Law', pp. 40–51.

[11] Hall, *Mandates*, p. 94.   [12] See Chowdhuri, *International Mandates*, pp. 43–44, 53.

[13] Hall, *Mandates*, p. 94.

[14] This scheme was the result of a confrontation between Wilson and several statesmen of the British Dominions – Smuts of South Africa and Hughes of Australia – as to the fate of the German colonies. The Dominions, supported by Britain, which at all times acted with the diplomatic tact born of much experience, demanded annexation of the territories in question. Wilson refused, and a compromise formula was finally adopted whereby the territories in question were divided into three categories: A, B, and C mandates. For an account of the confrontation between Hughes and Wilson, see Weeramantry, *Nauru*, pp. 41–54.

[15] League of Nations Covenant, Article 22, para. 3.

territories under the C regime. Mandatories over the most backward territories, the C mandates, were given especially extensive powers, as such territories were regarded as 'best administered under the laws of the Mandatory as integral portions of its territory', subject to the safeguards provided by the Mandate System on behalf of the inhabitants.[16] Apart from the broad stipulation contained in Article 22 of the Covenant regarding the 'sacred trust of civilization', the mandatory and the Council of the League of Nations entered into separate mandate agreements. These agreements outlined the obligations and powers of the mandatory in greater detail, and sought to strengthen further the protection of the natives. This was provided both by the general formula that the mandatory 'shall undertake to promote to the utmost the material and moral well-being and the social progress of its inhabitants'[17] and by the more detailed provisions that, for example, suppressed the slave trade and compulsory labour (except in special circumstances), controlled the sale of alcohol[18] and restricted the manner in which lands were to be disposed.[19] The mandatory was provided with broad powers for the purpose of performing its functions; few limits applied to the range of issues that the mandatory could examine in order to promote the material and moral well being of the inhabitants of the mandates. For example, the obligations outlined in Article 23 of the Covenant dealt with issues ranging from labour standards and traffic in women and children to trade in arms and ammunition.[20]

A proper mechanism for supervising the actions of the mandatory was essential for the efficient functioning of the system.[21] To achieve effective supervision, mandatories were obliged to submit an annual report to the League Council.[22] These were submitted in practice to the

[16] *Ibid.*, Article 22, para. 6.
[17] See, e.g., Wright, *Mandates*, p. 613 (citing Article 3 of the Mandate for Tanganyika).
[18] *Ibid.* (citing Article 6 of the Mandate for Tanganyika).
[19] *Ibid.* (citing Article 6 of the Mandate for Tanganyika). This Article required in part that laws that were enacted by the mandatory and dealt with lands 'take into consideration native laws and customs'. *Ibid.* It also required public authorities to consent to the creation of rights over land. This could be seen as an attempt to prevent unscrupulous private entities from persuading the natives to enter into agreements giving the entities extensive rights over those lands. This had been a very common practice in the past.
[20] League of Nations Covenant, Article 23.
[21] The excesses of the sort that had taken place in the Belgian Congo in the 1890s and early 1900s when the Congo was administered by the International Association of the Congo under King Leopold II of the Belgians suggest the difficulties connected with making such supervision effective. See Wright, *Mandates*, pp. 18–20.
[22] League of Nations Covenant, Article 22, para. 7.

Permanent Mandates Commission (PMC), the monitoring organ established to 'receive and examine the annual reports of the Mandatories,
and to advise the Council on all matters relating to the observance of
the mandates'.[23] The PMC was composed essentially of experts in colonial administration[24] who examined the annual reports presented by
the mandatory powers and advised the League Council on developments
within the territories.[25]

Finally, the supervisory mechanism was supported further by the stipulation, contained in all mandate agreements, that in the event of a
conflict between the mandatory and any other member of the League
of Nations as to the 'interpretation or application of the provisions of
the mandate', the dispute could be referred to the Permanent Court
of International Justice (PCIJ).[26] In this manner, different organs of the
League – the League Council (essentially a political organ that could be
regarded as the executive branch of the League), the PMC (an organ that
combined the functions of an administrative and expert body) and the
PCIJ (a judicial organ) – all brought their differing perspectives to bear
on the activities of the mandate. As a further supervisory measure, the
PMC instituted the practice of receiving petitions from the inhabitants
of the territories as to the implementation of the mandate. This system,
however, was far from successful.[27]

The League of Nations and the new international law

Sovereignty and the move to institutions:[28] the creation
of the League of Nations

The Mandate System was created in the context of a broader set of developments in international law and relations that occurred immediately
after the First World War.[29] Commencing a project that seems to follow

---

[23] *Ibid.*, Article 22, para. 9. For analyses of the relationship between the Council and
Commission, see Wright, *Mandates*, pp. 128–130, 146–155. These debates included issues
as to the competence of the Commission and the extent of its powers to direct the
administration of the territories.

[24] Wright, *Mandates*, pp. 140–141.   [25] *Ibid.*, p. 127.

[26] See *ibid.*, p. 620 (citing Article 7 of the Mandate for Nauru).

[27] See Hall, *Mandates*, p. 198.

[28] I have borrowed this phrase from David Kennedy's study of the establishment of the
League of Nations. David Kennedy, 'The Move to Institutions', (1987) 8 *Cardozo Law
Review* 841 at 884.

[29] For my overview of this period, I have relied principally on the classic work written by
Oppenheim and edited by Arnold McNair. See generally Lord Arnold McNair (ed.),

each major war,[30] international jurists of the League period set about
the task of creating a new international order based on respect for the
international rule of law.[31] Understandably, the maintenance of peace
was a major preoccupation of the time, sustained efforts were made to
further disarmament and to create regimes that would outlaw aggression. The great yet unfulfilled ambition to establish a system that would
foster the judicial resolution of disputes commenced with the creation
of the PCIJ.[32] Further, lawyers called for the codification of international
law and emphasized the importance of holding large international conferences at regular intervals to address the major international problems
of the time.[33]

International Law (4th ed, 2 vols., London: Longmans, Green & Co., 1928), I. Lord McNair
    became a Judge cf the ICJ.
[30] See Kennedy, 'The Move to Institutions', 846. I am indebted also to David Kennedy,
    'Some Reflections on the Role of Sovereignty in the New International Order',
    Presentation to the Canadian Society of International Law (October 17, 1992) (on file
    with the author).
[31] For important studies of this period, see generally Nathaniel Berman, 'A Perilous
    Ambivalence: Nationalist Desire, Legal Autonomy and the Limits of the Interwar
    Framework', (1992) 33 *Harvard International Law Journal* 353; Nathaniel Berman, '"But
    the Alternative is Despair": European Nationalism and the Modernist Renewal of
    International Law', (1993) 106 *Harvard Law Review* 1792; Nathaniel Berman, 'The
    Nationality Decrees Case, or, Of Intimacy and Consent', (2000) 13 *Leiden Journal of
    International Law* 265; Carl Landauer, 'J. L. Brierly and the Modernization of
    International Law', (1993) 25 *Vanderbilt Journal of Transnational Law* 881; David
    Bederman, 'The Souls of International Organizations: Legal Personality and the
    Lighthouse at Cape Spartel', (1996) 36 *Virginia Journal of International Law* 275, Martti
    Koskenniemi, *The Gentle Civilizer of Nations: The Rise and Fall of International Law 1870–1960*
    (Cambridge: Cambridge University Press, 2002).
[32] While many of these initiatives took on a particular importance immediately after the
    First World War, it should be noted that many of these projects, such as the judicial
    resolution of disputes, had an earlier history. In particular, the Hague Peace
    Conferences of 1899 and 1907 dealt with many of these questions. See Francis
    Anthony Boyle, *Foundations of World Order: The Legalist Approach to International Relations,
    1898–1921* (Durham, NC: Duke University Press, 1999), pp. 144–145. Boyle's important
    work focuses in particular on the contributions made by American jurists to
    international law in the period he studies.
[33] For accounts of some of the major issues of the period, see generally Manley O.
    Hudson, 'The Outlook for the Development of International Law', (1925) 11 *ABA Journal*
    102; Edwin D. Dickinson, 'The New Law of Nations', (1925–26) 32 *West Virginia Law
    Quarterly* 4; J. L. Brierly, 'The Shortcomings of International Law', (1924) 5 *British
    Yearbook of International Law* 4. For a more historical account, see McNair, *International
    Law*, I, §50. For an introduction to the Vienna School and the immensely important
    work of Hans Kelsen, see Josef L. Kunz, 'On the Theoretical Basis of the Law of
    Nations', (1924) 10 *Transactions of the Grotius Society* 115. For a later assessment of the
    period, see generally Wolfgang Friedmann, 'The Disintegration of European
    Civilization and the Future of International Law', (1938) 2 *Modern Law Review* 194; Hans

As McNair asserted, 'the outstanding feature of the period is the creation of the League of Nations, which is a serious attempt to organise the
international life of the family of nations'.[34] It was through this novel
apparatus, the international institution, that the international community as a whole attempted to address the classic problem of war and
peace and the more novel questions of economic and social welfare. The
existence of the League in itself challenged traditional positivist ideas
in at least two different respects. First, it challenged the positivist idea
that international law is the law governing states and that states are the
only actors in international law.[35] Second, and more importantly, the
existence of the League suggested new ways of approaching the problem of sovereignty, and led inter-war lawyers to question conceptions of
sovereignty that had been fundamental to the positivist international
law of the nineteenth century.[36] As previously discussed, according to
the positivists there was no authority superior to the sovereign state,
which was bound only by rules to which it had consented – if that – and
which enjoyed the unfettered and ultimate prerogative of waging war.[37]
For inter-war jurists, it was precisely this positivist international law,
however, with its exaltation of state sovereignty and its insistence on separating law from morality and society, that appeared to have endorsed, if
not facilitated, the tragedy of the First World War. Although the defective
amorality of positivism was apparent, it hardly was possible to return to
naturalism as a basis for international law, since positivists had inflicted

J. Morgenthau, 'Positivism, Functionalism and International Law', (1940) 34 *American
Journal of International Law* 260.
[34] McNair, *International Law*, I, §50c, p. 99.
[35] This problem is addressed in P. E. Corbett, 'What is the League of Nations?', (1924) 5
British Yearbook of International Law 119 at 119–123; McNair, *International Law*, I, §167c,
p. 321.
[36] For an interesting inter-war account of nineteenth-century concepts of sovereignty, see
McNair, *International Law*, I, §69. These concepts were more developed in the field of
what might be termed 'political theory' rather than international law. *Ibid.*
Oppenheim's remarks on sovereignty have an enduring significance:
> [I]t will be seen that there exists perhaps no conception, the meaning of which
> is more controversial than that of sovereignty. It is an indisputable fact that
> this conception from the moment when it was introduced into political
> science until the present day, has never had a meaning which was universally
> agreed upon.   (*Ibid.*, §66)
[37] These basic premises persisted despite the attempts made at the great Peace
Conferences held at the Hague in 1899 and 1907 to address the problems of war. On
the question of the sovereign prerogative to go to war, see generally Anthony Carty,
*The Decay of International Law?: A Reappraisal of the Limits of Legal Imagination in
International Affairs* (Manchester: Manchester University Press, 1986).

irreparable damage to that jurisprudence.[38] The inter-war jurists thus confronted the problem of devising a system that somehow effectively limited sovereignty even while recognizing that the sovereign state was the major, if not the only, actor in international law. Of course, this is the classic problem of international law restated: how is a plausible legal order to be created among sovereign states? This classic theme, however, was given a new significance by the emergence of a number of new institutions, virtually all of them derived from the League, which promised in some way to replicate, even if very tenuously, the institutions found in domestic systems: a legislature, judiciary and executive. International lawyers thus hoped, for example, that all disputes between states would be subjected to judicial resolution by the PCIJ.

The League itself lacked the power to bind its member states. Nevertheless, the League was a means of organizing states into a community, and it could therefore claim to represent, if not embody, the opinion and interests of the international community. Consequently, the sovereign actions of a state that deviated from norms prescribed by the League were considered not simply in terms of their impact on another state, which might be most affected, but rather in terms of their impact on principles that were thought fundamental to the maintenance of the larger international community.[39] The system of collective security that

---

[38] As McNair puts it, 'We know nowadays that a Law of Nature does not exist.' McNair, *International Law*, I, §59, p. 121. But it should be noted that many eminent international lawyers, such as Hersch Lauterpacht, attempted to formulate a more sophisticated naturalist international law. See, e.g., Hersch Lauterpacht's claim that positivism had been replaced by a more moderate natural law. *Ibid.*, §59, n. 2. For an illuminating account of Lauterpacht's own attempts to formulate such an approach, see Koskenniemi, *The Gentle Civilizer of Nations*. Several international lawyers who were sensitive to the history of their discipline, including Lauterpacht, turned to Grotius as a source of inspiration – for it was Grotius who, in the midst of a catastrophic war, established a plausible intellectual foundation for a peaceful world. In addition, Roscoe Pound's lecture delivered at Leiden also makes Grotius and his achievements a central figure in Pound's analysis of the problems confronting the international community in the aftermath of the war. Pound concludes his lecture by referring to Grotius and asserting: 'Our chief need is a man with that combination of mastery of the existing legal materials, philosophical vision and juristic faith which enabled the founder of international law to set it up almost at one stroke.' Roscoe Pound, 'Philosophical Theory and International Law', (1923) 1 *Biblioteca Visseriana Dissertationum Ius Internationale Illustrantium* at 73, 90. It is possible that Pound, the Carter Professor of Jurisprudence at Harvard at the time, saw himself – and his jurisprudence, which was developed principally in a domestic setting – in this larger role.

[39] Thus Dickinson's hope that '[t]he new law of nations . . . will place less emphasis relatively on the right of each separate nation to ignore its neighbor, exalt its own particular interest, or set the world aflame in seeking redress in its grievances. It will

the League attempted to establish the simple and yet profound notion that aggression against a particular state is aggression against all member states of the League – was the most significant expression of this idea. Article 10 of the League Covenant established the system of collective security.[40] Thus, even though the League could not bind sovereignty, it could coordinate sovereign states in its attempts to curb aggression.

International well being, it was hoped, would enter into the calculus of state action in this way,[41] as the regime perhaps aspired to affect the psychology of sovereignty.[42] This approach was combined with a focus on cooperation. Apart from the difficult and enduring problems of war and aggression, the less ambitious but nonetheless important function of the League was to foster cooperation among states.[43] The need for such cooperation seemed inevitable because states, 'whether they like it or not, are becoming every day more interdependent and more internationalised'.[44] International law could be created, not through the coercion of states, but rather by persuading them of the advantages of pursuing common goals through cooperation, particularly in the economic field. As McNair argued, more particularly and presciently, 'the more important international economic interests grow, the more International Law will grow'.[45]

From formalism to pragmatism

Positivism was attacked not merely because of its inadequate views of sovereignty, but also because of its formalism. This critique of positivism raised the familiar and yet novel debate of the relationship between law

---

lay increasing stress as time goes on upon the social interests of the great society.' Dickinson, 'The New Law of Nations', 32.

[40] For a discussion of Article 10, which Wilson characterized as the 'keystone of the Covenant', see McNair, *International Law*, I, §167m.

[41] This is perhaps to give a constructivist reading of these initiatives of the League. On constructivism, see Alexander Wendt, *Social Theory of International Politics* (Cambridge: Cambridge University Press, 1999).

[42] The notion that states possessed a consciousness and that this consciousness continuously changed and could find expression through the League of Nations was articulated by various international lawyers at the time. For the powerful argument that the success of the League depended on an 'international consciousness' that had not yet come into existence, see Alfred Zimmern, 'International Law and Social Consciousness', (1935) 20 *Transactions of the Grotius Society* 25.

[43] As McNair again puts it, 'While the family of nations was unorganised it did not, and could not, exercise any function, nor devote itself to the fulfilment of any tasks'. McNair, *International Law*, I, §167i.

[44] *Ibid.*, §150, p. 99.   [45] *Ibid.*, §51, p. 103.

and politics.[46] Positivism was viewed as a formalist system because it was based broadly on the view that international jurists, in their identification and application of rules, should focus on the strictly legal realm, as law existed independent of ethics or sociology.[47] It was by asserting the autonomy of law that positivists sought to give the discipline its scientific character. This resulted in formalism, since the positivist preoccupation with rules led to the conclusion that the life of the law was logic rather than experience.

To many inter-war jurists, the positivist preoccupation with legal materials to the exclusion of all other materials dealing with the political life of nations was intellectually flawed and morally dangerous because it posited a law that was devoid of social purpose and separated from the realities of social life. It was a common theme among eminent jurists on both sides of the Atlantic that the deficiencies and dangers of this approach had been revealed by the war.[48]

The new international law, by contrast, had thus to devote itself to furthering social goals. This did not mean, however, an international law that returned to the ethical system prescribed by naturalism, but rather an international law based on the social sciences – political science, sociology and international relations. Only by furthering social goals and developing a law that, far from being autonomous, was informed and shaped by social developments and that reflected the realities revealed by sociology and political science, was international law able to operate effectively and ethically.

In these different ways, what was required was a sociological jurisprudence.[49] American scholars were forceful in making these claims and

---

[46] Perhaps it would be more accurate to speak of 'debates', since the law–politics distinction emerged in a number of different settings.

[47] For a biting summary and critique of positivism, see Morgenthau, 'Positivism', 261–262. At this stage, Morgenthau still attributed an importance to international law, arguing that it should be more closely linked to politics. For a detailed critique of Morgenthau's work, see B. S. Chimni, *International Law and World Order: A Critique of Contemporary Approaches* (New Delhi, Newbury Park, CA: Sage, 1993), pp. 22–72.

[48] See, e.g., Manley O. Hudson, 'The Prospect for International Law in the Twentieth Century', (1925) 10 *Cornell Law Quarterly* 419 at 428–436 (discussing international law's failure to consider questions of social purpose).

[49] I have relied on Samuel Astorino's important discussion of the relationship between American sociological jurisprudence and international law in this period. See Samuel J. Astorino, 'The Impact of Sociological Jurisprudence on International Law in the Inter-War Period: The American Experience', (1996) 34 *Duquesne Law Review* 277. For a collection of works that embodies this tradition, see William W. Fisher, III, Morton J. Horwitz and Thomas Reed (eds.), *American Legal Realism* (New York: Oxford University

in developing this alternative jurisprudence, which might be termed 'pragmatism'.[50] The foremost American thinker on this subject in the domestic sphere was Roscoe Pound, who argued that the same approach was required in the international realm.[51] Indeed, according to Pound, Grotius himself understood the need to synthesise law with politics, and his achievement lay in doing this effectively, for Grotius' jurisprudence 'grew out of and grew up with the political facts of the time and its fundamental conception was an accurate reflection of an existing political system which was developing as the law was doing and at the same time'.[52] For Pound, the 'basis of a new philosophical theory of international law' could be achieved only by 'thinking of a great task of social engineering'.[53] This required a 'legal philosophy that shall take account of the social psychology, the economics, the sociology as well as the law and politics of today',[54] for only such a philosophy could give a 'functional critique of international law in terms of social ends'.[55] The theory of international law was to focus, then, not on whether it conformed to a formalist idea of 'science', but whether it was embedded within society and furthered social objectives.

These ideas were elaborated in the international sphere by a number of jurists, including Manley Hudson, Pound's colleague at Harvard, who argued that 'the future law of nations must seek contributions from

Press, 1993). For an account of the French jurists addressing the relationship between international law and sociology, see Koskenniemi, *The Gentle Civilizer of Nations*, pp. 266–353.

[50] For David Kennedy's account of this tradition and its significance for the international law tradition in the United States, see generally David Kennedy, 'The Disciplines of International Law and Policy', (1999) 12 *Leiden Journal of International Law* 9. Kennedy describes this tradition as involving a number of ideas that

> would include rule skepticism – a well-developed and ubiquitous practice of criticizing rules in the name of anti-formalism – and a blurring of the boundary between law and what United States lawyers call 'policy', a mix of expert arguments about how disputes should be resolved and institutions developed that opens legal analysis in the United States to all sorts of interdisciplinary input and social considerations which might elsewhere seem more like 'politics.'   (*Ibid.*, p. 26)

[51] As Astorino notes: 'Roscoe Pound wrote sparingly about international law; Cardozo did not write on this subject. Yet their philosophies of law, so closely intertwined otherwise, helped to provoke a profound debate about the nature of international law, the role of law in international relations and how Americans should respond to the twenty year crisis bracketed by the two World Wars.' Astorino, 'The Impact of Sociological Jurisprudence', 279 (citations omitted).

[52] Pound, 'Philosophical Theory', 76.   [53] *Ibid.* at 89.   [54] *Ibid.*

[55] *Ibid.* Morgenthau's famous 1940 article might be seen as such an attempt – as its title suggests. See Morgenthau, 'Positivism'.

history, from political science, from economics, from sociology, and from social psychology if it would keep pace with the society it serves'.[56] In relation to the specific subject of sovereignty, Robert Lansing's earlier writings were based on the same foundations, in that he argued that real sovereignty was based on the exercise of power. Thus, '[a]n equality among sovereigns to be *real* must be an equality of might, otherwise it is artificial, an intellectual creation'.[57] Lansing's concern to analyse law and sovereignty in terms of underlying sociological and political factors is to Kunz the hallmark of American pragmatism: '[Lansing] gives us considerations on sovereignty, not as a theoretical jurisprudent, but rather as a sociologist.'[58]

The same themes were sounded by a number of other scholars, including Alejandro Alvarez, the brilliant Chilean jurist who later became an outstanding judge of the International Court of Justice (ICJ), who asserted. 'Up to the present day, International Law has been considered an exclusively juridical science.'[59] Alvarez, framing his argument as belonging to the school of 'American International Law',[60] found that it was necessary to change this perspective and to adapt 'principles and rules and standards more directly to the service of the live, current needs of our present-day society'.[61] The strict application of rigid rules[62] was not conducive to this new jurisprudence of furthering social ends. Rather, it was by combining the legal and the political that important

---

[56] Hudson, 'The Prospect', 434–435. As Astorino notes, Hudson's critique of positivist jurisprudence followed very closely Pound's own critique of Langdell's legal science. Astorino, 'The Impact of Sociological Jurisprudence', 286. Hudson, of course, had a brilliant career in international law, was one of the major international jurists of his time, and served as a member of the PCIJ.

[57] Robert Lansing, *Notes on Sovereignty: From the Standpoint of the State and of the World* (Washington, DC: The Carnegie Endowment, 1921), p. 65 (emphasis in original).

[58] Kunz, 'On the Theoretical Basis', 138.

[59] Alejandro Alvarez, 'The New International Law', (1930) 15 *Transactions of the Grotius Society* 35.

[60] Alvarez announces the school as having emerged at the end of the nineteenth century: 'It consists of doctrines relating to both American and to universal interests that are professed by all nations of the New World, and that differ from those of the two preceding schools [Anglo-Saxon and Continental]. It is American International Law.' *Ibid.* at 44. Alvarez had written a lengthy article on this subject several years earlier. See Alejandro Alvarez, 'Latin America and International Law', (1909) 3 *American Journal of International Law* 269.

[61] Hudson, 'The Prospect', 435.

[62] Thus, Alvarez noted that 'juridical rules are exact, definite and rigid'. Alvarez, 'The New International Law', 47.

international problems could be resolved. For Alvarez, the disciplines of law and politics, instead of being in tension, strengthened and refined one another.[63] The fusion of law with politics, the 'harmony between politics and legal rules',[64] would assist in establishing a system that could address concrete problems. Alvarez further argued that such a fusion would result in 'the elimination from politics of all arbitrary notions'.[65] But this also required a law that did not consist simply of rigid rules, but rather of 'principles of morality and equity [that] are more pliable and elastic than legal rules and consequently, more adaptable to the solution of political problems'.[66]

The uniqueness of the Mandate System

In all these different ways, the conclusion of the First World War and the creation of the League questioned the formalist system of positivist international law that was based on an absolute sovereign. Nevertheless,

[63] *Ibid.*   [64] *Ibid.*

[65] *Ibid.*, 46. Scholars in the Anglo-Saxon tradition, such as Brierly, McNair and Lauterpacht, while recognizing the important links between law and politics, were more cautious in welcoming such a fusion, in part because this could result in the erosion of the idea of law itself. Thus, for example, Lauterpacht was emphatic in asserting that law prevailed, that law governed all disputes – whether they were characterized as political or legal in nature. See Hersch Lauterpacht, *The Function of Law in the International Community* (Oxford: Clarendon Press, 1933), pp. 434–447.

[66] Alvarez, 'The New International Law', 47. According to Alvarez, this division between law and politics was furthered in the academic sphere, where law *stricto sensu* was studied in law schools and international politics was studied in departments of political science. For Alvarez, it was only by combining the study of law and politics that it was possible to create an effective international law, a practical international law. Thus, Alvarez calls for the creation of 'the science of international relations', as this would enable the study of international law itself, 'not only in the realm of theory but especially to assure its practical realisation'. *Ibid.* at 38. Given the subsequently fraught character of the relationship between international law and international relations, it is interesting that, at this stage, Alvarez should see the complementarities between the fields – and, indeed, call for the creation of the field of international relations. American political scientists were equally keen to contribute their insights to the international realm and to examine international law for these purposes. See generally Pitman B. Potter, 'Political Science in the International Field', (1923) 17 *American Political Science Review* 381. Potter gives a fascinating account of the emergence of the subject of 'International Politics' in American universities. For a recent revival of the project of combining international law and relations, see generally Anne-Marie Slaughter Burley, 'International Law and International Relations Theory: A Dual Agenda', (1993) 87 *American Journal of International Law* 205. For a critique of this approach, see Martti Koskenniemi, 'Carl Schmitt, Hans Morgenthau and the Image of Law in International Relations', in Michael Byers (ed.), *The Role of Law in International Politics* (Oxford: Oxford University Press, 2000), p. 17.

in the final analysis, basic positivist principles were maintained;[67] states remained the major actors of international law despite the existence of the League of Nations. Furthermore, even as the inter-war jurists problematised sovereignty in seeking to dislodge its foundational significance for international law, these efforts also provoked increasingly sophisticated responses on the part of positivists who, with more or less credibility, attempted to account for the developments of the inter-war period by producing more thoughtful and nuanced versions of sovereignty doctrine and positivism. Thus, for more traditional and positivist scholars such as Corbett, the concept of sovereignty continued to possess a vital analytic value: all the major developments of the period, including the establishment of the League itself, could be seen as creations of sovereignty, as increasingly sophisticated exercises of the powers of sovereignty, and, in effect, as an elaboration of positivism rather than as a departure from it.[68]

Further, while the League represented a better and more efficient way by which states could express their consent and arrive at agreement, it did not obviate in any way the need for such consent.[69] State sovereignty was preserved. Indeed, somewhat ironically, it was upheld and celebrated by institutions that had been created in the hope that they somehow would curtail sovereignty. Thus, the PCIJ famously proclaimed: 'Restrictions upon the independence of States cannot therefore be presumed.'[70] Further, even in those circumstances where states had appeared to bind themselves, this, too, was characterized as an exercise of sovereignty.[71]

---

[67] Thus, Morgenthau, writing in 1940 at the end of the great experiments of the inter-war period, argued that none of the alternatives developed in the period had affected 'the predominance of positivist thought over the science of international law'. Morgenthau, 'Positivism', 264.

[68] Thus, Corbett argued that the League, far from being *sui generis* as McNair maintained, was explicable in positivist terms as a creation of states. See Percy Corbett, *The Growth of World Law* (Princeton: Princeton University Press, 1971), pp. 37–38 (discussing the importance of and emphasis on sovereignty of states in the creation of the League of Nations).

[69] McNair, *International Law*, I, §167t.

[70] *S. S. Lotus (France v. Turkey)*, 1927 PCIJ Ser. A, No. 10, at 18.

[71] In the first contentious case heard by the PCIJ, it stated: 'The Court declines to see in the conclusion of any treaty by which a State undertakes to perform or refrain from performing a particular act an abandonment of its sovereignty. No doubt any convention creating an obligation of this kind places a restriction on the exercise of the sovereign rights of the State, in the sense that it requires them to be exercised in a certain way. But the right of entering into international engagements is an attribute

In the Mandate System, however, the problem of sovereignty took a very different character. In the final analysis, the League was subordinate to the will of sovereign states. In the mandates, this relationship was radically altered. Here, international institutions, rather than being the product of sovereign states, were given the task of creating sovereignty out of the backward peoples and territories brought under the mandate regime.[72] The emergence of international human rights law during the UN period is axiomatically characterized in virtually all the literature on the subject as a revolutionary and unprecedented moment in the history of international law because it undermined the fundamental principle of territorial sovereignty, which had been in existence since the emergence of the modern European nation-state and the writings of Vattel.[73] It was only because of the emergence of the UN system of international human rights law that international law and institutions can regulate relations between a sovereign and its citizens. It is in this context that the truly extraordinary character of the Mandate System project, when put at its highest, becomes more apparent. It did not seek merely to qualify the rights of the sovereign,[74] but rather to create the sovereign.

Perhaps another way of understanding the unique character of the mandate project is to revert to the metaphor of 'consciousness' that is used repeatedly by the international lawyers of the period. Freud's work had a powerful impact on the inter-war lawyers.[75] It is thus unsurprising

of State sovereignty.' *S. S. Wimbledon (U.K., France, Italy, Japan v. Germany)*, 1923 PCIJ Ser. A, No. 1, at 25.

[72] It must be noted that the League exercised, in effect, a form of sovereignty over certain territories that it administered, such as the Saar for example. But it was not given the task of creating sovereignty, of transforming backwardness into modernity. See Corbett, 'What is the League of Nations?', 126–136.

[73] Jianming Shen, 'National Sovereignty and Human Rights in a Positive Law Context', (2000) 26 *Brooklyn Journal of International Law* 417 at 420–422.

[74] The Mandate System was not the only great experiment in nation building conducted by the League. At the same time, the League was seeking to manage the problem of nationalism in European states through the creation of minority treaty regimes. The great experiment of the minority treaty system – one of the important precursors of international human rights law – was animated by the idea of qualifying sovereign rights. For a superb account of this experiment, see generally Berman, 'Alternative', 1821–1873 (analysing the difficulties surrounding the nationalities problem and comparing the minority treaties with other alternatives by examining how they were applied to different nations in Europe). See also Berman, 'Ambivalence', 369–377 (comparing two decisions by the PCIJ that '[go] to the heart of the Versailles system for resolution of the nationalities question').

[75] For an important study along these lines, see generally Anthony Carty, 'Law and the Postmodern Mind: Interwar German Theories of International Law: The

that Brierly, for example, discusses the importance of the 'social consciousness' of states for international law.[76] And Butler, explicitly drawing the term from the emerging field of psychology,[77] uses the metaphor to describe the way in which a state's consciousness may evolve continuously: 'Interests within the subconscious sphere will demand admittance into the conscious sphere in ways that finally will find expression in international affairs, thus justifying international organization.'[78] Given Butler's own aim to erode the division between internal and external sovereignty, it may not be extending his metaphor too far to suggest that we could view the interior life of the state, its government, its social, economic and political organizations, as the subconscious.

Inter-war jurists were acutely aware that internal sovereignty and external sovereignty were intimately connected, and that the specific form of government within a state had a decisive impact on its international behaviour and hence was an important issue for international law. As Benedict Kingsbury points out, inter-war jurists were keenly aware of 'the importance in international relations of the links between sovereignty and domestic structures'.[79] Thus, one of the morals McNair deduces from the history of the development of the Law of Nations is that 'the progress of International Law is intimately connected with the victory everywhere of constitutional government over autocratic government, or what is the same thing, of democracy over autocracy'.[80]

Psychoanalytical and Phenomenological Perspectives of Hans Kelsen and Carl Schmitt', (1995) 16 *Cardozo Law Review* 1235.

[76] See J. L. Brierly, *The Law of Nations: An Introduction to the International Law of Peace* (2nd edn., Oxford: Clarendon Press, 1936), p. 35 (discussing the belief that elements of social consciousness are present in international life).

[77] Butler noted:

> We have heard much in recent times from the psychologists as to the existence of a subconscious sphere, whence flow into the consciousness of the individual motives and promptings, which, in certain circumstances dominate his action. In the light of this image and for the purpose of illustration only, we may visualise the nation state.
>
> (Sir Geoffrey Butler, 'Sovereignty and the League of Nations', (1920) 1 *British Yearbook of International Law* 35 at 42)

Freud's *The Interpretation of Dreams* had been published in German in 1900 and in an English translation by A. A. Brill in 1913. See Sigmund Freud, James Strachey (ed. and trans.), *The Interpretation of Dreams* (New York: Avon, 1965).

[78] Butler, 'Sovereignty', 44.

[79] Benedict Kingsbury, 'Sovereignty and Inequality', (1998) 9 *European Journal of International Law* 599 at 608 (referring to judicial decisions and arbitral awards). For an account of the different ways in which the boundaries between internal and external sovereignty were being challenged in the inter-war period, see *ibid.* at 608–609.

[80] McNair, *International Law*, I, §51.

McNair's view – which may be traced back to Kant's idea of the 'demo-cratic peace' – suggests that international jurists gradually were accept-ing the insights of political scientists and theorists. Nevertheless, the interior of the state remained outside the control or even scrutiny of international law, which could address state behaviour only when it emerged into the conscious sphere, as it were, when it manifested itself in the external actions of the state and thereby became a properly inter-national issue.[81] The frustration for inter-war jurists was that, while they could vaguely conceptualise the interior in various ways, they were unable to act upon it.[82]

The discovery of interiority is central to the phenomenon of moder-nity as a whole.[83] The great literature of modernity – the works of Joseph Conrad, T. S. Eliot, Henry James, James Joyce and Virginia Woolf – are preoccupied with mapping the interior, with tracing and examining the workings of an inner consciousness.[84] International jurists sensed that access to the interior of the state would revolutionise their disci-pline in much the same way that Joyce had revolutionised the novel and Freud had revolutionised our understanding of human nature. And yet, this inquiry was precluded by sovereignty doctrine. We might under-stand the monumental significance of international human rights law in these terms: it enabled international law and institutions to enter the interior, to address the unconscious, and thereby to administer 'civiliz-ing therapy' to the body politic of the sovereign state.

Whereas previously the internal character of the sovereign European state was immune from scrutiny, in the inter-war period it was precisely through the Mandate System that international law and institutions had complete access to the interior of a society. It was in the operations of the Mandate System, then, that it became possible for international law not merely to enter the interior realm, but also to create the social and political infrastructure necessary to support a functioning sovereign

---

[81] See text accompanying nn. 75–80.

[82] Freud's work, of course, had a far more direct relevance to international law and the whole question of war and aggression, as it sought to identify the origins of aggression and the death drive. See Sigmund Freud, James Strachey (ed. and trans.), *Civilization and Its Discontents* (New York: W. W. Norton, 1961).

[83] See generally H. Stuart Hughes, *Consciousness and Society* (New York: Knopf, 1958).

[84] See generally, e.g., Henry James, *The Portrait of a Lady* (Boston: Houghton, Mifflin & Co., 1881); Joseph Conrad, *Heart of Darkness* (Edinburgh: W. Blackwood & Sons, 1902); James Joyce, *Ulysses* (Paris: Shakespeare & Co., 1922); Virginia Woolf, *Mrs. Dalloway* (New York: Harcourt, Brace & Co., 1925); T. S. Eliot, *The Waste Land* (New York: Boni & Liveright, 1922).

state.[85] Here, then, sovereignty was to be studied not in the context of the problem of war and of collective security, but in a very different constellation of relationships that are central to the understanding of sovereignty in the non-European world.

Within the Mandate System, sovereignty is shaped by, and connected with, issues of economic relations between the colonizer and the colonized on the one hand, and comprehensively developed notions of the cultural difference between advanced Western states and backward mandate peoples, on the other. It was in the Mandate System that international law and institutions could conduct experiments and develop technologies that were hardly possible in the sovereign Western world. It was in the Mandate System, furthermore, that many of the interests of jurists such as Pound, Alvarez and Hudson could find expression. This was because the task confronting the Mandate System involved far more than the granting of a simple juridical status. Rather, international law and institutions were required to create the economic, political and social conditions under which a sovereign state could come into being. In this sense, law had to be combined with sociology, political science and economics in order to achieve the goals of the Mandate System. It was through international institutions that such a task of synthesis could be addressed. Precisely because of this, the aspirations of pragmatic jurists to make law more socially oriented could be given effect; international institutions made pragmatic jurisprudence a possibility in the field of international relations. It is, then, by studying how this occurred that we may gain an understanding of both the unique character of non-European sovereignty and, conversely, of the identities that international institutions developed in the course of bringing such sovereignty into being.

The Mandate System and colonial problems

Introduction

Although the Mandate System, in strictly legal terms, applied only to the territories formerly annexed to Germany and the Ottoman Empire, inter-war lawyers and scholars understood that it had a far broader

---

[85] Another relationship is suggested in seeing the mandate society as the unconscious. Most often, the encounter with the unconscious is characterized as a journey into the past, an encounter with the primitive: in this case, the backward mandate people. This is one interpretation of Marlow's journey upriver in *Heart of Darkness*. See Conrad, *Heart of Darkness*.

significance. It represented the international community's aspiration, through the League, to address colonial problems in general in a systematic, coordinated and ethical manner. At the highest level, it embodied 'the ideal policy of European civilization towards the cultures of Asia, Africa, and the Pacific'.[86]

The last major conference to be held on colonial problems was the Berlin Conference of 1884–5.[87] The character of the relationship between the European and non-European world had changed profoundly since that time as a consequence of numerous developments, including the First World War, the emergence of anticolonial movements and the condemnation of colonialism within the West itself. It was in these complex circumstances that the mandate had to legitimize its existence and demonstrate that the creation of international institutions would result in a better way of addressing colonial problems. More broadly, the Mandate System generated a debate among international lawyers on the role of their discipline in legitimizing colonial conquest. The creation and operation of the Mandate System, then, can be understood best in terms of these debates regarding colonialism and its significance for international law and relations.

Legitimizing the Mandate System: colonial problems in the inter-war period

By the end of the First World War, if not earlier, it was clear that many non-Western states would become sovereign states.[88] This point was most dramatically demonstrated by Japan's acceptance into the family of nations, which was followed in 1905 by the Japanese defeat of Russia, which marked not only Japan's military ascendancy but also its assumption of the role of a colonial power, as the war was fought essentially

---

[86] Wright, Mandates, p. vii.

[87] Although the largest conferences were held in 1885, Western powers held numerous other conferences relating to colonial problems between 1885 and 1912. Africa had the doubtful distinction of being the object of concern of many of these conferences. G. L. Beer, the American expert on Africa, stated that 'no other region had called forth more international cooperation or had been subjected to more comprehensive international control'. See Hall, Mandates, p. 103 (quoting G. L. Beer, African Questions at the Paris Peace Conference; With Papers on Egypt, Mesopotamia, and the Colonial Settlement, New York: The Macmillan Co., 1923, p. 193). Beer was among several American experts on colonial affairs; others included Colonel House, who accompanied Wilson to the peace talks.

[88] For an account of the non-European states that had been accepted, even if only partially, into the family of nations, see Kingsbury, 'Sovereignty', 607–608.

over Korea.[89] Japan participated in the Peace Conference as one of the major powers,[90] for with the conclusion of the First World War it was not only the United States but also Japan that emerged with greater strength.[91] Equally important, Siam and China[92] were signatories at the Treaty of Peace although, significantly, Islamic countries were initially excluded from the League.[93] Egypt won independence from the British in 1922.[94] All these events illustrated that non-European societies could become sovereign states despite the view powerfully promulgated prior to the war that Europeans alone had the capacity to govern.

The war, of course, had a profound effect on the issue of colonial relations at a number of different levels. It had not merely devastated Europe, but also severely weakened its claims to moral superiority – and, indeed, to be civilized.[95] In addition, the Allies had sought to justify themselves by arguing that the war was one of principle, fought for the preservation of freedom. Many colonies had sent soldiers to the war. At least 1.4 million Indians had been mobilised to serve in France, the Middle East and Africa;[96] in return, the Indian Secretary of State had promised to allow the gradual development of self-governing institutions for India within the overall framework of the Empire.[97]

Most significantly, nationalist movements were asserting themselves in colonial societies throughout the globe. Imperial powers, intent on

[89] See Carl F. Petry and M. W. Daly (eds.), *The Cambridge History of Egypt* (Cambridge: Cambridge University Press, 1998), p. 250.

[90] The five great powers at the Peace Conference, as listed by Oppenheim, were the British Empire, America, France, Italy and Japan. McNair, *International Law*, 1, §167a.

[91] Indeed, the United States and Japan emerged as imperial powers at approximately the same time, and sought to accommodate each other's ambitions. David B. Abernethy, *The Dynamics of Global Dominance: European Overseas Empires, 1415–1980* (New Haven: Yale University Press, 2000), p. 118. Thus, 'the Roosevelt administration formally acquiesced in the Japanese takeover of Korea in return for a free hand in the Philippines and an agreement to bar Japanese immigration to the United States'. Boyle, *Foundations*, p. 95.

[92] McNair, *International Law*, I, §167b.

[93] For an eloquent argument about this, see Syed Ameer Ali, 'Islam in the League of Nations', (1919) 5 *Transactions of the Grotius Society* 126.

[94] See Petry and Daly, *Cambridge History of Egypt*, p. 250.

[95] For detailed studies of this period, see V. G. Kiernan, *From Conquest to Collapse: European Empires from 1815 to 1960* (New York: Pantheon Books, 1982), pp. 191–207. See generally A. S. Kanya-Forstner, 'The War, Imperialism, and Decolonization', in Jay Winter, Geoffrey Parker and Mary R. Habeck (eds.), *The Great War and the Twentieth Century* (New Haven: Yale University Press, 2000), p. 231; Abernethy, *The Dynamics*. For an important study on which I have relied and which focuses specifically on the Mandate System, see Siba N'Zatioula Grovogui, *Sovereigns, Quasi Sovereigns, and Africans: Race and Self-Determination in International Law* (Minneapolis, MN: University of Minnesota Press, 1996), pp. 111–142.

[96] Abernethy, *The Dynamics*, p. 109.   [97] *Ibid.*

maintaining their Empires despite the war and its toll on their credibility and strength, now had to confront these movements, whose ambitions were expanding rapidly from requests for more participation in government to demands for outright independence – the result of broken promises and authoritarian rule by the imperial powers. The deliberations at Versailles occurred in the shadow of the massacre at Amritsar and Mahatma Gandhi's first *Satyagraha* campaigns. Protest, if not rebellion against colonial rule, took place in Sierra Leone, Saigon, the Congo, Egypt, Iraq, Kenya and South Africa.[98] Marcus Garvey's demand – 'Africa for the Africans' – caused great concern to colonial powers.[99] It was understandable then, that even at Versailles the A mandatories were characterized explicitly as well advanced in their progress toward independence.[100] Furthermore, as Grovogui argues, the Bolshevik Revolution in Russia gave inspiration to anticolonial struggles on the one hand, and made Western statesmen aware of the importance of offering greater voice to colonized peoples, on the other.[101] Anticolonial resistance, then, played a crucial role in shaping the League's policies toward the mandate territories.

Matters were complicated further by President Wilson's forceful promotion of the concept of self-determination, which he claimed was one of the major principles over which the war had been fought. Wilson's ideas had to be treated with respect. Consequently, the victorious European powers, intent on preserving, if not extending, their Empires, presented their claims in a manner that appeared to conform with Wilson's views.[102] Wilson's assertion that each distinctive culture was entitled to become an independent state was as relevant to the great colonial territories such as India as it was to the people of Europe to whom they primarily were addressed.[103] Consequently, Algerian, Vietnamese and Tunisian nationalist movements seized on the concept of self-determination to advance their claims for self-government.[104] Further, Grovogui argues, the recognition of the newly

---

[98] *Ibid.*, p. 129. For a good overview of anticolonial resistance during this period, see Young, *Postcolonialism*, pp. 161–181.

[99] Abernethy, *The Dynamics*, p. 129.

[100] This is suggested by the phrasing of Article 22, which asserts that these communities 'have reached a stage of development where their existence as independent nations can be provisionally recognized'. Wright, *Mandates*, p. 591 (citing Article 22 of The Mandate Articles of the League of Nations Covenant). For a larger discussion, see generally *ibid.*

[101] Grovogui, *Sovereigns*, p. 113.   [102] Kanya-Forstner, 'The War', p. 239.

[103] Wright, *Mandates*, p. 15.   [104] *Ibid.*, p. 242.

emergent Balkan states by the Western powers further gave impetus to nationalist demands for self-determination by the non-Europeans. In these ways, Wilson's condemnation of colonialism and his promotion of self-determination had far-reaching consequences that he could hardly have anticipated.[105]

Various criticisms of past colonialism made it vital for the League to establish that the Mandate System was not a form of veiled colonialism and that it could effectively protect native peoples, promote their interests and guide them toward self-government. Self-government had hardly been prominent in the colonial policies adopted by the traditional imperial powers.[106] The one example of a colonial power that professed itself intent on developing self-government and as acting in the interests of the native peoples was provided by one of the newest colonial powers, the United States, in its administration of the Philippines after the Spanish–American War of 1898. The character of this administration will be discussed in more detail in chapter 6. But it is clear that the US administration of the Philippines had some impact on the Mandate System, as it was Wilson himself, who had declared that the United States was a 'trustee of the Filipino people',[107] who had authored the Mandate System as well.

The Mandate System, by adopting the concept of trusteeship, justified the management of colonized peoples by presenting it as directed by concern for native interests and a desire to promote their self-government rather than by the selfish desires of the colonial power.

---

[105] The obscure young Vietnamese nationalist leader, Nguyen Ai Quoc (later to emerge as Ho Chi Minh), hopeful that Wilson would understand the aspirations of his people for liberation from France, attempted to meet him, but was shown the door. Kanya-Forstner, 'The War', p. 242; see also Mark Philip Bradley, *Imagining Vietnam & America: The Making of Post-Colonial Vietnam, 1919–1950* (Chapel Hill, NC: University of North Carolina Press, 2000), pp. 10–11.

[106] Hobson, at least, asserted: 'Upon the vast majority of the populations throughout our Empire we have bestowed no real powers of self-government, nor have we any serious belief that it is possible for us to do so.' J. A. Hobson, *Imperialism: A Study* (4th edn., London: George Allen & Unwin, 1948), p. 114. For a contrasting view, see Hall, *Mandates*, pp. 94–95. For a survey of of the different forms of government established in various British territories in the period immediately after the Second World War, see A. W. Brian Simpson, *Human Rights and the End of Empire: Britain and the Genesis of the European Convention* (New York: Oxford University Press, 2001), pp. 278–283.

[107] Wright, *Mandates*, p. 14, n. 24.

The economics of colonial relations in the inter-war period

Even as the colonies were demanding self-government and increased political freedoms, imperial powers were becoming acutely aware of the economic importance of their colonial territories. Until the latter half of the nineteenth century large trading companies, such as the British East India Company and the Dutch East India Company, had driven the colonial enterprise. The activities of these companies had embroiled European states in costly colonial conflicts, and, as a consequence, by the end of the nineteenth century, it was the imperial state that established economic links with its colonies on a sustained and organised basis.

Imperialism had always been motivated by economic gain. But whereas 'in 1880 a conscious policy of economic imperialism hardly existed',[108] by the end of the century this situation had changed dramatically, and imperialism had acquired a new and singular form. It was now the imperial European state, with its formidable powers and massive military and economic resources, that systematically set about the task of making profit out of the colonies.[109] This preoccupation with profit contrasted somewhat with the noble visions of Empire so evocatively produced by authors such as Kipling.[110] The commercial well being

---

[108] See Leonard Woolf, *Empire and Commerce in Africa: A Study in Economic Imperialism* (London: Allen & Unwin, 1920), p. 37.

[109] See *ibid.*, pp. 44–45. Woolf gives a pointed account of the singular nature of this form of imperialism. *Ibid.*, chapter 3. Woolf spoke with particular authority. He was a civil servant in Ceylon for seven years, during which time he developed a particularly intense dislike for the imperial system that he had very conscientiously administered and whose assumptions he did not entirely escape. Abruptly transported to the jungles of Ceylon from his beloved Trinity College and the company of his mentors and friends – who included G. E. Moore, Lytton Strachey and John Maynard Keynes – Woolf eventually resolved to live in Ceylon, looking after his district, but not as a Government Agent. His marriage to Virginia Stephen changed his plans. Woolf wrote one remarkable novel, set in Ceylon. See generally Leonard Woolf, *The Village in the Jungle* (London: Arnold, 1913).

[110] Orwell, who saw this dimension of imperialism only too clearly, explains Kipling's loss of popularity partly in these terms:

> He could not understand what was happening, because he had never any grasp of the economic forces underlying imperial expansion. It is notable that Kipling does not seem to realize, any more than the average soldier or colonial administrator, that an empire is primarily a money-making concern. Imperialism as he sees it is a sort of forcible evangelising. You turn a Gatling gun on a mob of unarmed 'natives' and then you establish 'the Law', which includes roads, railways, and a court house.

> (George Orwell, 'Rudyard Kipling', in *Dickens, Dali & Others*, New York: Reynal & Hitchcock, 1946, pp. 143–144)

of the European state and its national economy were perceived as being connected intimately with its overseas possessions and its ability to protect and expand its overseas markets. Indeed, the character and function of the European state itself was altered profoundly by this shift in emphasis. Joseph Chamberlain, as Secretary of State for the Colonies, made these points clear in a speech in 1895, where he asserted that the principal purpose of his government in effect was 'the development and maintenance of that vast agricultural, manufacturing and commercial enterprise upon which the welfare and even the existence of our great population exists'.[111] This involved 'finding new markets and . . . defending old ones',[112] and the Foreign Office, the Colonial Office, the War Office and the Admiralty were all involved, in their different capacities, in this great endeavour. Chamberlain went further in claiming that the promotion of such commerce was the principal function of government itself.[113]

By the beginning of the First World War, then, the central importance of colonial possessions for the economic well being of the metropolitan power was proclaimed widely and acted upon. The economic dimension of this new form of imperialism had been analysed by scholars such as Hobson years before the war,[114] and many scholars such as Woolf elaborated and refined these analyses immediately afterwards.[115] The war itself further demonstrated how important colonies were for the home state. Not only did the colonies provide soldiers to fight on the Western Front, but they also provided raw materials for the war effort including cotton, rubber, tin, leather and jute.[116] All this suggested that '[c]olonies

---

[111] Woolf, *Empire*, p. 7.   [112] *Ibid.*

[113] 'Therefore it is not too much to say that commerce is the greatest of all political interests, and that the Government deserves most the popular approval which does most to increase our trade and to settle it on a firm foundation.' *Ibid.*

[114] See generally Hobson, *Imperialism*. Hobson believed that '[i]mperialism is the endeavour of the great controllers of industry to broaden the channel for the flow of their surplus wealth by seeking foreign markets and foreign investments to take off the goods and capital which they cannot use at home.' *Ibid.* at p. 85. Hobson's view of imperialism focused more on the theme of colonies as markets than on the importance of colonies as a source of raw materials. His views of imperialism were powerfully shaped by the class struggle in England, and he argued that England would be better off if it invested in developing its own markets rather than in seeking them abroad.

[115] Lenin went a stage further in his analysis, which pointed to the centrality of colonialism to the entire capitalist system. See generally, V. I. Lenin, *Imperialism: The Highest Stage of Capitalism* (New York: International Publishers, 1939).

[116] Abernethy, *The Dynamics*, p. 112; Kanya-Forstner, 'The War', p. 247.

could be even more valuable in the future, so the thinking went, if their economic potential were realized'.[117] The economic importance of colonies was emphasized by the most eminent colonial administrators, Albert Sarraut and Frederick Lugard, who further distinguished between economic 'development' and what could be termed economic 'exploitation'.[118] The latter policy would exhaust the colony, whereas development would produce ongoing benefits to the metropolis.

It hardly was surprising, then, that the economic resources of the mandate territories were an important part of the debates regarding the structure of the Mandate System. The principal controversy focused on the 'open door policy'. The United States was opposed to becoming a mandate power;[119] nevertheless, it was implacable in asserting its economic interests by insisting that the 'open door policy' be implemented in all mandate territories. This would ensure that all states could trade and invest on an equal footing, and without fear of discrimination, in mandate territories. This was a manifestation of Point Three of Wilson's Fourteen Points.[120] Thus, the Mandate Agreements of B mandates contained provisions explicitly guaranteeing this.[121] Nevertheless, this hardly satisfied the United States, which had wanted the 'open door policy' to apply to the A mandates of the Middle East, and which

---

[117] Abernethy, *The Dynamics*, p. 112.

[118] Lugard's views are discussed later in this chapter. Sarraut argued: 'It is not by wearing out its colonies that a nation acquires power, wealth and influence; the past has already shown that development, prosperity, consistent growth and vitality in the colonies are the prime conditions for the economic power and external influence of a colonial metropolis.' Abernethy, *The Dynamics*, p. 112.

[119] The United States requested a reservation to the Mandate Article: 'Acceptance of a mandate is optional – no Power need accept a mandate unless it so chooses.' Cranston, *The Story of Woodrow Wilson*, p. 337. Other delegates protested, arguing that the United States should share the responsibility of managing backward territories. Colonel House, one of Wilson's advisers at the Conference on colonial affairs, responded by pointing out that Americans disliked acquiring 'imperial appendages'. *Ibid.*

[120] Point Three called for '[t]he removal, so far as possible, of all economic barriers and the establishment of an equality of trade conditions among all nations consenting to the peace and associating themselves for its maintenance'. President Woodrow Wilson, 'The Fourteen Points' (8 January 1918), reprinted in Cranston, *Woodrow Wilson*, pp. 461–463.

[121] Thus, the Mandate Agreement for Tanganyika, for example, included a provision stating: 'Further, the Mandatory shall ensure to all nationals of States Members of the League of Nations, on the same footing as to his own nationals, freedom of transit and navigation, and complete economic, commercial and industrial equality.' Wright, *Mandates*, p. 614 (citing Article 7 of the Mandate for Tanganyika). Generally, the 'open door policy' did not apply to A and C mandates, and this was a source of dispute for the United States. *Ibid.*, p. 236. See generally *ibid.*, pp. 476–480.

engaged in a long series of contentious negotiations with the British in order to gain access to the oil fields of Mesopotamia.[122] France and Great Britain were intent on gaining control over the oil resources in their Middle Eastern mandates and went so far as to redraw the boundaries of the mandate territories of Palestine, Mesopotamia and Syria in order to enable a more efficient exploitation of their oil reserves.[123] Protracted negotiations about access to these economic resources delayed confirmation of some of the mandates for several years.[124] Similarly, Australia and New Zealand did little to conceal their desire to annex the mandate territory of Nauru because of its valuable phosphate deposits.[125]

The paradox, then, was that colonial peoples were striving toward the ever more real goal of independence at precisely the time when their economic value and their significance for the metropolis were becoming increasingly evident. This was one of the fundamental tensions confronting the Mandate System, which simultaneously had to promote the self-government of the mandate territory, on the one hand, and a problematic form of economic development, on the other.

Reinterpreting the relationship between colonialism and international law

The liberal–humanist sentiment that animated Wilson's condemnation of colonialism was shared by a number of important international lawyers.[126] Further, jurists of the League period, including Wright and Lindley,[127] pointed out that many of their distinguished nineteenth- and early twentieth-century predecessors, such as Lawrence, Westlake and Oppenheim, had endorsed, if not authored, a system of international law that sanctioned conquest and exploitation.[128] The inter-war lawyers, then, sought not only to challenge the formalist law of their predecessors, but also to reform the international law that had legitimized the dispossession of non-European peoples.

In looking within their own discipline for jurists who could act as a foundation for such a humanist project, the League lawyers returned

---

[122] For an account of this dispute, see ibid., pp. 48–63.
[123] Ibid., p. 51. For a detailed study of the settlement of the Middle East by the Allied Powers following the Great War, see David Fromkin, A Peace to End All Peace (New York: H. Holt, 1989).
[124] See Wright, Mandates, pp. 48–56 (discussing negotiations over oil interests).
[125] See Weeramantry, Nauru, chapters 5–6.
[126] See, e.g., Lauterpacht, 'The Mandate', p. 39.
[127] See Wright, Mandates, p. 6.   [128] Ibid., p. 7.

to the work of Vitoria. They focused in particular on his argument that the Indians were the wards of the Spanish, and that Spanish governance of the Indians was to be dictated at all times by the interests of the latter. Vitoria, as discussed, characterized the natives as 'infants', further reinforcing the notion that they required guardianship. Consequently, the Mandate System was now presented as an elaboration of the important ideas first enunciated by Vitoria, that had been neglected and dismissed, together with so much else of value in international jurisprudence, as a result of the dominance of positivism, which now was itself discredited. The circle was complete: in seeking to end colonialism, international law returned to the origins of the colonial encounter. It hardly is surprising, then, that virtually every book written on the mandates makes some reference to Vitoria's work. To the League scholars, Vitoria was not so much the jurist legitimizing the Spanish war waged on the Indians as the committed advocate of Indian rights whose work suggested that international law, from its very beginnings, had been concerned with protecting the welfare of dependent peoples. Wilson, in arguing for trusteeship over backward peoples, was giving effect to ideas that Vitoria had elaborated centuries earlier.

The League's adoption of Vitoria's extraordinarily potent metaphor of 'wardship' had a number of effects. Most significantly, it reinforced the idea that a single process of development – that which was followed by the European states – was to be imitated and reproduced in non-European societies, which had to strive to conform to this model. This in turn justified and lent even further reinforcement to the continuing presence of the colonial powers – now mandatory powers – in these territories, as the task of these powers was not to exploit, but rather to civilize, the natives. This revival of Vitoria's rhetoric was combined through the Mandate System with a formidable array of legal and administrative techniques directed toward transforming the native and her society.

Since its inception, international law has been engaged in an ongoing struggle to manage colonial problems at both the practical and the theoretical level. In the nineteenth century, I have argued, the problem of accounting for relations between European and non-European societies threatened to negate positivist claims to establishing a coherent and comprehensive science of international law based on the behaviour of sovereign, European states. Similarly, the attempts of inter-war jurists to rid themselves of the colonial international law of the past was fraught with ambivalence, principally because it was precisely this colonial international law that had universalised a basically European international law. The positivist international law of conquest, which the League jurists sought to displace, had been directed toward extinguishing and invalidating the legal systems of non-European peoples and endorsing their replacement with the systems of law established by the colonizers. This basic feature of nineteenth-century international law remained unchallenged by the new international law of the mandates that now presumed the triumph of European international law and the unequal international relations that had arisen as a result.

The new international law, therefore, could embark on the next stage of the civilizing process of preparing non-European states for independence and emergence into the universal system of international law. The new universalizing mission of international law now acquired an even more powerful character: through the intervention of international tribunals, it took on the task of transforming the interior of non-European societies and peoples, ostensibly to liberate them. In this way, the universalizing mission of international law, by embracing the idea of trusteeship, could now be adapted to changed circumstances and anticolonial political sentiments, and still continue its task of ensuring that the Western model of law and behaviour would be seen as natural, inevitable and inescapable. In this sense, the Mandate System continued, rather than departed from, the grand nineteenth-century project of universalizing international law. Despite the ostensible changes in attitudes towards non-European societies, furthermore, it is also telling that the attempts by Baron Makino, the Japanese representative to the Peace Conference, to include a provision relating to racial equality in the Covenant of the League were emphatically opposed.[129]

The ambiguities of the inter-war period in relation to the colonial past – a past that was repudiated vehemently, even as the relationships of subordination that it established were to remain undisturbed – suggested a more specific ambiguity about the Mandate System itself: Was it designed to negate colonialism or recreate it in a different form?

---

[129] See Frank Furedi, *The New Ideology of Imperialism: Renewing the Moral Imperative* (London: Pluto Press, 1994), p. 5. The French and the Italians voted in favour of the inclusion of such a provision, but it was defeated by opposition from the United Kingdom and the United States. See Cranston, *The Story of Woodrow Wilson*, pp. 309–310. The Dominion powers, mindful of the impact of such a clause on their native populations, were especially opposed to such a provision.

The Mandate System and the construction of the non-European state

The mandates and the problem of sovereignty

The primary novelty of the Mandate System for many jurists of the inter-war period was its puzzling relationship to traditional sovereignty doctrine. Colonial territories had always posed a problem to conventional concepts of sovereignty.[130] For inter-war scholars, the central dilemma was that of determining who had sovereignty over mandate territories. The Axis powers lost their titles to their colonial possessions as a result of the peace settlement. While this much was agreed, the issue of where sovereignty over the mandates was vested was never resolved, although it was the subject of exhaustive debate and analysis among various jurists, such as McNair,[131] and Wright.[132] Possible candidates that were considered included the League, the mandatory power and the mandated territory – postulated here as possessing 'latent sovereignty' that would emerge in its actualised form upon the termination of the mandate. McNair also articulated this last position, initially argued in the 1930s, in his capacity as a Judge of the ICJ. McNair asserted: 'The doctrine of sovereignty has no application to this new system. Sovereignty over a Mandated Territory is in abeyance; if and when the inhabitants of the Territory obtain recognition as an independent State . . . sovereignty will revive and vest in the new State.'[133]

The inability of the jurists to resolve this question – despite which the Mandate System itself continued to function – justifies McNair's claim that the Mandate System was unique, as a result of which 'very little practical help [was] obtainable by attempting to apply existing concepts of sovereignty to such a novel state of affairs as the Mandate System present[ed]'.[134] But this was not the only reason why the Mandate System raised a unique set of problems regarding the character of sovereignty. Under the classic positivist international law, states came into being when they possessed certain attributes, such as territory, people, government and independence, and were recognized as an independent

---

[130] See W. W. Willoughby and C. G. Fenwick, *Types of Restricted Sovereignty and of Colonial Autonomy* (Washington, DC: Government Printing Office, 1919), pp. 5–13.

[131] McNair, *International Law*, I, §94f (discussing views in a textual note).

[132] Wright, *Mandates*, pp. 319–338, provides a customarily thorough analysis that reviews all the relevant literature of the period.

[133] *International Status of South-West Africa*, ICJ Reports 1950, No. 10, p. 128 at p. 150 (11 July) (separate opinion of Judge McNair).

[134] McNair, *International Law*, I, §94f.

state by other states.[135] Within this framework, international law played only a relatively passive role, merely outlining the characteristics of a state and leaving the matter to be decided by the states that proffered or withheld recognition. By contrast, in the Mandate System, international law and institutions actively engaged in the process of creating sovereignty – as conceptualised by pragmatist jurisprudence – by establishing the social foundation, the underlying sociological structure and the political, social and economic substance of the juridical state. This project supported the idea that sovereignty could be graded, as implied by the classification of mandates into A, B and C, based on their state of political and economic advancement.[136] This in turn assumed that sovereignty existed in something like a linear continuum, and that every society could be placed at some point along this continuum, based on its approximation to the ideal of the European nation-state. This model implicitly repudiated the idea that different societies had devised different forms of political organization that should command some degree of respect and validity in international law. As a consequence of this postulation of one model of sovereignty, the Mandate System further acquired the form of a fantastic universalizing apparatus that, when applied to any mandate territory – whatever its peculiarities and complexities – could ensure that such territories, whether the Cameroons in Africa, Papua New Guinea in the Pacific, or Iraq in the Middle East, would be directed to the same ideal of self-government and, in some cases, transformed sufficiently to ensure the emergence of a sovereign state.

The issue of where sovereignty resided with respect to the mandate territories was of great importance to mandatory powers. Those administering C mandates were especially prone to attempting to annex the mandate territory they controlled.[137] Significantly, however, it was, arguably, precisely because sovereignty over the mandate territory could

---

[135] In the case of the non-European states, of course, a further and more complex requirement, that of possessing 'civilization', was required.

[136] The acceptance of these divisions as somehow true rather than merely contingent on the peculiar battles waged by the statesmen at Versailles is suggested by the manner in which the PMC, for example, accepted these categories and proceeded to deal with the territories they were surveying accordingly. The superior sovereign status enjoyed by more advanced territories, the A mandates, was manifested in the form of greater autonomy given to these mandates.

[137] This strategy was repudiated by the argument that, whatever the uncertainties as to where sovereignty vested, it did not vest in the mandatory powers. See *Legal Consequences for States of the Continued Presence of South Africa in Namibia (South West Africa) Notwithstanding Security Council Resolution 276*, (1970), ICJ Reports 1971, p. 16.

not be located decisively in any one entity that the Mandate System could have complete access to the interior of that territory. It was for this reason that the League, rather than being restricted by assertions of sovereignty, could develop a unique series of technologies and techniques for entering and transforming the very recesses of the interior of the mandate territory in order to realize this pragmatist, sociological vision of the sovereign state.

The actual powers of the League to implement its vision of the sovereign nation-state were extremely limited and problematic. The fact remained, however, that the League, simply by virtue of creating the system with its unique purposes and its reporting and monitoring systems, could begin to conceive of deploying international law in completely new and ambitious ways. The nation-state was not so much created by the mandatories administering their particular territories as imagined, in elaborate and vivid detail, by the bureaucrats of the League.

The sociology of the non-European state and the new international law

The Mandate System has generated an extremely rich jurisprudence.[138] For the purpose of my argument, however, this analysis focuses on the administrative facets of the system. My argument is that the unique character of the Mandate System, and the principles the League formulated to guide its operations,[139] were developed largely through the work of the PMC, which had primary responsibility for supervising the operation of the system. Once the basic framework of the Mandate System had been established, it was the PMC that had the task of ensuring the progress of the mandate territories – and monitoring the everyday workings of the system. While the legal principles embodied in the mandate articles and mandate agreements purported to guide both mandatory powers and the League, these principles failed to provide any clear sense of the final end of the Mandate System. According to Article 22 of the Covenant, the primary purpose of the Mandate System was to secure the 'well-being and development' of the peoples of the mandate

---

[138] Issues relating to the Mandate System have been litigated extensively before the ICJ. See, e.g., *International Status of South-West Africa*, ICJ Reports 1950, No. 10, p. 128 (11 July); *South West Africa (Ethiopia v. South Africa; Liberia v. South Africa)*, ICJ Reports 1962, p. 319 (21 December) (preliminary objections, judgment); *South West Africa (Ethiopia v. South Africa; Liberia v. South Africa)* ICJ Reports 1966, p. 6 (18 July) (second-phase judgement); *Certain Phosphate Lands in Nauru (Nauru v. Australia)*, ICJ Reports 1992, p. 240 (26 June) (preliminary objections, judgement).

[139] The extent to which the Mandatory Powers actually complied with these principles is, of course, an entirely distinct question.

territories.[140] While this much could be agreed, it was far from clear what this involved in terms of the specific goals to be achieved. Nevertheless, a system had to be developed to monitor and assess the economic and social progress, however broadly defined, of a mandate territory. For such a project, as Wright points out, it was essential to formulate effective and workable standards.[141]

While the broad rhetoric of 'standards of civilization' may be traced back at least to Vitoria, the diversity of the mandate territories – and, even more importantly, their administration by the one centralised body, the League – raised the profound problem of developing and particularizing a set of standards that could be universally applicable. Civilization and progress could no longer be discussed in terms of vague standards haphazardly applied by different colonial powers. Rather, the Mandate System required the elaboration of a consolidated and detailed set of standards that could be applied to the massive range of social, economic and political phenomena examined by the League – whether this had to do with labour policy, systems of land holding, or trade relations – in determining the effectiveness of the mandatory's promotion of welfare, self-government and, ultimately in some cases, sovereignty.

While some colonial experts were sceptical about the possibility of formulating such standards, the broader view prevailed that no progress was possible in the mandate territories without 'some principle or standard of conduct or culture'.[142] The issue of standards was crucial according to Van Rees, a member of the PMC, who believed that '[t]he study of such questions by the Mandates Commission, with the object of gradually and methodically establishing for its own use what, in my opinion, would constitute its jurisprudence, seems to me to be not only of great value but really indispensable for its work in general'.[143]

The use of the term 'jurisprudence' suggests that the development and application of standards was essentially a legal enterprise. And yet, once it was decided that standards were necessary, the PMC was confronted with the question of whether these standards should take the form of strict legal norms or more flexible administrative guidelines. This division between the 'legal' and the 'administrative' was evident not only in the question of the character of the standards to be established, but also in the function of the PMC itself.

---

[140] League of Nations Covenant, Article 22, para. 1.   [141] Wright, *Mandates*, p. 190.
[142] *Ibid.*   [143] *Ibid.*, p. 221 (quoting Van Rees).

The PMC, on the one hand, saw its function in legalistic terms. It derived its authority from the Covenant, and its task was to give effect to Article 22. Thus, the interpretation of Article 22 and the relevant Mandate Agreements was a central preoccupation of the PMC.[144] The PMC, in this sense, adopted a strictly legal approach. It confined itself to studying the obligations undertaken by the mandatories and ensuring that these were discharged, as opposed to making its own suggestions, independent of these obligations, as to what the mandatory should be doing.[145] But the PMC also exercised an administrative function and control over the mandatory; this consisted of its role of receiving reports, providing and giving information based on these reports, questioning the representative of the mandatory power in the PMC and attempting to formulate a broader and overarching mandate policy in light of all this information.

As Wright argues, however, this apparent tension was resolved by the fusion of these two functions – a development he analyses in terms of the emerging discipline of public administration that required such a fusion. Some sense of how this took place is offered by an examination of the very different approaches adopted by two members of the PMC when outlining how the PMC should perform its duty of ensuring that welfare was being promoted. One member of the Commission, Van Rees, believed that this could be achieved by addressing a series of essentially legal questions:

Is it allowable to give the territory a political organization which would make it practically independent of the mandatory state? . . .

Do the clauses of the covenant and mandate oblige the mandatory powers to devote themselves to the development of the territory and its population exclusively in the interest of the native? . . .

What are the obligations which result from the principle that the mandatory powers, having been made trustees by the League of Nations, shall derive no profit from this trusteeship?[146]

Yanaghita, however, raised an entirely different set of questions that focused more on developments taking place in the mandates themselves

---

[144] See, e.g., M. Freire d'Andrade, Note, 'The Interpretation of that Part of Article 22 of the Covenant Which Relates to the Well-Being and Development of the Peoples of Mandated Territories'. *Permanent Mandates Commission, Minutes of the Seventh Session,* League of Nations Doc. C.648 M.237 1925 VI at p. 197 (1925) (hereafter *PMC, Seventh Session*). Lugard responded to the note. *See ibid.,* p. 206.
[145] Wright, *Mandates,* p. 226.   [146] *Ibid.,* p. 227 (quoting Van Rees).

than on the administrative, fact-finding function of the PMC. He sought information on matters such as the '[e]numeration of population according to tribal divisions, or to the stage of development attained by the various tribes . . . , [and the p]rogress of the development of the land, shown in reference to localities or native groups'.[147]

The PMC responded by combining these two approaches, thus creating a law incorporating both elements: first, the collection and systematization of information called for by Yanaghita and, second, the use of this information for the purpose of creating a set of standards that in turn is linked notionally to a broader legal framework. It was important for law and administration to become fused in this way because, as Wright points out, 'It is true the general principles of the Covenant and mandate may furnish guides, but clearly the main source for such formulations is not the documents, but the data, not deduction, but induction'.[148]

Legal principles were vital, but they had to be combined into a broader system that enabled the PMC to become cognizant of the 'facts'.[149] In effect, then, it is precisely because of the alliance between law and administration that the PMC was in a unique position to engage in an ongoing and evolving process of receiving, assimilating and synthesizing information from the mandate territories, and then using this information to develop more appropriate and effective standards, a task that fulfilled the legal dimensions of its operations even while giving the PMC enormous flexibility in its operations. This concern to retain flexibility, to be sensitive to empirical reality, was what led many PMC members to be opposed to the codification of standards.[150]

This synthesis of law and administration is illustrated by the list of questions the PMC presented to the Mandatory Powers.[151] Part N focuses

---

[147] *Ibid.*, p. 228 (listing suggestions of Yanaghita).   [148] *Ibid.*, p. 227.
[149] *Ibid.*, p. 220, n. 3 (quoting Merlin). Thus, when discussing how labour legislation should be framed, the Portuguese representative argued that 'an effort should be made to compile the fullest possible statistics, in order to ascertain what contribution the people may, without risk, be expected to make to the work of the community. These statistics should show not merely the number of natives, but also particulars of their physical powers, customs and psychology.' 'Draft Convention on Slavery', (1926) 11 *League of Nations Official Journal* 1542.
[150] Wright, *Mandates*, p. 220.
[151] 'List of Questions which the Permanent Mandates Commission Desires Should be Dealt with in the Annual Report of the Mandatory Powers', (1926) 10 *League of Nations Official Journal* 1322.

on questions regarding labour.[152] On the one hand, mandatories were required to provide detailed information as to the laws and regulations governing labour issues.[153] On the other hand, the PMC sought an immense amount of information in response to a series of questions regarding, among other topics, the adequacy of available labour for economic development; processes of recruitment; the nature of the work for which recruiting had occurred; whether private organizations were allowed to recruit; and whether local demand for labour was sufficient.[154] The list of questions embodies the synthesis of the approaches suggested by Van Rees and Yanaghita. This is, moreover, exactly the sort of exercise called for by political scientists and pragmatic jurists intent on adjusting the law in light of realities disclosed by empirical study.[155] Further, the new jurisprudence that developed through the Mandate System was extraordinarily self-generating precisely because it was based on acquiring increasing volumes of information on an expanding range of issues, a process that in turn led to demands for more information on further issues and the formulation of further standards.

None of this, however, undermined the legal character of the system. The entire structure of administration and supervision was still based on legal norms and gave rise to justiciable legal obligations on the part of the mandatory. This is the point made by Judge Jessup in comparing the broad phrases used in the mandate – 'material and moral well-being and the social progress of the inhabitants' of the mandate

[152] Other topics include: Status of the Territory, Status of the Native Inhabitants, International Relations, Public Finance, General Administration, and Trade Statistics. *Ibid.*

[153] Questions of this sort focused on laws regarding labour contracts and penalties; rates of wages and methods of payment; hours of work; disciplinary powers possessed by employers; housing and sanitary conditions for workers; inspection procedures for workshops; issues of compensation and insurance; and compulsory labour for essential public works. *Ibid.*, pp. 1325–1326.

[154] *Ibid.* The crucial link between labour and development is again emphasized in the list of questions: 'Does the local supply of labour, in quantity, physical powers of resistance and aptitude for industrial and agricultural work conducted on modern lines appear to indicate that it is adequate, as far as can be foreseen, for the economic development of the territory?' *Ibid.*

[155] This is the sort of science called for by Potter, who rejects a science of government based on abstract reasoning concerning the nature of man and of liberty, and instead calls for 'efforts to collect as much data as possible concerning actual forms of state organization and governmental methods, and efforts to analyse that data and discover therein the main lines of causation and the fundamental principles of politics'. Potter, 'Political Science', 381–391.

territory – to provisions in the US Constitution.[156] The full realization of the pragmatic, sociological international law comes into being, then, through international institutions that profoundly expand the tech-nologies of international law that are applied uniquely to the mandate territories.

We may see this system, then, as an embodiment of the new international law called for by Alvarez and Hudson. This is the system that addresses Alvarez's concern to develop a link between social reality and international law, between 'what is' and 'what must be'.[157] It is a project that fuses law with the social sciences by engaging in an empirical study of the phenomenon to be regulated.[158] Instead of abstract juridical rules that are exact, definite and rigid, the shift to standards creates the flexibility that enables this fusion between law and politics. This is the law that is governed, then, by 'new conceptions of economic, social and general utility'.[159] And it was because of the formidable adaptability of this new jurisprudence, its ability to adjust continuously to social realities as they became better disclosed through empirical study, that Hudson's vision of international law, which was in turn based on Pound's view of international law as a mechanism of social engineering, could progress towards realization. It was an international law based on 'a conscious process of adapting our rules and principles and standards more directly to the service of the live needs of our present day society'.[160]

[156] 'Certainly, courts can determine and have determined whether particular laws or actions comply with general broad criteria such as "due process," "equal protection" and "religious freedom".' *South-West Africa (Ethiopia v. South Africa; Liberia v. South Africa)*, ICJ Reports 1962, p. 319 at 428 (21 December) (dissenting opinion of Judge Jessup). This point is basically affirmed by the court in its Namibia Advisory Opinion. See *Legal Consequences for States of the Continued Presence of South Africa in Namibia (South West Africa) Notwithstanding Security Council Resolution 276 (1970)*, ICJ Reports 1971, p. 16 (21 June).
[157] Alvarez, 'The New International Law', 42.
[158] Alvarez thus claims that '[t]he establishment of this harmony between politics and legal rules is the greatest step which can be accomplished in International Law'. *Ibid.*, 47.
[159] *Ibid.*, 48. Alvarez makes his argument in the context of his larger project, which is 'above all, to "Americanise" these sciences [of international relations and international law], that is to say, take into account the doctrines, the practices and problems of the New World'. *Ibid.*, 38. It is clearly the American jurists who are most forceful in presenting a pragmatic international law. See Astorino, 'The Impact of Sociological Jurisprudence', for an important survey of this period and the significance of American pragmatism to the jurisprudence of the time.
[160] Hudson, 'The Prospect', 435.

It is perhaps only appropriate, then, that thirty years after his appearance before the Grotius Society, Alvarez, now a senior judge of the ICJ, characterized the new international law as being embodied by the Mandate System and the trusteeship system of the United Nations that succeeded it:

> But it is from the angle of international law that the creation of those institutions [the mandate and trusteeship systems] presents the greatest interest. The spirit and certain characteristics of what may be called the new international law have thereby been introduced in international law.[161]

It is difficult to assess how the ideas of jurists like Alvarez and Hudson affected the formation of international law and institutions. The simple fact was, however, that in creating international institutions, international law became capable, through the linkage between law and institutions[162] in the special context of the mandate project, to develop a formidable set of technologies to address particular problems. In the final analysis, the fusion between law and administration discussed by Wright is made possible only by the linking of international law with institutions. As a consequence of this, the Mandate System consisted not only of a set of rules, but also an entire system that, among other things, would collect information, analyse that information and formulate a policy.

A whole complex set of problem solving processes was devised and applied to colonial issues through the League, and I argue that these correspond closely with the ideas of advocates of the new international law. It is in the unique circumstances of the Mandate System – unique because of the connection between sociology and sovereignty, and unique because it gave institutions access to the interior of the state – that international law could develop a new set of technologies and methods of control to address colonial problems such as the gap between the civilized and the uncivilized, a gap that is transformed in the Mandate System into a difference between the advanced and the backward. The dynamic of difference is now created, not through the crude, inexact jurisprudence of nineteenth-century positivism, but rather through the sophisticated techniques and technologies of pragmatism. These technologies have an extraordinary power, range and penetration when

---

[161] *International Status of South-West Africa*, ICJ Reports 1950, No. 10, p. 128 at 174 (11 July) (dissenting opinion of Judge Alvarez).

[162] This is to accept the positivist argument that institutions are simply creations of international law.

exercised through standards, because these standards can create difference with respect to the most intimate and minute aspects of social life
in mandate territories – native 'customs, traditions, manner of living,
psychology, and even resistance to disease'.[163] Each rendition of difference in turn creates a project for the Mandate System, as the native's
deficiency must in some way be remedied. In the colonial setting, then,
the grand themes of law and politics played themselves out, not in the
attempts of international law to outlaw aggression or to establish collective security and to control the nationalist passions of Eastern Europe,
but rather in the less spectacular but relentlessly effective project of
acquiring more data on backward native peoples and their societies in
order to further the extraordinary project of creating government and
sovereignty in these territories. This project progressed even while the
system ensured that these territories continued to serve their traditional
purpose in the larger global economic system.

Government, sovereignty and economy

Introduction

The novel technologies devised by the League were designed to promote the 'well-being and development' of mandate peoples, protect the
natives, and 'promote self-government'.[164] This section examines the
character of the economic and social policies formulated by the PMC
through the actual operation of the system. My argument is that the
broad phrase 'well-being and development' was interpreted principally in
economic terms, and that a form of economic development that was disadvantageous to the mandate territories was instituted by the system as
a result. This preoccupation with economic development dominated all
other aspects of social policy in the mandate territories including, most
significantly, the character of the government created in mandate societies. Moreover, the discipline of economics itself became all-pervasive
and represented a new and powerful way of conceptualizing and managing the mandate territories and their peoples. Given that the ultimate
goal of the Mandate System was to promote self-government and even
to create sovereign states out of the mandate territories, the domination

---

[163] 'Draft Convention on Slavery', p. 1541.
[164] We recall here Hall's assertion that '[s]elf-government is the central positive
conception of the Mandate System set out in Article 22 of the League Covenant'. Hall,
Mandates, p. 94.

of economics resulted in what may be termed provisionally the 'economization of government' or the 'economization of sovereignty'.

The Mandate System and colonial administration

In attempting to formulate policies for the governance of mandate territories, the PMC almost inevitably prescribed and followed what was regarded as 'enlightened' colonial policy; simply, no other precedent or model existed. Thus, scholars such as Hall argued that a properly administered mandate territory was virtually the same as a properly administered colony[165] because in both territories there would be found the rule of law, personal liberty, security of property, trusteeship, indirect rule and the 'open door policy'.[166] In this way, the mandate was not a departure from colonialism as such; rather, it was a system of a progressive, enlightened colonialism, as opposed to the bad, exploitative colonialism of the nineteenth century.[167] This distinction between good and bad colonialism was important, for it helped to justify the French and British colonialism in Africa and Asia which naturally fell into the category of 'good colonialism'.

In its attempts to resolve the many problems of promoting welfare and development, the PMC focused on certain broad themes and organizing principles of colonial administration. Lugard had outlined these magisterially in his classic work on colonial administration, *The Dual Mandate in British Tropical Africa*, which first appeared in 1921, at precisely the time when the PMC was grappling with these concerns. The 'dual mandate' basically involved protecting the welfare of the natives by transmitting to them the benefits of civilization while expanding trade and international commerce in the colonized territories.[168] Equally significant, the basic function of the colony was seen in economic terms,

---

[165] Hall argued that 'an experienced observer, crossing over from an ordinary dependency in Africa into an adjoining mandated area administered by the same power, would be hard put to it to find any real distinctions between the one and the other'. *Ibid.*, p. 93.

[166] See *ibid.*

[167] Understandably, these developments led many scholars to represent the record of enlightened colonial powers as always having been guided by the principles embodied in the mandate. Thus, Hall, for example, argued that it was always the intention of enlightened British colonial policy to promote self-government, and it was only the backwardness of the natives that prevented this from being achieved. See *ibid.*, pp. 94–95.

[168] This basic idea is captured by the epigraph to Lugard's book, which quotes Joseph Chamberlain: 'We develop new territory as Trustees for Civilization, for the Commerce of the World.' In language that powerfully evokes the themes and opening

and as necessary for the well being of the West. Lugard argued that '[t]he democracies of to-day claim the right to work, and the satisfaction of that claim is impossible without the raw materials of the tropics on the one hand and their markets on the other'.[169]

The economic policies pursued under the Mandate System were governed by the same vision of the mandates as a source of raw materials, on the one hand, and markets, on the other. In examining the operation of the mandate, then, I have followed the PMC in drawing upon the literature relating to colonial administration as a whole.

Economic development and native welfare

While the two aspects of the dual mandate could be regarded as complementary, it was evident that economic progress and native welfare were often in tension with one another. The basic problem was identified by Orts:

> scenes of Conrad's *Heart of Darkness* by referring to Britain's Roman past, but lacking Conrad's irony, Lugard asserts:
>
>> As Roman imperialism laid the foundations of modern civilization, and led the wild barbarians of these islands along the path of progress, so in Africa to-day we are repaying the debt, and bringing to the dark places of the earth, the abode of barbarism and cruelty, the torch of culture and progress, while ministering to the material needs of our own civilization.
>>
>> (Lord Lugard, *The Dual Mandate in British Tropical Africa*, Hamden, CT: Archon Books 1965, p. 618)
>
> The term 'dark places of the earth' was used by Kipling, Conrad and Lugard to describe the barbaric, non-European world. The dual mandate also marked a different approach to colonialism from the colonialism practised up to the latter half of the nineteenth century. It succeeded the colonialism promoted by chartered companies and adventurers, who were unredeemable in their exploitation. As Furnivall puts it:
>
>> [t]he failure, economic and political, of the chartered companies in Africa, implied that the State, on taking over charge of the colonies, should intervene actively to promote economic development and to enhance native welfare. This new constructive policy with its double aspect came to be known as the 'dual mandate'.
>>
>> (J. S. Furnivall, *Colonial Policy and Practice: A Comparative Study of Burma and Netherlands India*, Cambridge: Cambridge University Press, 1948, p. 288)
>
> For a broad study, see D. K. Fieldhouse, *The Colonial Empires: A Comparative Survey from the Eighteenth Century* (London: Weidenfeld & Nicolson, 1966). Lugard himself had been such an adventurer, conquering many territories in Africa as a representative of the East Africa Company before acquiring fame and respectability first as a colonial administrator in Nigeria and then as the senior figure of the PMC. For an account of Lugard's earlier career with the East Africa Company, see Woolf, *Empire*, pp. 273–293. Woolf, who was not among Lugard's admirers, notes, 'Captain Lugard was one of those fortunate persons whose early life was chiefly occupied in killing things'. For a laudatory account of Lugard, see Hall, *Mandates*, pp. 96–97.

[169] Lugard, *The Dual Mandate*, p. 61.

The development of the mandated territories constituted for the mandatory Powers a duty, alongside their other duty of securing the welfare of the natives. These two duties must be reconciled, and the two tasks must progress side by side. For this purpose it was necessary to find a just criterion.[170]

The fundamental tension between development and welfare, and the further questions it generated, had become a central issue for colonial policy and appeared in one form or another in virtually all the major debates regarding the administration of the mandates. Labour policy posed the tension in its most basic form. Large infrastructure and development projects had become a central aspect of economic development policy as it had been formulated after the war. Technology such as the railroad had made the interior of the colonies far more accessible, and European mining, trading and agricultural companies significantly expanded their presence in the colonies in the inter-war period.[171] These projects, however, had a massively detrimental impact on the natives who were required to supply the labour,[172] and the PMC kept confronting the question of whether these projects were taking place at the expense of the native populations. The 'mortality of the natives engaged in certain work was very considerable'.[173] A number of

---

[170] *Permanent Mandate Commission, Minutes of the Sixth Session*, League of Nations Doc. C.386M.132 1925 VI at 47 (1925) (hereafter *PMC, Sixth Session*). This fundamental issue was a central preoccupation of PMC deliberations. Thus, Lugard begins his report on 'Economic Development of Mandated Territories in Its Relation to the Well-Being of the Natives' with the following assertion:

> That the economic development of African territories is no less a duty than that of securing the welfare of the natives is not questioned. The problem is how these two duties should be reconciled without, on the one hand, subordinating policy to a purely utilitarian outlook or, on the other hand, adopting a standpoint too exclusively philanthropic.
>
> (*PMC, Seventh Session*, p. 197)

[171] Abernethy, *The Dynamics*, p. 113. This approach to the development of colonies gave rise in the case of Britain to the Colonial Development Act of 1929 and the Colonial Development and Welfare Act of 1940. Furnivall, *Colonial Policy*, p. 433.

[172] As M. Freire d'Andrade asserts: 'Yet everywhere roads will have to be made, railways constructed, hospitals and schools built, and everything done that is indispensable to the well-being and development of the peoples. And where these large demands arise, it almost always happens that native labor is scarce and its output not very great.' *PMC, Seventh Session*, p. 202.

[173] *PMC, Sixth Session*, p. 48. It was noted that administrations were continuously required to provide more labour. *PMC, Seventh Session*, pp. 194–195. Noting with concern the significant mortality rates of the native populations, PMC members raised further questions as to whether this was due to liquor, to 'special diseases arising from the impact of civilization or . . . to an intensive effort to develop the country for purely economic reasons'. *Ibid.*, p. 195 (Rappard). Lugard, reporting on this matter, raised the

members of the PMC stressed the importance of bringing about gradual reform in mandate societies and ensuring that native well being
was not sacrificed for immediate economic gains.[174] Nevertheless, having made all these qualifying statements, the PMC concluded that the
development of the resources of the territories was crucial. Thus, even
Orts, who had drawn the attention of the PMC to the suffering endured
by the native populations, finally concluded: 'The present question was
to ensure in the general interest, not the preservation of this natural
wealth – which happily was not at issue – but the development of the
incomparable resources represented by the population of the countries
with which the Commission was concerned.'[175]

The development of the territories thus became the governing and
unquestionable principle of the Mandate System. Most significantly, the
resources of non-European territories were invariably and conveniently
characterized by European statesmen and colonial administrators as
belonging not only to the peoples of those territories, but also to the
larger 'international community'. This was indicated by Chamberlain's
very formulation of the dual mandate as developing new territories 'for
the Commerce of the World'.[176]

Despite the happy suggestion that both the natives and the world
in general would benefit from the exploitation of these resources,[177]
the fact that the terms of the exploitation were set by the colonial

---

possibility that '"sudden introduction of an industrial civilization" and the
consequent demand for native labour has not in some cases entailed too heavy a
burden on a population not yet accustomed to the new conditions and to European
methods'. *Ibid.*, p. 195.

[174] See *PMC, Seventh Session*, p. 195. 'In a word, the Administration, while assisting private
enterprise in every reasonable way, must not allow itself to be dominated by the
utilitarian spirit, for its special function is to frame its policy for the future and not
exclusively to immediate economic success.' *Ibid.*, p. 196.

[175] *PMC, Sixth Session*, p. 49.

[176] See *ibid.* These sorts of statements give some idea as to why the campaign for
Permanent Sovereignty over Natural Resources became so centrally important to
newly independent Third World states. The propensity of colonial powers to
characterize the resources of mandate territories as something akin to the 'common
heritage of mankind' is powerful and commonplace. Thus, the Portuguese
representative argued that '[s]ome people, having nothing at heart but the interests
of mankind as a whole, consider that it is the duty of colonising countries to exploit
the economic wealth of their colonies and that, unless they do so, they have no right
to retain those possessions'. 'Draft Convention on Slavery', p. 1541.

[177] Thus, Lugard himself claimed of the natives that 'their raw materials and foodstuffs –
without which civilization cannot exist – must be developed alike in the interests of
the natives and of the world at large'. Lugard, *The Dual Mandate*, p. 60.

powers or the mandatory powers inevitably led to the sacrifice of native interests.[178] Thus, while the sort of outright exploitation of native peoples by chartered companies that took place in the nineteenth century was condemned, the new regime of unequal exchange, officially sanctioned by the colonial state and embodied in legal regulations, was completely acceptable.

Several other reasons were advanced for giving primacy to economic development. PMC members argued that the suffering experienced by native populations was more than justified by the benefits they would derive.[179] Another alternative – that of viewing the whole issue from a native point of view – was considered explicitly and rejected by jurists. Van Rees, for example, asserted: 'It was clear that, in general, European civilization was based on principles diametrically opposed to those of the natives, and it resulted from this that a European administration had not and could not have the welfare of the natives, as conceived by the natives themselves, for its sole object.'[180]

The prevalence of the policy of economic progress was desirable for a number of additional reasons connected with the administration of the mandates. The PMC had been confronted with a number of complex questions about native cultures: Should special protection be given to native cultures in mandates with mixed populations? What aspects of native culture should be modified? The policy of promoting economic progress, it was opined, would resolve many of these issues. Economic progress appeared a neutral test that would decide objectively and effectively what traits of native cultures would survive and, according to some PMC members, whether they should survive at all. This was because economic progress, the determining standard, was not to be associated with a particular race or culture: transcending these specificities, it existed as a universal category. Thus d'Andrade – whose expertise was based on the Portuguese colonial model – argued: 'If there were races unable to work, then without any doubt the very impact of civilization would show them that they were not equipped for the struggle of life and they would end by disappearing.'[181]

---

[178] For a detailed contemporaneous study of this issue in relation to Africa, see generally Woolf, *Empire*. For a more recent study, see Walter Rodney, *How Europe Underdeveloped Africa* (London: Bogle-L'Ouverture Publications, 1972), pp. 147–203. For a detailed examination of the terms of exploitation in an actual mandate territory, see Weeramantry, *Nauru*.

[179] See d'Andrade's note in *PMC, Seventh Session*, p. 200.

[180] *PMC, Sixth Session*, p. 49.   [181] *Ibid.*, p. 50.

Economic progress, then, would bring about important social changes both directly and indirectly. For example, it would promote the emergence in mandate populations of modern, efficient communities[182] as well as the emergence of individualism – as opposed to the tribalism that was such a prominent feature of mandate societies and was understood to pose a serious obstacle to the advancement of mandate territories.[183] A particular structure of relationships emerges within the system of analysis adopted by the PMC. Within this system, the market is associated with modernity, progress, individualism and the universal. Culture, on the other hand, is connected with backwardness, tribal community and the particular. The introduction and development of the market had a profoundly undermining impact on native cultures.[184]

Economy, labour and the transformation of the native

The economic development of the mandate territories, once established as the guiding principle of mandate administration, possessed both international and local dimensions that were closely interrelated. At the broader, international level, the primacy of the economy was made explicit by a set of debates – regarding free trade and the mandates – that focused on the status of colonialism within the international economic system itself. Simply, colonialism was seen as both inefficient economically and destabilizing politically on account of its inhibition of free trade. Colonial powers established monopolies over the trade of their colonies, imposing severe restrictions on the ability of other nations to deal with these colonies, in terms either of procuring raw materials or opening markets. It was well recognized that these monopolies exacerbated international tensions and increased militarism.

---

[182] The promotion of 'efficient communities' was a major preoccupation of the Mandate System. Wright, *Mandates*, p. 231.

[183] These themes are made most explicit in the comments of d'Andrade in the PMC. d'Andrade was opposed to any protection being given to native cultures, even in mandate territories that had mixed populations of natives and European settlers. For d'Andrade, the 'ideal is the slow, unforced assimilation of weak or inferior communities by strong or more developed communities'. *Ibid.*, p. 233 (quoting d'Andrade). Furthermore, d'Andrade argued, the focus of the Mandate System was to be on the development of individuals, rather than communities; the market enabled individuals to emerge and escape the confines of their communities. See *ibid.*

[184] D'Andrade proved to be right; the absorption of native labour into the modern economy led to the phenomenon of detribalization observed by the PMC in relation, for example, to Papua New Guinea. See *Permanent Mandates Commission, Minutes of the Twenty-Seventh Session*, League of Nations Doc. C.251.M.123 1935 VI at 26–29 (1935).

It was partly for this reason that Wilson at Versailles had been vehement in stipulating that an 'open door policy' had to be provided for and secured within the terms of the mandates.[185] For the United States, the 'open door policy' was extremely important to ensure access to the oil deposits of the Middle East, which were to be subjected to French and British mandates. The League's failure to reach agreement on this matter was decisive in the final refusal of the United States to be party to the League.[186] Consequently, the mandate territories, like the colonies before them, were essentially integrated into the economic structures of the mandatory itself.

At the local level, the duty, as Lugard characterized it, to develop mandate territories required large infrastructure projects. The compelling need for 'arterial railways, with harbours and telegraphs, the public buildings and houses for staff',[187] in Lugard's words, 'justified any sacrifice'.[188] These public works further assisted in eliminating the slave trade and inter-tribal warfare; at the same time, they also expanded markets.[189]

This focus on economic development and efficiency had a radical effect on colonial policies in general; more particularly, it led colonial powers to view natives in terms of the labour and economic wealth they represented. Simply put, the native was no longer merely to be conquered and dispossessed; rather, he was to be made more productive. The link between the mandate provisions and this larger goal is made clear by Wright in his clear-sighted discussion of the link between humanitarianism and new perceptions of economic efficiency. Wright noted:

---

[185] Wilson's Third Point called for '[t]he removal, so far as possible, of all economic barriers and the establishment of an equality of trade conditions among all nations consenting to the peace and associating themselves for its maintenance'. President Woodrow Wilson, 'The Fourteen Points' (8 January 1918), reprinted in Cranston, *The Story of Woodrow Wilson*, p. 461. See also Wright, *Mandates*, p. 29; Grovogui, *Sovereigns*, pp. 129–130.

[186] See Wright, *Mandates*, pp. 48–56. The United States sought to deal with this problem simply by negotiating bilateral treaties enabling access to the mandatory territories.

[187] *PMC, Seventh Session*, p. 195.

[188] *Ibid.*

[189] Lugard also mentions the importance of private enterprise and capital: 'The plantation owner and the settler introduce new forms of culture of great value, such as coffee, cocoa, sisal and improved varieties of tobacco, cotton, sugar-cane etc.' Lugard points out as well that these enterprises are furthered by government infrastructure projects. *Ibid.*

[I]t began to be seen that the native was an important economic asset. Without his labor the territory could not produce. Thus the ablest administrators like Sir Frederick Lugard in Nigeria began to study the native and cater not only to his material but to his psychological welfare with highly gratifying economic results. Everywhere the devastating and uneconomic effects of trade spirits and firearms among the natives came to be recognized and their importation controlled. In some parts of Africa, especially the west coast, the more fundamental problems of an equitable land system and a liberal and humane labor policy were studied and in a measure solved.[190]

No longer were the formalist rules of positivism or the simple expedient of massacring the natives seen as adequate responses to colonial problems. Rather, a new regime of production came into being and proceeded on the basis of a new set of moral principles – liberalism and humanity – that established a new set of goals and objects as essential for its realization. This preoccupation with labour gave rise to a whole series of related issues that the League explored in detail. For example, complicated questions emerged as to whether natives were in fact capable of work and whether the reduction in native populations was due to disease or work.[191] Other issues included the question of the sacrifices required of natives in order to promote essential economic growth for the private sector.[192]

It was precisely these studies, however, that gave the pragmatist project, which called for empirical and interdisciplinary studies, a special significance here. Once the broad goal of native productivity had been identified, these technologies could be employed to achieve the desired results. The PMC, by monitoring the progress of labour policies in different mandate territories, was in a better position to develop appropriate standards that were all the more effective precisely because they were empirically based[193] and because they could take into account

---

[190] Wright, Mandates, p. 10.

[191] Labour questions were the central concern of the International Labour Office (ILO), which was also established by the Peace Conference of 1919. See generally James T. Shotwell (ed.), The Origins of the International Labor Organization (2 vols., New York: Columbia University Press, 1934), I. Some coordination existed between the ILO and the Mandate System. See Wright, Mandates, pp. 127, 140–141, 583. On how the ILO characterized the 'primitive', see generally Chris Tennant, 'Indigenous Peoples, International Institutions, and the International Legal Literature from 1945–1993', (1994) 16 Human Rights Quarterly 1.

[192] PMC, Sixth Session, p. 47.

[193] The PMC therefore sought more and better knowledge about how labour productivity could be assessed and properly utilised. Hence it was important, as the Portuguese government representative states,

so many different aspects of the problem, such as the physical capacity of the natives, their moral well being, their psychology and their vulnerability to disease. All of these initiatives helped devise legislation designed to make the natives more productive.[194]

'From the material side the natives' main assets are labor and land',[195] asserted Wright. And it was through all these initiatives focusing on native labour that the native was linked to the larger international economic system that was now coming into existence and that connected the native with economy, progress and capitalism.

The emergence of labour as a conceptual category was also important because of its broader implications for policy formulation. First, the analysis of labour could proceed on the assumption of universality:

The law of labor is a law of nature, which no one should be allowed to evade. And if this is true of organised and highly developed societies, the same must be admitted for peoples on the road to civilization and for countries which are on the threshold of development.[196]

Labour thus served the same purpose within the mandate scheme as the 'universal human being' postulated by Vitoria. It suggested that the discipline of economics being applied to the mandates in turn was universally valid, embodying a set of processes by which natives could be civilized.[197] Further, labour was connected so intimately with the physical existence of the native that it provided the League with a means of entering into the very being of the native, of disciplining and civilizing him. The latent capacity of the native to enter the universal realm of progress and modernity could be furthered precisely by using his labour to further economic development. The native and his surroundings were thus rendered in economic terms: economics and its related complex of concepts provided the vocabulary by which the essential

that an effort should be made to compile the fullest possible statistics, in order to ascertain what contribution the people may, without risk, be expected to make to the work of the community. These statistics should show not merely the number of natives but also particulars of their physical powers, customs and psychology.   ('Draft Convention on Slavery', p. 1542)
    The Portuguese government stressed that the relevant information was unavailable, and that the ILO should be given the task of compiling all of it. *Ibid.*
[194] These ideas are all to be found, for example, in the reply of the Portuguese government relating to the drafting of a convention on slavery. *Ibid.*, pp. 1539–1545.
[195] Wright, *Mandates*, p. 249.   [196] *PMC, Seventh Session*, p. 201.
[197] Wright, *Mandates*, pp. 252–254.

features common to all mandates could be both identified and then integrated into a programme of reform.

While labour was central to economic development, the problem remained of reconciling development policy with the promotion of native well being: a central goal, after all, of the Mandate System. Thus, for example, the PMC carefully charted the health policies adopted by mandatory powers in their respective territories and the amount spent on making improvements to health.[198] Crucially, however, health issues were discussed principally in terms of labour issues. Certain types of labour suffered from heavy mortality rates, for example.[199] The preoccupation with productivity and labour, then, was the prism through which questions of welfare in general were approached. Thus, 'colonial labour legislation [was] framed with a view to ensuring not merely the well-being of the native, but also his physical and moral development, and at the same time furthering the economic progress of the country, which is an essential condition of general prosperity'.[200]

This suggested a happy unity between welfare, on the one hand, and productivity and economic efficiency, on the other. The notion of welfare, however, became subsumed by the concern for productivity. The point was made explicit by Lugard:

It must, however, be admitted that these precautions for the welfare and increase of the native population are dictated by a utilitarian motive. The natives are regarded as the greatest 'asset' of the country because of their potential value as labourers. The same argument applies to the good treatment and good feeding of a horse or a plough-ox or to the increase of stock.[201]

'Welfare' thus meant, for example, requiring that work took place in hygienic conditions and that the PMC and the ILO[202] should collaborate in ensuring this. In this way, the new form of colonialism, based on preserving and developing the native and her territories as productive assets

---

[198] For an overview of health issues discussed by the PMC, see *ibid.*, pp. 552–554.
[199] See, e.g., *ibid.*, p. 553.   [200] 'Draft Convention on Slavery', p. 1541.
[201] *PMC, Seventh Session*, p. 196.
[202] See, e.g., *ibid.*, pp. 146–147 (discussing the report presented by the South West African Employers' Union to both the ILO and the PMC on 'Mortality in the Diamond Fields of South West Africa'). A representative of the ILO often attended PMC sessions (Mr Grimshaw in the Sixth Session), and the PMC often requested that the ILO supply certain information.

rather than exploiting and exhausting these assets, presented itself as an exemplification of humanist and liberal principles.

These reform projects, however, were accompanied by a number of ironies. European states had been especially proud of the abolition of slavery, regarding this as being among the major achievements stemming from their occupation of Africa. The mandate reaffirmed the importance of eliminating the slave trade; yet, ironically, infrastructure projects were of such central importance that the League Council permitted compulsory or forced labour for remuneration for 'essential public works and services'.[203] These took an enormous toll on native populations,[204] to the point where it became unclear as to which of these two practices – the primitive practice of slavery or the modern practice of development – had more devastating consequences.

The abolition of slavery liberated the native and enabled him to become a wage-earner. Despite the construction of the natives as economic assets, the broad ambition of the mandates to create an individualist and liberated economic man – 'economic man' as postulated by various political theorists – seemed conspicuously absent from many of the colonies. Much to the frustration of administrators such as Lugard, the natives were often indifferent to the prospect of amassing large amounts of wealth and engaging in the sort of consumer behaviour that would create large markets for goods from the colonial centre.[205] The simple fact nevertheless was that an extraordinarily powerful set of forces – the forces of international capitalist development – was transforming these societies. Not only labour, but also education and land

---

[203] This provision was included explicitly in a number of Mandate Agreements. Thus, in the Agreement for Tanganyika, for example, Article 5 reads in part:

Art. 5. The Mandatory:

(1) shall provide for the eventual emancipation of all slaves and for as speedy an elimination of domestic and other slavery as social conditions will allow;
(2) shall suppress all forms of slave trade;
(3) shall prohibit all forms of forced or compulsory labor, except essential public works and services, and then only in return for adequate remuneration . . .

The Tanganyika Mandate Agreement appears in full in Wright, *Mandates*, pp. 611–616. Similar provisions are found, for example, in the Ruanda-Urundi Mandate. See Hall, *Mandates*, pp. 353–358.

[204] See the discussion above.

[205] Thus, Van Rees noted that '[t]hey worked only so far as was indispensable for their own immediate needs, and sometimes less than was necessary for the satisfaction of those needs'. *PMC, Sixth Session*, p. 49.

reform, became a means by which native societies were transformed in such a manner as to integrate themselves into the overarching system of the market economy.[206]

Importantly, however, it was understood that change could not be imposed on the native. Rather, it was by educating the native and shaping her will that these transformations could take place most effectively and economically. Thus, '[i]n Africa and the Pacific the problem [was] to delay the economic development of the country until the native has wants which make him willing to aid voluntarily in that development'.[207] The idea, then, was to ensure that all these policies were desired and implemented by the natives themselves. New systems of disciplining the natives accompanied these new forms and ways of conceptualizing and managing native peoples.

Modernity, political institutions and native cultures

The League's ambition to promote self-government inevitably raised complex issues of mandate policy toward native cultures and political institutions, which had to be reformed if this project was to be made a reality. But this project was shaped powerfully by the fact that policies furthering economic development, as the previous section discusses, were the principal preoccupation of mandatory powers and the League itself. In two respects, then, the mandate project reproduced some of the central themes evident even in Vitoria's vision regarding the governance of non-European societies: first, barbaric customs had to be eliminated and, second, governance was to be directed at integrating the colony into the larger economic structure of the metropolitan power.

The Mandate System thus sought to extinguish certain customs. It had been decided 'in principle that certain native customs which conflict with humanitarian ideals should be abolished';[208] the natives had to be saved from the 'capricious jurisdiction of tyrannical chiefs'.[209] Those native laws that were not incompatible with civilization were to be allowed to remain in force at least for the moment.[210] Thus, while the mandatory power sought to replace native governance with modern

---

[206] Thus, in the case of education, the policy recommended by the PMC was education such that 'the native himself will be led to wish for an economic development of the region'. Wright, *Mandates*, p. 560.

[207] *Ibid.*, p. 558.

[208] Yanaghita, Note, 'The Welfare and Development of the Natives in Mandated Territories', *Permanent Mandates Commission, Annexes to the Minutes of the Third Session*, League of Nations Doc. A.19 (Annexes) 1923 VI at 282 (1923).

[209] *Ibid.*, p. 283.   [210] See *ibid.*, pp. 282–283.

political institutions in the long term, it was understood that a 'certain number of ancient customs, on which native life is founded, must
be preserved in the interests of peace in the territory'.[211] The difficulty
was that such a programme could not achieve its desired goal 'until
the natives [were] capable of distinguishing good from evil, and of comprehending the attitude of the administrators'.[212] The problem was that
the mandate peoples appeared incapable of appreciating their own best
interests, and accepted the offending custom as an integral part of their
own culture.

More particularly, native institutions and customs hindered the
project of economic development. But because the PMC recognized
that it was hardly possible to restructure these institutions radically
and immediately, they sought instead to advance the market precisely
through the partial adoption of existing native customs. Once again, the
PMC drew upon colonial experience in formulating an approach. The
concept of 'indirect rule',[213] which essentially called for the retention of
native political systems – provided that such systems served the overall
purpose of the colonial power – had been elaborated by Lugard.[214] And
within the PMC itself in the end, Lugard's view of a gradual transition of
native societies prevailed.[215] This policy decided debates as to whether
native governments should be promoted and reformed, or simply and
dramatically replaced. Yanaghita, a member of the PMC, suggested a

---

[211] *Ibid.*, p. 283.   [212] *Ibid.*

[213] Lugard is generally regarded as the authority on this subject. For his discussion of
'Methods of Ruling Native Races', see Lugard, *The Dual Mandate*, pp. 193–229. Lugard
was highly sceptical of the ability of native societies ever to acquire effective
self-government based on their own political traditions. *Ibid.*, pp. 197–198. I am
indebted to Dr Philip Darby of Melbourne University, who pointed out to me that
Lugard's ideas on self-rule emerged from his experiences in India, where he was born.

[214] For Lugard, it is clear that the native and colonial systems are not two separate,
parallel systems. Lugard remarks that
> the native chiefs are constituted as an integral part of the machinery of the
> administration. There are not two sets of rulers – British and native – working
> either separately or in co-operation, but a single Government in which the
> native chiefs have well-defined duties and an acknowledged status equally with
> British officials.   (*Ibid.*, p. 203)

[215] This is a recurring theme in the discussions of the PMC. Thus, Freire d'Andrade
argued:
> While keeping the native organisation as far as may be, it is also possible by
> degrees for the action of the native chiefs to be superseded by that of the
> administration of the Mandatory, which governs the community with the help
> of advisory or executive councils which include the principal natives, chosen
> either by the Administration or by the natives themselves.
> (*PMC, Seventh Session*, p. 201)

solution by which the native chieftains would be allowed to perform certain lesser functions in ways that furthered economic development: 'Scarcely aware of the fact that their little sovereignty has been transferred to a higher group, they will assist in the work of the mandatory government and will be content with the empty title and the modest stipend.'[216]

Both native quiescence and the progress of the mandatory policy were achieved by this strategy. The basic tactic involved here, then, was the familiar one of shifting the framework in which native society operated, as a consequence of which native procedures and practices became either purely ceremonial and ritualistic or a means by which they undermined the natives' own interests.[217] The mechanisms by which native authority was transformed and integrated into the larger political structures created by the Mandate System are revealed in the prosaic reports to the PMC by the mandatory for Tanganyika.

The Commission noted with satisfaction that the mandatory power, with the agreement of the chiefs as well as of their tribesmen, abolished the tribute and the compulsory labour formerly exacted by the chiefs, replacing them with a poll tax, part of whose proceeds were paid into the Native Treasuries from which the chiefs received a salary. The Commission also viewed approvingly the Administration's proposal to make it a legal offence for a chief to exact or attempt to exact taxes other than those legally authorised.[218]

---

[216] *Permanent Mandates Commission, Minutes of the Third Session*, League of Nations Doc. A.19 1923 VI at 283 (1923). This echoes Lugard: 'Develop resources through the agency of the natives under European guidance, and not by direct European ownership of those tropical lands which are unsuited for European settlement.' Lugard, *The Dual Mandate*, p. 506.

[217] The relationship between the market and native political institutions was dialectic. On the one hand, these institutions could assist in furthering the market; on the other, this process in itself would bring about desirable changes in native societies and customs. We may recall here d'Andrade's view that the furtherance of economic relations would result in the emergence of the individual and that weaker societies would be assimilated or even disappear. See the discussion in n. 183.

[218] See 'Work of the Permanent Mandates Commission', (1926) 10 *League of Nations Official Journal* 1306 at 1310. The massive changes that were made to native ways of life are somewhat obscured by the polite and calmly matter-of-fact language of international administrators:

> The Commission would be glad to have full information as to the further changes in the system of native administration which are foreshadowed in the report. The Commission will learn with interest of such arrangements as may be made by [the] Government of Tanganyika to assimilate the laws applicable to the Masai tribe in the reserves in Kenya and Tanganyika, in order to bring about greater co-ordination in the administrative policy applicable to the tribe as a whole.   (*Ibid.*)

Crucially, it was through the instruments furthering economic progress that this goal, too, was achieved. New regimes of taxation served the dual purpose of raising revenues and undermining native political institutions even while using those native institutions for collection.[219] The chiefs now became part of the administrative structure of the system, a system created to further economic progress. Rather than relying exclusively on traditional authority, they now became something akin to salaried officials.[220] In addition, the undermining of these traditional structures made 'free labour' available, as natives previously had seen their occupations as intimately connected with their traditional structures. This, in turn, was crucial because it helped meet the needs of the large infrastructure projects being undertaken at the time.

It must be noted, however, that the indirect approach was not always adopted. Thus, Belgium, the mandatory for Ruanda–Urundi, was far more explicit in its interventions in traditional structures: members of the PMC noted that 'a considerable number of sub-chiefs had again had to be removed from office or dismissed – twenty-four in Ruanda and thirteen in Urundi'.[221] The PMC also wondered how the Belgians could recruit 'Bahutu' chiefs while claiming that they were following traditional practices of appointing successors from the family of the previous chiefs, who generally belonged to the 'Asatuzi' people.[222]

---

[219] Often, traditional authority structures could be undermined and, indeed, deployed far more effectively through these indirect methods than through direct abolition or suppression of the structures. For a penetrating study of this phenomenon, see generally Nicholas B. Dirks, 'From Little King to Landlord: Colonial Discourse and Colonial Rule', in Nicholas B. Dirks (ed.), *Colonialism and Culture* (Ann Arbor: University of Michigan Press, 1992), p. 175.

[220] This strategy of transforming traditional chiefs into tax collectors is also evident in discussions as to various other government structures, for example, in the PMC's examination of the Annual Report on Ruanda–Urundi for 1934. See *Permanent Mandates Commission, Minutes of the Twenty-Eighth Session*, League of Nations Doc. C.439 M.228 1935 VI at 15–21 (1935) (hereafter *PMC, 28th Session*).

[221] *Ibid.*, p. 16.

[222] *Ibid.* The broader consequences of the colonial legacy for Rwanda are explored in Gérard Prunier, *The Rwanda Crisis: History of a Genocide* (New York: Columbia University Press, 1995), pp. 27–29. Rwanda, of course, continues to be the object of the international community's attempts to demonstrate its concern by establishing new institutions, in the form of an international criminal court, to deal with Rwanda's problems. For an important critical study of this theme, which places these initiatives in an historical perspective, see Jose E. Alvarez, 'Crimes of States/ Crimes of Hate: Lessons from Rwanda', (1999) 24 *Yale Journal of International Law* 365.

The consequences of the Mandate System for mandate societies

While the concept of 'backwardness' had a number of connotations, by the inter-war period it was understood primarily in economic terms.[223] An examination of PMC debates gives some idea of the logic and implications of the system of political economy that emerged in mandate territories as a result of the policies sketched in the previous section. The infrastructure projects begun in the colonies and mandate territories during this period basically were financed by the colonies/mandates themselves. For example, the people and territory of Ruanda–Urundi paid for the large projects that were essentially designed to extract the country's resources for the principal benefit of Belgium itself.[224]

It was a commonplace colonial practice to make colonies pay for their own exploitation and conquest. As Jawaharlal Nehru points out:

Thus, India had to bear the cost of her own conquest, and then of her transfer (or sale) from the East India Company to the British Crown, and for the extension of the British Empire to Burma and elsewhere, and expeditions to Africa, Persia, etc., and for her defence against Indians themselves.[225]

Consequently, the Belgian practice in Ruanda–Urundi, in itself, also would not have been objectionable to the PMC. Nevertheless, some members of the PMC were perceptive enough to raise questions about the extent of the debt allocated to the territory. The Belgian representative was adamant, however, that 'the loans made by the territory [Ruanda–Urundi] were not beyond its means and could not be called excessive, because the country's resources, and chiefly its mineral wealth, would make it possible later on to provide for the service and redemption of the public debt'.[226] This meant, however, that more mining and more extraction had to take place.[227] This in turn, of course, required more labour and, in order to get more labour, it was necessary to undermine the native political institutions and structures, as labour had traditionally been attached to functions served within those institutions,

---

[223] According to Wright, at the time it connoted a lack of Europeanization, a lack of self-determination, and a lack of industrialization. Of these, the economic dimension was prevalent. Wright, *Mandates*, p. 584.

[224] See *PMC, 28th Session*, p. 15.

[225] Jawaharlal Nehru, *The Discovery of India* (New York: The John Day Co., 1946), p. 305.

[226] *PMC, 28th Session*, p. 15. A similar system was adopted for the financing of the phosphate mining of Nauru. See generally Weeramantry, *Nauru*.

[227] Thus, the Belgian representative noted that between 1933 and 1934 the mining for gold and cassiterite had doubled. See *ibid*.

a point which the Belgian representative made explicit.[228] A cycle now becomes apparent: the native becomes the agent of his own exploitation, constructing the infrastructure that was designed to extract his own resources; furthermore, the greater the imperative to extract these resources, the more demands were made on the native, and the greater the imperative to destroy the traditional authority structures in order to create the liberated native who then could proceed to celebrate his new-found independence in the gold mines of Ruanda.[229]

All these developments had profoundly damaging effects on the mandate populations. As colonial experts at the time noted, the market, as it was constructed in colonial societies, became the central, dominant institution within those societies, distorting and undermining all other social institutions. Thus, Furnivall endorsed the view of J. H. Boeke, another colonial expert, that in tropical economies the impact of capitalist development was far more profound than in Western societies, where such development was relatively endogenous and gradual. In the tropical economies, by contrast, where capitalism was imposed from above,

there is materialism, rationalism, individualism, and a concentration on economic ends far more complete and absolute than in homogeneous western lands; a total absorption in the exchange and market; a capitalist structure, with the business concern as subject, far more typical of capitalism than one can imagine in the so-called 'capitalist' countries . . .[230]

Economic development was the supreme system to which all other social institutions were subordinated and that all other institutions had to serve. As Furnivall powerfully argues, once established within

---

[228] The Belgian representative saw this point clearly: he noted, in relation to Rwanda, that 'if the prestige of the chiefs and sub-chiefs were not to be destroyed, the system of forced tribute, in the provisions of labour, could not be touched except with the greatest circumspection'. See *ibid.*, p. 28.

[229] As Rodney notes, the infrastructure projects that were paid for by this extraction were not designed to meet the needs of the African peoples themselves. Rather, '[a]ll roads and railways led down to the sea. They were built to extract gold or manganese or coffee or cotton. They were built to make business possible for the timber companies, trading companies, and agricultural concession firms.' Rodney, *How Europe Underdeveloped Africa*, p. 209. For telling studies of the impact of colonial policies on contemporary African states, see Makau wa Mutua, 'Why Redraw the Map of Africa?: A Moral and Legal Inquiry', (1995) 16 *Michigan Journal of International Law* 1113; Obiora Chinedu Okafor, *Re-Defining Legitimate Statehood: International Law and State Fragmentation in Africa* (Boston: Martinus Nijhoff, 2000).

[230] Furnivall, *Colonial Policy*, p. 312 (quoting J. H. Boeke, *The Structure of Netherlands Indian Economy*, New York: International Secretariat, Institute of Pacific Relations, 1942, p. 412).

a colony, economic forces had a profound impact on native society that hardly could be reversed by the actions of the colonial government, no matter how solicitous and well intended. Social relations were transformed purely into economic relations, political authority became a means by which the market could be furthered, and with the dissolution of the traditional checks on behaviour 'there remain[ed] no embodiment of social will or representative of public welfare to control the economic forces which the impact of the West release[d]'.[231] Political advancement and independence hardly became a reality in these circumstances.

It was not only the systems of governance that were dictated by economic goals. The old model of colonialism suggested that economic progress was an end in itself and that welfare would be achieved by progress. The new model suggested instead that active state intervention was necessary to achieve welfare.[232] Native welfare was a principal preoccupation of enlightened colonial administrators and the PMC. And yet, as Lugard's own comments suggest, such concerns were entirely utilitarian: labour was an asset that had to be preserved.[233] Given the decisive importance of economic development to the whole project of colonial governance, it followed that economic development almost inevitably distorted the policies intended to protect native welfare. Thus, as Furnivall points out: '[T]he services intended to furnish the necessary protection function[ed] mainly to make production more efficient, and the services intended to promote welfare directly by improving health and education [had] a similar result; though designed as instruments of human welfare they [were] perverted into instruments of economic progress.'[234]

Economic development is crucial to the well being of any society. In this situation, however, economic progress was equated with the furtherance of a system of economic inequalities specific to colonialism. Analysing colonial economies in the period more generally, Abernethy soberly concludes that colonial economies were export oriented and specialised in the production of a few commodities. Furthermore, the systematic integration of the colonial economy into the metropolitan economy on disadvantageous terms created even greater ties of dependency and vulnerability in the colony.[235] In addition, of course, the native

---

[231] Ibid., p. 298. Furnivall's detailed and lucid exposition of the effect of individualism and market forces on traditional societies is all the more powerful for its notable lack of sentimentality or nostalgia for vanishing village communities. Ibid., pp. 297–299.

[232] See Furnivall, Colonial Policy, p. 288.

[233] See the discussion above.   [234] Furnivall, Colonial Policy, p. 410.

[235] As Abernethy soberly states: 'Because of such policies, the typical colony's economic prospects were unusually dependent on forces operating outside its boundaries and beyond its control.' Abernethy, The Dynamics, p. 114.

peoples hardly received the real value of the raw materials extracted from their territories.[236]

But these were not the only reasons why economic development had a devastating impact on native societies. Rather, the dominance of the economic, as discussed, profoundly altered the whole system of legitimacy, of authority, and of the meaning that held mandate societies together. The doctor and anthropologist W. H. R. Rivers, intent on identifying the cause of the massive population declines in Melanesia that accompanied the introduction of civilization to that region, argued that

> [i]t may at first sight seem far-fetched to suppose that such a factor as loss of interest in life could ever produce the dying out of a people, but my own observations have led me to the conclusion that its influence is so great that it can hardly be overrated.[237]

My argument has been that the economic and social policies actively endorsed by the PMC had profoundly damaging consequences for mandate peoples. It also must be noted, however, that in many instances, the PMC was unable to check abuses of the system by the mandatory powers themselves. Native cultures, as I have argued earlier, possessed no inherent validity for the PMC, but the PMC did recognize the importance of at least getting some impression of native views and responses. The Mandate System, however, failed to provide any formal mechanism by which the native could communicate meaningfully with, and represent herself before, the PMC. In basic terms, the native was spoken for by the mandatory power. Initially, Smuts argued for some native

---

[236] See generally Woolf, *Empire*; Rodney, *How Europe Underdeveloped Africa*. The topic of the economics of imperialism raises very complex questions. For a recent account see, e.g., B. R. Tomlinson, 'Economics and Empire: The Periphery and the Imperial Economy', in Andrew Porter (ed.), *The Oxford History of the British Empire: The Nineteenth Century* (Oxford: Oxford University Press, 1999), pp. 53–75. But focusing on a specific Mandate Territory, it was estimated that the three administering trustee powers (Australia, New Zealand and the United Kingdom) made a profit of about 165 million pounds from the exploitation of Nauru's phosphates while Nauru was a mandate and then a trust territory. For a detailed study of accounting issues relating to Nauru, see Weeramantry, *Nauru*, chapters 13, 16. Some idea of the scale of exploitation is suggested by the fact that in 1928, the people of Nauru received 2.6 per cent of the value of their phosphates. *Ibid.* at p. 235. It is likely that studies of the economies of other mandate territories such as Rwanda–Urundi would reveal similar, if not worse levels of exploitation and profiteering by the mandate power.

[237] W. H. R. Rivers, 'The Psychological Factor', in W. H. R. Rivers (ed.), *Essays on the Depopulation of Melanesia* (Cambridge: Cambridge University Press, 1922), pp. 84, 94. Rivers' work was discussed by the PMC. He is a central character in Pat Barker's superb *Regeneration* trilogy of novels – *Regeneration*, *The Eye in the Door* and *The Ghost Road*.

representation, at least to the extent of consulting the natives as to whether or not they were agreeable to the mandatory chosen. Only the advanced mandates participated in this process. For the rest, Smuts argued, consultation was simply inapplicable, on account of the backwardness of the peoples concerned.[238] The PMC attempted to establish a system by which petitions from the natives themselves could be received. The subject of petitions was treated, however, as a delicate one, liable to generate great tensions.[239] The compromise formula, arrived at in 1923, permitted the PMC to receive petitions from inhabitants of the mandate territories, but only through the mandatory, which appended comments prior to sending the petitions on to the Commission.[240]

The peoples of the mandate territories inevitably resisted the profound changes being made to their societies and ways of life. The people of Nauru, for instance, attempted in a number of different ways to prevent the phosphate mining that was destroying their island. Tragically, however, given the various limitations of the petition system, the actions of these peoples, at least at the international level, became largely what they were represented to be by the mandatory powers.

The ironies are made clear by the 1922 Bondelzwart riots in South-West Africa, which – certain members of the PMC observed with the restraint of seasoned diplomats – could be attributed to 'native grievances arising in part from legislative and administrative action in behalf of the white settlers'.[241]

Political and procedural factors – the PMC's practice of giving the mandatory large discretion when the issues involved were those relating to security – largely precluded PMC criticism of the measures adopted.[242] Indeed, the Commission, as reported by Wright, partially commended the South African response '"in taking prompt and effective steps to uphold government authority and to prevent the spread of disaffection", though because of the absence of native evidence no opinion could be expressed, "whether these operations were conducted with needless severity".'[243]

Within this system, native discontent could express itself only as rebellion, the meaning of which was interpreted and established by the League. The PMC response to the rebellion, however, simply confirmed

---

[238] See Smuts, 'The League of Nations', p. 28.   [239] Wright, *Mandates*, pp. 169–178.
[240] *Ibid.*, p. 169.   [241] *Ibid.*, p. 209.   [242] *Ibid.*
[243] Wright, *Mandates*, p. 198 (citing the PMC's statement from the Third Session).

the existence of grievances such as the lack of native participation in the Mandate System – 'the absence of native evidence',[244] to use Wright's phrase – which seems to have initiated rebellion in the first place. The meaning of this action is lost – assimilated into considerations of how the PMC should view situations where the mandate power ostensibly was acting in emergency conditions.

In the final analysis, the ambiguities of the mandate experiment were evident even to the most ardent supporters of the system who, while recognizing its contribution toward creating a new, universal order, could not ignore the underlying problem of pluralities that this assertion of a universal order attempted to obliterate. Did the Mandate System achieve the results it sought? Wright poses this question, and despite adopting his characteristically thorough and multiperspective approach – which includes assessing the scheme by using the 'judicial method', the 'technological method', the 'statistical method', and so forth – he offers no clear answer.[245] Instead, much of Wright's discussion is haunted by an awareness of the fact that the statistics, which he so assiduously compiled, could acquire a completely different significance in a different cultural setting. Does 'economic development' mean that the welfare of the natives is in fact being protected? What do 'wage levels' mean in a society where a subsistence economy prevails?[246] The doubts that Wright harboured were felt by members of the PMC, who nevertheless occasionally made bold assertions such as '[I]f the native races are dying out, it [is] clear that their moral and material welfare was being sacrificed'.[247] The irony of prescribing such standards is not lost on Wright, who queries the extent to which the mandates have advanced 'Security', 'Order and Justice', and 'Freedom' within the mandates.[248]

From the natives' point of view, freedom meant being let alone, an aspiration that seems doomed to disappointment in the 'strenuous

---

[244] Ibid.

[245] See ibid., p. 541. The difficulties that he encounters are suggested by Wright in his statement that '[b]ecause of the difficulties of statistical analysis and the presence of many imponderable factors, perhaps the subjective judgment of competent historians and observers in the areas is as reliable as the results of more refined methods'. Ibid., p. 549.

[246] See generally Wright, Mandates, pp. 540–581 (discussing achievements of the Mandate System).

[247] The comment was made by Rappard of the PMC. Wright, Mandates, p. 550.

[248] See ibid., pp. 563–564 (discussing Security), 564–568 (discussing Freedom) and 576–579 (discussing Order and Justice).

conditions of the modern world'.[249] 'Economic penetration can hardly be stopped, and if the native cannot adjust his own culture to meet it, that culture is likely to disappear altogether.'[250] Economic progress, then, is inescapable and culture must succumb accordingly. Wright reiterates: 'From the native point of view, security means continuance of traditional customs, and these are frequently opposed to economic and political development.'[251]

This reveals the double irony of the whole Mandate System: in seeking to liberate the mandate peoples from the 'strenuous conditions of the modern world',[252] the system instead entraps the mandate peoples within those conditions. The peculiar cycle thus creates a situation whereby international institutions present themselves as a solution to a problem of which they are an integral part. Such a situation is very much part of contemporary international relations.

This section has attempted to formulate a critique of the policies adopted and prescribed by the PMC. It is clear, however, that the PMC did often present what it perceived as a progressive and humane version of economic development, and that it was thwarted constantly in its efforts by intransigent mandatory powers that the PMC could not sanction effectively. Further, another question remains: whether the members of the PMC were acting in bad faith and deliberately set about the task of creating a new and better form of colonialism that complied with the ethos of the times and was all the more insidious precisely because it now expressed itself in the language of liberalism and humanism, the language of trusteeship. I cannot answer this question. But I am acutely aware of the care and conscientiousness with which some members of the PMC performed their duties, as they perceived them, and these members' clear-sighted understanding of the realities of what was occurring in many mandate territories such as Nauru. Indeed, the analysis of some members of the PMC was vital in assembling the case that Nauru subsequently made.[253] Perhaps, then, the members of the PMC simply could not escape the colonial assumptions – regarding the natives and the character of economic relations between the colony and the metropolis – that were powerfully held and were reformulated rather than extinguished by the model of trusteeship.

---

[249] League of Nations Covenant, Article 22, para. 1.
[250] Wright, *Mandates*, p. 567.   [251] *Ibid.*, p. 563.
[252] League of Nations Covenant, Article 22, para. 1.
[253] See Weeramantry, *Nauru*, pp. 101–122.

The mandate and the dissolution of sovereignty

Sovereignty, government and economic power

Sovereignty, in its most basic sense, is associated with power. The burden of my argument, however, is that the transference of sovereignty to non-European peoples, as undertaken by the Mandate System, was simultaneous with, and indeed inseparable from, the creation of new systems of subordination and control administered by international institutions. The relationship between 'sovereignty' and 'government' is key to understanding how this subordination was effected.

Formal sovereignty is based on the existence of effective government; and government, as conceptualised with regard to the mandate territories, was created principally for the purpose of furthering a particular system of political economy that integrated the mandate territory into the metropolitan power, to the disadvantage of the former. This was achieved by a technique of rendering the whole of mandate society in economic terms, by a process that might be called the 'economization' of government. These developments correspond closely with what Foucault, to whose work my discussion is indebted, analyses as a new and specific form of government that is based, not on the institutions of 'sovereignty', but on economy: '[T]he very essence of government – that is, the art of exercising power in the form of economy – is to have as its main objective that which we are today accustomed to call "the economy".'[254]

[254] Michel Foucault, 'Governmentality', in Graham Burchell, Colin Gordon and Peter Miller (eds.), *The Foucault Effect: Studies in Governmentality* (Chicago: University of Chicago Press, 1991), pp. 87, 92. Foucault's analysis of the crucial link between the emergence of political economy and the modern art of 'government' – as opposed to the earlier preoccupation with government, which had focused on relations of sovereignty – is especially illuminating for an understanding of the Mandate System. Foucault argues:

> The new science called political economy arises out of the perception of new networks of continuous and multiple relations between population, territory and wealth; and this is accompanied by the formation of a type of intervention characteristic of government, namely intervention in the field of economy and population. In other words, the transition which takes place in the eighteenth century from an art of government to a political science, from a regime dominated by structures of sovereignty to one ruled by techniques of government, turns on the theme of population and hence also on the birth of political economy.   (*Ibid.*, p. 101)

My reading of Foucault is indebted to Duncan Kennedy's analysis of the relationship between Foucault's work and that of the legal realist Robert Hale. See Duncan Kennedy, *Sexy Dressing Etc.: Essays on the Power and Politics of Cultural Identity* (Cambridge, MA: Harvard University Press, 1993), pp. 83–125.

In these terms, the Mandate System transferred only sovereignty to mandate peoples, not the powers associated with 'government' in the form of control over the political economy. Paradoxically, this denial of power took place even as the promotion of 'self-government' was officially proclaimed to be a central goal of the Mandate System. Rather, for mandate peoples, the acquisition of sovereignty, of political powers, was accompanied by the simultaneous withdrawal and transference of economic power to external forces.

The Mandate System, having transformed the native and her territory into an economic entity, proceeded to establish an intricate and far-reaching network of economic relationships that connected native labour in a mandate territory to a much broader network of economic activities extending from the native's village to the territory as a whole, to the metropolis and, finally, to the international economy. Integrated in this way into a dense and comprehensive network of economic power, the native – and, indeed, the entire mandate society – became vulnerable to the specific dynamics of the network. Given that the mandate territory was inserted into this system in a subordinate role, its operation inevitably undermined the interests of mandate peoples.

Pragmatic international law played a crucial role in establishing and sustaining this system. The complex economic network established by the Mandate System was supported and enabled by a comprehensive and flexible legal/administrative system, which corresponded with and undergirded the economic links.[255] A legal system – a new international law – now expanded to comprise norms, policies, standards, regulations and treaty provisions. It was a system that extended from the mundane, quotidian procedures of collecting information for the drafting of labour legislation in specific mandate territories to the great proclamations regarding the sacred trust of civilization made in Article 22, the foundation of the entire Mandate System itself.

Nor was the distinction between formal sovereignty and economic power lost on international lawyers of the inter-war period. As the PCIJ itself asserted in the *Austria–Germany Customs* Case[256] when elaborating on the concept of sovereign independence:

---

[255] An examination of the 'List of Questions which the Permanent Mandates Commission Desires Should be Dealt With in the Annual Reports of the Mandatory Powers' suggests all these links. See 'List of Questions', pp. 1322–1328.

[256] *Advisory Opinion No. 41, Customs Régime Between Germany and Austria*, 1931 PCIJ Ser. A/B, No. 41 (5 September).

[T]he independence of Austria, according to Article 88 of the Treaty of St. Germain, must be understood to mean the continued existence of Austria with her present frontiers as a separate State with sole right of decision in all matters *economic*, political, *financial* or other with the result that that independence is violated, as soon as there is any violation thereof, either in the *economic*, political, or any other field, these different aspects of independence being in practice one and indivisible.[257]

Similarly, in the *Lighthouses in Crete and Samos* Case,[258] the distinction between sovereignty and government is elaborated:

[S]overeignty presupposes not an abstract right, devoid of any concrete manifestation, but on the contrary, the continuous and pacific exercise of the governmental functions and activities which *are its constituent and essential element.*[259]

The relationships among sovereignty, government and economy have also been the subject of Foucault's analysis on the changing character of 'government'. For Foucault, this is evident in the shift from what he terms 'the constants of sovereignty' to 'the problem of choices of government', which once again he describes in terms that are recognizable from an analysis of the Mandate System. What Foucault describes is 'the movement that brings about the emergence of population as datum, as a field of intervention and as an objective of governmental techniques, and the process which isolates the economy as a specific sector of reality, and political economy as the science and the technique of intervention of the government in that field of reality'.[260]

It is in the Mandate System that we see international law developing a formidable set of institutions and legal techniques for addressing the issue of government, of the political economy of a non-sovereign entity. The crucial point is that, unlike the European state, which is Foucault's subject, the specific system of political economy that directs and shapes the government in these territories is a colonial political economy. This is evident from a study of the operation of the Mandate System and

---

[257] *Ibid.*, p. 12 (emphasis added). For a discussion of the meaning of economic independence in the inter-war period, see Weeramantry, *Nauru*, p. 323.

[258] *Lighthouses in Crete and Samos (France v. Greece)*, 1937 PCIJ Ser. A/B, No. 71 (8 October).

[259] *Ibid.*, p. 46 (separate opinion of Judge Séfériadès) (emphasis in original). Notably, Séfériadès was paraphrasing Max Huber in making this argument for his own purposes.

[260] Foucault, 'Governmentality', p. 102. While noting this shift, Foucault also points out that 'sovereignty is far from being eliminated by the emergence of a new art of government . . . on the contrary, the problem of sovereignty is made more acute than ever'. *Ibid.*, p. 101.

the writings of Lugard and other colonial administrators. The inequalities resulting from this system are analysed by Hobson and Woolf in the early twentieth century and have been the subject of ongoing work on the part of more recent scholars, such as André Gunder Frank[261] and Samir Amin.[262] Consequently, it was precisely the mandate peoples' ability to exercise 'governmental functions' effectively that was undermined profoundly by the type of government being created in mandate territories, even as these peoples were being guided ostensibly toward self-government and sovereignty.[263] These developments resulted in the instantiation of pervasive and structural economic inequalities in a system that claimed to provide formal political equality.

Sovereignty and the science of colonial administration

The Mandate System established novel forms of control by creating, in effect, new sciences of social and economic development that precluded the articulation or promotion of alternative systems of society or political economy within the mandate territories. In its efforts to promote self-government, supervise the mandate power and ensure the progress of the mandate territory, the PMC collected an unprecedented volume of information. The PMC dealt not only with conventional matters regarding legal status, but also with population, health, education, land tenure, wages, labour matters, external revenue, order and justice, public works and services.[264] The information gathered enabled Wright to provide comparative statistics on matters such as birth rates,[265] per capita

---

[261] See generally André Gunder Frank, *The Underdevelopment of Development* (Stockholm: Bethany Books, 1991). A study of the discussions and debates of the PMC lends considerable credibility to the work of dependency theorists, since those discussions make it clear that what is being created is a subordinate economy.

[262] See generally Samir Amin, *Imperialism and Unequal Development* (New York: Monthly Review Press, 1977).

[263] The creation and persistence of structured economic inequalities in a system of formal political equality is a concern of legal realist analysis that derives from Marx. See, e.g., Robert L. Hale, 'Coercion and Distribution in a Supposedly Non-Coercive State', in William W. Fisher, III, Morton J. Horwitz and Thomas Reed (eds.), *American Legal Realism* (New York: Oxford University Press, 1993), pp. 101, 108. The complex relationship between formal equality and racial and economic subordination is the subject of the pioneering work done by Critical Race Theory scholars.

[264] These are only some of the matters included in his Table of contents that Wright chooses to discuss on the basis of the available information provided. See Wright, *Mandates*, pp. xi–xiii.

[265] 'French investigations in Togoland indicate that each woman on an average gave birth to 4.03 children during her life, of which 3.02 live after fifteen years.' *Ibid.*,

health expenditures[266] and amounts spent on agriculture in different mandatories. A study of these details, the different types of information sought and the techniques by which this information could be manipulated attests to the Mandate System's aspiration to know the most intimate details of native life. The amount and classes of information collected from the mandates were massive, and expanded as the system developed over the years. In an annex headed *List of Questions Which the Permanent Mandates Commission Desires Should Be Dealt With in the Annual Reports of the Mandatory Powers*, the headings include: Status of the Territory; Status of the Native Inhabitants of the Territory; International Relations; General Administration; Public Finance; Direct Taxes; Indirect Taxes; Trade Statistics; Judicial Organisation; Police; Defence of the Territory; Arms and Ammunition; Social, Moral, and Material Condition of the Natives; Conditions and Regulation of Labour; Liberty of Conscience and Worship; Education; Public Health; Land Tenure; Forests; Mines; and Population.[267] The mandatories are presented with a number of more detailed questions under each of the headings; thus, under the heading Conditions and Regulation of Labour, the mandatories are presented with seventeen further questions.[268]

Knowledge was thus gathered from the furthest peripheries and consolidated by the League; it then was subjected to a number of interpretive and disciplinary processes, including the sciences of administration (through the PMC), legislation (through the Council), and adjudication (through the PMC in some limited capacity, in that it made comments as to whether or not the terms of the mandate were being fulfilled; and, more explicitly, through the PCIJ). This knowledge was assimilated and synthesised by the most eminent colonial administrators available. Thus, the Hon. W. Ormsby-Gore stated of the constituents of the PMC:

Its members must possess all knowledge – native law, native religion, native psychology, native customs, methods of combating disease and vice, understanding

p. 553. This preoccupation with understanding population in different ways exemplifies Foucault's point that population is a central concern of the government of political economy.

[266] '$0.07 in Togoland, $0.06 in Cameroons and West Africa, and $0.04 in Equatorial Africa'. *Ibid.*

[267] 'List of Questions', pp. 1322–1329.

[268] *Ibid.* And in turn each question can be quite detailed, e.g.: 'Does the local supply of labour, in quantity, physical powers of resistance and aptitude for industrial and agricultural work conducted on modern lines appear to indicate that it is adequate, as far as can be foreseen, for the economic development of the territory?' *Ibid.* at p. 1325.

of climate, geographical and economic conditions, principles of colonial administration throughout the world from the beginning.[269]

As a consequence of all this, for the purposes of the mandate, the
natives existed more vividly in Geneva, where all this information was
gathered and processed, than they did in the mandate territories themselves.[270] The use of these new techniques of monitoring and management created an entirely new science. As Wright again, very perceptively,
notes: 'Nothing less than a science of colonial administration based on a
deductive and experimental method was here contemplated. The discovery by such a method and verification by practical application of useful
principles and standards is probably the most important contribution
which the mandates system could make.'[271]

The mandate territories, then, provide both the information that is
synthesised into scientific models by the PMC and the laboratory in
which this new science may perfect itself through its 'deductive and
experimental method'. The science created out of these processes transcends the particularities and imperfections of specific types of colonial
administration in particular territories.

Economics was crucial for this project, for it was understood to
be a universal discipline that transcended the cultural particularities
of specific mandate territories. This was vital to the operation of the
mandate, which otherwise lacked the means of making sensible com-
parisons between Papua New Guinea in the Indian/Pacific region and
the Cameroons in Africa. It was only if Papua New Guinea and the
Cameroons, with their radically different cultures, could nevertheless
be assessed by the same criteria – economic criteria – that it appeared
intellectually valid to derive from the experiences of Papua New Guinea
a set of policies and principles that could be applied in some way to the
Cameroons. There was an important complement, then, between the
economization of government, which transformed all aspects of mandate territories into economic phenomena, and the emergence of this
science, which then could theorise and extrapolate upon the entities so
homogenised through the single discipline of economics.

The Mandate System is thus crucial for the emergence of this new
science: without its centralised authority, scholars concerned with

---

[269] Wright, *Mandates*, p. 137 (quoting Ormsby-Gore, *The League of Nations Starts, An Outline
by Its Organisers*, London: Macmillan & Co. Ltd., 1920, p. 119).
[270] For an example of how this operated to the disadvantage of the natives, see
Weeramantry, *Nauru*, pp. 172–173.
[271] Wright, *Mandates*, p. 229.

colonial problems had to rely on the cruder science of 'comparative colonial administration'.[272] Seen in this way, the Mandate System enabled the deployment of other disciplinary techniques – derived from psychology, for example – in the management of colonial relations; indeed, it created new disciplines. Further, these new and more powerful claims to create a science – Wright continuously uses the term – is crucial for the legitimization of this new, extraordinarily intrusive form of administration.

The invocation of 'science' and the involvement of the League provide a new justification and guise for colonial practices. The transformation of backward territories is no longer undertaken by colonial powers seeking to further their own interests. Rather, the civilizing mission is furthered by a disinterested body of colonial experts intent on acquiring detailed knowledge of native societies and economies, not for the purpose of exploiting them but to enable the formulation of the policies necessary to ensure the proper development of native peoples. Objective, disinterested scientific knowledge, then, justifies these practices.

This universal science enabled the League to deal with A, B and C mandates, with the British administration of Middle Eastern territories, on the one hand, and the French administration of the Cameroons, on the other. Each of these cases now merely exemplified aspects of, and was incorporated into, the larger science of administration by the League. Once this dynamic was established, the peculiarities of each territory and method of administration strengthened rather than disrupted the master science and the model of the nation-state it produced. Each peculiarity now represented an 'experiment' assimilated into the Mandate System that enabled it to adjust and perfect the League's model of the non-European nation-state and the science that created it. It also followed that if particular native practices were to justify themselves now, they had to do so against the massive system of scientific truth constructed by the mandates, which could now make new and more powerful claims to being universal.[273] We might discern here the origins of the modern science of 'development'.

---

[272] An example of this would be Furnivall's work that compared different colonies in South East Asia. See, e.g., Furnivall, *Colonial Policy*.

[273] See Michel Foucault, 'Two Lectures', in Michel Foucault, Colin Gordon (ed.), Colin Gordon *et al.* (trans.), *Power/Knowledge* (New York: Pantheon Books, 1980), pp. 78, 93. ('There can be no possible exercise of power without a certain economy of discourses of truth which operates through and on the basis of this association. We are subjected to the production of truth through power and we cannot exercise power except through the production of truth.')

The League's system of gathering, processing and interpreting information by an apparatus consisting of a carefully administered and synchronised set of bureaucrats and adjudicators is significant not only because it articulates a new version of the non-European state, but because it provides a function and justification for this new form of international institution. Once the master science of colonial administration is established, the Mandate System legitimizes itself by monitoring the progress of these backward territories, by devising ever more sophisticated ways of detecting deficiencies and by formulating new standards by way of remedy.[274] Basically, then, the continuing existence of these institutions is dependent on the existence of such deficiencies, which in turn are created by these institutions in more sophisticated ways. This science of colonial administration represents a formidable type of power simply because it defines, in compelling, detailed and ostensibly objective and scientific terms, the normal or desirable goal that all peoples should seek. It prescribes, further, elaborate techniques of achieving this desired state. This is what might be termed, once again following Foucault, 'disciplinary governance', by which society is controlled, not through the enforcement of the laws but rather by defining the normal, the standard and the truth against which deviations are identified and then remedied.[275]

Sovereignty and native will

The mandate project of transforming native peoples and territories was intimately linked with a further technique that was self-consciously developed and deployed by the Mandate System. Desirable native behaviour was to be promoted, not through physical punishment but through persuasion. The mandate rendered the native visible and amenable to the mechanisms and techniques of administration through the vocabulary of birth rates, productivity, wage rates and so forth. It was the ambition of the PMC to know the native in every detail: the native was to be studied in terms of psychology as well as 'his physical and

---

[274] I use this terminology and formulate this analysis in my thesis, Antony Anghie, 'Creating the Nation-State: Colonialism and the Making of International Law', unpublished SJD dissertation, Harvard Law School (1995), pp. 275, 283–284 (on file with the author).

[275] See Michel Foucault, Alan Sheridan (trans.), Discipline and Punish: The Birth of the Prison (Vintage Books 2nd edn., New York: Vintage Books, 1995, 1977), p. 170. 'These [the mechanisms of disciplinary governance] are humble modalities, minor procedures, as compared with the majestic rituals of sovereignty or the great apparatuses of the state.' Ibid.

moral development' since this was vital for 'furthering the economic progress of the country which is an essential condition of general prosperity'.[276] In essence, every detail of native life was collected, assimilated, processed, recombined and reconstituted in ways that pointed to new modes of understanding and reconstructing the native. This new mode of managing the native embodied the philosophy that 'the body becomes a useful force only if it is both a productive body and a subjected body'.[277]

Subjugation was to be achieved by discipline, not force. The study of the psychology of the native had a profound impact on the discipline of colonial administration. The techniques and policies formulated by the Mandate System were explained best by Wright's argument that '[h]uman action may in fact be directed by many methods other than coercion. The possibilities of these methods are just on the threshold of exploration.'[278]

This system of control is what Guha might term 'dominance without hegemony' – 'a dominance in which the movement of persuasion outweighed that of coercion without, however, eliminating it altogether'.[279] Nor was it the case that this method of persuasion was simply a part of the theory of experts; these techniques of control were understood and utilised by colonial officials.[280] The construction of the science of colonial administration is crucial to this project, then, because it is linked intimately with the task of normalization, of creating the universe against which the native will be found wanting and that will lead ultimately to reform desired by the native herself.

Sovereignty, difference and the new technologies

The significance of the Mandate System lies not only in the new system of control and management it brought into being, but also in the related

---

[276] 'Draft Convention on Slavery', p. 1541.   [277] See Foucault, *Discipline and Punish*, p. 26.

[278] Wright, *Mandates*, p. 269.

[279] Ranajit Guha, 'Introduction', in Ranajit Guha (ed.), *A Subaltern Studies Reader, 1986–1995* (Minneapolis, MN: University of Minnesota Press, 1997), pp. ix, xviii. Guha points out that this technique was used by the Raj; in the Mandate System, then, we might see the gradual internationalization of this technique.

[280] Thus, an Australian official seeking to get the people of Nauru to leave their phosphate-rich island for Australia and become assimilated as Australians asserted:

I believe that a policy of encouraging and helping assimilation can be pursued by us steadily and unostentatiously and that its prospects of success will not be affected *if we do not openly disclose it to the Nauruans as a deliberate policy*. Assimilation must develop from spontaneous choice by individual Nauruans and from opportunities presented. We can steadily help both of these to develop.   (Weeramantry, *Nauru*, p. 289)

question of the techniques and technologies devised and used by international law and institutions for this purpose. A central argument of this chapter has been that sovereignty doctrine and various important techniques of international law emerged out of the attempts made by international law to resolve the problem of cultural difference as it was understood by jurists in the inter-war period. A crude distinction may be made between 'doctrine' and 'technique', whereby 'doctrine' refers to a particular conceptualization of sovereignty, and 'technique' to the mechanisms developed by international law to make this concept a reality. In the case of the mandates, the conceptualization of sovereignty as something that could be created not only in its juridical form but also in its sociological form, provoked the development of a series of techniques including the fusion of law with administration and all its trappings. The relationship between the two issues of doctrine and technique is mutually reinforcing and dialectic. Indeed, in the final analysis, the distinction between the two appears artificial: the elaboration and development of technique enabled the League lawyers to conceive of sovereignty in new ways, just as these new ways of understanding sovereignty called forth new techniques and new interdisciplinary projects involving law, administration, psychology and economics. At a more intimate level, the same process occurred with respect to the native: the native both generated these techniques, disciplines and innovations and in turn was generated by them, for the application to the native of these techniques revealed further deficiencies in native society and practice. The process was continuous, self-sustaining and endless, given the premise that difference was deficiency and must be remedied, and given too that the Mandate System developed ever more sophisticated ways of registering difference.

I have argued that the problem of cultural difference has been crucial to the development of international law. The new technologies of the inter-war period give the dynamic of difference a very specific and far-reaching character in the Mandate System that might better be appreciated by a contrast between the positivist nineteenth-century regime and the pragmatist regime of the Mandate System. Whereas positivism insists on focusing on autonomous law, pragmatism posits a jurisprudence based on rules, standards, policies and administration. The classical positivist criteria for statehood – government, population and territory – are now rendered in the Mandate System, in detailed sociological terms. Thus, for example, in the Mandate System, territory is understood now in terms of resources and economic development; population is understood in terms of health issues, mortality rates, hygiene and labour concerns; and government is conceptualised in terms of the reform of native political institutions. Put another way, the formal positivist criteria of statehood – government, population and territory – are transformed from mere criteria, which have to be satisfied, into projects to be undertaken by the Mandate System. Because of the suppleness and penetration of pragmatic jurisprudence, the objects of administration within a territory can be isolated, refined, selected and reconnected in numerous ways. The dynamic of difference thus now operates with respect to the most intimate aspects of a native's life – his psychology, customs and health – all of which could be characterized as backward and deficient and requiring remedying. The imposition of sanctions following any failure of the natives to meet universally posited standards no longer takes the form of punishment alone; rather, the application of new and formidable disciplines of management seek to transform not the body but the soul of the native – 'a punishment that acts in the depth on the heart, the thoughts, the will, the inclinations'.[281]

Crucially, the problem of cultural difference was presented in the Mandate System not in terms of the distinction between the civilized and uncivilized, but rather in terms of the 'backward' and 'advanced'. This formulation opened a more comprehensive version of the dynamic of difference. For, as Wright notes, the concept of 'backwardness' connotes a lack of self-determination, a lack of Europeanization and a lack of economic progress;[282] of these three inter-related concepts, however, 'the economic sense of the term has been [the] most significant, the others tending to follow as consequences'.[283] Thus, whereas the dynamic in the nineteenth century employed principally racial and cultural concepts, the dynamic now establishes economic categories. It is in the Mandate System, then, that we arrive at this pivotal moment, when the 'uncivilized' are transformed into the economically backward; when international law begins to discard a vocabulary that appears racist and problematic and adopts a new series of concepts that appears neutral and universal because it is based on economics and on expression of scientific fact rather than on an assertion of cultural superiority by a European civilization that had come perilously close to destroying itself. While the nineteenth-century sciences that preoccupied themselves with issues of

[281] Foucault, *Discipline and Punish*, p. 16.   [282] Wright, *Mandates*, p. 584.
[283] *Ibid.* Wright proceeds to argue that economic backwardness was itself the 'byproduct of the industrialization of Europe', which led to the search for raw materials, markets, and opportunities for investment. *Ibid.*

racial superiority[284] have been discarded, the twentieth-century science of economic development is profoundly important to international relations. The dynamic of difference thus now acquires a new impetus, a new project, a new way of characterizing and supposedly remedying deficiency.

It is in the non-European world that international law acquires a different form – and, indeed, creates new types of control and management. We might see the operation of law in the Mandate System, in terms described by Foucault, who was concerned to show 'the extent to which, and the forms in which, the law (not simply the law, but the whole complex of apparatuses, institutions and regulations responsible for their application) transmits and puts in motion relations that are not relations of sovereignty, but of domination'.[285]

My argument, following Foucault, is that we see in the Mandate System the difficulties of applying conventional doctrines of sovereignty to those territories, of identifying the 'distillation of a single will',[286] the unitary sovereign. What we see in elaborate and stunning detail, however, is the role that international law and institutions plays in creating relations of domination, relations that almost render irrelevant the formal sovereignty for which these societies ostensibly were being prepared.

The legacies of the Mandate System: toward the present

The contemporary significance of the Mandate System may be understood at a number of different levels. Most immediately, it is noteworthy that Iraq, Palestine and Ruanda–Urundi were all mandate territories. The records of the PMC and the League more generally illuminate the attempts by international institutions to address these conflicts (sometimes, perhaps, exacerbating or indeed creating them), attempts that may be traced back to the origins of international institutions and the creation of the League itself. International law and institutions continue to grapple with the issue of administering certain territories. Attempts by the United Nations to administer Somalia, Cambodia, Timor and Kosovo are contemporary manifestations of a

---

[284] For an example of such writings, see Karl Peters, *New Light of Dark Africa* (London: Ward, Lock & Co., 1890); reprinted in Philip D. Curtin (ed.), *Imperialism* (New York: Harper & Row, 1971), p. 74. The writings of Lugard himself might be included in this category.

[285] Foucault, 'Two Lectures', pp. 95–96.   [286] *Ibid.*, p. 97.

project that began with the Mandate System and continued in a more refined and comprehensive form with its successor, the Trusteeship System.[287] As Ralph Wilde notes in his survey of these efforts, International Territorial Administration is seen as a response to two major problems – 'a perceived sovereignty problem' and a 'perceived governance problem'[288] – that are precisely the problems that the Mandate System attempted to address. The assumptions inherent in these projects – about the people and territories to be administered, the character of 'progress', and the actual legal techniques and instruments used by institutions to effect the transformations of these societies – all derive in important ways from that earlier, formative experiment.

It is clear that the Mandate System was an extraordinary innovation in the field of international law; it furthered the cause of international justice in extremely significant ways. The Mandate System played a profoundly important role in enabling the emergence of Namibia and Nauru, to name but two examples of former mandate territories, as sovereign, independent states.

Equally, however, the processes and mechanisms that transformed colonies into sovereign states had an enduring importance for the non-European state. As such, it is misleading to focus simply on the outcome, on the achievement of sovereign statehood, rather than on the unique character of non-European statehood that stems in part from the mechanisms that created it. The technologies devised in the Mandate System to manage relations between the colonizer and the colonized continue to play a profoundly important role in managing relations between their successors, the developed and undeveloped/developing. In strictly legal terms, the Mandate System was succeeded by the Trusteeship System. But in terms of technologies of management, it is the Bretton Woods Institutions (BWI) – the World Bank and the International Monetary Fund (IMF) – that are the contemporary successors of the Mandate System.[289] Indeed, whereas the Mandate System was confined in its application to the few specified territories, the BWI in effect have universalised the

[287] Ruth Gordon has contributed outstanding studies of some of these themes. See, e.g., Ruth Gordon, 'Saving Failed States: Sometimes a Neocolonialist Notion', (1997) 12 *American University Journal of International Law and Policy* 903; Ruth Gordon, 'Some Legal Problems with Trusteeship', (1995) 28 *Cornell International Law Journal* 301.

[288] Ralph Wilde, 'From Danzig to East Timor and Beyond: The Role of International Territorial Administration', (2001) 95 *American Journal of International Law* 583, 587.

[289] Antony Anghie, 'Time Present and Time Past: Globalization, International Financial Institutions, and the Third World', (2000) 32 *New York University Journal of International Law and Policy* 243 at 246.

Mandate System – in this way, Wright's conjecture about the significance of the Mandate System has become a reality – to virtually all developing states. All these states are in one respect or another subject to policies prescribed by these institutions. Fundamental aspects of the operations of the BWI derive in important respects from the Mandate System, and undermine Third World sovereignty in very significant ways. These are matters that I will discuss in greater detail in chapter 5.

My preoccupation here has been to point out the different ways in which these institutional disciplines and technologies have sought to control and manage the Third World. But the elaborate and cunning ways in which colonial relations are reproduced should not be taken to suggest that they invariably triumph. These systems of control are resisted inevitably by the people subject to their application as part of an ongoing struggle that subverted colonial institutions and their attempt to manage all aspects of native life.[290] Further, I do not intend this analysis to be deterministic, to suggest that a former colony never can succeed in escaping its origins. Rather, my hope is to identify some of the factors that inhibit such a metamorphosis.

If my analysis is correct, then the tragedy for the Third World is that the mechanisms used by international law to achieve decolonization were also the mechanisms that created neo-colonialism; and that, furthermore, the legal structures, ideologies and jurisprudential techniques for furthering neo-colonialism largely were in place before Third World states actually attained independence. The Mandate System had devised a set of technologies that would compromise that independence and maintain – indeed, entrench – the division between advanced and backward states. Having in this way ensured the existence of the division, international law and institutions nevertheless proclaimed themselves intent on bridging that division, on promoting global equality and justice. This project and the many initiatives that are a part of it are inherently problematic because it is sometimes precisely the international system and institutions that exacerbate, if not create, the problem that they ostensibly seek to resolve.

This point is illustrated by a reconsideration of the basic contradiction that afflicted the Mandate System, the contradiction between attempting to promote self-government while establishing an economic structure that recreated colonial relations. As Nehru, Furnivall, and others

---

[290] See generally, Laurel Benton, *Law and Colonial Cultures: Legal Regimes in World History 1400–1900* (Cambridge: Cambridge University Press, 2002).

recognized, however, the pursuit of such economic policy makes real self-government impossible because government is made subservient to unequal economic development. In these circumstances, the Western political institutions transferred to these territories, ostensibly for the purpose of promoting self-government, will very often fail to bring about the intended social and political benefits. This is because these institutions, too, become distorted in the colonial setting and serve largely to further economic inequalities. The function of the rule of law in the colonies, Furnivall observed, was to further commerce. but this version of the rule of law could hardly empower and unite a society when its very operation expanded commerce at the expense of the social and political integrity of that society.

Colonialism is a thing of the past. This is the broad understanding that informs the conventional narrative of international law. The principal concerns of this book are to question this assumption and to examine how this narrative sustains itself and how international law seeks to suppress its relationship with colonialism – a relationship that was, and continues to be, central to international law's very identity. An examination of the Mandate System makes it clear how colonialism continues. The colonial policies and management techniques formulated by Lugard were adopted and refined by the Mandate System, and these same practices continue today through the BWI. The shift from a discourse based on race to a discourse based on economics is crucial to the conventional narrative of international law. The characterization of non-Europeans as inferior based on racial categories is regarded as unacceptable and unscientific. But the civilizing mission of the BWI and the interventions such a mission requires can be justified on the basis that they are necessary in order to transform and improve the welfare of an economically deprived group of people. The neutral, scientific discourse of economics justifies these expanding and increasingly sophisticated forms of intervention. Race is distanced from international law in this way, even as an alternative vocabulary with which to characterize and reform the uncivilized as 'developing' emerges.

My argument is that we might see in both the Mandate System and in its successors, the BWI, the reproduction of the basic premises of the civilizing mission and the dynamic of difference embodied in the very structure, logic and identity of international institutions. Further, it may be the case that the basic premises of the civilizing mission are reproduced in a number of other arenas in which international institutions have played a crucial role in attempting to regulate international affairs. Jose Alvarez, for example, has shown how the structure of the international criminal tribunal for Rwanda served in important respects to obscure the West's complicity in the genocide that took place there.[291]

But I do not wish to suggest that international institutions invariably and inevitably reproduce this logic of the civilizing mission and always operate against the interests of the peoples of developing countries. A study of the Trusteeship System, which succeeded the Mandate System, shows, for example, how international institutions evolved to give voice to the peoples of the trust territories. An examination of the history of the Nauru Case reveals how the people of Nauru succeeded in protecting their interests, at least in part, through an astute use of these procedures.[292] This examination of the Mandate System is not intended, then, to be determinist. Rather, it attempts to outline certain historically based concerns that might enhance an understanding of the operation of international institutions and the role they play in contemporary international relations.

Conclusion

It is in the operation of the Mandate System that we might see, almost as in a fossil recording a crucial transition in the history of a species, a number of shifts in the history of international law: from positivism to pragmatism; from law to institutions; from sovereignty to government; from race to economics; from conquest to decolonization; from colonialism to neo-colonialism; from exploitation to development; and from England and France to the United States. While each of these themes is important, I have attempted to explore them in terms of my major concern to understand the distinctive character of non-European sovereignty. My argument has been that non-European sovereignty is distinctive on account of the mechanisms and processes that brought it into being, despite the appearance of equality between European and non-European sovereignty – an appearance that supports the dominant theoretical paradigm of international law, which examines the question of how order is created among equal and sovereign states, rather than attempting to question the character of this equality. I have argued that nineteenth-century jurists built racial discriminations into their conceptualization of sovereignty. Similarly, in the inter-war period,

[291] See Alvarez, 'Crimes of States', 391.
[292] On these issues, see generally Weeramantry, *Nauru*.

conceptualizations of sovereignty incorporated economic inequalities within it. As a consequence of this, non-European sovereignty suffered – and continues to suffer – a particular vulnerability that arises from the system of economic power into which it was integrated even as it became sovereign. The Mandate System did not succeed in implementing its grand ambitions of transformation. The great diversity of mandate territories, the different responses and resistance of the mandate peoples and the intransigency of mandate powers presented this from occurring. Nevertheless, the Mandate System created, however imperfectly employed, a new set of technologies for the management of colonial problems. This is perhaps the most significant and enduring legacy of the system.

Scholars examining the effects of nineteenth-century international law on colonial peoples have consistently argued that the formalist and positivist character of that law was ideally suited to support the imperial project. In short, formalism has been linked inextricably to imperialism. The further suggestion is that an antiformalist jurisprudence such as pragmatism would enable the negation of colonialism. My argument, however, is that pragmatism, itself a response against formalism and colonialism, gave rise to a new type of colonialism whose character may be identified by a study of the Mandate System.

The basic structures of colonialism, I conclude, are reproduced in all the major schools of international jurisprudence: naturalism, positivism and pragmatism. If this is the case, then we must surely rethink the prevalent history of the discipline, which sees each of these schools of jurisprudence as being significantly different from the others. My argument is that while these schools are distinctive, what is disturbing is that they all have served to reproduce colonial relations. It is in this sense that I argue that, far from being ancillary to the discipline, colonialism is central to its very constitution. Formal sovereignty is very important, and provides Third World states with a vital means of protecting and furthering their interests. But the enduring vulnerabilities created by the processes by which non-European states acquired sovereignty pose an ongoing challenge, not only to the peoples of the Third World, but also to international law itself.

SHOULD WE BE
SURPRISED THAT
LAW REPRODUCES
POWER RELATION-
SHIPS?

4   Sovereignty and the post-colonial state

Introduction

The whole attitude of the 'new' countries could be summarized in the liquidation
of imperialism in its widest meaning, with all its political, military, economic
and psychological implications.[1]

For the newly independent states, sovereignty is the hard won prize of their
long struggle for emancipation. It is the legal epitome of the fact that they are
masters in their own house.[2]

The great task initially begun by the Mandate System was to be continued by the United Nations, which made the issue of decolonization
one of its central concerns. The doctrine of self-determination, that
had been developed in the inter-war period principally in relation to
the peoples of eastern Europe, was now adopted and adapted by the
United Nations to further and manage the transformation of colonial
territories into independent, sovereign states. Virtually every facet of
the UN system participated in this project: the provisions in the UN
Charter that dealt with non-self-governing and trusteeship territories,
the famous General Assembly Resolutions articulating the right to self-
determination and the opinions of the International Court of Justice (ICJ)
in Western Sahara and Namibia, all addressed this question. The modern
doctrine of self-determination, then, was formulated in response to the
whole phenomenon of colonialism.

Decolonization supported the powerful claim that international law
had finally become, for the first time, truly universal. By the end of the

---

[1] R. P. Anand, 'Role of the "New" Asian–African Countries in The Present International
Legal Order', (1962) 56 *American Journal of International Law* 383 at 390.
[2] Georges M. Abi-Saab, 'The Newly Independent States and the Rules of International
Law: An Outline', (1962) 8 *Howard Law Journal* 95 at 103.

nineteenth century the international law which originated in Europe became universally applicable as a consequence of colonial expansion. With the emergence of the sovereign states of Africa and Asia, how- ever, international law became 'universal' in the more profound sense that Asian and African societies that had been excluded from the realm of sovereignty even while being subjected to the operation of interna- tional law, could now participate in that system as equal and sovereign states. Thus a true 'community of states' had finally come into being.[3] Within this system of international law, all societies could develop and act according to their own cultural traditions provided that they adhered to the minimal rules essential for the maintenance of international peace.[4]

These revolutionary developments did not, however, resolve colonial problems. Instead, the enduring consequences of colonialism became a central and inescapable issue for the discipline, rather than a periph- eral concern, as the emergence of these 'new states', as they were termed in the literature of the period, posed major questions to international law at both the theoretical and doctrinal levels. Was international law indeed universal? Given that international law was inherently European, how could it accommodate the new states which belonged to very differ- ent cultural traditions? What adjustments, if any, did international law have to make in order to address the concerns of Third World states?

---

[3] The existence of such a universal community is assumed in much contemporary theorizing. See, for example, Haskell Fain, *Normative Politics and the Community of Nations* (Philadelphia, PA: Temple University Press, 1987); James Mayall (ed.), *The Community of States* (London: Allen & Unwin, 1982).

[4] Robert Jackson has made the influential argument that decolonization resulted in the emergence of 'negative sovereignty', – that is, the creation of many Third World states that lacked the institutions that would make sovereignty real. These quasi-states exist primarily as juridical states because '[T]hey disclose limited empirical statehood: their populations do not enjoy many of the advantages traditionally associated with independent statehood. Their governments are often deficient in the political will, institutional authority, and organised power to protect human rights or provide socio-economic welfare.' Robert H. Jackson, *Quasi-States: Sovereignty, International Relations, and the Third World* (Cambridge: Cambridge University Press, 1990), p. 21. For a more recent elaboration of this line of argument, which also incorporates the literature on 'failed states', see Gerard Kreijen, 'The Transformation of Sovereignty and African Independence: No Shortcuts to Statehood', in Gerard Kreijen (ed.), *State, Sovereignty, and International Governance* (Oxford: Oxford University Press, 2002), p. 45. For accounts of the problems confronting African statehood which take into account the international dimensions of the issues, see Obiora Chinedu Okafor, *Re-Defining Legitimate Statehood: State Fragmentation in Africa* (Boston: Martinus Nijhoff, 2000); Makau wa Mutua, 'Why Redraw the Map of Africa? A Moral and Legal Inquiry', (1995) 16 *Michigan Journal of International Law* 1113.

198 IMPERIALISM, SOVEREIGNTY AND INTERNATIONAL LAW

These questions were addressed by prominent Western and non-Western jurists of the period, including Friedmann and Elias, Jenks, Roling and Anand, Fatouros, Abi-Saab and Castenada, McDougal and Falk.

International law had served the interests of the powerful Western states.[5] Inevitably, then, the new states would seek to regain control over their own economic and political affairs, and to change an international legal regime that operated to their disadvantage. The use of the newly acquired weapon of sovereignty was fundamental to these initiatives.[6] In this sense, the Third World was intent on furthering the project that had been commenced by the lawyers of the inter-war period, that of separating international law from its colonial past and reconstructing an anticolonial international law that would serve the interests of the entire international community.

In the realm of international law, the Third World states (or 'new states') adopted several basic strategies in their attempts to create an international law responsive to their needs.[7] The new states attempted to revise old doctrines to which they were ostensibly bound but which, they believed, were created to further the interests of Western states and which, furthermore, they had played no role in formulating. In addition, the new states attempted to create new doctrines, or adapt old doctrines, in order to further their own interests. The doctrine of permanent sovereignty over natural resources (PSNR) that is the focus of analysis here, is one such example. The West responded by attempting to negate these efforts, either by asserting that the new states were violating hallowed and classical principles of international law, or else by themselves formulating new doctrines that were often presented as a firmly established part of international law. Thus the law relating to self-determination, human rights, state responsibility, state succession, acquired rights, sources doctrine and the international law of development, may all be seen as involved, in one way or another, in this contest.

---

[5] For an overview of the literature, see Richard Falk, 'The New States and International Legal Order', (1966-II) 118 *Académie du Droit International, Recueil de Cours* 1–102 at 34 ff.

[6] As Sinha argues: 'Sovereignty is the most treasured possession of the newly independent States. On the one hand, it makes them the master of their own house, and on the other hand, it provides them with a legal shield against foreign incursions or attempts thereat by stronger States.' S. Prakash Sinha, 'Perspective of the Newly Independent States on the Binding Quality of International Law', (1965) 14 *International and Comparative Law Quarterly* 127. See also Georges M. Abi-Saab, 'The Newly Independent States and the Scope of Domestic Jurisdiction', (1960) 54 *American Society of International Law Proceedings* 84.

[7] See, e.g., Abi-Saab, 'The Newly Independent States and the Rules'.

Inevitably, and most significantly, given that so much importance was attached to the validity of these doctrines, the contest between new and old states eventually infiltrated the very foundations of international law, sources doctrine.

I examine these debates by attempting to analyse the different views of sovereignty, of its history and character, that were used by both sides – the West and the Third World – to support their position. My broad argument is that the formal acquisition of sovereignty and equality did not translate into the real power that the Third World states had hoped for. The exposure of the difference between formal and real equality is a familiar type of critique. Here, however, in elaborating the basic theme of this book, I seek to illustrate specifically how it is the continuing effect of the *colonial encounter* and the persistence of the structure of the civilizing mission that creates this discrepancy. The innovations and reforms of the UN period served in important ways to reproduce and reinstate the inequalities and power disparities that had characterized formal colonialism. These same issues informed my analysis of Mandate System in chapter 3, which attempted to examine why it was that non-European sovereignty was somehow destined to become distinctive and dependent and lacking in real economic power. Here, however, I examine similar themes by examining a different set of 'materials and initiatives', the attempts on the part of the Third World to use their sovereignty to create a New International Economic Order (NIEO) that would reverse the effects of colonialism. These campaigns, I believe illustrate the characteristics and limitations of Third World sovereignty. For if, as I have argued, sovereignty doctrine was forged in the colonial encounter, then questions emerge as to how successfully the Third World could deploy sovereignty for the purpose of revealing and remedying that past. It is through an examination of this confrontation between different views of sovereignty – the attempts, in effect, of the Third World to compel sovereignty to confront its own beginnings and, indeed, wrench it from its origins in colonialism – that we may acquire an understanding of the unique type of sovereignty that was inherited by the Third World and the new iterations of sovereignty doctrine that emerged in this phase of the colonial confrontation.

Decolonization and the universality of international law

Given that the Eurocentric character of international law had been emphasized since the nineteenth century, many scholars of the 1950s and 1960s attempted to outline ways in which the new states could be accommodated within the system, and the changes that had to be made for this purpose. Culture was the focus of scholars such as Verzijl and Kunz, who reiterated the concern that non-Western cultures were fundamentally different from the Western culture on which international law was based, and that, as a consequence, the entry of new states into the realm of an ineluctably Western international law would undermine that law.[8] Other scholars, such as Jenks and Friedmann, who produced major works addressing some of these issues, did not see the existence of diverse cultures as an insurmountable problem for the development of a truly universal international law. Thus, having attempted a survey, admittedly superficial, but revealing nonetheless, Jenks argued that it was possible to formulate a 'consensus of general principles' from legal systems ranging from common and civil law systems, Hindu law, Jewish law, Chinese and Japanese law.[9]

Further, and equally importantly, jurists from the new states, such as Anand, Castaneda and Sinha, while questioning the universality of international law, did not base their argument on cultural difference. In the first place, jurists such as Anand[10] and Elias argued that the legal traditions of their own societies had developed principles, relating to treaties, to the conduct of war – and, indeed, to the importance of law itself – which corresponded with principles which were already a part of international law. Thus, for example, Anand goes to considerable lengths to refute Northrop's argument that Asian societies were averse to the 'rule of law' because they preferred to settle disputes through negotiation and reconciliation: Anand concludes that 'Hindus, nay Indians, have all along believed in the rule of law and practiced it in their national affairs'.[11] In other cases, scholars argued that non-Western states had developed very advanced and comprehensive legal systems,

[8] For a review of these positions, see R. P. Anand, *New States and International Law* (New Delhi: Vikas Publishing House, 1972), pp. 6 ff. (quoting Julius Stone, *The Quest for Survival: The Role of Law and Foreign Policy*, Cambridge, MA: Harvard University Press, 1961, p. 88).

[9] C. Wilfred Jenks, *The Common Law of Mankind* (London: Stevens & Sons, 1958), p. 106.

[10] Anand, *New States and International Law*, pp. 9–11.

[11] Anand, 'Role of the "New" Asian–African Countries', 400. It must be noted that Northrop made this argument, not in order to claim that non-European states were incapable of becoming members of the international community (the argument made in the nineteenth century), but to suggest that international law had to adjust to reflect the characteristics of those other cultures. Falk, 'The New States', 38–39.

and that indeed international law could benefit from drawing upon them.[12]

The challenge to universality posed by the new states arose, then, not because of differences in culture, but differences in interest:[13] the difference between the developed and developing states. Thus, as Anand argues: 'It is this conflict of interest of the newly independent States and the Western Powers, rather than differences in cultures and religions, which has affected the course of international law at the present juncture.'[14] Broad agreement seemed to exist on this point, even though it was understood that culture did affect perceptions of interest and the manner in which interests were pursued.[15] In this context, for many jurists, from both the West and the new states, a universal international law reflecting the interests of the whole global community rather than that of the Western/European states alone, and the creation of such a system of law would in itself resolve the secondary problem of whether the rules of international law derived from a specific cultural tradition and how non-European states related to that tradition.

The need for compromise on both sides appeared to be accepted, at least in academic circles. It was hardly possible to dispute that international law had in fact subordinated the Third World. Further, international lawyers intent on ensuring the continuing relevance of the discipline, sought to develop an international law that was sensitive to the new social reality of a expanded international community which now comprised largely 'new states'. For these several reasons, the claims

[12] See, for example, Milton Katz's argument for drawing upon the older traditions of China, the Middle East and India, societies characterized as 'older and more mature legal systems which have dealt with a much greater range of human activity', in order to create a more just and workable international order. Jenks, *The Common Law of Mankind*, p. 77. Katz had been the Director of the Graduate Program at Harvard Law School.

[13] For a good account of this set of debates, see Falk, 'The New States', 38 ff.

[14] R. P. Anand, 'Attitudes of the Asian–African States Toward Certain Problems of International Law', (1966) 15 *International and Comparative Law Quarterly* 55 at 72. Anand further argues that 'National interest, rightly or wrongly understood, rather than cultural traditions, seem to be the decisive factor in the determination of policies toward international law and affairs'. Anand, *New States and International Law*, p. 51. Further, Anand argues that 'there is no noticeable tendency amongst Asian and African states to regard international law as a product of Western civilization or reject it on that basis'. *Ibid.*, p. 52.

[15] See A. A. Fatouros, 'International Law and the Third World', (1964) 50 *Virginia Law Review* 783 at 788, for arguments affirming the importance of culture. See also Julius Stone, 'A Common Law for Mankind?', (1960) 1 *International Studies* 414.

of the new states were initially regarded with a large degree of sympathy by many Western scholars who recognized the difficulties facing them, and the justice of their concern to create a different system of international law. At least in the 1950s and early 1960s, it was generally agreed that these differences could be resolved by creating a common law of 'welfare' and 'protection'.[16] Thus Jenks argued against the assertion of vested interests and called instead for a campaign 'to adjust conflicting interests on a basis which contemporary opinion regards as sufficiently reasonable to be entitled to the organised support of the universal community'.[17]

Equally, the new states made it evident that they were not intent on rejecting international law wholesale. Scholars from the new states such as Elias, Sinha and Anand, Castaneda and Abi-Saab, while powerfully articulating the position of the new states in relation to various aspects of international law, adopted, on the whole, a conciliatory position: the aim was to reform international law rather than dispense with it. Indeed, it was through the use of international law itself that the new states sought to further their own interests and to redeem the discipline from its colonial past, by excising from the body of international law those doctrines and elements which created and furthered colonial relations. The new states were intent on challenging, principally, those doctrines of existing international law, such as state responsibility, which had furthered colonial relations and which hindered the new states from meeting their aspirations.[18]

The general understanding of the impact of colonialism on international law was muted, for a number of reasons. Thus, for Jenks, international law expressed the highest ideals of a proper and responsible colonial policy.[19] The problem was, however, that these ideals were disregarded in practice, by unhappy conflicts between 'precept and practical realization'.[20] The proper implementation of international law, then, was

---

[16] See, for example, B. V. A. Roling, *International Law in an Expanded World* (Amsterdam: Djambatan, 1960), p. 10; Falk, 'The New States', 35. Anand, *New States and International Law*, pp. 60 ff.

[17] Jenks, *The Common Law of Mankind*, p. 85. See also Jorge Castaneda, 'The Underdeveloped Nations and the Development of International Law', (1961) 15 *International Organizations* 38.

[18] See Sinha, 'Perspective of the Newly Independent States', 121.

[19] See Jenks, *The Common Law of Mankind*, p. 243, where he asserts that international law since Vitoria onwards embodied a 'recognition by the powers concerned of their own moral responsibilities'.

[20] *Ibid.*, 231.

the solution. Further, the understanding that developed and developing states had 'different interests',[21] while no doubt true and accurate in suggesting the problems caused by colonialism, also reduced their most radical implications: after all, historically, among European states, it was precisely the purpose of international law to reconcile differing interests. Seen in this way, the 'challenge' presented by the new states was not particularly novel or especially daunting, for the new states were really presenting another variation of a very familiar problem, that of reconciling the interests of particular sovereign states with the broader concerns of the international community.

This view was reinforced by the argument that whatever the differences in culture and interest separating societies, the emergence of the modern nation-state in these new states created a certain uniformity in the international system which assisted the effective operation of a universal international law. Thus, as Friedmann argues:

Further, whatever the differences may have been in the past, the facts of modern state organization and international life have completely overshadowed any traditional differences of outlook and philosophy. The representatives of Asian values have become modern nation states, of greater and lesser power, organised on the lines developed by the European nations in previous centuries, and seeking to realize national aspirations. In so doing, they are subjected to the same tensions between international community interests, reflected in international law, and national aspirations, reflected in the power politics of states.[22]

Third World scholars adopted a very similar approach, arguing, in effect, that while the new states had certain distinctive concerns and attitudes about international law, they were equally concerned about the peaceful resolution of disputes and providing their populations with a decent standard of living that could be achieved through development.

As a consequence of these dramatic changes in the international system, the dynamic of difference acquired, once again, a new form. The achievement of development became the central and defining preoccupation of the new states, as reflected by the fact that these states

---

[21] Thus scholars such as Falk and Roling asserted that 'as a consequence of their underdeveloped condition, the new states have interests fundamentally different from those of the European states', Falk, 'The New States', 35.

[22] Wolfgang Friedmann, 'The Position of Underdeveloped Countries and the Universality of International Law', (1963) 2 *Columbia Society of International Law Bulletin* 5–12, cited in Fatouros, 'International Law and the Third World', 788.

were also termed 'developing states'. It was principally in the language
of development, then, that the new states approached the problem of
balancing interests and creating a truly universal international law. Consequently, the gap between the colonizers and the formerly colonized
was no longer located in juridical distinctions between the civilized and
the uncivilized, but in economic distinctions between the developed and
the developing.

This shift is hardly surprising for, as chapter 3 has argued, the effect
of the Mandate project was, precisely, to transform cultural differences into economic differences, to translate the categories of civilization and non-civilization into the categories of the advanced and the
backward, the developed and the developing and to develop a richly
textured and detailed vocabulary by which these differences could be
assessed and administered. The distinction between the developed and
developing became central to the operation of institutions such as the
Bretton Woods institutions (BWI) which, following their predecessor, the
Mandate System, formulated new techniques with which to bridge this
difference. Most significantly, the vast majority of new states, while differing on how development was to be achieved, believed that modernization and industrialization were key to the futures of their people,
and their vision of the nation-state corresponded in important respects
with the vision propounded by the Mandate System. The dynamic of
difference persisted in this form. Uniquely, however, the character of
the dynamic was now profoundly challenged by the ability of Third
World states to exercise their sovereign powers and to articulate their
own vision of international law. As a consequence of all this, Friedmann
argued, 'the whole field of international economic development illustrates most pregnantly the central problem in the reorganization of
international legal studies in our time'.[23]

Development, nationalism and the post-colonial state

The body of this chapter deals with the external aspect of the newly
acquired Third World sovereignty and examines how the Third World
state attempted to use its sovereignty to change the international order.
Even as it launched this campaign in the international arena, however,
the Third World confronted the simultaneous challenge of consolidating

---

[23] Wolfgang Friedmann, 'The Changing Dimensions of International Law', (1962) 62
   Columbia Law Review 1147 at 1165.

its sovereignty internally. The nationalist struggles that led to the independence of Third World states did not conclude with decolonization. Rather, the Third World state itself became a site of conflict, as it often contained within its territory many different ethnic groups, some of which aspired to be independent peoples with their own state. These difficulties were especially severe in Africa, where colonial boundaries were drawn with little regard for the integrity of the pre-colonial indigenous political entities.[24] These communities had joined together – with varying degrees of success and credibility – in opposing colonial rule. The advent of independence, however, directly posed the question of what factors united these disparate communities other than a shared opposition to colonial domination. Thus, the problem of cultural difference emerged once again, this time in the form of the difference between the post-colonial state and the entity that sought to secede from it. We might consequently see the dynamic of difference as operating within the interior of the post-colonial state, and being played out through the doctrines and technologies developed by the United Nations to address the profound problems of statehood and ethnic violence – doctrines such as self-determination, *uti possidetis* and minority rights regimes.

How was the post-colonial state to assert its unity when confronted with contending ethnic groups intent on becoming independent states? Development, which had become a central – indeed, defining – preoccupation of the post-colonial state offered one solution to the problem because, as Partha Chatterjee argues, 'It was in the universal function of "development" of national society as a whole that the post-colonial state would find its distinctive content'.[25] The state was the agent of development. And development appeared to offer a means of transcending cultural divisions and justifying the intervention of the development state into the many social, economic and cultural spheres that had been previously governed by the traditions of the particular community involved. Since development planning affected the whole of the society, as Chatterjee further argues, it was to be premised on the existence of one consciousness, that of the state, and 'Particular interests needed to be subsumed within the whole and made consistent with the general

---

[24] Makau wa Mutua, 'Why Redraw the Map' 1113–1176. This article reviews much of the literature dealing with this ongoing problem.

[25] Partha Chatterjee, *The Nation and Its Fragments: Colonial and Postcolonial Histories* (New York: Oxford University Press, 1994), p. 205.

interest'.[26] The development state thus represented universal interests that would prevail against the interests of minorities that were absorbed and assessed by criteria which were often externally determined and which purported, with formidable force, to be universal.

Development was understood by the new states principally in terms of the furtherance of industrialization and modernization, and these processes were expected to marginalize ethnic identity. The success or failure of state building was assessed in these terms. Economic integration, centralised administration, mass public education systems, improved communications and the expansion of modern legal systems were all directed at consolidating the state and furthering development. Equally importantly, these programmes were intended to make compelling a concept of citizenship which made the state, and not the ethnic group, the source of authority and the recipient of allegiance.

Many of these assumptions, however, proved unfounded. The 'development' state, rather than operating as a neutral institution that represented a modern, rational, universal culture, and which could therefore mediate between rival ethnic groups, became instead the arena in which these groups conducted their battles. Seizure of the formidable power of the state was a means by which one ethnic group could dominate another.

Ethnic violence, of course, continues to afflict the Third World. In this context, however, international law offers little doctrinal support for minorities seeking to preserve their culture. Article 27 of the International Covenant of Civil and Political Rights, which purports to protect the rights of minorities, is based, significantly, on the rights of individuals belonging to minorities and, does little to protect minorities as a collectivity. As James Crawford argues: 'Article 27 provides little more than that the rights, which the rest of the International Covenant says that everyone has, are not to be denied to members of certain minorities.'[27] In effect, then, international law endorses the assimilation of minorities into the 'universal state'. In this respect, the minority treaty system of the League of Nations provided minorities with more significant rights. Important debates continue about autonomy regimes as a means of addressing the grievances of minorities without endorsing secessionism.

---

[26] Ibid., p. 204.

[27] James Crawford, 'The Right to Self-Determination in International Law: Its Development and Future', in Philip Alston (ed.) Peoples' Rights (New York: Oxford University Press, 2001), pp. 7–67 at p. 24.

My broad point, however, is that we might see the relationship between the state and minorities, as it has been characterized in international law, as reproducing the dynamic of difference; the minority is characterized as the 'primitive' that must be managed and controlled in the interests of preserving the modern and universal state. These were the interests that were subordinated by the Third World state to assert and consolidate itself.

Development and the reform of international law

The achievement of development was urgent and desirable. This much could be agreed upon. Nevertheless, the First and Third Worlds held widely contrasted versions of how this was to be achieved. Inevitably, these competing versions were based on very different understandings of the nature and history of colonialism, the causes of underdevelopment and the appropriate remedy, on how to bridge the gap between the developed and developing.

The Mandate System had produced a comprehensive and ostensibly scientific account of the causes of underdevelopment in the non-European world, and these ideas were widely adopted and expanded on by scholars in the West from the 1950s onwards. In broad terms, this view held that the lack of development was attributable to the backward cultural, political and economic systems in the Third World. Of course, it was recognized that colonial excesses might have hindered progress; but once these were negated – and this was achieved, it was asserted, by granting independence to colonial states – then indigenous conditions and incapacity were to blame. This set of views was embodied by 'modernization theory', as it was termed by political scientists and economists, who then formulated the corresponding policies necessary to modernise backward societies.[28] The Mandate System had continuously posited integration into the global economy as being the best means of achieving this goal of becoming 'internationalised'; almost inevitably, this also became the purpose of the development and international financial institutions (IFIs) which came into being in the 1940s – most evidently, the two BWIs which could be regarded in many respects as the direct successors of the Mandate System: the International Monetary Fund (IMF)

---

[28] The classic works on modernization theory include Walt W. Rostow, *The Stages of Economic Growth: A Non-Communist Manifesto* (Cambridge: Cambridge University Press, 1960) and Lucian W. Pye and Sidney Verba (eds.), *Political Culture and Political Development* (Princeton: Princeton University Press, 1965).

and the World Bank.[29] In terms of international law, this view held that while the international system required some adjustments, the full and responsible participation of independent Third World states in the international system would ensure the appropriate changes.

For the Third World, the problem of development was inextricably linked with the colonial past. According to this view, Third World deficiencies, while attributable in part to backward social and economic systems, were also caused in important respects by the systematic exploitation of Third World countries over the centuries. Further, this exploitation created a set of economic and political relations which favoured the colonial powers and which continued to operate even in the post-colonial era. These relations were embodied and perpetuated by a system of international law which continued to operate after the achievement of independence by the Third World. This common history united the otherwise disparate members of the Third World, and provided the foundation for the establishment of various organizations that were designed to further Third World interests in the international arena.[30] R. P. Anand summarizes the strategy adopted by the new states as follows:

They have launched an 'anti-colonial, anti-racist crusade' which has put colonial Powers on the defensive. Placing a measure of responsibility for their retarded development on those nations whose 'overdevelopment' was accomplished, at least in part, by collecting a vast amount of wealth from their territories and by preventing their industrialization, they not only now demand restitution, but reformation of the relationship between themselves and their erstwhile superiors. They not only demand full freedom to restructure their societies, but unconditional help for their economic and industrial development.[31]

These differing views of development, and how it was to be achieved, resulted in a number of debates and controversies in the legal arena.

---

[29] The actual legal successor to the mandate system was the UN trusteeship system, which assumed responsibility – with some exceptions – for all the mandate territories. For discussion of the continuities between the mandate system and the World Bank, see *infra*.

[30] This provided the basis of the Group of 77, the Non-aligned movement. See Karl P. Sauvant, *The Group of 77: Evolution, Structure, Organization* (New York: Oceana Publications, 1981).

[31] R. P. Anand, 'Attitude of the Asian–African States Toward Certain Problems of International Law', (1962), in F. Snyder and Surakiart Sathirathai (eds.), *Third World Attitudes Toward International Law: An Introduction* (Boston: Martinus Nijhoff, 1987), pp. 5–22.

Many of the controversies regarding the impact of the new states on the rules of international law emerged in pointed form in the disputes generated by the doctrine of state responsibility as it related to the protection of foreign investment. According to the West, the law basically stipulated that host states were bound by international minimum standards with regard to their treatment of foreign investment, even in a situation where these international standards exceeded the standards prescribed by domestic law. A failure on the part of a state to abide by such international standards would give rise to state responsibility under international law. Much of this body of law had been generated by disputes between American and European investors on the one hand, and Latin American states, on the other, and the latter insisted that the investment was governed entirely by local, national law. Further, an Argentine jurist, Carlos Calvo, developed the famous 'Calvo Clause', under which the investor was required to settle all disputes in accordance with national law and to refrain from seeking the assistance of its own government.[32] European and American jurists disputed the validity of the clause on the basis that a private party could not surrender the sovereign's power to exercise its right of diplomatic protection.

The Latin American states, which had won independence many decades prior to the states of Africa and Asia, confronted the problem that although they were sovereign, they lacked economic and political power, and had to contend with a system of international rules that they regarded as biased against their interests. The new states of Africa and Asia now found themselves confronting a set of issues that their Latin American counterparts had already experienced, and it was perhaps at this point that the distinctive history of Latin American international law merged with the histories of the new states. Given their experience with these issues, many distinguished Latin American lawyers were at the forefront of efforts to create a different law of state responsibility.

The Western position on the law of state responsibility was consequently disputed by the new states, and became a focus for the question: what rules of international law were binding on new states? The Third World argued that all international law, including the law of state

---

[32] For a discussion of the international law surrounding such a clause, see *United States of America (North American Dredging Co. of Texas) v. United Mexican States*, 4 U.N.R.I.A.A. 26 (1926).

responsibility, was part of an international law which they had played no role in formulating and which was not, therefore, binding on them. Guha-Roy suggested, however, that

If . . . the existing law [of state responsibility] with suitable modifications could be applied only to rights and interests to be created now or after the adoption of a new law of responsibility, a good deal of the objectionable features of this law from the point of view of the victims of colonialism are likely to disappear.[33]

Guha-Roy in effect asserted a sovereignty which was capable of beginning anew and constructing a system based on the real consent of states which had finally become sovereign and which were now in a position to assert principles of law which corresponded with their own interests. The West, however, emphasized the conditionality of sovereignty, arguing that the new states' entrance into and participation in the international system implied their acceptance of the existing rules of international law, including the law of state responsibility.[34]

One solution to the issue was to create a universal standard that the Third World could play a role in creating. The new field of human rights law offered one such possibility, as it was a law that developed at the same time as the emergence of the new states. As such, it could not be subjected to the criticism that the new states had played no role in formulating the law by which they were being bound. The difficult question, of course, was whether the principles of 'international minimum standards' applicable to individual human beings could be extended to corporations. In these ways, the Third World became aware of the urgent need to create a new system of international relations that would reflect their aspirations. The rules of state responsibility were only one part of a more formidable system that the new states perceived as acting to their disadvantage. By the 1970s, in consequence, the new states set about a comprehensive restructuring of the rules governing

---

[33] S. N. Guha-Roy, 'Is the Law of Responsibility of States for Injuries to Aliens a Part of Universal International Law?', (1961) 55 *American Journal of International Law* 863 at 883. On the broad issue of state responsibility see, e.g., C. F. Amerasinghe, *State Responsibility for Injuries to Aliens* (Oxford: Clarendon Press, 1967).

[34] Falk, 'The New States', 27, quotes D. P. O'Connell, who argued that 'in asserting the faculties of statehood, the new state is accepting the structure and system of Western international law, and it may not, without offending all juristic doctrine, pick and choose the acceptable institutions'. D. P. O'Connell, 'Independence and Problems of State Succession', in W. V. O'Brien (ed.), *The New Nations in International Law and Diplomacy* (New York: Praeger, 1965), pp. 7–41 at p. 12.

the international economic system, this in an effort to establish a NIEO[35] and a corresponding set of rules of international law. The Third World could make its presence most felt, in international forums, in the General Assembly of the United Nations. And it was through the work of the Assembly that the Third World attempted to reform international law.

Permanent sovereignty over natural resources and the New International Economic Order

The formulation of the doctrine of PSNR[36] was one of the principal mechanisms by which the new states hoped to regain control over their own resources and, in this way, promote development. As such, the propagation and establishment of the doctrine of PSNR constituted one of the most important aspects of the campaign for a NIEO. Indeed, the idea of PSNR was closely tied to the concept of self-determination, which in itself suggests the close links between political sovereignty and economic sovereignty.[37]

As chapter 2 on the nineteenth century suggests, imperial expansion was powerfully motivated by the desire of colonial states to exploit the resources of non-European territories. During the colonial era, Western trading and mining companies acquired concessions for the exploitation of extremely valuable mineral resources within the colony, often at extraordinarily favourable terms. More often than not, these concessions were obtained through direct coercion or else by 'agreements' which,

---

[35] On the NIEO, see the pioneering work of Mohammed Bedjaoui, *Towards a New International Economic Order* (New York: Holmes & Meier, 1979). The NIEO was advanced through a number of key General Assembly resolutions and declarations including the Charter of Economic Rights and Duties of States, G. A. Res. 3281, 29 GAOR, Supp. 30, U. N. Doc. A/9030 at p. 50 (1974), and the Declaration on the Establishment of a New International Economic Order, G. A. Res. 3201, Sixth Spec. Sess. GAOR, Supp 1, U. N. Doc. A/9559 (1974).

[36] See Nico Schrijver, *Sovereignty Over Natural Resources: Balancing Rights and Duties* (Cambridge: Cambridge University Press, 1997), for a magisterial treatment of the history of PSNR, to which I am indebted. See also B. S. Chimni, Review Article, 'The Principle of Permanent Sovereignty Over Natural Resources: Toward A Radical Interpretation' (Review of Nico Schrijver, *Sovereignty Over Natural Resources: Balancing Rights and Duties*), (1998) 38(2) *Indian Journal of International Law* 208–217; Kamal Hossain and Subrata Roy Chowdhury (eds.), *Permanent Sovereignty Over Natural Resources* (New York: St Martin's Press, 1984).

[37] U. O. Umozurike, *Self-Determination in International Law* (Hamden, CT: Archon Books, 1972).

while possessing a legal form, were hardly comprehensible to the natives who were ostensibly signatories to them.[38]

The importance of the raw materials to the global economy was always well understood by the more powerful states. Thus it is unsurprising that the Atlantic Charter of 1941, which looked to the period beyond the war, emphasized the importance of these materials, and stressed that the Allies:

> will endeavour . . . to further the enjoyment by all States, great or small, victor or vanquished, of access, on equal terms, to the trade and to the raw materials of the world which are needed for their economic prosperity.[39]

Given that the raw materials so referred to were located principally in the developing world, what is evident here is the continuation of the rhetoric of the mandate era, which characterized the resources of the mandate territories as somehow belonging to humanity as a whole. It was in this context that the developing states, commencing in the early 1950s, attempted to assert their right to control and exploit their own resources. These efforts were inevitably connected with other issues, including the right to nationalise, the relationship between control over natural resources and economic development and the connections between the principle of PSNR and the emerging body of human rights law, most significantly, the right to self-determination.[40]

The attempts of the new states to regain control over their natural resources generated a number of complex debates about several doctrines of international law. Simplifying considerably, however, the West and the Third World presented very different views of international law and sovereignty in presenting their positions. First, the Third World argued that the natural resources of a territory had always belonged to the people of the territory, and that this ownership continued through the colonial episode.[41] In essence, Third World peoples asserted a sovereignty over their resources which preceded the colonial encounter; this argument implied that 'native sovereignty' survived the international law of colonialism. Secondly, they argued that the colonized states were entitled, upon independence, to review the concessions

---

[38] See Bengt Broms, 'Natural Resources, Sovereignty Over', in R. Bernhardt (ed.), *Encyclopedia of Public International Law* (4 vols., New York: Elsevier, 1997), III, pp. 520–524.

[39] Cited in Schrijver, *Sovereignty*, p. 37. Interestingly Schrijver points to corresponding principles in the Articles of Agreement of the IMF and the World Bank, and the preamble of the GATT.

[40] For an account of these debates, see Schrijver, *Sovereignty*, pp. 49 ff.

[41] See discussion *infra*.

which had been granted by the colonial powers to trading companies exploiting the resources of colonial territories. Mohammed Bedjaoui, for example, argued that 'a concessionary contract must end with the extinction of the ceding state and could survive the change of sovereignty only at the express wish of the new authority'.[42] This position was understandable as colonial powers and trading enterprises often acquired 'rights' over these resources through duress and deception, and the concessions had often never been the subject of meaningful consent on the part of the Third World peoples. The review would examine the legality of the manner in which the concessions had been obtained and, further, the profits made by the colonial power or trading company from the exploitation of the resources. These factors could then be taken into account in assessing the compensation to be paid to the nationalised enterprises. Finally, the Third World argued that nationalization was to be determined according to national rather than international standards, thus attacking once again the rules of state responsibility relating to foreign investment.[43]

The West differed from the Third World on each of these issues. First, it argued in effect that the only sovereignty enjoyed by the Third World was the sovereignty provided by European international law; this international law legitimized conquest and dispossession, as a result of which no remedy was available to the victims.[44] Secondly, the West argued that the new states were bound by established international law, and that the Third World state's control over its natural resources had to comply with the doctrines of state succession and acquired rights which stipulate that a new state must respect the obligations undertaken by a predecessor state.[45] Accordingly, it followed, contrary to Bedjaoui, that the newly independent countries were legally bound to honour the concessionary rights to their natural resources which trading companies had acquired prior to independence. Finally, the former colonial powers

---

[42] Mohammed Bedjaoui, 'First Report on Succession of States in Respect of Rights and Duties Resulting From Sources Other Than Treaties', UN Doc. A/CN.4/204, in *Yearbook of the International Law Commission*, II, 1968, UN Doc. A/CN.4/SER.A./1968 Add 1 at p. 115.

[43] *Ibid.*, p. 116.

[44] Chief Justice Marshall asserts the point in its most implacable form: 'The title by conquest is acquired and maintained by force. The conqueror prescribes the limits.' *Johnson v. McIntosh*, 21 U.S. (8 Wheat.) 543 (1823).

[45] On acquired rights, see Daniel P. O'Connell, *The Law of State Succession* (Cambridge: Cambridge University Press, 1956). For a general overview of the debates, see the various essays collected in Richard B. Lillich (ed.), *The Valuation of Nationalized Property in International Law* (Charlottesville, VA: University Press of Virginia, 1975).

did not dispute the right of a sovereign to nationalise property *per se*.[46] Rather, they argued that nationalization was legitimate provided that a number of conditions were met, the most significant of these being payment of compensation according to internationally determined standards. The West relied on sources doctrine for this argument, asserting that the international standard of compensation was established by customary international law which was binding upon the new states once they became independent, and that the 'national standard' asserted by the Third World lacked any such legal foundations.

The various doctrines – state succession, acquired rights and sources doctrine – are related to each other in complicated ways. Simplifying once again, Western and Third World characterizations of these doctrines reveal fundamental differences in the ways in which each side understood the history of sovereignty doctrine and its engagement in the colonial encounter. For instance, acquired rights doctrine, when considered in the context of state succession which was so central to the debate involving Third World countries, essentially asserted that the rights granted by a sovereign to a private entity had to be respected by the successor sovereign.[47] In this way, it seemed to provide sovereignty doctrine with a past by establishing that the obligations of a predecessor state to a private party were binding on a successor state. Beyond the minimalist assertion as to the continuity of obligations, it failed to provide any more complex or substantive means of comprehending the relationship between the predecessor and successor sovereign. As a consequence, it denied the Third World's attempts to recount a complex history in which colonial powers had, in a number of respects, deliberately compromised the nascent sovereignty of the colonial territory. As an example, several colonial powers sought to protect their interests by manipulating the essential expression of the Third World state's

[46] See, e.g., Francesco Francioni, 'Compensation for Nationalisation and Foreign Property: The Borderland Between Law and Equity', (1975) 24 *International and Comparative Law Quarterly* 255, 260–261.

[47] 'When a certain status or legal right has been acquired under the municipal law of a State, such status or right must be respected as a matter of international obligation.' Francioni, 'Compensation', 259. I have discussed acquired rights in the context of state succession, as it was in this context that the doctrine was especially significant to the new states. However, as Francioni points out, the doctrine has developed in different ways in different areas of law. For an extended examination of acquired rights in the context of a dispute over the ownership of resources in a colonial territory, see Christopher G. Weeramantry, *Nauru: Environmental Damage Under International Trusteeship* (New York: Oxford University Press, 1992), pp. 307 ff.

sovereignty, its constitution. These colonial powers did so by incorporating provisions protecting fundamental rights and freedoms in the constitutions to be inherited by the newly independent states; the purpose of such provisions was not simply to enhance liberal-democratic institutions in the newly independent states, but also to protect their own property interests. In crucial respects, then, Third World sovereignty was manufactured by the colonial world to serve its own interests.[48] In addition, as Okon Udokang points out, countries such as France adopted the practice of entering into an agreement with one of its colonies shortly before that colonial state acquired its independence; under the terms of these agreements, the nascent new state undertook to protect all rights acquired with respect to its territory prior to independence.[49] The same method was used by America with respect to the Philippines and the Netherlands with respect to Indonesia.[50] As a consequence, the vulnerable new states often surrendered important rights in order to achieve independence.

Acquired rights, however, remains agnostic to these events; instead it simply focuses on sequence, the succession of one state by another, rather than on the historical and political factors which compromised the sovereignty asserted by the Third World. The manner in which sovereignty is brought into being, the complex political and economic forces which finally shape the appearance of an equal and sovereign state is thus suppressed by the doctrine. As with nineteenth-century positivist jurisprudence, the real work of sovereignty doctrine occurs at a level which is beyond the scrutiny of any approach to these issues which is based on a question of how order is maintained among 'sovereign states'. The presumption that states are sovereign and equal prevents an examination of the processes by which sovereignty is shaped in such a way as to preclude scrutiny of its historical engagement in the colonial encounter. The contradiction was that even while the West asserted that colonialism was a thing of the past, it nevertheless relied precisely on those relationships of power and inequality that had been created by that colonial past to maintain its economic and political superiority which it then attempted to entrench through an ostensibly neutral international law.

From a legal point of view, this entailed emphasizing and expanding those doctrines of international law which prevented those unequal

---

[48] See Okon Udokang, *Succession of New States to International Treaties* (New York: Oceana Publications, 1972), pp. 462–464.
[49] *Ibid.*, p. 465.   [50] *Ibid.*, pp. 465–466.

colonial relations from being re-examined and remedied. Indeed, in its most extreme form, acquired rights doctrine appeared to suggest that the effects of those unequal relations would have been legally valid and this would have to be accepted by the post-colonial state and be given continuing legal effect.[51]

The 1962 Resolution on PSNR

Confronted with the many legal difficulties that impeded their effective exercise of independence, the Third World attempted to change the relevant international law. The new states enjoyed a significant majority in the General Assembly, and it was through the mechanism of General Assembly resolutions that the new states launched their campaign to establish the principle of PSNR, which culminated in General Assembly Resolution 1803 of 1962, that is seen as the most complete expression of the principle up to that time.[52] This resolution is the focus of many of the legal disputes that arose from nationalizations by the new states. The links between natural resources and sovereignty are suggested by the legal instruments which elaborate PSNR doctrine. The 1962 General Assembly Resolution on PSNR declares that: 'The right of peoples and nations to permanent sovereignty over their natural wealth must be exercised in the interest of their national development and the well-being of the people concerned.'[53] Para. 7 of the same Resolution states that:

Violation of the rights of peoples and nations to sovereignty over their natural wealth and resources is contrary to the spirit and principles of the Charter of the United Nations and hinders the development of international economic cooperation and the maintenance of peace.[54]

Crucially, the same resolution stipulated that in the event of a nationalization, 'the owner shall be paid appropriate compensation, in accordance with the rules in force in the State taking such measures

---

[51] Thus, for example, in debates relating to the drafting of a resolution on Permanent Sovereignty Over Natural Resources, the Netherlands asserted that 'as a general rule, old investments should not be jeopardised by new laws and should be protected in accordance with the generally recognized principle of international law of respect for legally acquired rights'. Karol Gess, 'Permanent Sovereignty Over Natural Resources', (1964) 13 *International and Comparative Law Quarterly*: 398, 442–443.

[52] Permanent Sovereignty Over Natural Resources, G. A. Res. 1803, 17 GAOR, Supp. 17, U. N. Doc. A/5217 at p. 15.

[53] *Ibid.*, Article 1.   [54] *Ibid.*, para. 7.

in the exercise of its sovereignty and in accordance with international law'.[55]

The clear link between sovereignty and PSNR was also emphasized in the realm of human rights, by Article 1(2) of the International Covenant on Civil and Political Rights and the International Covenant on Economic, Social and Cultural Rights both of which describe the right of a people to control its natural resources in the following terms:

> All people may, for their own ends, freely dispose of their natural wealth and resources without prejudice to any obligations arising out of international economic co-operation, based upon the principle of mutual benefit, and international law. In no case may a people be deprived of its own means of subsistence.[56]

The use of the term 'people' in this context could be compared with the articulation of a right of 'peoples to self-determination', the right of an entity which had not yet acquired independence to some sort of recognition and protection by the international legal system.

These terms of Resolution 1803 raise several interpretive problems. The provision leaves unexplained the content of the right and the meaning of the word 'people'. But the term 'people' refers at least to 'people' under colonial rule, and further suggests that these people possess a latent sovereignty over resources and, therefore, an accompanying right to their natural resources. This in turn raises the issue of what obligations, if any, are imposed on an administering colonial power by this right.

Some of these issues are illuminated by the General Assembly's approach to the rights of the people of Namibia, who had been placed under the protection of the Mandate System. The view that dependent peoples, and not merely states, had a right to their natural resources was affirmed, for example, by the General Assembly, which reproduced some of the phraseology of Resolution 1803 in seeking to protect the interests of the Namibian people who were struggling to win independence from South Africa. The Assembly stated that it 'Reaffirms that the natural resources of Namibia are the inviolable heritage of the Namibian

---

[55] Ibid., Article 4. The United States and the United Kingdom successfully fought for this inclusion of a reference to 'international standards'. For the debates surrounding the drafting of this resolution, see generally Gess, 'Permanent Sovereignty', and Stephen M. Schwebel, 'The Story of the UN's Declaration on Permanent Sovereignty Over Natural Resources', (1963) 49 American Bar Association Journal 463.

[56] International Covenant on Civil and Political Rights, New York, 16 December 1966, in force 23 March 1976, 999 U.N.T.S. 171; International Covenant on Economic, Social and Cultural Rights, New York, 16 December 1966, in force 3 January 1976, 993 U.N.T.S. 3.

people' and that the systematic plunder of those resources by foreign economic interests, in collusion with South Africa, presented a 'grave threat to the integrity and prosperity of an independent Namibia'.[57] The same Resolution declared that any state violating the rights of the Namibian people over their natural resources would be in violation of the UN Charter.

The use of the term 'people' – the Resolution refers to 'peoples and nations' – in both the Resolution and the Covenants suggests, then, that even those colonized peoples who had not as yet become independent were granted certain rights that could protect their resources. If indeed a dependent people had a right to sovereignty over their natural resources, then it could be further argued that nationalization of its resources, once those people became an independent state, was one way in which this right was being exercised. Further, the violation of such a right to natural resources arguably gave rise to claims of compensation for colonial exploitation. It was precisely on the basis that the people of Nauru were sovereign over the phosphates found in that island even prior to acquiring official independence that the state of Nauru took action against Australia, arguing that Australia and the other partner governments had violated these rights.[58] I cannot examine in detail here the important question of reparations for colonial exploitation that has once again become a focus of international attention. Arguably, however, the wording of the 1962 Resolution could have been used as a basis for peoples seeking compensation for colonial exploitation upon becoming independent, sovereign peoples, capable of presenting claims in international law, particularly because Resolution 1803 is widely recognized as stating customary international law.

Scholars and jurists of the period were aware of these possibilities, and an examination of some of their arguments as to the interpretation of the resolution illuminates the ways in which concepts of Third World sovereignty, acquired rights and colonialism are inter-connected in complex ways. In his authoritative study of the drafting of the 1962 declaration, Karol Gess makes the character of the personality of Third World sovereignty central to his argument. He commences by focusing on the assertion that colonial peoples had sovereignty over their resources

[57] Question of Namibia, G. A. Res. 35/227, U. N. Doc. A/RES/35/277, adopted on 6 March 1981.
[58] For an account of the litigation, see Antony Anghie, 'The Heart of My Home: Colonialism, Environmental Damage, and the Nauru Case', (1993) 34 *Harvard International Law Journal* 445.

even while subject to colonial rule. His argument requires quotation at length:

To the extent to which the peoples and nations in whom the right of self-determination – a concept basic to that of sovereignty over natural resources – is vested are those of the colonial administrative units which came into being between the middle and end of the nineteenth century, and to the extent to which these units bear little or no relation to such former territorial or tribal sovereignties (if any), it is difficult to uphold the notion of a title to permanent sovereignty of peoples and nations over natural resources which lay dormant during the colonial era and which can be revived upon accession of the colonial administrative unit to independence.[59]

Gess' argument takes the West's position on sources doctrine and consent a stage further. Not only are newly independent states bound by international law as a condition of becoming sovereign states; but they possess no history or existence which may be asserted in international law until that precise time when they are 'created' by colonialism. They enter the international realm by being conquered – that is, they come into existence as a result of the very act which nullified their sovereignty. Title presupposes the existence of personality to exercise it. Colonial territories had no pre-colonial personality cognizable by international law; as a consequence, their resources were unprotected by international law. In this sense they belonged to no one and could, presumably, be appropriated by the colonial state even as it brought into existence the unit, the 'people' to which PSNR ostensibly refers.

Against Gess, it could be argued that if the tribes of Africa lacked personality to own their own resources then, presumably, they also lacked the personality to consent in any meaningful manner to the appropriation of these resources by Western trading interests by means of 'concession' agreements. Thus, the agreements had no validity. This is the issue I discussed in some detail in chapter 2 in relation to the nineteenth century.

Gess demurs again. Colonial peoples were not completely lacking in capacity during the colonial era; sovereignty in resources was not vested only upon the accession of these peoples to sovereign statehood. Rather, as Gess puts it, there was a period of 'transition or evolution' during which time 'territorial legislatures and governments came into being and began to take over functions representing the exercise of territorial sovereignty, however limited their scope might have been'. Whatever the

---

[59] See Gess, 'Permanent Sovereignty', 446–447.

'limitations', however, they do not preclude the peoples from entering into valid concessions. With the arrival of independence, territorial title was passed to the newly independent state which thus became bound by its predecessor. Gess concludes:

> Such transfers of territorial title traditionally safe-guard acquired rights and we may conclude that contracts entered into with respect of such territories – and from a practical viewpoint equally important *by* such territories acting in the exercise of a limited but nevertheless existing sovereignty during the above-mentioned transition period – are performable by the successor State.
>
> (Emphasis in original)[60]

The line of argument is familiar; it is articulated by Vitoria in the sixteenth century, and by Westlake in the nineteenth. The elisions and transitions in Gess' argument are evident in the last paragraph: territories are transformed from mere passive arenas which are demarcated by colonial powers, into subjects, actors (contracts are entered into 'by territories acting') who possess both the volition and now, suddenly, the sovereignty necessary to justify the imposition of obligations. Gess attributes to colonial territories just that degree of sovereignty necessary to make the concessions binding. Thus the essential manifestation of self-determination, the assertion of sovereignty, becomes primarily a surrender to obligations. Personality, as in the case of Vitoria, is invented in order to be bound.

The crucial point is not only the recurrence of this form of argument, the mechanism by which sovereignty doctrine repeats the same steps when dealing with the colonial past; but, rather, that these arguments continue to have a vital significance in contemporary international relations and law. Gess, after all, was writing in the 1960s. This then, is the paradox: that Western international lawyers relied on the past by insisting that these concessions had to be respected by the new states. And, yet, the version of the past on which this argument relied curiously denied the realities of colonialism even while relying on the effects of such realities – as suggested by an examination of Gess' argument.

The 1974 Charter of Rights and Duties Among States

While the 1962 Declaration is seen as an important initiative by the new states to further and protect their economic interests, a number of the

---

[60] *Ibid.*, 448.

provisions in that declaration appeared to weaken the Third World position. Thus, Resolution 1803 stated that in the event of expropriation, owners would be paid 'in accordance with international law';[61] the reference to international standards here arguably affirmed the traditional law of state responsibility, which had been continuously questioned by Third World states and which maintained that standards of compensation would be determined by international rather than local law. Further, the same resolution appeared to empower corporations by the use of the phrase that 'Foreign investment agreements entered into by or between sovereign States shall be observed in good faith'.[62] The reference to agreements entered into 'by . . . States' appeared to encompass agreements between states and corporations. Ironically, then, the 1962 Resolution may have harmed rather than furthered the interests of the new states.

By the 1970s, some of these defects with Resolution 1803 were apparent, and far more explicit and strongly worded provisions were included, in subsequent resolutions, most prominently in the 1974 Charter of Economic Rights and Duties of States.[63] The provisions on nationalization that appeared in the Charter, while affirming the right of a state to nationalise foreign property, made no reference to international standards of compensation, stating instead that in the event of a controversy regarding compensation, 'it shall be settled under the domestic law of the nationalizing State and by its tribunals', unless all concerned States agreed on some other peaceful alternative.[64]

This resolution, which provides the nationalizing state with expansive powers, was closely examined in the celebrated arbitration involving Libya and Texaco.[65] Professor Dupuy, in his famous arbitral decision, explored the legal significance of these resolutions and concluded that they were not binding on capital exporting states; while the relevant provision had been passed by large majorities of Third World states, it had been opposed by many industrialised states.[66] Dupuy, relying on a

---

[61] G. A. Res. 1803 at para. 4. [62] Ibid. at para. 8. [63] G. A. Res. 3281.

[64] Res. 3281, para. 2(c); the reference to states is significant as this seemed to diminish the importance of corporations.

[65] *Texaco Overseas Petroleum Co. & California Asiatic Oil Co. v. The Government of the Libyan Arab Republic*, 53 ILR 389 (Preliminary Award 27 November 1975; Award on the Merits 19 January 1977) (hereafter Texaco Award).

[66] Paragraph 2(c) of Article 2 was subject to a separate vote. 104 states voted in favour, with sixteen against and six abstentions. Texaco Award, p. 489. The major capital exporting states were among the sixteen dissenters.

considerable literature analysing the status of General Assembly resolutions, concluded that the relevant provision was not law, and even more broadly, that 'Article 2 of this Charter must be analysed as a political rather than as a legal declaration concerned with the ideological strategy of development and, as such, supported only by non-industrialised states'.[67]

The validity of the reasoning and legal status of this decision has been widely questioned.[68] The ramifications, which have been much extracted and analysed, are several. In effect, the decision starkly asserts that the new states, whatever the numbers they possessed, were incapable of changing international law if those changes were opposed by the industrialised states. Such opposition was inevitable, given that the old rules had in effect been created by those industrialised states to further their own interests during the colonial period. Even more significantly, the decision presents as decisive the Western version of the old rules of state responsibility that were so vehemently attacked by the new states; these were the old rules that Dupuy applied to the dispute – despite the fact that the new states, by voting for Article 2, had clearly demonstrated that they no longer regarded themselves as bound by the old law. The stark contrast that I have been attempting to illuminate, between Third World and established sovereignty, is clearly demonstrated once again; the resistance of the old states to the emerging law of development is upheld as a valid exercise of sovereignty. According to Dupuy, however, the new states were powerless to change the law that they had played no role in creating and which profoundly undermined the sovereignty they were supposed to enjoy.

These were the legal techniques used to oppose the attempts of the new states to use the General Assembly to create a different type of international law. In effect, then, the efforts made by both Western and Third World lawyers in the 1960s, to create an international law that could accommodate the legitimate aspirations of the new states, was contested in these different ways. Indeed, it is arguable that the new states were unable even to use the 'old' law to their advantage, because of the emergence of a new arena and a new type of law in which development issues were to be resolved. The West not only negated Third World attempts to use the General Assembly as a means of transforming a colonial international law, but set about using a new legal framework,

---

[67] Texaco Award, p. 492.

[68] See discussion *infra* of the views, for example, of Ian Brownlie and M. S. Sornarajah.

suggested by the term 'transnational law', to further undermine the economic sovereignty of the new states.

Colonialism and the emergence of transnational law

Both the West and the new states alike understood that private actors, multinational corporations (MNCs), played a vital role in achieving development. While the new states possessed rich natural resources, their exploitation required the investment and expertise of foreign MNCs. As a consequence of this emphasis on the importance of MNCs for development, the whole project of achieving development intersected with several other major contemporary debates in international law, which focused not only on the emergence of the Third World but on the emergence of non-state entities as significant actors in the international arena, and the effects of these non-state entities on international law.

The theme was more explicitly taken up in Philip Jessup's notable work, *Transnational Law*,[69] which examined the impact of these entities and sketched a legal framework appropriate for the regulation of these new realities. Such a framework, Jessup argued, could be provided by 'transnational law', a system that comprised a complex combination of domestic law, private international law and public international law. As the developing field of transnational law was in many respects created to account for the emergence of actors such as MNCs, it had a particular significance for Third World states because it was precisely in those states that the activities of these corporations generated new and complex problems that required legal resolution. Understandably, then, Jessup alluded in his work to a series of famous Middle Eastern arbitrations of the early 1950s. These arbitrations arose out of disputes between Western-based corporations, and Middle Eastern states that had granted these corporations concessions to exploit the oil in their territories. Further, the increasing engagement of MNCs in the economic affairs of Third World states led to the emergence, in American law schools, of the subject 'the international law of foreign investment', a topic which studied relations 'between sovereigns and private investors – a field almost automatically excluded from the traditional study of international law,

---

[69] Philip Jessup, *Transnational Law* (New Haven: Yale University Press, 1956). It should be noted that Jessup himself spoke forcefully against the furtherance of a neo-colonial international law, arguing that 'Economic imperialism is not consistent with the modern concepts on which the United Nations is built and should function'. Philip Jessup, *A Modern Law of Nations* (New York: Macmillan, 1948), p. 117.

which recognizes only states as subjects of international law'.[70] At a number of levels, then, it was broadly claimed that these new developments required the formation of a new set of rules and processes – and, indeed, academic disciplines. All these facts suggest, perhaps, the colonial origins of foreign investment law as an academic discipline.

While the arguments regarding the novel challenges posed by MNCs were valid in some respects, it could hardly be claimed that MNCs were new actors in the international arena. Traditional international law had developed a number of doctrines to deal with the relationships between MNCs and host governments, including the doctrine of diplomatic protection and state responsibility for injury to aliens. Examined in the context of colonial history, furthermore, the MNCs were in many respects successors to entities such as the Dutch and British East India Companies which, after all, had been central to the whole imperial project. Indeed, these companies, far from being new actors in international relations, had enjoyed sovereign powers under the international law of the nineteenth century. Grotius, the father of international law, had also served as the lawyer for the Dutch East India Company, and had written several of his most important works as a justification for advancing their interests. Further, even after they were deprived of such sovereign status, these metropolitan companies had firmly and expansively entrenched themselves in the economic affairs of the colonies by entering into concession agreements with the colonial authority for the exploitation of the colonial territory's resources. No real legal difficulties were created by these entities and their transactions, however, because their dealings with the colonial government were regulated by the laws of that government. These agreements were not, of course, the subject of international law since they fell within the scope of the domestic jurisdiction of the colonial state.

The acquisition of sovereignty by the new states profoundly changed these comfortable arrangements and assumptions, for these foreign corporations were now regulated by the municipal law of the new state intent on regaining control over its natural resources. This municipal law was arguably subject to international minimum standards, the issue of ongoing controversy between the West and the new states. Nevertheless, in asserting the primacy of national laws over corporations

---

[70] Wolfgang Friedmann, 'The Changing Dimensions of International Law', (1962) 62 *Columbia Law Review* 1147 at 1148. As Friedmann points out, this gave rise to the discipline of international economic law, a field he describes as 'new and largely experimental'.

operating within their territory, the new states were merely asserting certain incontrovertible and classic principles regarding sovereignty and domestic jurisdiction.

It was precisely these classic principles, however, that were questioned and challenged by the new phenomenon of transnational law, which was used to attempt to abridge the powers of the sovereign Third World state in a number of important respects. The particular techniques used for these purposes, and their impact on Third World sovereignty, may be understood by an examination of a series of seminal arbitral decisions that were handed down in the 1950s. Arbitration, of course, was a venerable institution for the resolution of international disputes, and it was a particularly favoured means of resolving disputes between states and private foreign actors. Much of the law of state responsibility had been developed through arbitration. Now, with the concentrated focus of the international community on development, and the corresponding generation of foreign investment agreements on an unprecedented scale, arbitration was given an extraordinarily important role in formulating the law relating to these agreements. Many arbitral decisions adopted the position that these agreements, because they were unique 'economic development agreements', and because they involved the state on the one hand and a non-state actor, a foreign corporation, on the other, had to be regulated by a new type of legal framework – the framework eventually described and analysed as transnational law. In effect, a significant aspect of the project of economic development that was so crucial to Third World countries was to take place in this new arena, the transnational arena, which required to be structured and managed through new legal doctrines.

In sketching the impact of arbitration on the emergence of the law of development, and on the classical principles of sovereignty that the Third World sought to rely upon, I have focused on some of the arbitral decisions handed down in the 1950s which have been the subject of extensive discussion and analysis because of their founding significance for the law of international arbitration.[71] The decisions include the

[71] See Amr A. Shalakany, 'Arbitration and the Third World: A Plea for Reassessing Bias Under the Specter of Neoliberalism', (2000) 41 *Harvard International Law Journal* 419; Patrick M. Norton, 'Law of the Future or Law of the Past? Modern Tribunals and the International Law of Expropriation', (1991) 85 *American Journal of International Law* 474; M. S. Sornarajah, *The Settlement of Foreign Investment Disputes* (The Hague: Kluwer Law International, 2000), pp. 249ff; Jan Paulsson, 'Arbitration Unbound: Award Detached from the Law of Its Country of Origin', (1981) 30 *International & Comparative Law Quarterly* 358; Jan Paulsson, 'Delocalisation of International Commercial Arbitration: When and Why it Matters', (1983) 32 *International & Comparative Law Quarterly* 53.

Arbitration involving Petroleum Developments (Trucial Coast) Limited and the Ruler of Abu Dhabi,[72] and the Arbitration between the Ruler of Qatar and International Marine Oil Company.[73] These decisions have acquired a certain notoriety in the field of arbitration, and are now regarded with a certain embarrassment.[74] But I focus on them because they raise, in a very explicit form, the crucial issues raised by this emerging field of transnational law for the sovereignty of new states and the evolution of the techniques used to resolve them. These techniques were to some extent obscured by the later, more diplomatically worded, arbitral decisions. The common theme uniting these arbitral decisions was their conclusion that the contracts between the new states and foreign corporations were not governed by the municipal law of thecountry. Rather, the contracts were characterized as being internationalised.[75] These arbitral decisions in turn have been succeeded by a number of others, the most notable of which was the decision handed down by Arbitrator Dupuy in the 1977 *Texaco* Case, which appears to be regarded in the literature as a classic statement and culmination of a series of legal developments which focused on identifying the unique character of these contracts and then formulating the principles of law which applied to their operation. Dupuy's decision may be regarded as a classic, furthermore, for reasons elaborated in more detail below, because not only does it outline the characteristics of this new law but it also illuminates the relationship between this law and Third World attempts to use the much-prized sovereignty to pursue their own interests.

Sources of law and international contracts

The concession agreements between Arab states and Western MNCs that were the subject of the disputes contained arbitration clauses that provided, in the event of a dispute, for the resolution of the dispute by an arbitral tribunal that was to be established in the manner provided for in the clause. It was uncontested that in usual circumstances, the

---

[72] *Petroleum Development Ltd. v. The Sheikh of Abu Dhabi* (1951) 18 I.L.R. 144 (hereafter Abu Dhabi Award).
[73] *Ruler of Qatar v. International Marine Oil Co.* (1953) 20 I.L.R. 534 (hereafter, Ruler of Qatar award).
[74] Jan Paulsson, 'Third World Participation in International Investment Arbitration', (1987) 2 ICSID Rev. 19 at 21.
[75] I am indebted to the expert discussion of the techniques of internationalization provided by M. S. Sornarajah, 'The Climate of International Arbitration', (June 1991) 8 *Journal of International Arbitration* 47.

agreements would be governed by the laws of the host state. Thus, in the words of the arbitrator, Lord Asquith of Bishopstone, in the *Ruler of Abu Dhabi* Case:

What is the 'Proper Law' applicable in construing this contract? This is a contract made in Abu Dhabi and wholly to be performed in that country. If any municipal system of law were applicable, it would prima facie be that of Abu Dhabi.[76]

This position, which is no more than a restatement of the classic principles of international law,[77] was, however, rejected by Lord Asquith, who magisterially pronounced that the domestic law of Abu Dhabi was inapplicable because

no such law can reasonably be said to exist. The Sheikha administers a purely discretionary justice with the assistance of the Koran; and it would be fanciful to suggest that in this very primitive region there is any settled body of legal principles applicable to the construction of modern commercial contracts.[78]

While basically arriving at the same conclusion that the local law was inapplicable, Sir Alfred Bucknill, in another Middle Eastern arbitration, observed, with more restraint, that 'I have no reason to suppose that Islamic law is not administered there strictly, but I am satisfied that the law does not contain any principles sufficient to interpret this particular contract'.[79]

The basic reasons for departing from the clearly established principle that the applicable law is the law of the host state are further developed and elaborated by Lord McNair in a notable article that appeared in the *British Yearbook of International Law*. McNair argued that there is a

---

[76] Abu Dhabi Award, p. 149.
[77] *The Case Concerning Various Serbian Loans* establishes this point:
> Any contract which is not a contract between States in their capacity as subjects of international law is based on the municipal law of some country. The question as to what this law is forms the subject of that branch of law which is at the present day usually described as private international law or the theory of conflict of laws.
>> (*Case Concerning Various Serbian Loans Issued in France* (1929), PCIJ Ser. A, No. 20 at p. 41, cited by Dupuy in the Texaco Award at p. 443)
This is the orthodox, classical position which was transformed by the emergence of transnational law.
[78] Abu Dhabi Award, p. 149.
[79] Ruler of Qatar Award, p. 545. Sir Alfred further concluded, after hearing the testimony of two experts, that in Islamic law as applied in Qatar there was no settled body of legal principles applicable to modern commercial contract law of this kind. *Ibid.*, p. 544.

'strongly marked contrast both in content and stage of development' in the laws of, basically, Western countries and 'the law of many Asiatic countries'.[80] The domestic law of these new states 'has not yet been developed to deal with this particular type of transaction'.[81] Given the enormity of the departure from classic principles of international law and the quite sweeping assertion that a law adequate for the purposes of dealing with such complex contracts did not exist in the domestic sphere of the non-European state, McNair sought to strengthen his argument by asserting that the state itself would not have intended the contract to be governed by its own non-existent law; rather, McNair suggests, it could be inferred that the government did not intend the applicable law to be that of its own state

The question then emerged: what was the law applicable to such a contract? Public international law could not govern these agreements because they were entered into by states and private entities. Nor was private international law helpful in these circumstances, because it was used for the purposes of determining which systems of municipal international law applied to the contract. The three categories of law recognized by the PCIJ in the 1929 *Serbian Loans* Case – public international law, private international law and municipal law – did not apply in these circumstances. In short, a new system of law, which had an international character but which was not public international law, had to be developed to deal with these special cases.

Despite this, McNair argued, the new legal framework had close affiliations with public international law, as it shared with public international law a common source of recruitment and inspiration, namely, 'the general principles of law recognized by civilized nations'.[82] Having thus established a source of law applicable to these new types of transactions, McNair promptly proceeds to identify the applicable substantive principles: 'respect for the private property and the acquired rights of foreigners undoubtedly constituted one of these "general principles"'.[83] Another such principle was the principle of 'unjust enrichment' – when the corporation was denied its rights and the host state profited unjustly

---

[80] Lord Arnold McNair, 'The General Principles of Law Recognized by Civilised Nations', (1957) 33 *British Yearbook of International Law* 1.

[81] *Ibid.*, p. 4.

[82] *Ibid.*, p. 6. 'General principles' are referred to as a source of law in Article 38(1)c of the Statute of the International Court of Justice. In addition, of course, McNair could have drawn on the argument that international law prescribed certain standards for the protection of aliens – and their private property.

[83] *Ibid.*, p. 15.

from this action. The application of this principle to colonial rule and the exploitation it enabled received significantly less scholarly attention at the time.

Once the category of 'general principles' had been established as a source of law, municipal systems could come into play. Thus, as Lord Asquith argued:

> But albeit English municipal law is inapplicable as such, some of its rules are in my view so firmly grounded in reason, as to form part of this broad jurisprudence – this 'modern law of nature'.[84]

A new 'natural law' of contracts emerges, a law by which the law of the Third World state is in effect selectively replaced by the law of England through the invocation of 'general principles of law'. Startling consequences follow from this reasoning: not only is the concession *not* governed by the law of Abu Dhabi, but it could, rather, be governed by the law of England because that law represented the 'modern law of nature'. As mentioned, these early decisions are now regarded as an embarrassment by arbitrators who now, like their counterparts in the field of public international law, have attempted to distance themselves from the colonial origins of their particular specialization, international arbitral law.[85]

Nevertheless, the fundamental principles outlined in these decisions attempting to profoundly negate Third World sovereignty have been elaborated and further refined by subsequent arbitral decisions. These subsequent decisions have developed three basic themes that are first evident in these earlier decisions. First, the view that these concession agreements were unique agreements, economic development agreements that were not governed by the municipal law of the host state but rather, had been internationalised. Second, that the state had acquiesced in various ways to these contracts being governed by a law other than its own municipal law; and, third, that a new type of law which was connected with both municipal and international law but which was different from both, governed these contracts. This new law, which might be

---

[84] Abu Dhabi Award, p. 149. Notably, however, English law had to be selectively applied. Thus, interestingly, Lord Asquith refuses to apply the English law favouring the sovereign, the 'rule that grants by a sovereign are to be construed by the grantee' on the basis that this rule was a peculiar product of English history and was of 'little relevance to conditions in a protected State of a primitive order on the Persian Gulf'. *Ibid.*, p. 150.

[85] See Shalakany, 'Arbitration', 430.

seen as an embodiment of transnational law, was variously termed the 'international law of contracts' and 'international commercial law';[86] or, more broadly, when international law was established as governing these arrangements, it was an international law 'found in the general principles of civilized nations'.[87]

Each of these themes has been carefully analysed by M. S. Sornarajah, who has produced a sustained and erudite body of work directed at revealing the problems associated with these new arguments that asserted 'principles hitherto unknown in international law'.[88] As Ian Brownlie argues, for instance: 'Before the Second World War the view that concession contracts operated on the plane of international law was heretical.'[89] Indeed, even shortly after the war, the ICJ, in the 1952 case between Iran and the United Kingdom (*Anglo Iranian Oil Co.* Case), declared in effect that an agreement between a state and a corporation was simply a concessionary agreement and could not be elevated to the international level.[90] It was precisely this proposition that the new international law of contracts sought to undermine.

By the time of the *Texaco* decision, the basic problems that had been so crudely addressed in the earlier decisions could be resolved with far greater elaboration. It is clear that arbitral decisions and scholarly writings influenced the nature of the arbitral clauses that were used in concession agreements. Whereas the earlier arbitral clauses made no specific reference to international law as governing the arbitration clauses in subsequent concessions, agreements usually made reference to dispute resolution through arbitrations that would apply 'general principles of law'[91] – a category which by now enabled the effortless transposition of Western concepts of law that provided for the comprehensive protection of private property. Consequently, it became far easier for arbitrators to conclude that the contract had indeed

---

[86] Texaco Award, p. 448.   [87] *Ibid.*, p. 449.

[88] M. S. Sornarajah, *The International Law on Foreign Investment* (Cambridge: Cambridge University Press, 1994), p. 21.

[89] Ian Brownlie, *Legal Status of Natural Resources in International Law (Some Aspects)* (Alphen aan den Rijn: Sijthoff & Noordhoff, 1980), p. 308.

[90] *Anglo-Iranian Oil Co. Case (U.K. v. Iran)*, ICJ Reports 1952, p. 93. But see Schrijver, *Sovereignty*, p. 42.

[91] See Texaco Award, p. 453; the arbitral clause in the Texaco Award provided for the application in the first place of Libyan law common to the principles of international law, failing which, the law applicable was 'the general principles of law, including such of those principles as may be applied by international tribunals'. *Ibid.*, p. 450. This was interpreted in effect to mean the application of 'international law to the legal relations between the parties'. *Ibid.*, p. 453.

been internationalised, even when reference was made to local law and, secondarily, to 'general principles of law'.

Thus the 'international' could be established as governing this trans-action in a number of different ways, and a whole repertoire of argu-ments were developed by jurists apparently intent on demonstrating their virtuosity by elaborating on the many ways in which this interna-tionalization had been achieved. For Dupuy, a reference to 'international arbitration' in the contract meant not only that any dispute had to be resolved through international arbitration, but that the law applied by the arbitral body was the new international law of contracts. It was in this broad sense that the contract had been internationalised for Dupuy:

> It is therefore unquestionable that the reference to international arbitration is sufficient to internationalise a contract, in other words, to situate it within a specific legal order, the international law of contracts.[92]

Dupuy, further supported his argument by asserting that the contract could also be seen as internationalised if it included any reference to 'general principles of law'.[93] Indeed, even more startlingly, the mere fact that the contract was a particular type of agreement, an 'economic development agreement' elevated it to the international level, even when explicit reference was made to the municipal, national law as the gov-erning law.[94] Dupuy characterizes these agreements as long-term agree-ments requiring considerable investment by the foreign party, who thus becomes associated 'with the realization of the economic and social progress of the host country'.[95]

These factors resulted in the formation of agreements which were sub-ject, not to domestic law, but to *sui generis* rules or to a system which is properly 'an international law system'.[96] As Derek Bowett argues, as against this view, developed states entering into foreign investment

---

[92] See *ibid.*, p. 455.

[93] *Ibid.*, p. 453. Dupuy further pointed out that the inadequacy of domestic law was not the only reason for the internationalization of the contract and a recourse to 'general principles of law'; in addition, resort to general principles was seen as a means by which contractual equilibrium could be achieved between the state and the investor, and the latter could be 'protected against unilateral and abrupt modifications of the legislation in the contracting State'. *Ibid.*, p. 454. In other words, contractual relations could prevail even as against legislative power.

[94] *Ibid.*, p. 455. The further suggestion appears to be that even if the contract made municipal law explicitly applicable, the contract might still be internationalised as a consequence of the fact that it is an economic development agreement. See *ibid.*, p. 460.

[95] *Ibid.*, p. 456.   [96] Texaco Award, p. 457.

agreements did not accept this theory of internationalization, which 'raises the question of why such contracts are only "internationalised" if concluded by developing States'.[97]

Further, by entering into such contracts, Third World states, in effect, were investing foreign corporations with international personality, providing them with the 'certain capacities which enable [them] to act internationally in order to invoke the rights which result to [them] from an internationalised contract'.[98] In addition, provisions within such agreements were designed precisely to prevent the state from exercising its usual sovereign powers:

The investor must in particular be protected against legislative uncertainties, that is to say, the risks of the municipal law of the municipal law of the host country being modified, or against any government measures which would lead to an abrogation or rescission of the contract.[99]

The argument that the contracts had been internationalised was further advanced by characterizing the transaction between the Third World state and the corporation in two different ways. First, it was argued that these agreements were akin to 'quasi treaties'.[100] The agreement thus existed between two international entities, the Third World state and the corporation which, by implication, had international personality, and to that extent, a quasi-sovereign status which enabled it to take action against the Third World state on the international plane. Secondly, and contrastingly, these agreements were characterized as contracts – but not as contracts between a state and a private actor, but a contract between two equal private actors.

The basic significance of an agreement between a state and a private entity is that the state retains certain residual powers with respect to the

---

[97] Derek Bowett, 'State Contracts With Aliens: Contemporary Developments on Compensation for Termination or Breach', (1988) 59 *The British Yearbook of International Law* 49–74.

[98] Texaco Award, p. 459.

[99] *Ibid.*, p. 456. The clauses that provided for this stasis were known as 'stabilization clauses'. For criticisms of Dupuy's award, see Brownlie, *Legal Status of Natural Resources*, pp. 308–309; Bowett, 'State Contracts', 50–51.

[100] Friedmann, 'Changing Dimensions', 1158 (citing Jessup, Berle and Schwarzenberger). Further, the British government argued an agreement between the Anglo-Persian Oil Company and the Iranian Government has a 'double character, the character of being at once a concessionary contract between the Iranian Government and the Company and a treaty between the two Governments'. *Anglo-Iranian Oil. Co.*, 1952 ICJ at p. 112; cited in Jessup, *Transnational Law*, p. 14. It is noteworthy that the Middle Eastern arbitrations feature in several of Jessup's examples: see, e.g., pp. 19–20, 31–32; 81–82 (Abu Dhabi Award).

contract, which powers it would exercise in the interests of its people. The right of the state to organise its own economic system was continuously reiterated, even by Dupuy.[101] The right to nationalise property is an example of such a residual right that all sovereign powers possess. While it was quite commonplace for government contracts to be legally modified by a government legally exercising its sovereign powers, the ability of a state to unilaterally amend the obligations embodied in a treaty with another country were much more limited.[102] Thus, if the agreement was a treaty, or a quasi-treaty, then the ability of a state to change the terms of the agreement would be significantly restricted precisely because then, as Dupuy goes on to assert in ringing tones, the most sacrosanct principles of international law, *pacta sunt servanda*, applied to these contracts. Seen in this framework, the characterization of the agreement as a quasi-treaty had the simultaneous effect of restricting the powers of the Third World state, on the one hand, while implicitly on the other, elevating the private actor to an entity that has certain rights under international law, and to that extent bestowing such entities with a quasi-sovereign status.[103]

As a consequence, we return, then, to a situation where Western corporations operating in the developing world, like their predecessors, the East India company and other such trading companies, acquire a quasi-sovereign status. In the nineteenth century, 'sovereign' corporations acquired sovereignty over native peoples by entering into treaties with them – a practice which gave rise to the argument that these native entities were in some respect sovereign – if only for the limited purposes of transferring their sovereignty to the corporation. Now, the reverse relationship was being enacted: the Third World state, by contracting with the corporation, was providing it with a quasi-sovereign status – which gave it significant powers, not least of which was an elevation of its status to the international plane.[104] The right of sovereign Third World states to grant corporations such quasi-sovereign status was staunchly

---

[101] Texaco Award, pp. 470–471.

[102] See Brownlie, *Legal Status of Natural Resources*, pp. 308–309.

[103] See the discussion by Dupuy in the Texaco Award, pp. 458–459. Dupuy states that 'for the purposes of interpretation and performance of the contract, it should be recognized that a private contracting party has specific international capacities'. Texaco Award, p. 458.

[104] This point could be of some interest in the context of current debates as to the status, in international law, of MNCs. See, e.g., Steven R. Ratner, 'Corporations and Human Rights: A Theory of Legal Responsibility', (2001) 111 *Yale Law Journal* 443. Generally, it appears that it is corporations which operated in non-European states that enjoyed this peculiar quasi-sovereign status according to the law as outlined by these jurists. Corporations operating in European states are unlikely to have enjoyed this status.

234 IMPERIALISM, SOVEREIGNTY AND INTERNATIONAL LAW

defended by scholars and arbitral tribunals, just as nineteenth-century scholars had argued in favour of the proposition that non-European entities had a legal status sufficient to enable them to properly transfer their rights to European states.

Even as the contract was characterized as a quasi-treaty, jurists also simultaneously characterized it, by contrast, as a contract between two private parties. The application of the framework of contract transformed the state into a private actor that was merely contracting with another private actor, and could not rely on any residual sovereign powers to amend the terms of the contract, whatever the demands of public welfare. The application of contract principles in a situation where the Third World state was deprived of its one major source of bargaining power, sovereignty, considerably shifted the relative strengths of the two parties.

The sovereignty of new states was further undermined by stabilization clauses. Under these clauses, once the new state had entered into a contract, it was taken to have consented to suspend the exercise of its usual public functions, its legislative powers, to the extent that they affected the contract; consequently, any agreement between the state and the corporation could be changed only with the mutual assent of the two parties. This position was supported by the argument that a state could exercise its sovereignty by binding itself to a particular arrangement – as famously asserted by the PCIJ in the 1923 S. S. Wimbledon Case.[105] Nevertheless, as Brownlie pointed out, such a position was a radical departure from the legal position that prevailed in capital exporting countries, where government contracts were susceptible to unilateral amendment.[106] Furthermore, as Brownlie argued, it would be unrealistic to 'treat this contract as a fundamental law, overriding the power of the legislation within the State concerned and producing rigidity in the economy'.[107]

Thus, on one hand, the Third World state elevated the corporation to the international level, and the concession was a quasi-treaty. On the

---

[105] S. S. Wimbledon (U.K., France, Italy, Japan, Germany) 1923, PCIJ Ser. A, No.1. It is difficult to overlook the fact, when reading this case and the principle it stands for regarding the rights of a sovereign state to assert its sovereignty by binding itself, that the state whose rights to surrender its sovereignty was being upheld was the vanquished and defeated state of Germany.

[106] Ian Brownlie, 'Legal Status of Natural Resources in International Law', (1979-I) 162 Académie du Droit International, Recueil de Cours 245–318 at 309. See also Bowett, 'State Contracts', 55–56.

[107] Brownlie, 'Legal Status of Natural Resources', 309.

other, the state, by entering into these concessions, is taken to have acted almost as a strictly private party, dealing with equals.[108] Whether a quasi-treaty between a sovereign and a quasi-sovereign entity, or a contract between two private parties, what is common to both characterizations is the real reduction of the powers of the sovereign Third World state with respect to the Western corporation. The Third World state was thus subjected to unique constraints that were especially unconscionable because it was the new states that most urgently needed the flexibility necessary to achieve development after years of exploitation and dependency.

Overview and conclusions

My broad argument has been that traditional principles of international law, particularly sovereignty doctrine, take on a different form when applied to the non-European world. I pursue the same line of inquiry in this chapter. Now the non-European world presents itself not as the tribal chief whose legal personality has to be determined, or the mandate peoples seeking self-government, but a sovereign entity intent on reversing the effects of imperialism by changing the rules of international law in order to achieve development. Consequently, the West had to confront the challenge of preventing the disruption of the international order which would follow from the developing world's campaign to articulate its history of exploitation and to change the rules of international law that had both justified and furthered this system of exploitation. The non-European world, the Third World, must be distanced now, not because it is barbaric or threatening or undeveloped – although these ideas continue to have a powerful residual influence – but because it seeks these changes. But how does the West attempt this, now that the Third World has acquired sovereignty, the most powerful instrument of international law?

The West responded by negating the Third World campaign for a NIEO on the one hand, and by elaborating a new transnational law of international contracts on the other. As a consequence, not only was the Third World attempt to reform international law largely thwarted, but it had to contend with a new set of rules, the 'international law of contracts', that sought to expand the powers of MNCs well beyond the powers those corporations had enjoyed under the traditional law of state

---

[108] See the discussion in the Texaco Award, pp. 466–467.

responsibility. The *Texaco* decision illustrates both these themes. Even while seeking to negate the effect of General Assembly resolutions and relying on the classic law of state responsibility to establish the principle that compensation was determined by international rather than local standards, it proceeded well beyond the traditional law of state responsibility by further asserting that the entire contract was governed by a putative international law and that, further, the foreign corporation had the necessary international personality to pursue its claims in the international realm.

Many aspects of the debates I have examined here remain controversial and unresolved. The rules of state responsibility and the effect of bilateral investment treaties on the customary international law applicable to these treaties, for example, continue to be the subject of analysis and debate. The character of this debate has altered profoundly, however, as a consequence of the emergence of neo-liberal development policy and the fact that Third World countries are now competing intensely with each other to attract foreign investment. It would seem that whatever the failures of the NIEO,[109] it did at least serve the purpose of challenging the Western view of state responsibility.

The issues I have been examining here seem moot in many respects. The use of bilateral investment agreements, the acceptance by the majority of Third World states of international arbitration and of the legal provisions desired by investors, in order to attract foreign investment, the creation and expanding use of the International Center for the Settlement of Investment Disputes (ICSID) – all these developments have gone far towards resolving many of the practical questions that created the debates I have examined here.[110] My main interest, however, has focused,

---

[109] For a moving and powerful account of the failure of the Third World to establish the concept of the 'common heritage of mankind' to advance its own interests in the Law of the Sea, another area in which the Third World hoped to reform international law, see Moragodage C. W. Pinto, '"Common Heritage of Mankind": From Metaphor to Myth and the Consequences of Constructive Ambiguity', in Jerzy Makarczyk (ed.), *Theory of International Law at the Threshold of the 21st Century: Essays in Honour of Krysztof Skubiszewksi* (The Hague: Kluwer Law International, 1996), pp. 249–268.

[110] For contrasting assessments of the current situation, see, e.g., Charles Brower, 'Notes and Comments: International Arbitration and the Islamic World: The Third Phase', (2003) 97 *American Journal of International Law* 643–656; M. S. Sornarajah, 'Economic Neo-Liberalism and the International Law on Foreign Investment', in Antony Anghie, Bhupinder Chimni, Karin Mickelson and Obiora Okafor (eds.), *The Third World and International Order: Law, Politics and Globalization* (Leiden: Martinus Nijhoff, 2003), pp. 173–191.

not so much on establishing the current law relating to this area, but on the ways in which the newly emergent Third World challenge was met by the West, and what these debates reveal about sovereignty doctrine in terms of the history I have attempted to sketch.

By arguing that the area of foreign investment contracts required a new legal framework, arbitrators could choose the principles of private and public international law that were in their view most appropriate to deal with this novel situation. The existence of an 'international law of contracts' continues to be questioned. Nevertheless, to the extent it exists, the law of international contracts, as traced through the writings and reasoning of McNair and Dupuy, was shaped profoundly by the post-colonial encounter between metropolitan states and investors on the one hand, and the new states on the other. Sources doctrine was the crucial arena of contestation in the attempts to develop this law, because many jurists asserted that the principles embodied in this international law of contracts derived from 'general principles of law'. One of the aspirations of the new states was to expand the range of international law and to contribute towards its formation by drawing upon Article 38(1)(c) of the Statute of the International Court of Justice which mentions general principles as a source of law. As Abi-Saab argued:

This source of international law is very important from the point of view of the newly independent states. It is through it that they hope their legal systems will contribute to the development of international law. This would widen its base and increase its material sources. It would also give the newly independent state the satisfaction of participating in the creation of the law they are supposed to observe.[111]

These efforts, pursued through the General Assembly, for example, have been largely resisted, although Third World jurists such as Judge Weeramantry continue to attempt to make Third World jurisprudence a part of international law.[112] 'General principles', however, was precisely the source used by jurists such as McNair and Dupuy to develop not so much international, but transnational, law.

As scholars such as Friedmann and Fatouros pointed out, the West and the new states had very different ideas regarding the relationship between the state and property. Recognizing the intention of the Third World to change the property arrangements established by colonial rule,

---

[111] Abi-Saab, 'The Newly Independent States and the Scope', p. 109.
[112] See, e.g., Judge Weeramantry, separate opinion, *Case Concerning the Gabcikovo-Nagymaros Project (Hungary v. Slovakia)*, ICJ Reports 1997, p. 7.

Fatouros argued that 'there is no implicit understanding on the legal position of private property whether owned by the aliens or the citizens'.[113] These views, of course, are reinforced by the clear positions staked out by the new states in the General Assembly. Strangely, then, 'general principles of law' relating to contracts and the protection of property were being asserted at precisely the time when the Third World was clearly rejecting such principles. It is one thing to say that the West is not bound by Assembly resolutions; it is something else to entirely overlook those resolutions when presenting so-called 'general principles' of international law. What is then relied upon is something like the natural law of contracts or, to use the language of Lord Asquith, 'the modern law of nature' that transcends, and prevails against, the objections of numerous states.

What is equally clear, then, is that while the international law of contracts was proclaimed to be universal, it was a law which was specifically devised to deal with a type of agreement to which only Third World states were parties – i.e. economic development agreements. There is thus a double movement evident in the construction of this law: it is proclaimed to be 'universal', through recourse to general principles, in order to overcome Third World assertions of sovereignty; at the same time, this 'universal' law has a very particular and specific application to the new states, because it is only these new states which enter into these unique types of agreements. As in the case of Vitoria's jurisprudence, the principle of universality creates, even as it encompasses, the difference that must be sanctioned; universality is created to disempower the party to which it applies. Indeed, the construction of the universal and the international is not by any means an innocent act for here, it would seem, the 'international' is formulated precisely in order to subordinate the Third World. The international law of contracts does not apply to the West itself, for as Bowett, among other scholars, points out, many of the crucial elements of the international law of contracts – relating to the governing law and the validity of stabilization clauses – have been rejected by developed states.[114] The reasoning and validity of *Texaco* has been questioned both by scholars and subsequent arbitral decisions. But for my purposes, its real significance lies in what it reveals of the strategies that could be used to negate Third World sovereignty, and the resemblance between those strategies and the sort of reasoning found in Vitoria.

---

[113] Fatouros, 'International Law', 811.   [114] Bowett, 'State Contracts'.

In very broad and no doubt simplistic terms, one of the major responses of the West to the challenge of the Third World was to entrench neo-imperial economic relations in the private sphere.[115] In the field of international economic law, it is this 'post-colonial' encounter that reconstitutes the division between the private and public sphere, establishes the content of each and proceeds to demarcate the boundaries between the private and the public that have to be maintained and elaborated. Colonialism, of course, had been furthered not simply in the realm of public international law that had, in the nineteenth century, excluded non-European peoples from the realm of sovereignty, but also through private law regimes of contract and property that justified the dispossession of the native peoples by Western individuals and corporations. The new states, then, sought to use their sovereign powers to transform the private law rules that played such a significant role in creating and furthering colonial inequalities. But rather than an expansion of public power over the private realm, transnational law was deployed for the purpose of achieving the reverse: of establishing that private law was not susceptible to amendment by the state.

Indeed, public international law, transformed by the medium of transnational law, was then used to further solidify the private realm and to enhance the immunity of private actors. This is reflected by the emphasis on the importance of 'acquired rights' which now assumed the status of a 'general principle of international law', and respect for private property. A further aspect of this use of public law to protect private rights is suggested by Friedmann, who argued that 'Private law may become public law, and a comparative study of a particular subject may become the prelude for an international convention'.[116] Further, international organizations were becoming increasingly involved in 'their role in developing new bodies of law or transforming private law and rules into norms of public international law'.[117] It was through this mechanism that a 'whole new body of international commercial public law is developing'.[118]

Apart from stressing the universality of the international law of contracts, the jurists developing this body of law focused on legal doctrines which bind sovereigns, the most prominent of these being, of course, *pacta sunt servanda*. In justifying these radical transformations in

---

[115] I am indebted here to Amr Shalakany's work on the private–public distinction and its effects on the law of international commercial arbitration. See Shalakany, 'Arbitration'.

[116] Friedmann, 'Changing Dimensions', 1153.   [117] *Ibid.*, 1157.   [118] *Ibid.*, 1158.

established doctrines of jurisdiction and sovereign powers these jurists relied heavily on the basic principles of contract. Leaving aside the complications of acquired rights and state responsibility, the simple fact remained that the sovereign Third World state had agreed to be bound by the terms of the contract, and the arbitrators were doing no more than enforcing those terms.

It is hardly surprising then, that *pacta sunt servanda* and the *S. S. Wimbledon* are cited in the *Texaco* decision, because in many of these decisions Third World sovereignty is most firmly asserted in the context of its ability to transfer it. As Grovogui points out, the 'right of the natives to dispose of themselves' was a principle that was asserted from the time at least of the Berlin Conference.[119] The whole discourse of contracts as it applied to the Third World has, since the nineteenth century, focused on two main themes: the construction of 'consent' on the part of the non-European entity; and the power that contracts bestow on a non-European entity, whether a tribe or a sovereign state, to transfer whatever resources it possesses. These are the themes evident in the nineteenth century – and the same themes are found even in the most important provisions of the PSNR. Thus, for example Resolution 1803, the Third World's foundational resolution, talks of the rights of people to 'dispose of their natural resources' in language that eerily reflects that proposed at the Berlin Conference in 1884–5, by Kasson, the American representative, who asserted the 'right' of native peoples to 'dispose of themselves'. Resolution 1803 also talks of 'contracts freely entered into' by the state, in a situation where the whole idea of the 'freedom' of the Third World state had been rendered extremely problematic by the whole burden of colonialism. Curiously, then, the Third World itself appears to have accepted this characterization, strenuously affirming its powers of transfer even as it affirms its sovereignty.

The problem, of course, is that for the vast majority of Third World states, particularly in this era of neo-liberalism which is characterized by intense competition among Third World states for foreign investment and an intensifying inequality of bargaining power, whether with respect to private actors or international financial institutions, the whole discourse of contracts conceals the enormous inequalities in power between parties. The device of 'contract' and 'consent' played a crucial

[119] Siba N'Zatioula Grovogui, *Sovereigns, Quasi Sovereigns, and Africans: Race and Self-Determination in International Law* (Minneapolis, MN: University of Minnesota Press, 1996), p. 80.

role in sustaining this set of ideas and creating and enforcing limits on sovereignty through, for example, stabilization clauses. Now unequal treaties are created not because of force, but because of economic power-lessness, a feature prominent – indeed, inescapable – in the international system, and yet, incapable of remedy, at least through international law. This, of course, is a familiar and unsurprising point, but it remains a real one. It was in some ways unnecessary for the 'international law of con-tracts' to prevail as the legal framework applicable to concession agree-ments because all the crucial elements of this law could be achieved sim-ply by including the appropriate provision within the agreement itself. Thus contractual provisions would ensure that the MNC had standing and that the contract was internationalised.

Law encounters great difficulties in coherently redressing naturally arising inequalities in power. To the extent that international law presents the image of contractual principles being free of the suspi-cion that accompanied the doctrines of state responsibility or conquest that were unmistakable tools of imperialism that had been so compre-hensively attacked by the new states, the view is misleading.

I have argued that international law continuously attempts to efface its complicity with colonialism. Contractual approaches to international law further serve to obscure the imperial past. The whole framework of contracts is crucial to the attempt to establish that international law is neutral, that the arbitrators are doing no more than enforcing the agreements that had been freely entered into by sovereign states on the one hand and MNCs on the other. The point, however, is that it is inter-national law that legitimized, through doctrines of conquest and by upholding unequal treaties, the imbalances and inequalities in social and political power that are inevitably reflected in international con-tracts which are then characterized as expressing the free will of the parties. The old international law of conquest creates the inequalities that the new international law of contracts perpetuates, legalises and substantiates when it 'neutrally' enforces the agreements, however one-sided, entered into by sovereign Third World states. It is in this way that the 'old' international law of imperialism, based on conquest, is connected with the new international law of imperialism, based on con-tract.

The sovereignty of the non-European entity is determined in nineteenth-century international law by applying the standard of civ-ilization to determine the status of that territory; the sovereignty of the non-European entity in the post-colonial period is determined by the framework of contracts. There is a broad shift, then, from status to contract.

It is not only through the device of contract, but in the complex relationship between sovereignty doctrine and its own past that we might better understand this period and the debates which took place within it. The Third World aspired to transcend colonialism through its exercise of sovereignty. In responding to this challenge, scholars such as Gess and Dupuy, in their analysis of GA resolutions, although writing in very different settings, basically adopt the same position. The Third World comes into existence only through colonialism; it is bound by the rules of international law that prevailed at the time, the laws of the nineteenth century, and is powerless to change these rules unless the states whose interests are threatened by these attempts to change the rules take the unlikely step of acquiescing to such changes. What is particularly interesting is that it is precisely when the Third World threatens the existing system that that system reveals most clearly the mechanisms of control on which it relies. Gess' arguments focused on the validity of acquired rights and Dupuy on the issue of sources; but when followed to their logical conclusion, each argument returns inexorably to that founding moment, almost in the mode of a paroxysm, that moment when the Third World enters the international realm to be bound. This is the moment when the non-European world enters the realm of international law as a 'colonial subject', a phrase which, as opposed to an alternative term, 'colonial object', suggests the recognition of the native for the sole purpose of effecting his subordination and dispossession in a manner which appears legally coherent. In some peculiar way, then, the Third World's acquisition of sovereignty appears conditional upon its repudiation of its colonial past. Sovereignty is coeval with acceptance of 'international standards' of state responsibility and the doctrine of acquired rights. Whatever the other freedoms and empowerments offered by sovereignty, limitations apply. The colonial past is unredeemable in international law, however powerful its effects may be on the futures of the peoples of the former colonies.

The same logic is evident in arbitral decisions. Lord Asquith dismissed Abu Dhabi as having no law in the 1950s. By the time of the AMINOIL arbitration in 1982, the arbitrators insist by contrast that another Middle Eastern state, Kuwait, possesses a very sophisticated legal system. They assert that 'Kuwait law is a highly evolved system', even while gracefully making the transition to international law on the basis that 'established public international law is necessarily a part of the law of Kuwait' and, further, that 'general principles of international law are part of public international law'.[120] The international law that proclaims general principles that protect acquired rights is thus transformed into the law of Kuwait itself. It is only at this point, when these self-negating, colonizing principles of acquired rights have become an integral part of its foundation, that the Kuwaiti legal system is recognized as having any validity. The outcome, then, for the Arab states is the same, whether through the reasoning of Lord Asquith (Middle Eastern states have no sophisticated laws) or the arbitrators in AMINOIL (Middle Eastern states have very sophisticated laws). The Middle Eastern state is bound by an international law that nullifies its sovereignty.

It is in this way that sovereignty doctrine denies its history and appears to exist in a continuous present. It is in this way that the divide between First and Third Worlds is maintained. And it is for these reasons that sovereignty offers itself to the scrutiny of scholars in the form of the problem: how is order to be maintained among sovereign states? It is because of these conservative arguments that it becomes difficult, even in this ostensibly post-colonial era, to speak of the attempts of the discipline to rid itself of its colonial origins, for the consequence of this resistance to changing the rules of international law that were clearly inequitable is the continuation, if not intensification of the rules that produce inequality.

The jurists who sympathised with the plight of the new states believed that, although international law had furthered colonialism, it could be reformed. This assumed that colonialism was localised in specific doctrines – such as state responsibility.[121] My argument, however, is that colonialism is somehow pervasive, foundational in international law; and this is suggested in the way that the battle over state responsibility shifts to another area of international law, sources doctrine.

Even more disconcertingly, it is not only the case that reform was resisted; but, rather, colonialism reconstructed itself through new techniques – as I have attempted to suggest in my examination of transnational law – even while reproducing the fundamental structure of the civilizing mission. In this sense, the colonial encounter has

---

[120] *Award in the Matter of an Arbitration Between Kuwait and the American Independent Oil Company (AMINOIL)* [1982] 21 ILM 976, 997–998.

[121] For a telling analysis of this approach, which he terms the 'weak' form of anti-colonial scholarship, see James Gathii, 'International Law and Eurocentricity', (1998) 9 *European Journal of International Law* 184–211.

ineluctably shaped the fundamental doctrines of international law – sources and sovereignty. Further, it has created an international law which, even when it innovates, follows the familiar pattern of the colonial encounter, the division between civilized and uncivilized, the developed and the developing, a division that international law seeks to define and maintain using extraordinarily flexible and continuously new techniques.

5 Governance and globalization, civilization and commerce

Introduction

Few of the NIEO initiatives had an enduring impact on international law and the international economic system. Rather, through the 1980s, neo-conservative economic and development policy became the norm, and the collapse of the Berlin Wall and the end of the Cold War were taken to signal the ultimate triumph of capitalism and its decisive emergence as the one economic system that every society had to follow if it was to prosper and progress. Following this, 'globalization' became one of the dominant themes of the 1990s. While the term 'globalization' is the subject of intense discussion and debate,[1] and globalization has had an impact on virtually every aspect of life – cultural, political and social – I use the term here to refer principally to an economic phenomenon, the internationalization of production and financial services. For the Third World, more specifically, globalization has signified the dominance of neo-liberal economic policies, the 'Washington Consensus', promoting privatization and liberalization; these policies have been forcefully advanced by the three major international economic institutions, the World Trade Organization (WTO), the World Bank (hereafter, 'the Bank') and the International Monetary Fund (IMF).

The relationship between globalization and imperialism has been the subject of considerable scholarship. Globalization, for Michael Hardt and Antonio Negri, has created a particular global order 'a new logic and structure of rule – in short, a new form of sovereignty',[2] a sovereignty

---

[1] See David Held and Anthony McGrew, 'The Great Globalization Debate: An Introduction', in David Held and Anthony McGrew (eds.), *The Global Transformations Reader: An Introduction to the Globalization Debate* (Cambridge: Polity Press, 2000), pp. 1–44.

[2] Michael Hardt and Antonio Negri, *Empire* (Cambridge, MA: Harvard University Press, 2000), p. xi.

which they call 'Empire',[3] an Empire which, while it resembles old empires in various ways, is significantly novel in part because of its all encompassing character: 'Empire's rule has no limits.'[4] For Samir Amin, by contrast, globalization can be viewed as yet another stage of imperialism which has in common with its predecessors the goals of achieving 'the control of the expansion of markets, the looting of the world's natural resources, the superexploitation of the labor reserves in the periphery'.[5] More specifically, B. S. Chimni argues that 'The threat of recolonisation is haunting the world . . . Indeed, international law is the principal language in which domination is coming to be expressed in the era of globalisation'.[6]

Globalization, as it emerged in the 1990s, was accompanied by a series of initiatives undertaken by international law and institutions that were directed at bringing about 'good governance', the creation of political institutions and formulation of principles appropriate for the governance of a globalised world. The concept of good governance, in turn generated more specific programmes focusing on how international law and institutions could promote 'democratic governance' and 'legitimate governance'. The purpose of this chapter is to examine globalization and governance in terms of the issues and themes I have previously outlined, the management of the non-European world by international law and institutions, a task now undertaken through the techniques and technologies generated by globalization and governance. I attempt here to examine how globalization and governance have been accommodated and reproduced through, specifically, international human rights law. Further, I examine the relationship between globalization and good governance by focusing on the manner in which the IMF and the World Bank, the world's two major international financial institutions (IFIs), use the concept of governance to expand their activities through, in part, their articulation of a novel relationship between their activities and international human rights law mediated through the concept of governance. My focus on the IMF and the Bank is in part determined by the fact that these institutions have an enormously important impact on

---

[3] *Ibid.*, p. xii.   [4] *Ibid.*, p. xiv.

[5] Samir Amin, 'Imperialism and Globalization', (June 2001) *Monthly Review*, 6–24 at 9.

[6] B. S. Chimni, 'Third World Approaches to International Law: A Manifesto' in Antony Anghie, Bhupinder Chimni, Karin Mickelson and Obiora Chinedu Okafor (eds.), *The Third World and International Order: Law, Politics and Globalization* (Leiden: Brill Academic Publishers, Martinus Nijhoff, 2003), pp. 47–75 at p. 47 (footnotes omitted). In a similar vein, see Peter Fitzpatrick, *Modernism and the Grounds of Law* (Cambridge: Cambridge University Press, 2001), pp. 212–215.

the peoples of the Third World. The IFIs exercise enormous power over the workings of the international financial system, as reflected by the fact that half the world's population and two-thirds of its governments are bound by the policies they prescribe.[7]

[handwritten margin note: Ground in Theory]

Globalization is an inescapable and complex phenomenon, about which it is hardly possible to generalise. But there is considerable evidence that globalization, in its current form, despite the opportunities and advantages it is supposed to create, has intensified inequalities between the West and the Third World.[8] For the majority of Third World states at least, it is clear that development has failed, and this is reflected by declarations of the Non-aligned movements and the attempts within the UN to establish and achieve 'Millennium Development Goals' that would bring real advancement to Third World peoples, yet another in a long series of such initiatives.

Good governance and the Third World

'Good governance' is, like 'development' before it, a broad term which has a number of meanings.[9] Like development, furthermore, 'good governance' has a very powerful and apparently universal appeal: all peoples and societies would surely seek good governance – in much the same way that all peoples and societies were seen as desiring development. Good governance may be seen in many ways as an 'essentially contested term' which could justify a whole series of very different, and perhaps inconsistent, projects and initiatives. The profound changes that have occurred in the international system as a consequence of globalization have generated extensive discussions about how the basic issues of governance – accountability, transparency, participation – may be resolved in the context of a global economy. Thus, for example, Richard Falk has conceptualised humane governance as 'the effective realization

[7] Ute Pieper and Lance Taylor, 'The Revival of the Liberal Creed: The IMF, The World Bank, and Inequality in a Globalised Economy', in Dean Baker, Gerald Epstein and Robert Pollin (eds.), *Globalization and Progressive Economic Policy* (Cambridge: Cambridge University Press, 1998), p. 37.

[8] See Held and McGrew, 'The Great Globalization Debate', pp. 30–31.

[9] For different treatments of 'governance', see, for example, Richard Falk, *On Humane Governance: Toward A New Global Politics* (Cambridge: Polity Press, 1995); Commission on Global Governance, *Our Global Neighborhood: The Report of the Commission on Global Governance* (Oxford: Oxford University Press, 1995); Edward Kofi Quashigah and Obiora Chinedu Okafor (eds.), *Legitimate Governance in Africa: International and Domestic Legal Perspectives* (The Hague: Kluwer Law International, 1999).

of human rights, including economic and social rights, and the extension of participatory mechanisms and accountability procedures to the arenas of decision in which geopolitical and market forces are operative'.[10] This project deals with the issues of governance at a both global and national level.

The term 'governance' has no technical meaning in international law. Rather, the concept of 'good governance' is in some senses a term which combines a number of different areas and principles of international law. In very broad terms, 'good governance' involves the creation of a government which is, among other things, democratic, open, accountable and transparent, and which respects and fosters human rights and the rule of law. Thus good governance is linked very prominently with international human rights law[11] and, more specifically, with particular understandings of human rights law that emerged at the end of the Cold War, an event which heralded arguments that extended and particularised human rights law to support initiatives relating to democratic governance[12] and legitimate governance.[13] As a consequence of these developments, human rights lawyers have focused on the ways in which human rights norms regarding political participation,[14] free speech and so forth may be used to achieve the overarching goal of good governance.[15]

At the national level, the concept of good governance, particularly because of its reliance on universal international human rights norms, may appear to be a neutral concept that is potentially applicable to all

[10] Falk, On Humane Governance, p. 125.

[11] For a good example of a study of the relationship between human rights and good governance, see Linda C. Reif, 'Building Democratic Institutions: The Role of National Human Rights Institutions in Good Governance and Human Rights Protection', (2000) 13 Harvard Human Rights Journal 1–69.

[12] See the major articles: Henry J. Steiner, 'Political Participation as a Human Right', (1988) 1 Harvard Human Rights Yearbook 77–134; Thomas Franck, 'The Emerging Right to Democratic Governance', (1992) 86 American Journal of International Law 46–91; Gregory H. Fox, 'The Right to Political Participation in International Law', (1992) 17 Yale Journal of International Law 539–607; Christina M. Cerna, 'Universal Democracy: An International Legal Right or the Pipe Dream of the West?', (1994–5) 27 New York University Journal of International Law and Politics 289–329.

[13] Obiora Chinedu Okafor, Re-Defining Legitimate Statehood: International Law and State Fragmentation in Africa (Boston: Martinus Nijhoff Publishers, 2000).

[14] Steiner, 'Political Participation as a Human Right', 77–134.

[15] For examinations of the extent to which human rights norms relating to good governance have been incorporated in treaties and institutionalised within the UN system, see, e.g., Fox, 'The Right to Political Participation', 539–607; Cerna, 'Universal Democracy', 289–329.

states. Whatever the political crises and corruption and election irreg-
ularities afflicting advanced industrial states, however, these are rarely
if ever discussed in terms of internationally articulated norms of 'good
governance'. In practice, then, good governance is a concept that has
developed, at the international level, principally in relation to Third
World states, for these are the countries that lack governance. Indeed,
even those East and South-East Asian countries which had achieved significant levels of economic development were criticized by international
institutions for lacking 'good governance' and, more specifically, 'good
corporate governance'. The task of international law and institutions,
then, is to promote good governance in these societies. Consequently,
important international actors – international human rights groups and
IFIs such as the Bank and the IMF – have, within their own spheres of
competence, sought to promote 'good governance'. The view that a lack
of development may be attributed to the absence of 'good governance'
is now both powerful and commonplace. And unlike the important
project of humane governance that is still evolving, the project of good
governance has been given a specific, detailed and institutional form
precisely because it is being formulated and advocated by these extraordinarily powerful institutions, such as the IFIs, that are in a position
to implement their understandings of governance and development in
Third World states.

Good governance, then, provides the moral and intellectual foundation for the development of a set of doctrines, policies and principles,
formulated and implemented by various international actors, to manage,
specifically, the Third World state and Third World peoples. Attempts by
Western states to promote 'good governance' in the Third World – and
this involves far-reaching transformations, relating to the promotion of
democracy, free markets and the rule of law – are directed at reproducing in the Third World a set of principles and institutions which are
seen as having been perfected in the West, and which the non-European
world must adopt if it is to make progress and achieve stability.[16]

Many scholars and international institutions present the good governance initiative as a new and important development in the history
of international relations. My argument is, however, that this initiative
merely replicates the 'civilizing mission' that has been such a prominent

---

[16] For a telling examination of this phenomenon in relation to 'democracy promotion',
see William P. Alford, 'Exporting the Pursuit of Happiness', (2000) 113 *Harvard Law
Review* 1677–1715.

feature of the international relations system at least since the time of
Vitoria. My further argument is that we might understand the extent
to which the Western narratives of international law have shaped the
discipline precisely by examining further the reasons why this initiative
is presented as a new development representing the progress of international law. Indeed, the view that 'good governance' is a new initiative
suggests to me evidence for the argument I have been trying to develop
here: that the imperial character of international law is disregarded even
when it is being reproduced in a way that powerfully shapes contemporary international relations.

The claims for the novelty of the twin projects of 'good governance'
and 'democratization' are intimately connected with the emergence
of international human rights law. Under classic nineteenth-century
international law, respect for the sovereignty of a country prevented
international law from scrutinizing or legally assessing the character of
government of a state. In particular, the relationship between a government and its citizens was a matter entirely outside the proper scope of
international law. As Gregory Fox argues, in his important work on the
right to political participation:

States in the nineteenth century, caught increasingly in the throes of aggressive
nationalism, saw their domestic political institutions as essential components
of a unique national culture. In order to protect these institutions from external
pressures, the dominant states of Europe shaped an international law that carved
out an exclusive sphere of domestic jurisdiction. A fortress-like conception of
state sovereignty endowed governments with 'a monopoly over fundamental
political decisions, as well as over legislative, executive and judicial power'.[17]

Seen in this way, concepts of good governance or the right to political
participation, which intervene in what has been regarded as within the
domestic jurisdiction of a state, represent a fundamental departure from
classic international law.

If we examine the concept of good governance from the perspective
of the history of the Third World state, however, it is clear that jurists
have been concerned about how international law can create proper
government since at least the beginnings of the modern discipline in
the sixteenth century. Equally importantly, these ideas have been developed principally in relation to governance in the non-European world.
Vitoria, for example, even while recognizing that the Indians had their
own form of government, provided, as I have discussed in chapter 1, a

---

[17] Fox, 'The Right to Political Participation', 545.

detailed assessment of the inadequacy and inferiority of Indian societies stemming from their lack of proper governance when measured by universal standards.[18] This lack necessitated the intervention of the Spanish who acted as the agents, the enforcement mechanisms, of universal natural law. The Spanish would establish proper governance in the Indies, through conquest if necessary.

For Vitoria, however, internationally administered governance is not merely about reforming the primitive or rescuing the innocent. Accompanying these arguments, which rely heavily on images of backwardness and barbarity, are an equally if not more compelling set of ideas which focus on property, trade and commerce. Vitoria's arguments are based on the concept of property, which is intimately connected in his thought with issues of legal personality and sovereignty. Thus the crucial consequence of being recognized as a legal person, as possessing reason, is the acquisition of the right to own property.[19] With regard, more broadly, to commerce, as previously discussed, Vitoria argues that the right to travel in Indian lands, and the right to trade, are fundamental principles of natural law to which the Indians must adhere: 'it is an apparent law of the *jus gentium* that foreigners may carry on trade, provided they do no hurt to citizens.'[20] Vitoria further argued that 'The Spaniards have a right to travel to the lands of the Indians and to sojourn there, so long as they do no harm, and they can not be prevented by the Indians'.[21] Taken together, these statements go very far towards asserting that non-European sovereignty is subject to a foreigner's 'right to trade'. Crucially, then, one of the major functions of government was to ensure that international commerce would be furthered. Since the beginning of the discipline, the creation of norms regarding good government has been inextricably connected with commerce and a 'right to trade' that, in reality, legitimates the presence of foreigners in non-European territories. Once European powers conquered African and Asian societies, however, this 'right to trade' often ceased to exist, and inter-European rivalries intensified

[18] 'Although the aborigines in question are (as has been said above) not wholly unintelligent, yet they are little short of that condition, and so are unfit to found or administer a lawful State up to the standard required by human and civil claims. Accordingly they have no proper laws nor magistrates, and are not even capable of controlling their family affairs.' *De Indis*, para. 407, p. 161.

[19] This is reflected in Vitoria's extensively argued position that since the Indians possess reason, they were 'true owners alike in public and private law before the advent of the Spaniards among them'. *De Indis*, para. 303, p. 115.

[20] *De Indis*, para. 389, p. 152.   [21] *De Indis*, para. 383, p. 150.

precisely because French traders, for example, were denied access to British colonies.

The 'right to trade' and the assessment of non-European government in terms of its recognition of the right to trade has been a continuous theme of the discipline. When companies such as the British East India Company, exercising sovereign rights, administered the territories of non-European peoples, they established systems of law and governance that were directed at furthering the commercial relations that were the very *sine qua non* of their existence. Commerce and governance were not merely complementary but identical: a corporation exercised the power of government. The governance of non-European territories was assessed principally on the basis of whether it enabled Europeans to live and trade as they wished. Thus, according to Westlake, non-European states were uncivilized unless they could provide a system of government 'under the protection of which . . . the former [Europeans] may carry on the complex life to which they have been accustomed in their homes'.[22] If such government was lacking, Westlake argued, 'government should be furnished'.[23] Capitulation systems, protectorate arrangements and outright conquest could remedy the situation.

The explicit association between governance and commerce was gradually elaborated over time to establish a more morally nuanced justification for commerce and colonialism, after the decline of trading companies and the direct engagement of European governments in the imperial enterprise. Thus, during the Berlin Conference – which was preoccupied precisely with the orderly exploitation of Africa by the great European powers – commerce was characterized by Bismarck as a crucial means of spreading civilization itself. The link between commerce and civilization was further elaborated, of course, through the concept of the dual mandate, as developed by Chamberlain and Lugard: 'We develop new territory as Trustees of Civilisation for the Commerce of the World.'[24] In these ways, the expansion of European commerce was not understood as a mechanism for the economic exploitation and subordination of non-European peoples, but rather, a means of effecting the entry of the backward peoples into the world of civilization. Humanitarian goals were furthered precisely through the expansion of commerce,

---

[22] John Westlake, *Chapters on the Principles of International Law* (Cambridge: Cambridge University Press, 1894), p. 141.

[23] *Ibid.*, p. 142.

[24] Lord Lugard, *The Dual Mandate in British Tropical Africa* (Hamden, CT: Archon Books 1965), epigraph.

and appropriate systems of government had to be formulated for this purpose. Even while driven by commerce, the humanitarian aspect of the rhetoric of governance developed an extraordinarily complex and resilient character such that, in the new framework of the dual mandate, all manner of economic policies, could now be justified and refined as advancing humanitarian causes.

My overall argument, then, is that the non-European world is different, that the governance of these societies has been intimately shaped, since the very beginnings of the colonial encounter, by international actors, imperial European states, whose actions have been sanctioned and enabled by international law. It is hardly surprising, then, that the governance of non-European societies was a subject of considerable scholarship, and that authors such as M. F. Lindley compiled, described and analysed these techniques of governance in 1926, in a book revealingly titled, for example, *The Acquisition and Government of Backward Territory in International Law*.[25] At a time when government within European states was entirely immune to regulation by international law, government in non-European states was a matter which international law could dictate. It must be noted that the purpose of this exercise was often to grant the indigenous peoples some measure of protection. But the fundamental purposes animating governance, of furthering civilization and commerce, remained the same.

Contemporary debates on governance focus largely on the relations between the governors and the governed, the relations between the state and its citizens, the individuals whose democratic rights must be protected, or whose standards of living must be elevated. My argument, however, is that, historically, the international legal discourse on government has been shaped not so much by a concern for the governed – although invariably some reference is made to them – but by a concern to impose 'universal standards' that essentially furthered European/Western interests. This history of governance exerts an enduring and powerful pressure on the present. The relationship between globalization and governance can be seen, I suggest, in the same way: governance is now designed to provide the political institutions that will enable the furtherance of globalization. Specifically, this is to be achieved through the international human rights norms that are seen

---

[25] For other examples of this genre, see Charles G. Fenwick, *Wardship in International Law* (Washington, DC: Government Printing Office, 1919); Alpheus H. Snow, *The Question of Aborigines in the Law and Practice of Nations* (New York: Putnam, 1921).

as prescribing universally accepted international standards and which are used as a basis to further governance.

Governance, human rights and the universal

The emergence of international human rights law is among the most significant developments to have occurred in the field of international law and relations during the UN period which has been termed, 'The Age of Rights' by Louis Henkin. Human rights law is revolutionary because it purports to regulate the behaviour of a sovereign within its own territory. The emergence of Third World societies, as independent sovereign states, was simultaneous with the creation of international human rights law, which significantly conditioned the character of that sovereignty. The sovereign non-European state, then, never possessed the absolute power over its own territory and people that was exercised by the nineteenth-century European state. Further, to the extent that international human rights law and nationalism represent Western ideas of the individual, state and society they both create the paradox that Third World sovereignty was exercised through, and shaped by, Western structures.

Given the universality of human rights and its aspiration to regulate state action with respect to the individual, it is unsurprising that 'good governance' should be conceptually and operationally linked with international human rights law and that it enjoys a certain legitimacy and coherence as a result. While the question of the universality of international human rights law has always been debated, developments following the end of the Cold War raised this issue in a particularly contentious way. This occurred in part because Western governments and other entities sought to universalise the political institutions of the liberal democratic state by elaborating models of 'democratic governance' and 'legitimate governance' through international human rights law. In his scrupulous examination of Article 25, the Right to Political Participation enunciated in the International Covenant on Civil and Political Rights (ICCPR), Henry Steiner concluded in 1988 that Article 25 was an open and programmatic right that could be tailored in various ways to the particular social and cultural conditions and traditions of a society.[26] By contrast, in his 1992 article on the same matter, Gregory

---

[26] Steiner, 'Political Participation'.

Fox argued that human rights prescribed a fairly specific form of government.[27] In the same year, Thomas Franck's article on the Right to Democratic Governance argued that the collapse of the Berlin Wall and all that followed from it indicated the existence of an emerging norm of democratic governance.[28]

These developments corresponded, in the sphere of human rights, with Francis Fukuyama's argument that liberal democracy had established itself as the one universal model, that the 'End of History' had arrived and that all that remained was the task of making liberal democracy a reality for all other societies. Asian countries and scholars heatedly contested these claims, asserting that they ignored significant differences between Western and other understandings of universal human rights. Thus a dialogue was essential to establish 'a balance between a pretentious and unrealistic universalism and a paralyzing cultural relativism'.[29] The 'Asian Values' debate is too complex to consider in detail here, but the essential point is that international human rights law, now developed, recast and animated by the broad concepts of 'democratic governance' and 'legitimate governance' acquired a far more intrusive and comprehensive character, than had previously been the case. The 'Asian Values' debate raises important questions on the relationship between culture and human rights,[30] and who speaks for Asian culture; clearly, furthermore, extreme forms of the argument could effectively negate the protections human rights is designed to provide.

The Asian Values argument, further, was based in many ways on the issue of what human rights system was appropriate to achieve development. Advocates of the Asian Values approach pointed out that the East and South East Asian countries had achieved very significant economic development that had enhanced the welfare and hence the human rights of the people in those countries.[31] The attack on these Asian systems of governance, through the arguments relating to 'democratic governance' and 'legitimate governance' was seen, then, as an attempt to undermine the conditions that had resulted in this Asian success,

---

[27] Gregory Fox, 'The Right to Political Participation'.
[28] Franck, 'The Emerging Right'.
[29] Bilhauri Kausikan, 'Asia's Different Standard', (1993) 92 *Foreign Policy* 24–41.
[30] Karen Engle, 'Culture and Human Rights: The Asian Values Debate in Context', (2000) 32 *New York University Journal of International Law* 291–333.
[31] 'East and Southeast Asia are now significant actors in the world economy. There is far less scope for conditionality and sanctions to force compliance with human rights.' Kausikan, 'Asia's Different Standard'.

which challenged the view that the collapse of the Soviet Union decisively established the universal and enduring validity of the Western liberal-democratic system. Equally importantly, the Asian model of development, which had relied on strategic protectionist policies, deviated from conventional theories, prescribed by the Bank, as to how development was to be achieved.[32] These were the complex circumstances in which the Asian Values debate occurred, and the 'democratic government' and 'legitimate governance' debates can be seen as countering the challenges presented by Asian economic success to the 'end of history' thesis. The collapse of the Asian economies in 1997 was thus hailed as a vindication of that thesis, an affirmation of the argument that only development achieved through 'legitimate governance' was enduring.

Rather than adopt the 'Asian' position in the Asian Values debate, it is possible to formulate another critique of the initiatives of democratization and good governance, both of which appear intent on transforming human rights law into a mechanism to further a particular version of the market. The dangers involved have been powerfully outlined by Upendra Baxi:

I believe that the paradigm of the Universal Declaration of Human Rights is being steadily supplanted by a trade-friendly, market-friendly, human rights paradigm. This new paradigm reverses the notion that universal human rights are designed for the dignity and well being of human beings and insists, instead, upon the promotion and protection of the collective rights of global capital in ways that 'justify' corporate well being and dignity over that of the human person.[33]

Human rights is the one area of international law that is explicitly committed to the protection and furtherance of human dignity. Globalization, with the inequalities it promotes, challenges if not threatens the integrity of human rights law, precisely because it uses human rights as a means of furthering itself. Examined in a historical context, furthermore, the new alliance between globalization and the neo-liberal version of human rights described by Baxi is hardly novel or surprising: commerce has, since, the time of Vitoria, furthered itself through an invocation of 'civilization'. Similarly, as Susan Marks has argued, 'democratization' initiatives are informed by a very shallow concept of democracy,

---

[32] Robert Hunter Wade, 'Japan, the World Bank, and the Art of Paradigm Maintenance: The East Asian Miracle in Political Perspective', (May 1996) 217 *New Left Review* 3–36.

[33] Upendra Baxi, 'Voices of Suffering and the Future of Human Rights', 8 *Transnational Law and Contemporary Problems* 163–164 (1998), 125–169.

'low intensity democracy' that is an inadequate mechanism for truly transformative politics.[34]

For Third World countries, as they experience the operation of these initiatives, good governance acts as a 'bridging concept', linking human rights to development in a specific way. Similarly, democratic governance has been asserted to be indispensable for development.[35] Explicit attempts to link international human rights law with development can be traced back to at least the attempts of the Third World to use the vocabulary of rights to further their most imperative need by establishing an 'international right to development'. This right, which was articulated in 1986,[36] complemented the Third World stress on economic and social rights in its efforts to improve the living standards of Third World peoples. This initiative was resisted in a number of different ways – on the basis that the right to development was a 'collective right' and was therefore incommensurate with human rights law which was explicitly individualistic in orientation and, secondly, on the basis that the right to development would be used in such a manner as to suppress civil and political rights.[37] While the right to development has been articulated and elaborated in subsequent UN documents, its implementation confronts immense difficulties,[38] and the principles it outlines have been largely disregarded by the major international economic institutions, the WTO, Bank and IMF.[39]

Governance, now, can be seen as a 'bridging concept' that provides an alternative articulation of the relationship between human rights and development in the context of globalization and the collapse of the Soviet Union. The character of that relationship, and the manner in which 'governance' can be used to project particular ideas of development, can best be illuminated by an examination of the Bank and its attempts to further the project of 'good governance'. The Bank is the major development institution in the international system and, further,

---

[34] Susan Marks, *The Riddle of All Constitutions: International Law, Democracy and the Critique of Ideology* (Oxford: Oxford University Press, 2000), pp. 74–75.

[35] Balakrishnan Rajagopal, 'From Modernization to Democratization: The Political Economy of the "New" International Law', in Richard Falk, Lester Edwin J. Ruiz and R. B. J. Walker (eds.), *Reframing the International: Law, Culture, Politics* (New York: Routledge, 2002), pp. 136–162.

[36] Declaration on the Right to Development, adopted by the UN General Assembly, 4 December 1986, GA Res. 41/128 (Annex), UN GAOR 41st Sess. Supp. no 53 at 186, UN Doc. A/41/53 (1987).

[37] Anne Orford, 'Globalization and the Right to Development', in Philip Alston (ed.), *Peoples' Rights* (New York: Oxford University Press, 2001), pp. 136 ff.

[38] *Ibid.*, p. 172.   [39] *Ibid.*, p. 146.

has been particularly eloquent in articulating and elaborating different aspects of 'good governance' and the relationship between governance and the achievement of development. Unlike the Third World attempts to establish a right to development, then, 'governance' as formulated, institutionalised and acted upon by extraordinarily powerful entities (the Bank and the IMF), has had a profound impact on the peoples and states of the Third World. This is a consequence of the fact that the IFIs make the financial assistance they provide to Third World countries conditional upon those countries making profound changes to their economic, political and financial systems.

International financial institutions, human rights and good governance

The Bank and the IMF were essentially created in 1944 at the Bretton Woods Conference for the broad purpose of coordinating and managing international monetary and financial matters. The Bank focuses on promoting development and foreign investment, while the IMF focuses on monetary policy. Both the IFIs now provide loans to Third World (and, in recent times, Eastern European) countries which are subject to various 'conditionalities'. The system of IFI control established in this way has been likened to the nineteenth-century system of capitulations,[40] and it is through this mechanism that the IFIs play an extremely important role in the formulation of Third World economic policies.

The IFIs are creations of international law, specifically, international treaty law. Their constituent documents, their respective Articles of Agreement, provide them with independent legal personality and a system of governance, outline a set of functions and provide them with specific powers to enable them to perform those functions. In broad terms, the law governing the IFIs may be found in two distinct realms: first, in the Articles of Agreement, the constituting documents of the institutions and, second, in the larger universe of international law which creates the environment in which these international institutions operate and which bestows on them certain rights and responsibilities.[41]

---

[40] David Fidler, '"A Kinder, Gentler System of Capitulations?" International Law, Structural Adjustment Policies, and the Standard of Liberal, Globalized Civilization', 35 *Texas International Law Journal* 387 (2000).

[41] It is general international law which gives these institutions certain rights which extend beyond the rights which are explicitly bestowed in their Articles of Agreement.

The basic governance structure of the two IFIs is very similar. The Bank has a President,[42] and all the powers of the Bank are vested in a Board of Governors;[43] the day-to-day running of the Bank is entrusted, however, to the Executive Directors of the Bank.[44] Similarly, the IMF is headed by a Managing Director and is administered by its Executive Directors. Both institutions have adopted a weighted voting system which is based on contributions made by the members. Under this system, the United States exercises roughly 17 per cent of the vote; China and India exercise roughly 3 per cent of the vote each.

It is clear now that both IFIs have in effect become managers of economic policies of the vast majority of developing countries. In this capacity, the IFIs have required developing countries seeking their assistance to embark upon the radical restructuring of their economies through 'structural adjustment programmes' (SAPs). 'Structural adjustment', in broad terms, involves reduction in government spending, liberalisation of the economy, privatisation and devaluation.[45] These programmes are designed to increase efficiency, expand growth potential and increase resilience to economic shocks.[46] These programmes have important distributional consequences for the societies in which they are implemented and women, in particular, have suffered considerable disadvantage because of them.[47] Critics of such programmes have further argued that they are designed with little regard for the specific needs of the particular country concerned (the 'cookie cutter' approach), and as such are inherently defective. The SAPs often have massively detrimental consequences for the most disadvantaged in recipient countries; health services are affected, food and fuel prices increase and unemployment intensifies. 'IMF riots' have taken place in African and Latin American

---

[42] There is an understanding that the head of the Bank, the President, would be selected by the United States; and the head of the IMF, the Managing Director, would be selected by European countries. As this indicates, the origins of the BWIs as creations of the Allied powers continue to play an important role in their governance structures.

[43] Articles of Agreement of the World Bank, Article V.2.   [44] Ibid., Article V.4.

[45] See Poul Engberg-Pedersen et al. (eds.), Limits of Adjustment in Africa: The Effects of Economic Liberalization, 1986–94 (Copenhagen: Centre for Development Research in association with James Currey, 1996), p. ix.

[46] Sigrun I. Skogly, 'Structural Adjustment and Development: Human Rights – An Agenda for Change', (1993) 15:4 Human Rights Quarterly 751–778, citing a Bank paper.

[47] See Kerry Rittich, Recharacterizing Restructuring: Law, Distribution and Gender in Market Reform (The Hague: Kluwer Law International, 2002).

countries where these programmes were implemented.[48] Despite the social and political instability caused by these programmes, they have also produced uncertain benefits. Indeed, it has been argued that the neo-liberal policies promoted by these organizations have intensified the impoverishment of the Third World countries for which they were prescribed.[49] Despite these criticisms, however, the IFIs have been firmly committed to promoting globalization.

Human rights scholars have argued that IFI neo-liberal policies, involving SAPs – which aim to reform the economies of the recipient Third World state through devaluation, trade liberalization and privatization – effectively undermine, if not violate, important economic and social rights because of the impacts of SAPs. Rights set out in the Covenant on Economic and Social Rights, which include the right to health and education, for example, have been undermined by IFI SAP policies.[50] Further, many of the African countries which submitted to IFI structural adjustment policies are now even worse off than they were initially and are deeper in debt, and the IFIs have given priority to debt repayment as opposed to the provision of the basic welfare services necessary for survival.[51] Further, the Articles of Agreement of the Bank, the constituent document of the organization, require the Bank to base its lending policies strictly on economic criteria. As such, the Bank is arguably prohibited from taking the human rights record of a particular state into account when deciding whether or not to make a loan to that country.

Although criticized for being indifferent to human rights issues, the Bank has in recent times formulated a series of arguments as to how its policies can further human rights.[52] The Bank claims that: 'The world

---

[48] See Michel Chossudovsky, *The Globalization of Poverty: Impacts of IMF and World Bank Reforms* (London: Zed Books, 1997); and Skogly, 'Structural Adjustment', 763.

[49] Chossudovsky, *The Globalization of Poverty*. Chossudovsky argues that. 'The late 20th century will go down in world history as a period of global impoverishment marked by the collapse of productive systems in the developing world, the demise of national institutions and the disintegration of health and education programmes.' Michel Chossudovsky, 'Global Poverty in the Late 20th Century', (Fall 1998) 52 *Journal of International Affairs* No. 1 at 293.

[50] J. Oloka-Onyango, 'Beyond the Rhetoric: Reinvigorating the Struggle for Economic and Social Rights in Africa', (1995) 26 *California Western International Law Journal* 1–71.

[51] Thus in Tanzania, 'where 40 per cent of people die before the age of 35, debt payments are six times greater than spending on health care'. David Ransom and Margaret Bald, 'The Dictatorship of Debt', (1999) 46:10 *World Press Review* 6, 7.

[52] International Bank for Reconstruction and Development (World Bank), *Development and Human Rights: The Role of the World Bank* (Washington, DC: World Bank, 1998).

now accepts that sustainable development is impossible without human rights. What has been missing is the recognition that the advancement of human rights is impossible without development.' Basically, then, the Bank claims to be promoting human rights by promoting controversial development policies that have achieved somewhat questionable success. In any event, human rights law is not an independent category of norms and principles that govern the way in which development should take place. Rather, human rights should be assimilated into development, achieved through development.

'Good governance' has played a crucial role in enabling the Bank to link its actions to human rights at several other levels. In recent times, the Bank has blamed the failure of its development policies on the absence of 'good governance' in the recipient states. As a consequence, the Bank argues, the achievement of real development can occur only through the creation of good governance, and this the Bank seeks to promote. The linkage between governance, development and human rights that is thus established is suggested by the Bank:

> The World Bank helps its client countries build better governance. This assistance in improving the efficiency and integrity of public sector institutions – from banking regulation . . . to the court system – has a singularly important impact on creating the structural environment in which citizens can pursue and continue to strengthen all areas of human rights.[53]

In this way, the Bank powerfully suggests that its good governance agenda complements, supports and furthers the human rights agenda formulated by scholars and activists who focus on the importance, for example, of democratic governance.[54] In addition, however, the shift to governance has massively expanded the range of domestic issues that can be subjected to IFI management. The Bank is prohibited by its Articles of Agreement from interfering in the political affairs of a recipient state.[55] Now, however, by asserting that economic development depends on good governance, on the political system of a country, the Bank can justify formulating an entirely new set of initiatives that seeks explicitly to reform the political institutions of a recipient state, on the basis that such reform is necessary to achieve development, the central concern of

---

[53] *Ibid.*, p. 11 (Report No. 23188).

[54] For an example of such an argument, see Ibrahim F. I. Shihata, 'Democracy and Development', (1997) 46 *International and Comparative Law Quarterly* 635–643.

[55] Article 10 of the Bank's Articles of Agreement explicitly asserts that 'the Bank shall not interfere in the political affairs of any member'. Articles of Agreement of the World Bank, Article IV.10.

the Bank. Thus the Bank asserts that 'at least as important as the policies and the resources for development are the efficiency and transparency of the institutions that carry out the policies'.[56] Consequently, the Bank's governance campaign has focused on creating a system of government which is accountable, transparent and democratic; this includes initiatives to reform judiciaries, enhance participation in decision making, formulating environmental policy, restructuring the public service and governmental auditing functions and even strengthening the role and effectiveness of the press.[57] If, as the Bank claims, it may exercise its powers over any aspect of a country's policies and practices which impinge on 'development', then there is virtually no aspect of a country's affairs that will remain outside the Bank's scrutiny. The ambitions of the project are sweeping. As Nira Wickremasinghe has put it: 'In this new approach [the project of good governance] the aim is nothing less than to change the world-system by reforming the fundamental institutions of the recipient state.'[58]

The concept of good governance, then, is used as a 'bridging concept' by institutions such as the Bank to articulate a new relationship between human rights and development. The vision of governance thus produced suggests that the IFIs, rather than participating in the violation of international human rights law, further and promote that law. In addition, the IFIs use the concept of governance to deflect criticisms directed at the policies they impose on Third World countries, shifting blame for the absence of development in recipient countries to those countries themselves. As James Gathii has argued in relation to the Bank's embrace of good governance: 'This association has given a measure of credibility to the neo-liberal macro-economic programmes of the Bretton Woods institutions and their powerful western industrial members.'[59] It is in these ways that the IFIs combine governance and globalization, heralded as new initiatives, to reproduce once more the very old project of civilization and commerce.

The IFIs are required, by their Articles of Agreement, to act impartially and independently when recommending and implementing

---

[56] World Bank, *Development and Human Rights*, p. 11.   [57] See *ibid.*, p. 17.

[58] Nira Wickremasinghe, 'From Human Rights to Good Governance: The Aid Regime in the 1990s', in Mortimer Sellers (ed.), *The New World Order: Sovereignty, Human Rights and Self-Determination of Peoples* (Oxford: Berg Publishers, 1996), pp. 305–326 at p. 306.

[59] James Thuo Gathii, 'The Limits of the New International Rule of Law on Good Governance', in Quashigah and Okafor (eds.), *Legitimate Governance in Africa*, pp. 207–233 at p. 230.

economic policy in recipient states, and the legitimacy of the IFIs is heavily dependent on the extent to which they succeed in this endeavour. Now, the rich industrialised states that essentially control the IFIs have used the IFIs as a mechanism for advancing their own interests.[60] Quite apart from the consequences of following the embrace of the rhetoric of 'good governance', the IFIs have in recent times used their enormous power to transform Third World societies to satisfy the interests of the rich, industrialised countries.

International financial institutions and the Mandate System

In essence, then, governance serves the function of legitimating globalization by seeking to create the political institutions, the system of government, that would further a particular set of economic arrangements, those prescribed by neo-liberal development policies. A distorted, economistic version of human rights is one of the principal mechanisms being used for this purpose. But it is not only in the reproduction of the civilizing mission, through the rhetoric of good governance, that the colonial past is being replicated by the IFIs. The whole massive IFI project of transforming the Third World reproduces the ideas and systems of management initially established by the Mandate System.

In strictly legal terms, the Mandate System was succeeded by the Trusteeship System. But in terms of technologies of management, it is the IFIs, the Bank and the IMF which are the contemporary successors of the Mandate System. Indeed, whereas the Mandate System was confined in its application to the few specified territories, the IFIs have in effect universalised the Mandate System to virtually all developing states and, more recently, to the transition states of Eastern Europe, as all these states are in one respect or another subject to policies prescribed by these institutions.

The IFIs, like the Mandate System, seek to ensure the 'well being and development' of Third World countries, and attempt to do so by integrating their economies into the international economic system in ways

---

[60] As *The Economist* notes, 'in recent years, the Fund and the Bank have been hijacked by their major shareholders for overtly political ends. Whether in Mexico in 1994, Asia in 1997, or Russia throughout the 1990s, the institutions became a more explicit tool of Western, and more particularly American, foreign policy'. 'Sick Patient, Warring Doctors', *The Economist*, 18 September 1999, 81. For further discussion of this issue, see Antony Anghie, 'Time Present and Time Past: Globalization, International Financial Institutions, and the Third World', (2000) 32 *New York University Journal of International Law and Policy*, 267–270.

which are often disadvantageous to Third World peoples.[61] The techniques, justifications and legitimating devices they use for these purposes derive in fundamental ways from the Mandate System. The significance of the Mandate System lies, I have argued, in its creation of new systems of control, new sciences of management which rely upon new and more sophisticated models of legitimacy. The new 'science of colonial administration' that the mandates brought into being is, in its most important elements, the new 'science of development' which provides the legitimating foundation of contemporary development institutions such as the Bank. It is in the Mandate System that a centralised authority is established for the task of collecting massive amounts of information from the peripheries, analysing and processing this information by a universal discipline such as economics, and constructing an ostensibly universal science, a science by which all societies may be assessed and advised on how to achieve the goal of economic development.[62] Indeed, it is arguable that this 'science' could not have come into being without a central institution such as the Mandate System. In this sense, the Mandate System not only enabled the deployment of other disciplinary techniques – derived from psychology, for example – in the management of colonial relations, but indeed, *created* new disciplines. Had it not been for the existence of the Mandate System, scholars and officials concerned with colonial problems would have had to rely on the cruder science of 'comparative colonial administration'.[63] It is in this sense that the operation of the Mandate System, whatever its actual limitations and failures,was fundamentally important to the creation of the science of development itself.

This novel system of management and control inaugurated by the system is accompanied by a correspondingly novel system of legitimation, based on the concept of 'science', for these massively intrusive practices. The transformation of colonial territories is no longer undertaken by colonial powers seeking to further their own interests; rather, it is undertaken by a disinterested body of colonial experts intent on acquiring the

---

[61] The negative impact of BWI policies on Third World countries has been extensively documented. See, e.g., Chossudovsky, *The Globalization of Poverty*.

[62] For an important critical approach to development theory, see Chantal Thomas, 'Critical Race Theory and Postcolonial Development Theory: Observations on Methodology', (2000) 45 *Villanova Law Review* 1195–1220.

[63] Furnivall's work, which compared, for example, different colonies in South East Asia, is an example of this. See, e.g., J. S. Furnivall, *Progress and Welfare in South-East Asia: A Comparison of Colonial Policy and Practice* (New York: Secretariat, Institute of Pacific Relations, 1941).

knowledge of native practices, customs, psychology, native institutions and economies, not for the purpose of furthering profits but to enable them to formulate the policies necessary to ensure the proper development of native peoples. Objective, disinterested scientific knowledge, then, justifies these practices.

All these features are crucial aspects of the contemporary science of development: and all emerge, for the first time, in however crude and undeveloped a form, in the Mandate System. These are precisely the technologies and techniques, now refined and elaborated, which are used, for example, by the Bank to legitimize its activities and expand the range of issues it deals with.[64] The basic intellectual division of labour instantiated by the Mandate System persists in the operations of institutions such as the Bank and the IMF. The developing countries provide raw materials, not only in the form of primary commodities, but in the form of information, which is then processed by the Bank into knowledge, theories of development and best practices, which are then promoted as scientific, authoritative truths. As commentators have noted, the production of knowledge is becoming crucial to the Bank, which aspires to maintain its authority and legitimacy by becoming sovereign over the entire subject of development – as reflected by the Bank report titled, precisely, 'Knowledge for Development'.[65] The construction of these 'truths' is then used to discipline deviation by developing countries. The science of development is then used to monitor the native, to assess and check deviations. Further, any deviation is often accompanied, by economic disciplining, as international markets often require states to adopt IFI policies.[66] The fact that the Third World states thus administered by the IFIs are ostensibly sovereign states which can decide their own policies is negated by the fact that these states have only doubtful control over their economies – a situation exacerbated by globalization.

The Mandate System represented the inaugural encounter between international institutions and non-European territories: and the techniques of management developed through that encounter continue in these different ways. My broader point is that there is a unique relationship between international institutions and the non-European world – a

[64] I have elaborated on this theme in Anghie, 'Time Present and Time Past', 243–290.
[65] International Bank for Reconstruction and Development (World Bank), *World Development Report, 1998/99: Knowledge for Development* (New York: Oxford University Press, 1998).
[66] See Wade, 'Japan, the World Bank', 217.

uniqueness which was evident when the League was first established,[67] and which continues today. It continues to be the case that it is only in the non-European world that these technologies are applied in their extraordinarily intrusive form – for it is the condition of 'undevelopment' which calls for these technologies. Further, as in the case of the Mandate System, the people who are the objects of this system, the peoples of the Third World, are denied any effective decision making power. The governance structure of the IFIs ensures that it is the rich industrialised countries which control them and which use this control to pursue their own interests while ostensibly promoting development. The current Bank concern to promote 'good governance' and 'democratization' resembles in important respects the Mandate preoccupation with promoting 'self-government'; in each case, these projects of creating government are secondary to economic considerations, in that they seek to further economic policies which are in the interests of the metropolitan powers.[68]

My preoccupation has been to point out the different ways in which these disciplines have sought to control and manage the Third World. But the elaborate ways in which colonial relations are reproduced should not be taken to suggest that they invariably triumph. These systems of

---

[67] See discussion on pp. 147ff.

[68] See the important body of work by James Gathii which outlines the genealogy of the Bank's good governance project, its connections with the Bank's neo-liberal economic policies and the impacts of these initiatives on African states. See, e.g., James Thuo Gathii, 'Good Governance as a Counter Insurgency Agenda to Oppositional and Transformative Social Projects in International Law', (1999) 5 *Buffalo Human Rights Law Review* 107–174; Gathii, 'Retelling Good Governance Narratives on Africa's Economic and Political Predicaments: Continuities and Discontinuities in Legal Outcomes Between Markets and States', (2000) 45 *Villanova Law Review* 971–1035 at 971. It might be argued that the Mandate System was more advanced than the BWIs. First, the most senior figures of the system, such as Lugard, had an intimate knowledge of the colonial societies for which they prescribed policies – whatever might be said about the uses to which this knowledge was put. The heads of both the IMF and the Bank rarely possess any intimate knowledge of developing countries. Second, the operations of the Mandate System were subject to judicial scrutiny: issues arising from possible breaches of the laws governing the creation and operation of the Mandate System could be referred to the Permanent Court of International Justice (PCIJ). The BWIs are not subject to such independent scrutiny – despite the fact that many of their policies, particularly in recent times, clearly appear to violate their constituent documents, their Articles of Agreement. This development illustrates the ways in which law can create systems of management and control which, once established, elude conventional legal techniques of accountability. The IMF and Bank, which are creations of international law, are not in any meaningful way subject to the control of international law. See Anghie, 'Time Present and Time Past'.

control are inevitably resisted by the people to whom they are applied as part of an ongoing struggle which, as Balakrishnan Rajagopal has persuasively argued, have powerfully shaped the character of contemporary international institutions.[69]

The 'dynamic of difference' that was understood in the nineteenth century in terms of the categories of race, was transformed in the League period by the characterization of the non-European world as economically backward. It is this dynamic, a dynamic founded on the concept of 'developed' versus 'undeveloped', that remains with us, and which continues to provide the impetus for international law and institutions which ostensibly seek to bring about development and alleviate poverty.

In the context of the Mandate System, I have argued, it was inevitable that the 'rule of law' and the other institutions of Western government took on a different character when transported to the mandate society and consequently failed, very often, to bring about the intended social and political benefits. Within the Mandate System, this failure was often attributed to the backwardness of the mandate people and the pathologies of traditional societies – a view that raises a different set of questions about the universal applicability of Western forms of government. But the further point is that this transference of institutions is inherently problematic because the broader goals of the mandate project – to create independent societies capable of withstanding the demands of the 'modern world' – are undermined by the system of economic relations the mandate creates. The function of the rule of law in the colonies, Furnivall observed, was to further commerce; this version of the rule of law, itself so problematic, can hardly keep a society together when its very operation undermines the social and economic integrity of the society simultaneously being fragmented by the many policies of the Mandate System – and now the IFIs – directed at promoting a dubious form of economic development. The problem, then, is not only the clash between modernity and tradition, on the one hand, but between the different and ultimately conflicting goals of the Mandate System, political independence on the one hand, and economic subordination on the other. A failure to recognize this basic contradiction is crucial to the

---

[69] See Balakrishnan Rajagopal, 'International Law and the Development Encounter: Violence and Resistance at the Margins', (1999) 93 *American Society of International Law Procedure* 16–27; Balakrishnan Rajagopal, 'From Resistance to Renewal: The Third World, Social Movements, and the Expansion of International Institutions', (2000) 41 *Harvard International Law Journal* 529–578.

notion that colonialism is a thing of the past, that neo-colonialism does not exist.

Similar contradictions haunt the efforts made by the Bretton Woods Institutions (BWIs) to eradicate poverty and promote development. The IFIs understand poverty and underdevelopment to arise from factors which are purely endogenous to developing societies, as a consequence of which all their initiatives and programmes – of good governance, transparency and anti-corruption – are directed towards reforming the backward developing country. The IFIs' make no effort to reform the fundamental structures of the international economy itself – structures which operate largely to the disadvantage of developing countries. Nor, unsurprisingly, do the IFIs choose to recognize the crucial role they play in maintaining these structures. If, then, the causes of poverty are located at least in part at the international rather than the purely local level, the IFIs focus on national reform is misplaced and, as in the Mandate System, 'good governance' and 'rule of law' projects can only achieve partial and often unpredictable results in bettering the conditions of Third World peoples. Nevertheless, it is precisely because of this inevitable failure that the IFIs can propose new initiatives and new approaches to development – participation, governance, anti-corruption and transparency – which further their reach and their powers of intervention into the deepest recesses of the supposedly sovereign Third World state.

Conclusions and overview

The colonial history of international law is concealed even when it is reproduced. This, I argue, is why the initiatives of globalization and governance, which bear such striking resemblances to the earlier initiatives of commerce and civilization, have been hailed as novel developments in international law and relations. This argument of novelty is based on an understanding of the history of international law viewed in terms of the history of the European state, even when the European state remains immune, on the whole, from the particular initiatives in question, at least in terms of the specific connection between globalization and governance that I have attempted to outline here. Paradoxically, then, European history is invoked to help explain developments that are experienced most vividly, immediately and tragically, by the people of the Third World. Once again, the history of the Third World is explained by categories that emerge from the West.

I have tried to argue that an approach to these initiatives that focuses instead on the history of the experiences of the non-European world suggests, by contrast, that the important aspects of the 'novel' phenomena of governance and globalization can be traced back at least to the work of Vitoria and the beginnings of the modern discipline of international law. As I have argued, Third World sovereignty is distinctive; Western sovereignty was protected against the intrusion of international law, whereas non-European societies have invariably been subject to international law. As a consequence, it is understandable, given the porous character of non-European sovereignty, that the powerful set of ideas developed over the centuries as to how international law can bring about 'good government' have been conceptualised and elaborated in relation to the alleged absence of good government in non-European societies. A focus on this 'other history', the history of the non-European world, also suggests that while international law proposes systems of government designed ostensibly to further the well being of Third World peoples, to enhance their prosperity and protect them against tyrannical leaders, the theme that repeats itself over the centuries is that government must further and enhance commerce and trade in ways that protect and advance the interests, on the whole, of the West. Whatever the rhetoric, as to humanism and the welfare of the non-European peoples, commerce has been the controlling preoccupation of colonial governance. The situation is not significantly different now. Western states are immune from the operations of the IFIs although they engage in forms of protectionism, for example, that have been targeted by the IFIs when present in Third World societies. Further, as I have attempted to argue, the rhetoric of governance, as articulated by the West and the IFIs, is driven significantly by economic considerations. The powerful discourse of human rights has been used for this purpose.

The idea that societies which do not possess certain economic systems and corresponding political institutions should be regarded as outlaws that must be appropriately disciplined and reformed is a very old one. In a famous passage, Vattel makes clearer how a particular form of economic governance, a particular set of economic practices, is central to the integrity of a state:

The cultivation of the soil . . . is an obligation imposed upon man by nature. The whole earth is designed to furnish sustenance for its inhabitants; but it cannot do this unless it be cultivated. Every Nation is therefore bound by the natural law to cultivate the land which has fallen to its share . . . Those peoples such as the ancient Germans and certain modern Tartars, who, though dwelling in fertile countries, disdain cultivation of the soil and prefer to live by plunder, fail in their duty to themselves, injure their neighbors and deserve to be exterminated like wild beasts of prey . . . Thus . . . while the conquest of the civilized Empires of Peru and Mexico was a notorious usurpation, the establishment of various colonies upon the continent of North America might, if done within just limits, have been entirely lawful. The peoples of those vast tracts of land rather roamed over than inhabited them.[70]

What Vattel describes is something akin to an economic 'rogue state', a state that must be exterminated. The 'cultivation of the soil' is the principal criterion by which such rogue states were to be identified in the eighteenth century. Now, however, such deviant states are to be identified by all the economic criteria formulated by the IFIs; states that are protectionist, inefficient and encumbered by bureaucracy and government regulations must be eliminated, as it were, through SAPs that will bring about their transformation into proper international citizens.

In 2003, the US Treasury Undersecretary asserted that the US government believed that the ability to transfer capital 'freely into and out of a country without delay and at a market rate of exchange' is a 'fundamental right'.[71] The use of the rhetoric of 'rights' here, together with the assertions of a 'right to globalization',[72] appears to exemplify precisely the developments critiqued by Baxi. At the same time, such assertions rely on the very old tradition. It is, of course, commonplace that human rights theory has been significantly shaped by an idea of possessive individualism that focuses on economic rights, most notably the right to property. But if we return to Vitoria, and examine his work, not only as representing the colonial origins of international law but the colonial origins of international human rights law, then another theme becomes evident. What we see in the discourse of human rights that has been developed in relation to the non-European world in Vitoria's writings, for example, is that these rights are defined in *economic terms* – the right to engage in commerce, to trade, to travel; but, equally significantly, these economic rights are enjoyed, in effect, in their most comprehensive form, by *foreigners* – by the Spanish, rather than the

[70] Emer de Vattel, Joseph Chitty (ed.), *The Law of Nations: Or, Principles of the Law of Nature, Applied to the Conduct and Affairs of Nations and Sovereigns* (6th American edn., Philadelphia: T. & J. W. Johnson, 1844), I.7. 81, pp. 37–38; see also pp. 85–86.
[71] Robert Hunter Wade, 'The Invisible Hand of American Empire', (2003) 17(2) *Ethics and International Affairs* 77–88 at 86.
[72] Michael D. Pendleton, 'A New Human Right – The Right to Globalization', (1999) 22 *Fordham International Law Journal* 2052–2095.

Indians. This point becomes evident when Vitoria stipulates that just as the Spanish could enter the territory of the Indians to trade, so too could the Indians enter Spain for the same purpose. The Asian values argument asserts – with some basis – that human rights are Western in orientation, and that it is inappropriate to impose these rights on societies that have very different ideas of the individual, the state and society. But Vitoria suggests a somewhat different and additional point, the point that concepts of human rights not only have an economic dimension, but that these rights are designed to protect Westerners trading in foreign countries. The doctrine of state responsibility for injury to aliens, as asserted by the West, reproduced this structure, whereby foreigners enjoyed more extensive economic rights than locals who could not assert their claims at the international level or invoke international standards. Equally illuminatingly, scholars suggested that international human rights law offered a way of resolving the conflict over international standards by prescribing certain minimum standards that were applicable universally to local and foreigner alike. The same theme is evident in the international protection of intellectual property rights. The Trade Related Intellectual Property Rights (TRIPs) agreements requires all members of the WTO, including Third World states, to provide wide-ranging protection for intellectual property within their domestic legal systems. However, in most Third World countries, foreigners are far more likely to benefit from such protections than the locals, whatever the claims made on behalf of indigenous knowledge and local artists and producers. It is not only the Western individual who acts as the basis for 'universal' human rights but, particularly in the case of economic human rights, Western entities that seek to establish themselves in Third World countries.

It is in the midst of these contending positions, regarding governance, the rule of law and democracy, that Third World peoples are left with the task of fighting to create a system of human rights true to the original promise of human rights to protect human dignity, and advance social justice in the face of a hostile state and an inequitable economic system. The challenge remains to articulate such a system as an alternative to the authoritarian Third World state, and 'Asian Values'-type arguments, on the one hand, and neo-liberal versions of human rights, on the other. The task of refusing the established positions which, while presented as oppositional, nevertheless rely on and reinforce each other, is both necessary and challenging. Thus James Gathii's attempts to formulate a Third World approach involves developing an international law that decentres the 'Euro-American opposition between liberal internationalism and neo-conservative realism'.[73] This same approach is exemplified, in a somewhat different context, by Celestine Nyamu's proposal of a system of 'critical pragmatism' that seeks to use both Kenyan custom *and* international human rights for the protection of the property rights of women in Kenya.[74]

In attempting to demonstrate the imperial dimensions of these initiatives, then, I am not arguing that we should dispense with the ideals that inform them – the ideals of 'good governance', the 'rule of law' and 'democracy'. Rather, the attempt here is to contest imperial versions of these ideals, and to seek their extension to all areas of the international system. It is remarkable, for example, that the Bank and the IMF are not subject to any 'rule of law', in a context when the Bank has continuously extolled the virtues of the rule of law and when serious questions have arisen as to whether these institutions are adhering to their constituent documents, their Articles of Agreement.[75] As Susan Marks puts it, in her own searching attempt to develop a meaningful, substantive idea of 'democratic governance', 'When ideals begin to seem like illusions, we can jettison and replace them. Or we can reassert and reclaim them.[76]

[handwritten margin note: IT SURE SOUNDS LIKE ANGHIE WANTS TO DISPENSE W/ THESE IDEALS! SEE NOTE ON P. 104]

[73] James Thuo Gathii, 'Neoliberalism, Colonialism and International Governance: Decentering the International Law of Governmental Legitimacy', (2000) 98 *Michigan Law Review* 1996–2054 at 1997.

[74] Celestine Nyamu, 'How Should Human Rights and Development Respond to Cultural Legitimization of Gender Hierarchy in Developing Countries?', (2000) 41(2) *Harvard International Law Journal* 383–418.

[75] Anghie, 'Time Present and Time Past', 263–272.

[76] Susan Marks, *The Riddle of All Constitutions*, p. 119.

6   On making war on the terrorist: imperialism as self-defence

According to Buddhism there is nothing that can be called a 'just war' – which is only a false term coined and put into circulation to justify and excuse hatred, cruelty, violence and massacre. Who decides what is just and unjust? The mighty and victorious are 'just' and the weak and defeated are 'unjust'. Our war is always 'just' and your war is always 'unjust'. Buddhism does not accept this position.[1]

Introduction

Imperialism has once again become the focus of analysis in international relations, initially, as a consequence of the victorious emergence of the United States as the single global superpower intent on exercising its unprecedented influence to ensure its own security and further its own interests and, following 9/11, the commencement of a 'war against terrorism' (WAT) animated by principles and policies that, when taken together, closely resemble, if not reproduce, imperialism.[2] For many scholars who have focused on the history of the non-European world – and, I suspect, for many people in the Third World – imperialism has never ceased to be a major governing principle of the international system, and the only novelty of current developments lies in the fact that it has re-asserted itself in such an explicit form that it has become

---

[1] See Legality of the Threat or Use of Nuclear Weapons, Advisory Opinion, ICJ Reports 1996, p. 226 at p. 481 (Dissenting Opinion of Judge Weeramantry, citing Walpola Rahula, 'What the Budhha Taught').

[2] In broad terms, classical 'colonialism' denotes the actual conquest, occupation and settlement of a country, whereas 'imperialism' suggests a broader set of practices, including those by which a great power in essence governs the world according to its own vision, using a variety of means that may or may not include actual conquest or settlement.

unavoidably central to any analysis of contemporary international relations.

Third World sovereignty suffers from a number of deficiencies that can be attributed to the operation of colonialism within international law. At the very least, however, international law facilitated the transformation of colonial territories into sovereign states whose formal sovereignty was protected by a number of fundamental norms, including those prohibiting intervention in the internal affairs of the state and the use of force except in extremely limited circumstances. Significantly, then, recent examples of humanitarian intervention, and the new imperialism, challenge and undermine those doctrines. International law is now being subjected to various pressures that might ultimately result in the emergence of an international system that permits, if not endorses and adopts, quite explicitly imperial practices. The purpose of this chapter, then, is not to examine an ostensibly neutral set of practices – such as those associated with globalization – and reveal their imperial character. Rather, it is to examine the particular character of contemporary imperialism, to sketch out ways in which it both resembles and departs from the imperialism of the past, and to identify the particular strategies and doctrines used to further it and alter the existing framework of international law. These contemporary developments exemplify in many ways the themes I have been exploring in this book: international law is created in part through its confrontation with the violent and barbaric non-European 'other'; and the construction of the 'other' and the initiatives to locate, sanction and transform it disrupt existing legal categories and generate new doctrines regarding, very significantly, sovereignty and the use of force. In short, the WAT reproduces what I have sketched as the 'dynamic of difference'.

The war against terrorism

The terrorist attacks of 9/11 have now generated a 'war on terrorism' (WAT), the character of which will profoundly shape both international law and relations. The recourse to the language of 'war' to characterize the attacks and the response to them, was not, however, self-evident or inevitable. Thus, several scholars argued that the 9/11 atrocities should be thought of as criminal acts that would be addressed by policing actions directed at bringing the perpetrators to justice,[3] rather than

---

[3] Michael Howard, 'What's in a Name? How to Fight Terrorism', (2002) 81 No.1 *Foreign Affairs* 8–13; Mark Drumbl, 'Victimhood in Our Neighborhood: Terrorist Crime, Taliban

as an 'armed attack' that could justify war in self-defence.[4] The differences between these characterizations are significant because, as Tawia Ansah argues, 'the resort to the language of war as "natural" and "starkly simple" as it is, nevertheless has a profound impact on how the law's intervention is shaped, or how the laws governing the transnational use of force are interpreted to accommodate a "war" on terrorism'.[5]

Notwithstanding these doubts and issues, the debate has now entered a phase where the United States has emphatically asserted the language of war to justify its actions following 9/11. The WAT is now firmly and irrevocably in place, raising important questions as to how this WAT relates to the rich and old tradition of 'just war' theory. The sense that we are now moving back, in some curious fashion, to pre-modern times is also suggested by the fact that the terrorist bears important resemblances to the peoples of the Muslim world that have, for centuries, been the enemy against whom this theory has been applied. President Bush himself made this clear shortly after the attacks of 9/11, when he referred to the emerging battle against terrorism as a 'crusade'.[6] And it is precisely in the Middle East that the war is being waged in its most extreme form.

The WAT might be crudely understood in terms of three concepts: the doctrine of pre-emptive self-defence (PESD); the concept of 'rogue states' the most prominent of which constitute an 'Axis of Evil'; and the idea of democracy promotion in order to transform these violent and threatening entities.

First, and importantly, this war, in all its magnitude and reach, is being characterized as a war of self-defence; and self-defence is permitted under Article 51 of the UN Charter. Controversially, however,

---

Guilt, and the Asymmetries of the International Legal Order', (2002) 8 *North Carolina Law Review* 1–113.

[4] See Antonio Cassese, 'Terrorism is Also Disrupting Some Crucial Legal Categories of International Law', (2001) 12 *European Journal of International Law* 993–1001; Alain Pellet, 'No, This is Not War!', http://www.ejil.org/forum_WTC/ny-pellet.html; Georges Abi-Saab, 'The Proper Role of International Law in Combating Terrorism', (2002) 1 *Chinese Journal of International Law* 305–314 at 307–308.

[5] Tawia Ansah, 'War: Rhetoric & Norm-Creation in Response to Terror', (2003) 43 *Virginia Journal of International Law* 797–860 at 799. See also Frederic Megret, 'War? Legal Semantics and the Move to Violence', (2002) 13 *European Journal of International Law* 361–399.

[6] That this religious perception was not peculiar to President Bush but was, rather, shared more widely within the administration was suggested by the divine character of the mission to be undertaken, as suggested by the name of the campaign, 'Operation Infinite Justice'. Elizabeth Becker, 'A Nation Challenged: Renaming an Operation to Fit the Mood', *The New York Times*, September 26, 2001, 3.

the United States has declared its intention to act in pre-emptive self-defence where necessary. The basic character of pre-emptive self-defence has been outlined in the National Security Strategy (NSS) of the White House. President Bush has declared that:

> For centuries international law recognized that nations need not suffer an attack before they can lawfully take action to defend themselves against forces that present an imminent danger of attack. Legal scholars and international jurists often condition the legitimacy of preemption on the existence of an imminent threat – most often a visible mobilization of armies, navies and air forces preparing to attack. We must adapt the concept of imminent threat to the capabilities and objectives of today's adversaries.
>
> The United States has long maintained the option of preemptive actions to counter a sufficient threat to our national security. The greater the threat, the greater is the risk of inaction – and the more compelling the case for taking anticipatory action to defend ourselves, even if uncertainty remains as to the time and place of the enemy's attack. To forestall or prevent such hostile acts by our adversaries, the United States will, if necessary, act preemptively.
>
> The United States will not use force in all cases to preempt emerging threats, nor should nations use preemption as a pretext of aggression. Yet in an age where the enemies of civilization openly and actively seek the world's most destructive technologies, the United States cannot remain idle while dangers gather.[7]

The doctrine of pre-emptive self-defence as articulated in what might be termed the 'Bush doctrine' appears to extend the concept of self-defence well beyond traditionally understood boundaries of Article 51 of the UN Charter. The commonly accepted view of self-defence is that if preemptive self-defence is permitted at all, it is permitted only if an attack by an adversary is imminent.[8] President Bush, however, suggests that the concept of an 'imminent threat' should be expanded to correspond with modern realities and, in addition, that 'emerging threats' could also be subjected to pre-emptive self-defence. This extends the scope of

[7] President George W. Bush, 'The National Security Strategy of the United States of America', September 17, 2002, Part V, www.whitehouse.gov/nsc/nssall.html.

[8] The famous words of Daniel Webster are often cited in this context; Webster argued that self-defence should be confined to cases in which there was 'a necessity of self-defence, instant, overwhelming, leaving no choice of means, and no moment of deliberation'. Letter from Daniel Webster, US Secretary of State, to Henry Fox, British Minister in Washington (April 24, 1841), 29 *British and Foreign State Papers 1840–1841* (London: James Ridgway & Sons, 1857), pp. 1129–1139 at p. 1138. The issue of whether anticipatory self-defence is permitted remains controversial. For discussion of this doctrine, see, e.g., Thomas M. Franck, *Recourse to Force: State Action Against Threats and Armed Attacks* (Cambridge: Cambridge University Press, 2002).

self-defence considerably, particularly given that this 'emerging threat' is presumably to be assessed by the state seeking to use force.

The second major element of the war against terrorism was made clear in President Bush's speech regarding the Axis of Evil, where he referred to North Korea, Iran and Iraq in the following terms:

> States like these, and their terrorist allies, constitute an Axis of Evil, arming to threaten the peace of the world. By seeking weapons of mass destruction, these regimes pose a grave and growing danger. They could provide these arms to terrorists, giving them the means to match their hatred. They could attack our allies or attempt to blackmail the United States. In any of these cases, the price of indifference would be catastrophic.[9]

This speech seemed to suggest that certain 'rogue nations' that possessed weapons of mass destruction (WMD) – or were suspected of possessing weapons of mass destruction, or were even intent on developing or acquiring WMD – could be the subject of legitimate attack by the United States.[10] Finally, the WAT, as it unfolds in Iraq, suggests that these rogue nations, once defeated, must be transformed into democratic states.[11] Democracy plays a crucial dual role in this process: it liberates the oppressed people of Islamic states and it creates law-abiding societies that would be allies rather than threats to the United States. The NSS seeks to promote 'moderate and modern government, especially in the Muslim world to ensure that the conditions and ideologies that promote terrorism do not find fertile ground in any nation'.[12] Terrorism is thus closely associated with the primitive and the Muslim world. Further, on 6 November President Bush made a speech in which he argued that the absence of democracy turned Arabs towards Islamic extremism. This argument, however, is complicated by the fact that America is widely seen as the supporter of repressive regimes in the Middle East.[13]

---

[9] President George W. Bush, 'State of the Union Speech: The Axis of Evil', in Micah L. Sifry and Christopher Cerf (eds.), *The Iraq War Reader: History, Documents, Opinions* (New York: Touchstone Books, 2003), p. 251.

[10] This, of course, leaves open the question of how such 'rogue nations' are to be defined. Scholars have attempted, subsequent to the attack on Iraq, to glean from those events a set of principles that might be applied to international law generally.

[11] This transformation is consistent with Ileana Porras' argument that 'terrorism has come to be the thing against which liberal Western democracies define themselves'. Ileana Porras, 'On Terrorism: Reflections on Violence and the Outlaw', in Dan Danielsen and Karen Engle (eds.), *After Identity: A Reader in Law and Culture* (New York: Routledge, 1995), pp. 294–313 at p. 295.

[12] Bush, 'The National Security Strategy', Part III.

[13] 'They Say We're Getting a Democracy', *The Economist*, 15 November 2003, 9.

WELL
SUMMED
UP

In short, the current US position appears to be that <u>PESD against</u> <u>any rogue regime is legal</u> and that, furthermore, the <u>transformation</u> <u>of the offending society into a democracy is the most effective way of</u> <u>ensuring that it will pose no future threat.</u> The WAT has been given concrete form in the wars conducted against Afghanistan and Iraq. Each of these actions raises troubling legal issues under the law of the UN Charter which have already been the subject of extensive analysis. For instance, the war against Afghanistan raised the question of whether the US action could be regarded as self-defence, which is legal, or reprisal, which is not; and further problems arise from the fact that Afghanistan was attacked for actions committed by Al Qaeda. In the case of Iraq, questions arise as to whether US action was authorised by the Security Council or whether, rather, the United States was exercising a right to PESD, on the basis that Iraq possessed 'weapons of mass destruction'.[14]

It is clear then, that the WAT is challenging and extending, if not violating, the existing laws of war.[15] For the purposes of my argument, what is significant now is that this 'other', the terrorist, is constructed, not only in terms of the discourse of race (the nineteenth century) or the discourse of economics (the Mandate System) but the discourse of war, characterized as self-defence compelled by emerging threats. It is princi-pally through the language of war-as-self-defence that the 'other' is con-structed, excluded from the realm of law, attacked, liberated, defeated and transformed. In enacting these manoeuvres, however, the language of self-defence is not only transformed into PESD but, rather, it collects together and deploys a series of other doctrines and principles – relating, for example, to human rights, humanitarian intervention and democ-racy – to complete this structure of preemptive war. The additional and major complication, of course, is that the war is waged against a nebu-lous entity, the terrorist. Terrorism is notoriously difficult to define, as indicated by the absence of a clear legal definition of the term (which is partly why the attempts of Sri Lanka, Turkey and India to include terror-ist acts as offences punishable by the International Criminal Court (ICC) were defeated).[16] Further, the war against terrorism seeks to neutralise

---

[14] See for example, Lori Fisler Damrosch and Bernard H. Oxman, 'Agora: Future Implications of the Iraq Conflict: Editors' Introduction', (July 2003) 97 *American Journal of International Law* 533–557.

[15] Sienho Yee, 'The Potential Impact of the Possible US Response to the 9–11 Atrocities on the Law Regarding the Use of Force and Self-Defence', (2002) 1 *Chinese Journal of International Law* 280–287.

[16] Antonio Cassese, 'Terrorism', 993–1001 at 994.

279 WAS A FAILED STATE

states that are seen to support or harbour terrorists – and, indeed, Arab states that promote certain forms of Islam.

The United States and imperial democracy

The unfolding events in Afghanistan have led Michael Ignatieff to conclude that 'In fact, America's entire war on terror is an exercise in imperialism'.[17] Further, the logic of the doctrine of preemption, and the actual example of Iraq, seem to exemplify and correspond with the arguments made by a number of scholars that the threat of terrorism can be addressed only by the reconstruction of a new, imperial order. Thus Robert Cooper argues that if rogue 'pre-modern states' became 'too dangerous for established states to tolerate', it will become necessary to inaugurate a 'defensive imperialism'.[18] This furthermore, is 'a new kind of imperialism, one acceptable to a world of human rights and cosmopolitan values'.[19] Niall Ferguson has reiterated this position, arguing that the United States should take on this imperial role: 'The hypothesis, in other words, is a step in the direction of political globalization, with the United States shifting from informal to formal empire much as late Victorian Britain once did.'[20] Ferguson's concern is that the United States may not have the staying power of the British. Colonial rule became necessary, because, a state – such as Iraq – will be particularly dangerous if left in a state of civil war and chaos, as it is precisely in these circumstances that terrorists will flourish. A 'failed state' could pose far more difficulties to the WAT than a dictatorial state.

US imperialism, as it is being practised through the WAT, will, then, have a significant if not decisive impact on international law and relations. Notably, however, whatever the other divisions separating the different members of the Bush administration, the one position on which they have united is that America is not an imperial power and has no imperial ambitions. My attempt then, is to understand the particular character of American policies and their relationship to imperialism – indeed, their denial of imperialism – as these are the

---

[17] Michael Ignatieff, 'Nation-Building Lite', *New York Times Magazine*, July 28, 2002, 28.

[18] Robert Cooper, 'The New Liberal Imperialism', *The Observer*, 7 April 2002, http://observer.guardian.co.uk/comment/story/0,6903,680093,00.html.

[19] *Ibid.*

[20] Niall Ferguson, *Empire: The Rise and Demise of the British World Order and the Lessons for Global Power* (New York: Basic Books, 2003), p. 368.

policies that are, in important ways, driving the new conceptualizations of preemptive self-defence and which are giving concrete form to
the WAT.

The United States denies imperial ambitions because, it claims, it
is not intent on colonizing the Iraqi people but rather, on restoring
their sovereignty by guiding them towards self-government. In his presentation to the UN General Assembly, in September 2003, President
Bush used the language of self-government and forcefully opposed any
attempts on the part of the UN to quickly transfer power to the Iraqi
people:

> The primary goal of our coalition in Iraq is self-government for the people
> of Iraq, reached by orderly and democratic process. This process must unfold
> according to the needs of Iraqis, neither hurried, nor delayed by the wishes of
> other parties. And the United Nations can contribute greatly to the cause of Iraq
> self-government.[21]

'Self-government' here stands for the massive transformations entailed
in turning Iraq into a democratic state. This is, of course, the familiar
language of trusteeship, according to which the United States acts simply
as a trustee; sovereignty in Iraq resides with the Iraqi people;[22] and the
US occupation of Iraq is directed towards furthering the well being of
the Iraqi people until such time as they become sovereign.

While the goals of the US administration are comparable to the goals
of the Mandate System and the UN Trusteeship system, the United States
apparently intends to unilaterally manage the Iraqi progress towards
sovereignty and self-government rather than hand it over to international control, although this position, like so much else with Iraq, in
terms of both policy and academic analysis, is very likely to change. As
such, the project of creating self-government in Iraq might be best compared with the US occupation of the Philippines, a wholly American
enterprise whose precise purpose was to bring about self-government.
The United States took control over the Philippines after defeating the

---

[21] President George W. Bush, 'Speech to the United Nations General Assembly, September
23, 2003', www.whitehouse.gov/news/releases/2003/09/20030923–4.html. The escalating
violence in Iraq subsequently persuaded the US administration to establish a
programme for a swifter transfer of power.

[22] See Security Council Resolution 1511 (2003). It reads in part: '*Underscoring* that the
sovereignty of Iraq resides in the State of Iraq, *reaffirming* the right of the Iraqi people
freely to determine their own political future and control their own natural
resources.' Thus, the debate that took place as to who had sovereignty over the
mandate territories will not arise in the case of Iraq.

Spanish in 1898: while this war proclaimed that it was directed at liberating the Filipinos from the iniquities of Spanish imperial rule, it eventually and peculiarly metamorphosed into a war waged against the Filipino nationalists who had initially welcomed the arrival of the United States. The war resulted in approximately 200,000 deaths, the enormous majority of them Filipino civilians.[23] The US Secretary of War, who pursued the campaign against the Filipinos with ruthless efficiency, despite the growing concerns within the United States generated by the atrocities committed by US forces, and the great unease among many Americans about engaging in war that seemed colonial in character, was Elihu Root.[24] Root, who was later to become the first President of the American Society of International Law,[25] was given the task of formulating American policy towards the Philippines after the defeat of the Filipino nationalist forces. Root's policies took the form of a set of instructions that he authored, and which were issued by President McKinley to William Howard Taft – who was himself to become President – the head of the commission appointed in effect to inquire into American governance of the Philippines.[26]

Root had exhaustively studied English colonial policy, particularly British rule in India,[27] and he was emphatic in asserting that the US approach to the Philippines that he was authoring was distinctive:

It has differed from all other colonial experiments that I know anything about in following consistently as one of its fundamental rules of conduct the purpose to fit the Filipinos themselves for self-government.[28]

---

[23] The history of the war is told in Stanley Karnow, *In Our Image: America's Empire in the Philippines* (New York: Random House, 1989).

[24] Root's remarkable life is the subject of a two-volume biography by Philip Jessup. Philip C. Jessup, *Elihu Root* (New York: Dodd, Mead & Co., 1938). Root was awarded the Nobel Peace Prize for his efforts to create a permanent court to settle international disputes. See Jessup, *Root*, II, p. 504.

[25] For the argument that American interest in international law which led to the creation of the American Society of International Law was powerfully shaped by its emergence as a colonial power following the war against Spain in 1898, see Francis Anthony Boyle, *Foundations of World Order: The Legalist Approach to International Relations, 1898–1922* (Durham, NC: Duke University Press, 1999), pp. 18–19.

[26] Elihu Root, 'President McKinley's Instructions to the Commission to the Philippine Islands', in W. Cameron Forbes, *The Philippine Islands* (Boston: Houghton Mifflin Co., 1928), II, appendix VII. Taft himself, heavily influenced by his reading of Tocqueville's *Democracy in America*, regarded the New England town as central to the democratic project and sought to create a similar system in the Philippines. See Karnow, *In Our Image*, p. 228.

[27] *Ibid.*, p. 345.   [28] *Ibid.*, p. 371.

Given the history of the United States, and its own anti-colonial struggles against the British, it was inevitable that the US approach to colonialism would differ markedly from that of the European colonial states. Indeed, the US occupation of the Philippines was extremely controversial precisely because it appeared to violate sacrosanct principles of American identity.[29] Simply, how could the United States, which was born out of a war of independence against colonialism, itself become an imperial power?[30] This anti-colonial sentiment might explain in part why the United States was never intent on formal political control of colonial territories. Rather, as its position at the Berlin Conference of 1884–5, for example, made clear, the United States was intent on trading with colonial territories and furthering its economic power.[31]

The argument that the United States was intent on promoting self-government in the Philippines was crucial to the argument that the United States was not an imperial power, and Root set about the task of making self-government a reality. Crucially, this task was understood as reconstructing the Philippines along the lines suggested by the history of the United States itself; self-government meant government that operated according to the principles established in the US Constitution. Indeed, the question of whether the US government was legally required to provide the people of the Philippines with the rights guaranteed by the Constitution, on the basis that 'the Constitution followed the flag', was an issue considered by the Supreme Court,[32] whose decision led Root to conclude that 'as near as I can make out the Constitution follows the flag – but doesn't quite catch up with it'.[33]

Quite apart from the strictly legal issues, however, Root recognized that his policy raised an even more far-reaching issue. Was the model of the US Constitution an appropriate one for the people of the Philippines?

---

[29] See Karnow, *In Our Image*, pp. 78–138.

[30] For a classic examination of this broad theme, see Ernest R. May, *Imperial Democracy* (New York: Harcourt, Brace & World, 1961).

[31] See Antony Anghie, 'Finding the Peripheries. Sovereignty and Colonialism in Nineteenth Century International Law', (1999) 40 (1) *Harvard International Law Journal* 1–80 at 60–61 for the US position at Berlin.

[32] The series of cases which focused on the question of the applicability of the US Constitution to the various territories the United States acquired following the Spanish War of 1898 has been given the term the 'insular cases'. For a detailed discussion of these cases, see Peter Fitzpatrick, *Modernism and the Grounds of Law* (Cambridge: Cambridge University Press, 2001); and Efren Rivera Ramos, 'The Legal Construction of American Colonialism: The Insular Cases', (1996) 65 *Revista Jurídica Universidad de Puerto Rico* 225–328.

[33] Jessup, *Root*, I, p. 348.

On the one hand, Root was of the view that rights enjoyed within the United States could not be extended to the Philippines because

the provision of the Constitution prescribing uniformity of duties throughout the United States was not made for them, but was a provision of expediency solely adapted to the conditions existing in the United States upon the continent of North America.[34]

Here, Root understood the Constitution to be a peculiar and unique product of the history and conditions existing in North America. On the other hand, Root could not ignore the universalist claims embodied in the Constitution, that articulated rights that were proclaimed to be rights belonging to all men.[35] The Constitution, while being the peculiar product of US history, prescribed limits to what *any* government could do. Root studied these issues in considerable detail and attempted to resolve them by providing the Philippines with all the rights contained in the Bill of Rights, with the exception of the right to trial by jury in criminal cases and the right to bear arms.[36]

Further, Root proposed a number of concrete measures to promote self-government: locals were to manage their own affairs 'to the fullest extent of which they are capable';[37] municipal authorities were to be selected by the people; government was to take place with proper regard for Filipino customs, habits and prejudices 'to the fullest extent consistent with the accomplishment of the indispensable requisites of just and effective government'.[38] The administration was to be directed, not towards US well being, but to 'the happiness, peace and prosperity of the Philippine Islands'.[39] Seen in this way, colonialism, for Root, was a relationship of trusteeship, and was therefore a burden.[40] Further, Filipino traditions were to be accommodated within this system to the extent that they were consistent with the universal principles embodied by American structures of government. Nevertheless, this munificence was not entirely disinterested. While locals were to be incorporated into the administration, they had to demonstrate, as Root implacably ordained, 'an absolute and unconditional loyalty to

[34] Jessup, *Root,* I, p. 347.   [35] Jessup, *Root,* I, p. 347.
[36] See Karnow, *In Our Image,* p. 170; Root, 'President McKinley's Instructions', p. 443.
[37] Root, 'President McKinley's Instructions', p. 440.   [38] *Ibid.,* p. 442.   [39] *Ibid.,* p. 442.
[40] Moreover, it was through the concept of trusteeship that the United States could seek to resolve a fundamental contradiction: how could the United States, born out of a war of independence against colonialism, itself become a colonial power? The American occupation of the Philippines generated enormous controversy precisely for this reason. See Karnow, *In Our Image,* chapters 4–5.

the United States'.[41] Filipino self-government and independence, then, meant complete affinity with the United States at all these different levels.

The US commitment to self-government was such that Congress had declared that the Philippines would receive independence 'as soon as stable government can be established'.[42] The Philippines became an independent nation on 4 July 1946,[43] the date, of course, further reinforcing the narrative that appeared to sustain the whole American enterprise in the Philippines – that all societies to achieve true independence must replicate, however problematically and partially, the defining experience of the United States which represents the universal model that all societies are destined to follow. Within this scheme, it is the US Constitution that provides the blueprint.

Philip Jessup termed Root's instructions to the commission as 'the most important document in American colonial history',[44] and while this statement may initially appear extravagant, US policies in Iraq suggest that it is a valid assessment. Further, as William Alford has noted, the United States has a long history of attempting to 'enlighten, if not save, our foreign brethren by exporting ideas and institutions that we believe we have realized more fully'.[45] It is perhaps in the writings of Root that we see the first comprehensive articulation of this project, manifested today in various projects of good governance and democracy promotion that have been initiated by the United States and which play such a large role in contemporary international affairs.

Root's position is marked by ambivalences arising from simultaneous repudiation of colonialism and his insistence that a particular model of government and society is valid universally, and that less enlightened peoples whose systems of government do not comply with the American model must be transformed accordingly. A similar ambivalence afflicts the US position on Iraq, which attempts to repudiate the claim that it is in any way 'imperial' by repeatedly proclaiming that it is intent simply on promoting self-government, thus eliding the fact that the whole campaign of using massive force to conquer a territory as a prelude to attempting to civilize and liberate its people by recreating them in the

---

[41] Root, 'President McKinley's Instructions', p. 442.

[42] Quincy Wright, *Mandates Under the League of Nations* (New York: Greenwood Press, 1968), p. 14, n.4.

[43] Karnow, *In Our Image*, p. 323.   [44] Jessup, *Root*, I, p. 354.

[45] William P. Alford, 'Exporting "The Pursuit of Happiness"', (2000) 113 *Harvard Law Review* 1677–1715 at 1678.

image of the conqueror is one of the defining aspects of colonialism over many centuries.

Root's belief that American principles of government represent 'the immutable laws of justice and humanity'[46] is a fundamental premise of current American policies. Similarly, in referring to the core principles of the American Constitution, President Bush argues that 'Many other nations, with different histories and cultures, facing different circum-stances, have successfully incorporated these core principles into their own systems of governance';[47] this incorporation suggests the universal validity of these principles and might even justify their imposition when that becomes necessary.

The character of US-created self-government, however, is problematic, and not only because its exercise must, as Root stipulated, be allied to the United States. Whereas, in chapter 5, democracy was seen as essential to development, it now presents a solution to terrorism. The concept of 'democracy', however, remains extremely controversial, given that it can take many different forms, and its implementation is very problematic. Further, and more basically, US understanding of self-government must surely be brought into question by the fact that even as Mr Bush was com-mitting himself to furthering self-government, crucial decisions were already being made about the Iraqi economy. As *The Economist* notes in an article blithely entitled 'Let's All Go to the Yard Sale', all Iraqi industries, except for the oil industry, have been privatised;[48] all this well prior to any official democratically elected Iraqi government being in place, and while the Security Council continues to affirm that the resources of Iraq 'belong to the Iraqi people'. Thus, as in the Mandate System, while 'self-government' in Iraq is presented as a mechanism by which the sovereign people of Iraq finally liberate themselves from the tyranny of Saddam Hussein, it is being shaped, in important ways, by various external eco-nomic imperatives that undermine the interests of the Iraqi people and which will make them subject to foreign control for the foreseeable future. A comparison between the ideas of colonial rule expressed by Root, on the one hand, and his contemporary, Lugard, on the other, suggests the distinctiveness of the US approach. Both men formulated types of colonial rule that sought to transform colonial societies. Root's ideas, however, were in many respects more intrusive as they aspired to transform all the political institutions of the colonial territory to bring

---

[46] Jessup, *Root*, I, p. 332.   [47] Bush, 'The National Security Strategy', Part II.
[48] 'Let's All Go to the Yard Sale', *The Economist*, 27 September 2003, p. 44.

them into accordance with the universal principles laid down by the US Constitution. Lugard's model of 'indirect rule', by contrast, attempted to integrate existing native political institutions, albeit in a modified form, in the system of colonial governance. Lugard saw little prospect of English systems of government working in Africa whereas Root believed that the American system of governance was applicable to all societies.

But Root's private view might be more complex than his official positions might suggest. It is interesting then, that Root himself privately concluded, on the one hand, that the Filipinos were not capable of self-government as he defined it and, on the other, that American expertise and technologies were inadequate for the purposes of devising an appropriate system of government for foreign peoples. Thus, he declared – when Congress was discussing the question of what system of government would be appropriate for the people of Samoa – 'I should think that an exchange of professors of governmental science between Tutuila and Boston would be particularly advantageous to the people of the last mentioned city'.[49]

While the American governance of the Philippines might suggest these parallels, however, the situation now confronting the United States in Iraq is, of course, very different in vital respects. The task of promoting self-government in Iraq has an urgency that was hardly present in the Philippines, the occupation of which provided the United States with all the pleasures of being a colonizer even while asserting its moral superiority as against the squalid behaviour of European imperial powers. This project of promoting self-government in Iraq is now no longer seen merely in terms of effecting the salvation of backward peoples – although that idea, of course, continues to be of great importance – but, rather, of ensuring the safety and security of the American people. Backwardness is now associated not merely with economic deprivation, but terror. It is imperative to support and promote 'moderate and modern government, especially in the Muslim world, to ensure that conditions and ideologies that promote terrorism do not find fertile ground in any nation'.[50] Somewhat lacking in this analysis is any sense of US actions that could generate resentment in the Middle East.

Within this structure of ideas, of course, certain forms of Islam are seen as dangerously and radically different, and it is for this reason

[49] Jessup, Root, 1, p. 349.   [50] Bush, 'The National Security Strategy', Part III.

that the transformation of these societies becomes so important. At the same time, it is suggested that democracy is compatible with Islam – and, indeed, more specifically, with American forms of government. This notion is based on the powerful idea that the particular form of universalism espoused by democracy and the American system can accommodate difference. Thus, 'America's experience as a great multi-ethnic democracy affirms our conviction that people of many heritages and faiths can live and prosper in peace'.[51]

Ultimately, of course, the character of the 'self-government' established in Iraq will be determined far more by political exigencies than the lofty visions of a Middle East transformed by democracy. The transfer of sovereignty to the Iraqi people is not in itself incompatible with US control of the country. Both the nineteenth century and the League period illustrate the many technologies and techniques that can be deployed to effectively control what were ostensibly sovereign states. Quite apart from any measure taken to ensure that the people who govern Iraq are sympathetic to the United States, treaty arrangements based on the principles, if not the explicit form, of the nineteenth-century colonial protectorate can create a 'sovereign' Iraq over which the United States can retain significant control. Indeed, the experience of Iraq itself, once a mandate territory, suggests the character of such a treaty. Under the 1922 treaty between Iraq and His Britannic Majesty, the basic provisions of the Constitution of Iraq were provided for, and Britain undertook to 'support and assist' the 'armed forces' of the King of Irak, when this was necessary, and to provide guidance and advice to the King of Irak – who agreed to 'fully consult' with Britain – on how to manage the economy and finances of the country.[52]

If the history of the United States is to establish the terms by which other societies are to be assessed, and the US Constitution is the system of governance to which they should all aspire, then an examination is required of the complex and contradictory character of that history and system of government, rather than an idealized and selective version of it. The view that America was in important respects anti-colonial, overlooks the violence of the colonization of North America, the wars against the Native Americans, their dispossession – in violation of the

---

[51] Bush, 'The National Security Strategy', Part II.
[52] Treaty Between His Britannic Majesty and His Majesty the King of Irak, Signed at Bagdad, 10 October 1922, in Wright, *Mandates*, p. 595.

treaties that had been made with them – marginalization and disem-powerment.[53] Further, of course, the history of racism and slavery raises the important question of how a set of principles that were defined to be the rights of all men did not apply to blacks, for many years. The encounter between American principles of government and the foreign Islamic world might be illuminated by an examination of the encounter between American principles of government and the foreign Native Americans and African Americans who were incorporated into that system.

One of the main arguments I have been advancing in this book is that certain structures of thought regarding the 'foreign' or the 'unciv-ilized', which arise from particular and identifiable historical circum-stances, have an enduring presence. As a consequence, these patterns are often reproduced, albeit in somewhat modified form, in later encoun-ters with people deemed to be uncivilized and violent. It is in this way that the Native American is connected with the Iraqi. Both have been seen as threats to the security of the United States. Both challenge an American system of government that is extended to incorporate them, even while ostensibly enabling them to retain important aspects of their own identity. American approaches to 'the other' have been importantly shaped by its own historical encounters with the Native American. Thus, Wilson's idea of international trusteeship on which the Mandate System was based, derived in part on Root's model of colonialism as trustee-ship for the Philippines, that in turn was heavily influenced by the trust relationship between the US government and the Native Americans. The connections between the US actions in Iraq and these earlier histories are suggested at a number of levels:

To wondering Puerto Ricans, the American troops who brazenly seized their island in 1898 advertised themselves not as an army of occupation but as angels of deliverance – fairy godmothers with leggings and Springfield rifles, benignly bestowing all the virtues of utopian democracy . . .

This was not conquest, [General] Miles insisted, but liberation. The vanquishers marched in 'bearing the banner of freedom'. They extended to Puerto Ricans 'the fostering arm of a nation of free people, whose greatest power is in justice and humanity to all those living within [its] fold'. These beneficent new rulers, he vowed, with a euphoric flourish, would confer 'the immunities and blessings of

---

[53] The literature on this subject is enormous. For an examination of the relationship between America's emergence as a colonial power and its policy towards the Indians, see, for example, Robert N. Clinton, 'There is no Federal Supremacy Clause for Indian Tribes', (2002) 34(1) *Arizona State Law Journal* 113–260 at 164.

the liberal institutions of our Government ... [and] the advantages and blessings of enlightened civilization'.[54]

The resemblances between the earlier attitudes towards Puerto Rico and the occupation of Iraq are hard to ignore. Even more intimately, many of the American troops who fought against the Spanish in 1898 were veterans of wars against the Native Americans.[55] It is not coincidental that current debates occurring in the *American Journal of International Law* regarding the applicability of international humanitarian law to alleged terrorists resemble a similar debate that appeared in the same journal in 1927 on the broad topic of 'How to Fight Savage Tribes', when the tribes discussed included the Indian tribes which, like the terrorists, were savage, barbarous and backward and therefore disqualified from the protections offered by international law.[56]

The projection of American democracy as a universal solution to the problems of governance depends crucially on the assumption that America has overcome the histories of slavery and conquest that are such an integral part of the American experience. Seen in this way, whatever the problems affecting American democracy, they are relatively minor, and the greater and more urgent task is that of expanding outwards and liberating other peoples. These are precisely the assumptions that have been searchingly questioned, among others, by Critical Race scholars and Lat-Crit scholars, who point out the different ways in which exclusion and subordination are reproduced in a situation where equality, tolerance and accommodation are proclaimed to have been decisively achieved. Critical Race Theory, for instance, attempts to uncover 'the ongoing dynamics of racialised power and its embeddedness in practices and values which have been shorn of any explicit, formal manifestations of race'.[57] It is for this reason that the work of Critical Race Theory

[54] Peter C. Stuart, *Isles of Empire: The United States and its Overseas Possessions* (Boston: University Press of America, 1999), p. 329.

[55] See generally, Stuart, *Isles of Empire*.

[56] Elbridge Colby, 'How to Fight Savage Tribes', (1927) 21 *American Journal of International Law* 279–288. Colby was responding to Quincy Wright's contrary argument. In addition, of course, it could be argued that the circle is now complete: Western approaches to the American Indian were shaped by Christian approaches to the pagans of the Middle East, as Robert Williams has shown. Robert A. Williams, Jr., *The American Indian in Western Legal Thought: The Discourses of Conquest* (New York: Oxford University Press, 1990). Now, through the US intervention in Iraq, the descendants of those same peoples of the Middle East are being thought of in terms developed in relation to the American Indians.

[57] Kimberle Crenshaw (ed.), *Critical Race Theory: The Key Writings That Formed the Movement* (New York: New Press, 1995), p. xxix. For different aspects of this rich body of work,

scholars, who have focused precisely on the consequences of American Empire as it has manifested itself within what is now the United States itself, is important to an understanding of these current projects of Iraq and beyond. As Henry Richardson has argued.

Intersecting racial narratives, both global and national, are integral to U.S. hegemonic claims, as well as to community responses about them, including the racial implications of the new U.S. Preemption and Supremacy doctrine toward Southern Tier governments and their peoples.[58]

And if the parallel between the Indian and the Muslim holds, then the words of Chief Justice John Marshall – who had accumulated an enormous wisdom on the complex relationship between American systems of government and the Native Americans – might be illuminating. The enemy poses a dilemma that Marshall identifies as follows:

But the tribes of Indians inhabiting this country were fierce savages, whose occupation was war, and whose subsistence was drawn chiefly from the forest. To leave them in possession of their country, was to leave the country a wilderness; to govern them as a distinct people, was impossible, because they were as brave and as high spirited as they were fierce, and were ready to repel by arms every attempt on their independence.[59]

Similarly, Iraq cannot be left to its own devices, but nor can the US colonize it. Creating a form of self-government that is still subordinate to the larger powers of the United States might be one solution to the

see also Natsu T. Saito, 'Crossing the Border: The Interdependence of Foreign Policy and Racial Justice in the United States', (1998) 1 *Yale Human Rights and Development Law Journal* 53–84; Henry J. Richardson, III, 'Gulf Crisis and African–American Interests Under International Law', (1993) 87 *American Journal of International Law* 42–82; Isabelle R. Gunning, 'Modernizing Customary International Law: The Challenge of Human Rights', (1991) 31 *Virginia Journal of International Law* 211–247; Elizabeth M. Iglesias, 'Global Markets, Racial Spaces and the Role of Critical Race Theory in the Struggle for Community Control of Investments: An Institutional Class Analysis', (2000) 45 *Villanova Law Review* 1037–1073; and Adrien Katherine Wing, 'A Critical Race Feminist Conceptualization of Violence: South African and Palestinian Women', (1997) 60 *Albany Law Review* 943–976. For important collections of work in these traditions which also provide guidance to the literatures, see, on Critical race theory and international law, 'Symposium, Critical Race Theory and International Law: Convergence and Divergence', (2000) 45 *Villanova Law Review* 827–970; on Lat crit theory, see 'Colloquium, International Law, Human Rights and LatCrit Theory', (1997) 28 *University of Miami Inter-American Law Review* 177–302.

[58] Henry J. Richardson, III, 'US Hegemony, Race and Oil in Deciding United Nations Security Council Resolution 1441 on Iraq', (2003) 17(1) *Temple International and Comparative Law Journal* 101–157 at 103 (footnote omitted).

[59] *Johnson v. McIntosh*, 21 US (8 Wheat) 543 (1823) at 590.

problem, and it remains to be seen how Iraqi self-government succeeds in this respect. The projection of American values and systems of government to other parts of the world cannot be seen in isolation, I argue, from the complex factors, the densely interwoven histories, that I can only sketch here, that are inextricably linked with those values and systems. These are the factors that might shape in part, the US approach to Iraq and the WAT in general, a war in which America is projecting not only democracy, but its entire history of encounters with the 'other', within the United States and also in its previous imperial ventures.

Historical origins: war, conquest and self-defence

The WAT includes several unilateral initiatives that the United States is intent on taking regardless of international support. Inevitably however, the United States seeks to legitimize its claims within a broader international environment. It is almost compelled to do so, however unwillingly, because it requires international support for the WAT. Further, as Detlev Vagts notes, in relation to hegemonic powers 'the historical record shows that it can be convenient for the hegemon to have a body of law to work with, provided that it is suitably adapted'.[60] The United States, then, can work most effectively if it transforms the international legal and institutional order in such a manner as to enable the furtherance of its policies. Despite its criticisms of the UN, then, the United States relies on it for the condemnation of 'rogue states' such as Iran and Security Council resolutions directed against terrorism. How then, does the United States, with its own unique vision of the WAT and the civilizing mission it embodies, seek to alter the international system to further its war against terrorism? More particularly, how is this new imperialism, 'imperialism as self-defence', to be accommodated within an international law that is posited as being firmly anti-colonial? What is the conjunction, the relationship, between imperialism and international law in these circumstances, at the beginning of the third millennium?

The crisis of 9/11 has led to claims that this event is entirely unprecedented, that it is a 'constitutional moment' or a 'transitional moment' that will require an entirely new approach to international law and international law making. This issue of what this new international system will be is the subject of discussion and analysis now, not only by

---

[60] Detlev F. Vagts, 'Hegemonic International Law', (2001) 95 *American Journal of International Law* 843–848 at 845.

legal scholars, but by the United Nations itself, where Secretary-General Annan has inaugurated a series of initiatives designed to bring about the institutional changes that may be necessary for this new system.

Many aspects of 9/11 are unprecedented. Nevertheless, to the extent that the outlines of a new international order designed to respond to 9/11 are clear, they resemble in many ways a very old structure. The civilizing mission whose basic character I have previously attempted to identify is now being reproduced in the mode of self-defence which is all the more powerful because it has been combined with a series of other doctrines to establish the new legal framework for the WAT. This framework combines the doctrines of human rights and humanitarian intervention, democratic governance and trusteeship, to create a new and formidable system of management – that of 'defensive imperialism' – that, far from being new, derives its power and resonance in part through its invocation of a very old set of ideas, those of the 'civilizing mission', thus affirming the enduring hold of these formations on the structure and imagination of international law. As David Kennedy has argued, then, the attempts to renew international law often repeat similar patterns.[61]

Classically, the sovereign state precedes international law, and international law is constructed through the will of sovereign states. Self-defence is the foundational right of states, a basic attribute of sovereignty, as no state can be truly sovereign unless it has the right to preserve itself through self-defence if necessary. The concept of self-defence in this sense precedes the law – and, indeed, significantly shapes the legal universe. Thus Vitoria argues that 'In war everything is lawful which the defence of the common weal requires. This is notorious, for the end and aim of war is the defence and preservation of the State'.[62] Seen in this way, not only is self-defence fundamental but whatever self-defence requires is legal. The defining significance of self-defence in any system of order is reiterated by Grotius, who argues that:

In the first principles of nature there is nothing which is opposed to war; rather, all points are in its favour. The end and aim of war being the preservation of life and limb, and the keeping or acquiring of things useful to life, war is in perfect accord with those first principles. If in order to achieve these ends it

[61] David Kennedy, 'When Renewal Repeats: Thinking Against the Box', (2000) 32 *New York University Journal of International Law and Politics* 335–500.
[62] Franciscus de Victoria, *De Indis et de Ivre Belli Relectiones* (Ernest Nys ed., John Pawley Bate trans., Washington, DC: Carnegie Institution of Washington, 1917), p. 171.

is necessary to use force, no inconsistency with the first principles of nature is involved.[63]

The primordial importance of self-defence is emphasized, then, not only in the nineteenth-century positivist system with its exaltation of sovereignty but, as Vitoria and Grotius suggests, within natural law itself. Understandably then, the UN Charter itself terms the right of self-defence an 'inherent right'. The foundational character of self-defence has also been suggested in recent case law through the argument that it prevails against every consideration and competing international norm.[64] Thus Judge Higgins, in her dissenting opinion in the *Nuclear Weapons* Case, arguing that the threat or the use of nuclear weapons was legal under international law, seemed to suggest that self-defence would take primacy even in the event of a conflict between the use of such weapons and international humanitarian law, in order to prevent an 'unimaginable threat'.[65] If the right of self-defence has such power, of course, it becomes imperative for any system of legal order to carefully define what is meant by 'self-defence'.[66]

The doctrine of preemption, which extends the concept of self-defence by asserting that war against an imminent wrongdoing is legitimate, has been the subject of extensive analysis since at least the time of the Roman Empire, as Richard Tuck points out in his valuable and prescient analysis of this issue.[67] The precise contours of the doctrine of preemptive self-defence remain unclear and problematic.[68] As Tuck points out,

---

[63] Hugo Grotius, *De Jure Belli ac Pacis Libri Tres*, Francis W. Kelsey, ed. (Oxford: Clarendon Press, 1925), p. 52. The consequences of this position are explored in illuminating detail in Richard Tuck, *The Rights of War and Peace: Political Thought and the International Order From Grotius to Kant* (New York: Oxford University Press, 1999).

[64] But compare Judge Weeramantry's dissenting opinion in the *Nuclear Weapons* Case, who argues that international humanitarian law applies even in the case of self-defence. *Legality of the Threat or Use of Nuclear Weapons*, Advisory Opinion, ICJ Reports 1996, p. 226 at pp. 429–555.

[65] *Legality of the Threat or Use of Nuclear Weapons*, Advisory Opinion, ICJ Reports 1996, p. 226 at p. 529 (Dissenting Opinion of Judge Higgins). The majority decision was more equivocal.

[66] Franck, *Recourse to Force*; Christine Gray, *International Law and the Use of Force* (New York: Oxford University Press, 2000).

[67] Tuck, *The Rights of War and Peace*, pp. 18–31. Tuck argues that a distinction may be made between two different traditions which adopted very different approaches to war, the 'theological' or 'scholastic' tradition which forbade preemption, and the 'humanist' or 'oratorical' tradition which permitted it. *Ibid.*, p. 16.

[68] The legal adviser to the Department of State has offered a relatively restrained version of the character of PESD as stated in the National Security Strategy, asserting that the right arises:

however, even in its more restrained versions the doctrine of preemption is 'clearly a morally fraught matter, as by definition the aggressor has not been harmed, and his judgment about the necessity of his action might well be called into question both by the victim and the neutral observer'.[69] And if Iraq is regarded as an example of PESD,[70] then the implications are especially far-reaching, however qualified the character of that doctrine may be by the particular factual elements surrounding the Iraqi action.[71] For example, the International Court of Justice (ICJ) has held that the use of nuclear weapons may be permissible for the purposes of self-defence, and the question then arises whether nuclear weapons may be used also for the purposes of PESD.

War, waged in the PESD mode may now become the vehicle for a new form of imperialism, defensive imperialism. As Pagden argues, 'as all European empires in America were empires of expansion, all at one stage or another, had been based on conquest and had been conceived and legitimized using the language of warfare'.[72] Inevitably then, it is through the law of war that conquest has been most readily justified. As Vitoria observes, 'the seizure and occupation of those lands of the barbarians whom we style Indians can best, it seems, be defended under the law of war'.[73] Equally importantly, however, Vitoria emphatically asserts that 'Extension of empire is not a just cause of war'.[74] Rather, Vitoria, argues, it is through waging a defensive war that Spanish imperial rule could be legitimized. The attacks by the Indians on the Spanish who entered their territory, ostensibly for peaceful and legitimate purposes, would justify the Spanish in defending themselves – and this action could necessitate the complete conquest of the Indians and their territory, as it was only in this way that the Spanish could ensure their own safety. 'It is

> After the exhaustion of peaceful remedies and a careful consideration of the consequences, in the face of overwhelming evidence of an imminent threat, a nation may take preemptive action to defend its nationals from unimaginable harm.
>
> (William H. Taft, IV, Legal Adviser, Department of State, The Legal Basis for Preemption, November 18, 2002, <http://www.cfr.org/publications>)

[69] Tuck, The Rights of War and Peace, p. 18.

[70] See John Yoo, 'International Law and the War in Iraq', (2003) 97 American Journal of International Law 563–576; Ruth Wedgwood, 'The Fall of Saddam Hussein: Security Council Mandates and Preemptive Self-Defence', (2003) 97 American Journal of International Law, 576–585.

[71] William H. Taft, IV and Todd F. Buchwald, 'Preemption, Iraq, and International Law', 97 American Journal of International Law 557–563.

[72] Anthony Pagden, Lords of All the World: Ideologies of Empire in Spain, Britain and France c.1500–c.1800 (New Haven: Yale University Press, 1995), p. 63.

[73] Vitoria, De Indis, p. 165.   [74] Ibid., p. 170.

undeniable that there may sometimes arise sufficient and lawful cause for effecting a change of princes or for seizing a sovereignty . . . when security and peace cannot otherwise be had of the enemy and grave danger from them would threaten the State if this were not done.'[75] Vitoria, of course, as I have already argued, establishes a legal framework which makes it entirely legitimate for the Spanish to enter Indian territory, and trade within and occupy that territory, thus making inevitable the tensions that later manifest themselves between the Spanish and the Indians. While providing extraordinary comprehensive rights of war, however, Vitoria continuously reiterates that a just reason for war must exist: 'Wrong done is the sole and only just cause for making war.'[76] For Vitoria, a just war is a defensive war. Thus, even in relation to the Indians who are regarded as only nominally human, Vitoria attempts to prescribe limits.

The relationship between law and self-defence poses enduring problems that Kant addresses in his attempts to construct a perpetual peace. He famously dismisses Grotius, Pufendorff and Vattel as the sorry comforters who 'are still dutifully quoted in justification of military aggression', on the basis that, in the final analysis, the principles they lay down 'cannot have the slightest *legal* force, since states as such are not subject to a common external constraint'.[77] Kant, by contrast, seeks to provide such a constraint, in part by focusing on the internal constitutional order of states. Kant, among his contemporaries, was particularly eloquent in his recognition of the evils of colonialism, and his analysis of the hypocrisy of European states 'who make endless ado about their piety, and who wish to be considered as chosen believers while they live on the fruits of iniquity'[78] has an enduring validity.

PESD, as Tuck pointed out, is problematic because the party seeking to exercise it has not been injured. The relationship between injury and war is discussed by Kant:

It is usually assumed that one cannot take hostile action against anyone unless one has already been actively *injured* by them. This is perfectly correct if both parties are living in a *legal civil state*. For the fact that one has entered such a state gives the required guarantee to the other, since both are subject to the same authority. But man (or an individual people) in a mere state of nature robs me of any such security and injures me by virtue of this very state in which he

---

[75] *Ibid.*, p. 186.   [76] *Ibid.*, p. 163.
[77] Hans Reiss (ed.), *Kant: Political Writings* (Cambridge: Cambridge University Press, 1991), p. 103.
[78] Immanuel Kant, 'Perpetual Peace', in Reiss, *Kant*, p. 107.

coexists with me. He may not have injured me actively (*facto*) but he does injure me by the very lawlessness of his state (*statu iniusto*), for he is a permanent threat to me.[79]

By making this argument, Kant enlarges the justifications for war to a quite extraordinary extent by expanding the concept of an 'injury'; those societies, which lack a 'legal civil state', by their very existence, injure their neighbours, thus justifying the use of force against them. What this permits – indeed, requires – then, is the development of a set of ideas relating to how we should understand a legal civil state and the formulation of a set of criteria for distinguishing a civil state from a not-civil state, a task that evolved into the nineteenth-century project of distinguishing civilized states from non-civilized states. As Anne-Marie Slaughter has argued in illuminatingly applying Kant's theory of the liberal peace to international law, a distinction between liberal and non-liberal states is crucial to this system:

> The most distinctive aspect of Liberal international relations theory is that it permits, indeed mandates, a distinction among different types of States based on their domestic political structure and ideology.[80]

The definition of non-civil states takes on a particular importance because those states, by their very character, present a threat to humanity and exist either outside the given laws, or else in violation of them. International law can be said to operate only among liberal states, while non-liberal states operate in a zone of lawlessness, untrammelled either by international or by domestic law – and it is precisely for this reason that Kant feared such states. This basic division between the civilized and the uncivilized has existed in the discipline since at least the time of Vitoria. The vocabulary of international human rights law, democracy and the rule of law – and, indeed, market oriented economies – have now become the markers of a 'civil state', and it is for this reason that Cooper, for example, makes a distinction between pre-modern and post-modern states, and calls explicitly for different standards to apply to these two categories. The fundamental premise of this argument – that liberal-democratic states comply with international law while non-liberal states do not – has been searchingly challenged by Jose Alvarez.[81]

[79] *Ibid.*, p. 98.
[80] Anne-Marie Slaughter, 'International Law in a World of Liberal States', (1995) 6 *European Journal of International Law* 503–538 at 504.
[81] Jose Alvarez, 'Do Liberal States Behave Better? A Critique of Slaughter's Liberal Theory', (2001) 12 *European Journal of International Law* 183–246.

Kant's solution to the existence of the non-civil state does not immediately and explicitly call for war; rather, 'I can require him either to
enter into a common lawful state along with me or to move away from
my vicinity'.[82] What globalization has ensured, of course, is that it is no
longer possible to distance oneself from the uncivil state. Thus it is only
the first possibility that remains, and it is that delicate word 'require'
that now comes into question. Kant's anti-imperial position, then, exists
in tension with his arguments in favour of self-defence – and, indeed,
a version of self-defence that appears to make conquest of the non-civil
state imperative.

Now, the particular criteria that define an uncivil state – or a 'rogue
state', to use a more contemporary term – have been suggested by
Anne-Marie Slaughter, who has argued that the Security Council should

adopt a resolution recognizing that the following set of conditions would constitute a threat to the peace sufficient to justify the use of force: 1) possession
of weapons of mass destruction or clear and convincing evidence of attempts to
gain such weapons; 2) grave and systematic human rights abuses sufficient to
demonstrate the absence of any internal constraints on government behaviour;
and 3) evidence of aggressive intent with regard to other nations.[83]

The doctrine of PESD can be institutionalised within international law
through this mechanism. But the proposal, despite its careful wording,
raises complex questions as to whether the Security Council can legit-
imately pass such a sweeping resolution, who can decide whether the
conditions have been met (there is an arguable case that the United
States itself meets the first and third of these criteria, and perhaps even
the second) and who would use force in response.

It is not only by recourse to the doctrine of self-defence, of course,
that the current US strategy is attempting to displace various doctrines
of international law that limit the use of force and prohibit intervention and aggression. Rather, as the action against Iraq has demonstrated,
these policies are buttressed by a series of inter-related arguments that
are based on human rights considerations which allude in various ways
to Kosovo and the example it provided of 'humanitarian intervention'
that was 'illegal but legitimate'. The attack on Iraq is principally an
attack on a 'rogue state'; but it is also an act of liberation of the people
of Iraq from a dictator who subjected them to extreme abuse. The Iraqi,

[82] Kant, 'Perpetual Peace', p. 98.
[83] Anne-Marie Slaughter, 'A Chance to Reshape the UN', *Washington Post*, April 13, 2003,
B7.

then, is both dangerous and oppressed, but conquest is the appropriate response in either event, the difficulty being that this might succeed in producing a liberated terrorist. These simultaneous and varying characterizations of the non-European are, again, familiar from Vitoria's time.[84] Vitoria provides a useful approach to Iraq, not only because the arguments he presents are being so closely replicated, but because he provides a variety of possible reasons for exercising legitimate title over the uncivilized.

Importantly, however, in the contemporary setting the humanitarian arguments are inextricably connected with – fused with – self-defence, rather than seen purely as alternative and adjunct arguments. This is because, following the logic of Kant, security can now be achieved only through the transformation of the uncivil state into a civil state, and in a globalised world awash with WMD, the 'other' ceases to be a threat only once it is transformed into an 'us'. It may maintain its 'difference' only to the extent sanctioned by Western understandings of tolerance and plural identities, all of which have to conform, largely, to the liberal-democratic state.

The transformation of 'the other' has been the continuous goal of the 'civilizing mission', but this task has acquired an unprecedented urgency, an imperative character, precisely because it is now so powerfully linked to the idea of self-defence and survival, not only of the United States but of civilization itself. Within this scheme, cultural differences in themselves may become a marker for an armed attack justified as self-defence. The new imperial imperative created in these new circumstances, while promising to establish perpetual peace, may very well instead result in endless war.

Terrorism and the United Nations: a Vitorian moment

What, then, is the relationship between this imperial WAT and the existing law of the United Nations?[85] How is American hegemony affecting

---

[84]   Another possible title is founded either on the tyranny of those who bear rule among the aborigines of America or on the tyrannical laws which work wrong to the innocent folk there, such as that which allows the sacrifice of innocent people or the killing in other ways of uncondemned people for cannibalistic purposes.   (Vitoria, *De Indis,* p. 159)

[85] See speech of Kofi Annan to the UN General Assembly, September 2003, where it is clear that the US concerns have animated a whole series of initiatives within the United Nations, including the establishment of special groups to investigate these

the basic doctrines of international law?[86] Some aspects of these issues can be illuminated by examining three instances of actions directed against international terrorism: the action against Libya arising from the Lockerbie bombing; the US action against Afghanistan; and the US action against Iraq.

The very invocation of 'the terrorist' suggests a threatening entity beyond the realm of the law that must be dealt with by extraordinary emergency powers, or even extra-legal methods. In the *Lockerbie* Case, the spectre of terrorism was invoked to justify recourse by the Security Council to its emergency (Chapter VII) powers, under which the Council decided that Libya had to take a series of measures to 'cease all forms of terrorist action and assistance to terrorist groups' and, in effect, to surrender two Libyan nationals accused of plotting the Lockerbie bombing.[87] The ICJ held – in the provisional measures hearing of the dispute – that the resolution prevailed against the rights that Libya alleged it possessed under the Montreal Convention, under which Libya claimed it had the right to try the suspects themselves.[88] Here, the extraordinary measures taken under Chapter VII prevailed against established treaty rights but were nevertheless taken in a manner compatible with the Charter which explicitly provides for such measures.

Following the 9/11 attacks the Council, on 12 September 2001, passed Resolution 1368, which simultaneously recognized the right of individual and collective self-defence, while expressing its 'readiness to take all necessary steps to respond to the terrorist attacks'.[89] Antonio Cassese acutely argued that '[t]his resolution is *ambiguous and contradictory*',[90] and the Council 'wavers between the desire to take matters into its own hands and resignation to the use of unilateral action by the US'.[91]

In Security Council Resolution 1373, passed on 28 September 2001, the Security Council appeared to give states the broad power to '[t]ake the necessary steps to prevent the commission of terrorist acts'.[92] The 'necessary steps' arguably included the use of force for the very broadly stated

matters. Kofi Annan, Speech to the United Nations General Assembly, 23 September 2003, Press Release SG/SM/8891, www.un.org/News/Press/docs/2003/sgsm8891.doc.htm.
[86] Michael Byers and Georg Nolte (eds.), *United States Hegemony and the Foundations of International Law* (Cambridge, Cambridge University Press, 2003).
[87] SC Res. 748 (1992).
[88] *Questions of Interpretation and Application of the 1971 Montreal Convention Arising from the Aerial Incident at Lockerbie (Libya v. US)*, ICJ Reports 1992, p. 114.
[89] SC Res. 1368 (2001). [90] Cassese, 'Terrorism', 996.
[91] Cassese, 'Terrorism', 996. [92] SC Res. 1373 (2001).

purpose of preventing terrorism.[93] It was not clearly established in international law that force could be used by a state attacked by terrorists against the state which simply harboured terrorists. Indeed, the rules of state responsibility suggest that a number of conditions have to be satisfied before the actions of a private actor can properly be attributed to the state and thereby give rise to responsibility on the part of the state.[94] Even if the Security Council resolution could be read as authorizing the use of force against states such as Afghanistan, a profound question remains as to whether the Security Council had the legal power to issue such a permission. Nevertheless, in his analysis of Resolution 1373 and its relationship to the US actions against Afghanistan, Michael Byers argued that the United States, rather than relying on Council authorization, justified its actions on the basis that self-defence permitted the use of force against states 'which actively support or willingly harbour terrorist groups who have already attacked the responding State'.[95] Byers further concludes that this principle has now become a part of customary international law.[96] The attack on Iraq, of course, takes this trend a step further, as the action was not explicitly authorised by the Security Council, but might arguably be justified as an exercise of preemptive self-defence.[97]

What is evident in the developments from the *Lockerbie* Case to Iraq is the gradual subordination of the UN system and its emergency, Chapter VII powers in responding to terrorism, to the unilateral use of force ostensibly in self-defence. In *Lockerbie*, the United Nations controlled the situation; in Afghanistan, a system of UN control seemed to co-exist with unilateral action; and with Iraq the United States took unilateral action. The WAT, if it is to be accommodated within international law, has such far-reaching consequences that it can be seen, in effect, as creating a new international jurisprudence, of 'national security', that

---

[93] Michael Byers suggests that the phrasing could be used as an argument to justify the use of force, while disagreeing that such an argument would be valid. Michael Byers, 'Terrorism, the Use of Force and International Law after 11 September', (2002) 51 *International and Comparative Law Quarterly* 401–414 at 402.

[94] Byers, 'Terrorism, the Use of Force', 408–409; Sean Murphy, 'Terrorism and the Concept of "Armed Attack" in Article 51 of the UN Charter', (2002) 43 *Harvard International Law Journal* 41–51 at 50.

[95] Byers, 'Terrorism, the Use of Force', 409–410 (footnote omitted).   [96] *Ibid.*

[97] See, for example, Yoo, 'International Law and the War in Iraq'. Others argue that the Council resolutions while not explicit, nevertheless permitted the use of force. My own position is that the US action was illegal.

recreates the sort of Hobbesian universe whose defining character is fear,[98] and which will be based on the right of the world's one super-power, the United States, to wage unilateral, preemptive war, rather than the system of the United Nations. While the right to preemptive self-defence articulated by the United States might be couched in general and universal terms, political realities would suggest that it is a right, in effect, that can be exercised only by extremely powerful states.

These basic characteristics of the WAT suggest, I would argue, why we could be seen as living in what might be termed a 'Vitorian moment' – that is, a moment when the conceptualization of 'the other' – the terrorist, the barbarian – invokes a response that combines doctrines of violation, self-defence, intervention, transformation and tutelage that threaten the existing law and could result in a dramatic shift in the character of the law. The terrorist is in various ways connected with fundamentalist Islam and the Muslim world which has, since the time of the Crusades at least, represented the extreme 'other' against whom the civilized West must respond. The measures taken in the WAT have tested, if not undermined, international human rights law, international humanitarian law and, most significantly, the law relating to the UN Charter and the use of force.[99] And just as the novelty of the threat posed by terrorism is invoked to justify departures from the UN system, so too was the novelty of the Indian reiterated and emphasized by Vitoria in his attempts to justify and elaborate a new jurisprudence that was based on secular natural law rather than on a religious law administered by the Pope. While subtly incorporating aspects of that papal jurisprudence within the new scheme he was developing, Vitoria's work marginalized the Pope and expanded the realm of operation of the new secular law that was administered by the sovereign. Now, the UN Charter is threatened with displacement, much as the Pope was, and the power to administer the decisive natural law is transferred to the individual sovereign – the United States acting in self-defence. Sometimes, of course, it is the United States that appears to be assuming the powers of the Pope, God's representative on earth who will decree what is just and unjust and punish wrongdoers. Confusingly, on other occasions, the

[98] See Anthony Carty, 'The Terrors of Freedom: The Sovereignty of States and the Freedom to Fear', in John Strawson (ed.), *Law After Ground Zero* (London: The Glass House Press, 2002), pp. 44–56 at p. 45.

[99] Vaughan Lowe, 'The Iraq Crisis: What Now?', (2003) 52 *International and Comparative Law Quarterly* 859–871.

United States itself seems to be God, the God of the Old Testament who speaks through his prophets in their regular appearances on CNN and who is slow to anger but, once aroused, terrible in his vengeance which turns night into day, stunning the people of Babylon into shock and awe.

The *Lockerbie* Case, together with a number of other actions taken by the Security Council in the 1990s, raised a number of crucial legal issues – whether the actions of the Security Council could be reviewed by the ICJ and whether in fact the Security Council was bound in any way by international law, and the question of the powers of the Security Council to act, in effect, like a legislature. Those important questions have been replaced by another set of issues in which it is not the ICJ alone, but the Security Council and the United Nations itself that might be undermined by the imperatives of the WAT and the doctrines devised by the United States to conduct that war.

What these developments might bring about, then, is not the shift from natural law to positivism, or from positivism to pragmatism, but a law, once again initiated and animated by the invocation of the 'uncivilized' and the 'barbaric' that, in the name of security, produces a new form of imperialism. Self-defence is, for the reasons I have outlined above, in many ways the most problematic and delicate doctrine of international law, the one doctrine that is inherently connected with unilateral action. It is precisely through the doctrine of self-defence that the entire structure of the 'civilizing mission' is being recreated. This new jurisprudence of security does not, however, completely repudiate international law, just as, in Vitoria's new jurisprudence, papal law continued to play a role in the system. Rather, the new international law of security invites international law and institutions, appropriately amended, to join with it in this great task of protecting civilization.

This new international law seeks to further itself at a number of different levels. It furthers itself jurisprudentially by exploiting all the techniques and distinctions that undermine the idea of law and its formally binding quality, through recourse to ethics and international relations.[100] It seeks to elaborate the ambivalences and uncertainties, that have been generated by the agonizing question of how international law should respond to the threat of genocide in Kosovo by asserting that

[100] See Martti Koskenniemi, *The Gentle Civilizer of Nations: The Rise and Fall of International Law 1870–1960* (Cambridge: Cambridge University Press, 2002); Martti Koskenniemi, '"The Lady Doth Protest Too Much", Kosovo, and the Turn to Ethics in International Law', (2002) 65 No2 *Modern Law Review* 159–175.

the actions in Iraq, similarly, could be 'illegal' and yet 'legitimate'. In institutional terms, it seeks to make a reconfigured and compliant United Nations a crucial actor in this war against terrorism. Thus the United Nations is invited by the United States to make available all its resources to recreate the state of Iraq – and, in effect, legitimize the violation of its own founding principles. Further, the new imperialism of national security law infuses and seeks to deploy all the other areas of law, such as human rights and democracy, to further itself. Human rights is deployed as both an argument for invasion and then, that invasion having been completed, as an argument for transformation, in which international human rights law – as a proxy for the law of the United States – stands for the norms that must be achieved in order to bring about a 'civil state' thus, supposedly, bringing about international stability. The attraction for human rights scholars is considerable, especially given the atrocities committed by Saddam Hussein, because what human rights law has notoriously lacked is enforcement. It is in this way, through the invocation of human rights, that what might be seen as an illegal project of conquest is transformed into a legal project of salvation and redemption.

This new imperialism seeks, then, to further itself jurisprudentially (by using the recourse to 'international relations' and 'ethics', both of which have been deployed to undermine the idea of a formal and binding law), doctrinally (principally through the new version of self-defence and then through human rights and humanitarian intervention) and institutionally (for example, through the use of the enforcement mechanisms of the United Nations and its nation-building capacities, and the use of the Security Council to change international law itself, most prominently the law relating to the use of force).

Terrorism, self-defence and Third World sovereignty

The Third World, I have argued through this book, lacks effective sovereignty because of the manner in which sovereignty doctrine has been developed in international law. Nevertheless, at the very least, Third World peoples did acquire political sovereignty, an important development that was consolidated through the evolving law of self-determination and the passage of a series of resolutions that elaborated and reaffirmed the principle of non-intervention. The *Nicaragua Case* could be seen as a landmark in the progress of this trend, as it reaffirmed the character and integrity of the sovereignty of a Third

World state that was being threatened by a superpower, the United States. As the ICJ reiterates in the *Nicaragua* Case:

The Court cannot contemplate the creation of a new rule opening up a right of intervention by one state against another on the ground that the latter has opted for some particular ideology or political system.[101]

In all these different ways, Third World sovereignty was asserted and established, whatever the inequalities of power that compelled Third World states to enter into treaties to their disadvantage and agree, for instance, to wide-ranging and extraordinarily intrusive IFI authored programmes. At least in this most basic sense, then, the United Nations developed a system of international law that outlawed conquest and affirmed the right of a state to establish a particular ideology or political system. It is precisely this set of ideas that is being threatened by the new developments that I have termed 'imperialism as self-defence'.

Self-defence is a crucial right of states. Indeed, the self-defence of the United States is of such massive significance that the attempts to ensure it have resulted in all the profound consequences that I have attempted to trace here. The anxieties of many states regarding their own self-defence are no greater than the anxieties experienced by the United States. In this era of massively sophisticated and destructive technology, 'weapons of mass destruction', arguably, are essential for any state's self-defence. Certainly, the established nuclear powers show very little sign of relinquishing their weapons. On the contrary, some of them vehemently argued, in the *Nuclear Weapons* Case, that they had every right to use them in self-defence. Nevertheless, any attempt by states that could be characterized by the United States, at its own discretion, as 'rogue states' to acquire WMD – broadly defined – appears to make it a potential target of attack. Vitoria's jurisprudence established that the right to wage a just war is a fundamental right; nevertheless it is to be enjoyed only by Christian states. It now appears that the right of self-defence, which surely implies the right to arm oneself, is a fundamental right, affirmed in every jurisprudence, but exercisable only by Western civilized states.

This emerging position regarding the significance of WMD in the context of the war against terrorism furthers a trend that was evident to judges more sensitive to the Third World position in the *Nuclear Weapons* Case, who confronted the peculiar situation that would arise if the use

---

[101] *Military and Paramilitary Activities in and against Nicaragua (Nicaragua v. United States)*, ICJ Reports 1986, p. 14 at p. 133.

of nuclear weapons in self-defence was found to be legal, in a situation where the use of less damaging but no less horrifying weapons such as chemical weapons that would be more readily available to poor countries would be deemed illegal. As Judge Weeramantry pointed out in that case, there are injustices inherent in a view where nuclear states could be subjected to one regime and non-nuclear states to another with respect to international humanitarian law.[102] The fundamental principle of international law that stipulates that all sovereigns are formally equal would posit that any right of PESD that develops in international law should be enjoyed by all states, as it derives from the inherent right of all states to self-defence. The development of the doctrine in the context of the WAT, however, suggests that it is only certain states, powerful states that would enjoy such a right.

The UN system risks being gradually distorted as a result of all these developments. Its considerable enforcement mechanisms are now being used, in effect, to prevent certain states from developing nuclear weapons through Security Council monitoring of the Non-Proliferation Treaty, while established nuclear states are not subject to any comparable pressure to dispense with their weapons. Similarly, the United States continues to attempt to use the Security Council as an international legislative power even while asserting its right to disregard the Council and the United Nations when it thinks fit. Not the least of the consequences of the WAT is the possibility that it will establish an imperial Security Council that exists permanently in a Chapter VII mode and that will purport to legislate all manner of international activities in the name of the WAT. These developments suggest a dual process: the further expansion, ostensibly within the framework of the UN Charter, of the powers of the large states, and a corresponding diminution in the powers of the smaller states. The United Nations, if it accedes to the US position about its proper role, runs the risk of being transformed, to an even greater extent, into the Bank or the IMF: that is, into an institutional mechanism by which certain powerful states can impose on the rest of the international community a law by which they do not regard themselves

---

[102] See *Legality of the Threat or Use of Nuclear Weapons,* Advisory Opinion, ICJ Reports 1996, p. 226 at pp. 526–527 (Dissenting Opinion of Judge Weeramantry); 'Least of all can there be one law for the powerful and another law for the rest.' *Ibid.* Further, Weeramantry points out: 'A legal rule would be inconceivable that some nations alone have the right to use chemical or bacteriological weapons in self-defence and others do not. The principle involved, in the claim of some nations to be able to use nuclear weapons in self-defence, rests on no different juristic basis.' *Ibid.,* p. 527.

as bound. Even the UN Security Council's current record in the WAT surely raises several problematic questions. The vital questions raised by the *Lockerbie* litigation regarding, for example, the powers of the Council and the extent to which the Council itself is bound by international law and the law of the Charter, are now especially significant. Was it legally open for the Security Council to purport, however obliquely, to authorize so quickly the use of force against Afghanistan?

To argue for the continuing validity of the current UN system is not meekly to acquiesce to terrorism. In exploring the way in which language creates the 'other' I am not, of course, in any way, attempting to suggest that the killing of thousands of innocent people in attacks that have deliberately targeted civilians is in some way 'unreal' or negligible or condonable. Rather, as many scholars and commentators almost immediately after 9/11 pointed out, different ways of understanding and characterizing those events had a profound impact on how to address them. The resolve of the international community to address the problems and threats of terrorism is surely evident in the many steps the United Nations has taken to address these problems. Some views of the Non-aligned movement on the issue of terrorism needs to be quoted in full:

119. The Heads of State or Government rejected the use, or the threat of the use of armed forces against any NAM [Non-aligned movement] country under the pretext of combating terrorism, and rejected all attempts by certain countries to use the issue of combating terrorism as a pretext to pursue their political aims against non-aligned and developing countries and underscored the need to exercise solidarity with those affected. They affirmed the pivotal role of the United Nations in the international campaign against terrorism. They totally rejected the term 'axis of evil' voiced by a certain State to target other countries under the pretext of combating terrorism, as well as its unilateral preparation of lists accusing countries of allegedly supporting terrorism, which are inconsistent with international law and the purposes and principles of the United Nations Charter. These actions constitute on their part, a form of psychological and political terrorism.[103]

This emphatic assertion on the continuing importance of the United Nations is surely significant, not only because of the large number of countries that belong to the NAM, but precisely because many of them have suffered the worst consequences of terrorism. Thousands

---

[103] Final Document of the XIII Conference of Heads of State or Government of the Non Aligned Movement, Kuala Lumpur, 24–25 February 2003, para. 119, www.nam.gov.za/media/030227e.htm.

of people have died in these countries as a result of terrorism, without those deaths ever being so exalted as to represent an attack on 'civilization' itself. Nor have these countries, despite these ongoing tragedies, sought to dismantle the existing system of international law. Indeed, when taking action against terrorism they have been continuously condemned by the very states that now disregard foundational international norms relating to international humanitarian law and international human rights law in their own WAT. Terrorism is universally condemned. The great danger of the war against terrorism, however, is that it will fragment the international community to such an extent that the coherent global action needed to respond to the real problems of terrorism will become impossible.

Scholars and policy makers confidently recommending imperial rule characterize it as both desirable and easily achieved. There is a presumption in much of this writing that imperialism is simply a matter of will, that the Western states, in a moment of weakness and delusion, provided independence to backward native peoples who – being incorrigibly backward despite their years of colonial tutelage – lacked the capacity properly to exercise it. As events in Iraq have suggested, imperialism may not be so easily implemented. The consequences of imperialism are unpredictable for both the ruler and the ruled. Edmund Burke, for example, argued that imperialism had an inevitably corrupting effect on the polity of the imperial power.[104] Since the time of Kant, at least, international relations literature has either implicitly or explicitly characterized democratic governments as being more responsible, mature and far-seeking in their judgements. As Jose Alvarez has suggested in his searching article on the subject, liberal democratic states do not always behave better.[105] The United States and United Kingdom justified going to war in Iraq, despite the absence of any UN authorization, on the basis that Saddam Hussein possessed WMD. The absence, so far, of any such weapons, and the complex questions surrounding the failure of intelligence and the manner in which available intelligence was used by the

---

[104] See Uday Singh Mehta, *Liberalism and Empire: A Study in Nineteenth Century British Liberal Thought* (Chicago: University of Chicago Press, 1999), pp. 152–189. Mehta's study contrasts Burke's approach to empire, on the one hand, with that of John Stuart Mill, and J. S. Mill on the other, both of whom, despite their commitment to liberalism, were staunch supporters of empire.

[105] Surveying the issues of compliance, Alvarez argues that 'we still have little reason to be confident that the levels of compliance across the range of subjects covered by international obligations fall along "liberal"/"non-liberal" lines'. Alvarez, 'Do Liberal States Behave Better?', 210.

two governments as they proceeded towards war, must surely suggest that democratic states are entirely fallible. The fact that a state is democratic and proclaims itself to be acting from the highest motives does not make its violation of international law any the less excusable. It is not only imperialism as such but, compounding matters, an imperialism promoted as indispensable for self-defence that distorts and undermines the democratic process and the principles of accountability and transparency it is supposed to ensure.[106] The distinct possibility has now arisen that the war in Iraq may not only fail to deliver democracy to Iraq but, instead, undermine it in the United States and United Kingdom. Imperialism corrupts both the ruler and the ruled.

The perspective of the ruled might also have some bearing on the workability and desirability of empire. A reading of Frantz Fanon's *The Wretched of the Earth* suggests disturbing parallels between the terrorist and the colonized, if we seek to trace the genealogy of the violence that we associate with terrorism:

> The violence which has ruled over the ordering of the colonial world, which has ceaselessly drummed the rhythm for the destruction of native social forms and broken up without reserve the systems of reference of the economy, the customs of dress and external life, that same violence will be claimed and taken over by the native at the moment when, deciding to embody history in his own person, he surges into the forbidden quarters. To wreck the colonial world is henceforward a mental picture of action which is very clear, very easy to understand and which may be assumed by each one of the individuals which constitute the colonized people.[107]

This implications of this argument are radical – and to many, unacceptable – because it might be taken to 'justify' terrorism.[108] But the passage may be read instead as a way of attempting to understand terrorist violence, not as an expression of an inherent and inalienable fanaticism, but as a phenomenon that must be studied in historical terms. Fanon's characterization of the colonized as 'deciding to embody history in his own person' has, of course, a peculiar and disconcerting resonance in this age of suicide bombings, in the context of Fanon's broader point that history is ineluctably connected with violence. It is

---

[106] Pratap Bhanu Mehta, 'Empire and Moral Identity', (2003) 17(2) *Ethics and International Affairs* 49–62.

[107] Frantz Fanon, *The Wretched of the Earth*, Constance Farrington trans. (Harmondsworth: Penguin Books, 1982), p. 31.

[108] See Chalmers A. Johnson, *Blowback* (New York: Metropolitan Books, 2001), a work that was attacked precisely because it seemed to make this sort of an argument.

IMPERIALISM AS SELF-DEFENCE

in this context, furthermore, that it becomes crucial to argue that imperialism has *always* governed international relations, rather than seeing imperialism as having ended with formal decolonization. The latter view suggests that the unruly and chaotic world requires the re-imposition of imperial order. The former view suggests that many communities around the world, the large majority of the world's population, already experience themselves as marginalized and impoverished by an imperial international system; and a WAT, which simply reinforces this imperialism, is most likely to produce an endless war. The crucial question remains, then, of whether international law and the UN system can resist this drive towards a new imperialism even while adapting to the new challenges facing the international community.

My broad argument is that the WAT represents a set of policies and principles that reproduces the structure of the civilizing mission. Further, it is precisely by invoking the primordial, imperial structures latent within international law that this supposedly new initiative seeks to disrupt and transform existing international law. It is a novel initiative that relies for its power on a very ancient set of ideas – regarding self-defence humanitarian intervention and conquest. It is almost as though any attempt to create a new international law must somehow return to and reproduce, the colonial origins of the discipline. What is perhaps distinctive about the dynamic of difference as it is asserted in the WAT, however, is the belief that, in a globalised world, the transformation of the 'other' is essential for the defence, the very survival of the Western self. This could give rise to a uniquely dangerous situation and a continuous and self-sustaining violence.

Conclusion

[T]o him the meaning of an episode was not inside like a kernel, but outside, enveloping the tale which brought it out only as a glow brings out a haze, in the likeness of one of those misty halos that sometimes are made visible by the spectral illumination of moonshine.[1]

The Peace of Westphalia has a defining significance for the discipline of international law. It is the 'Westphalian model' of sovereignty, created as a means of resolving conflicts among European powers, that has preoccupied international lawyers over the centuries in their analysis and elaboration of the founding concept of the subject. This model, which asserts that all sovereigns are equal and exercise absolute power within their own territory, has in time produced the haunting problem: how is order created among sovereign states? It is the 'Westphalian model' of sovereignty, further, that has generated histories of the discipline that broadly present the non-European world in terms of the process by which sovereignty, established in the European centre, extends to incorporate that non-European world. I have attempted in this book to sketch an alternative history of sovereignty, a history that focuses not on events in Europe but on the colonial confrontation between non-European and European societies.

This book argues that colonialism was central to the constitution of international law and sovereignty doctrine. In developing this argument, I focus on the rhetoric of the 'civilizing mission' that was such an indispensable part of the imperial project. This mission furthered itself by postulating an essential difference – what might be termed a 'cultural difference' – between the Europeans and non-Europeans, the Spanish and the Indians, the civilized and the uncivilized. This basic distinction

---

[1] Joseph Conrad, *Heart of Darkness* (Edinburgh: W. Blackwood & Sons, 1902), p. 493.

310

has been reproduced, in a supposedly non-imperial world, in the distinctions that play such a decisive role in contemporary international relations: the divisions between the developed and developing, the pre-modern and the post-modern and now, once again, the civilized and the barbaric. My argument is that the 'civilizing mission', the maintenance of this dichotomy – variously understood in different phases of the history of international law – combined with the task of bridging this gap, provided international law with a dynamic that shaped the character of sovereignty – and, more broadly, of international law and institutions. Vitoria's formulation of the problem of cultural difference, and his attempts to resolve it, occur at the very beginnings of the modern discipline of international law. The problem of cultural difference, then, antedated the problem of how order is maintained among sovereign states, the problem that has preoccupied the discipline since at least the Peace of Westphalia and the emergence of the modern state system. Indeed, it could be argued that the Peace of Westphalia was precisely an attempt to resolve this problem of difference, the internecine warfare resulting from religious divisions within Europe. Sovereignty, I argue, did not precede and manage cultural differences; rather, sovereignty was forged out of the confrontation between different cultures and, at least in the colonial confrontation, the appropriation by one culture of the powerful terms 'sovereignty' and 'law'. Perhaps, then, Westphalia and the model of colonial sovereignty structured by the 'civilizing mission' that I have sketched here might be understood as two different responses to the same problem of cultural difference.

My argument is that the traditional focus on the problem of order among sovereign states commences its inquiries by assuming the existence of a sovereign Europe. It therefore lacks the conceptual apparatus to interrogate fundamental characteristics of the colonial encounter, the construction of the non-European society as primitive violent, uncivilized and therefore non-sovereign. Sovereignty is formulated in such a way as to exclude the non-European; following which, sovereignty can then be deployed to identify, locate, sanction and transform the uncivilized. This is the series of manoeuvres, the reflex, that I have termed the 'dynamic of difference'. Consequently, it is primarily in the peripheries, in the non-sovereign, non-European world that sovereignty is completely unfettered, directed and controlled only by its ingenuity in constructing the uncivilized in ever more innovative ways which then call for new elaborations, applications and refinements in sovereignty. The unique operation of sovereignty doctrine in the colonial encounter suggests that it is seriously misleading to think of sovereignty as emerging in Europe and then extending – stable, imperial in its reach and control, unaltered, sovereign – into the colonial world. The creation of international law in its necessarily endless drive towards universality is based on the compelling invocation of this 'other'. The drive is necessarily endless, I have argued, because even while seeking to create a universal system it generates the difference that makes this task impossible and, further, because these imperial projects inevitably provoke rebellion and opposition.

Pioneering Third World jurists have attempted to transform the old, Eurocentric, international law into an international law responsive to the needs, the interests and the histories of the developing world. In the 1960s and 1970s these jurists, while formulating a very powerful anti-colonial stand, adopted the strategy of asserting similarities with the European world – claiming, for example, that traditional Asian and African societies had formulated certain principles which were also fundamental principles of international law. More recently, developing country jurists have relied on the rhetoric of 'difference' in intense debates regarding, for example, human rights and cultural relativism. They assert their uniqueness and insist on the need for international law to acknowledge and accommodate this.

The point of this book is that whatever the claims made, whether the Third World is characterized as different, similar, or a combination of the two, it must contend with the history of international law that is sketched here, a history in which international law continuously disempowers the non-European world, even while sanctioning intervention within it – as when Vitoria characterizes the Indians as 'infant', thereby simultaneously diminishing the Indians and justifying their subjection to Spanish tutelage.

The underlying premise of my argument is that the structure of sovereignty, the identity of sovereignty, no less than the identity of an individual or a people, is formed by its history, its origins in and engagement with the colonial encounter. But sovereignty doctrine, I have argued, is formidably ingenious in concealing this intimate relationship. Indeed, international law remains oblivious to its imperial structures even when continuing to reproduce them, which is why the traditional history of international law regards imperialism as a thing of the past. My attempt, then, is to illuminate the processes, the barely visible thoroughfares by which this colonial history insinuates itself into the discipline with enduring and far-reaching effect. This colonial

history shapes the underlying structure of sovereignty doctrine; it creates within sovereignty doctrine juridical mechanisms in the form, for
example, of sources doctrine, personality doctrine, consent doctrine and
so forth, which resist any challenge being made to the colonial past
and sovereignty's role within it. The New International Economic Order
(NIEO) constituted the most important international law initiative taken
by the developing world in attempting to remedy colonial inequities. Its
attempted negation by traditional international law demonstrated how
the juridical mechanisms created by the colonial encounter continue
to operate in the present. Traditional sources doctrine was deployed to
oppose Third World formulations of new standards of compensation, for
example. Principles of 'consent' were used to argue that colonial societies, in becoming sovereign, independent, states had in effect agreed to
abide by the given rules of customary international law that they played
no role in formulating; and that they had, furthermore, surrendered any
right to question the effects or the character of the sovereignty they were
now privileged to enjoy. It is in this way that the legal doctrines of the
nineteenth century – and the relations of inequality they created – continue to affect the present, for these economic inequalities remain in
place, and these doctrines impede current attempts to seek reparations
for colonial exploitation.

My argument, however, is not only that the colonial origins of international law have, in this way, an impact on the present. Rather, as I
attempt to show in chapter 6 on the WAT, on many of the occasions on
which international law seeks to institute a new order it reproduces, in
effect, the colonial structures of international law. It is for this reason,
I have argued, that striking parallels exist between the legal worlds of
Vitoria and the present, the twenty-first century, as it proceeds towards
an uncertain future. The colonial origins of the discipline are re-enacted
whenever the discipline attempts to renew itself, reform itself. At one
level, then, the old doctrines created to further colonialism are difficult
to reform; at another level, new international law doctrines somehow
reproduce the structure of the 'civilizing mission', as I have attempted
to show in my examination of such ostensibly new initiatives as 'good
governance'. In other cases, the re-emergence of a very old doctrine, such
as preemptive self-defence (PESD), deployed to create a new international
law, appears rather to simply reproduce the structure of the 'civilizing
mission' once again. The further conclusion I draw from this last example is that the techniques and methods of imperialism are never consec-
utive, as it were: that is, all the techniques and methods of imperialism

continue to co-exist in the present and, in given circumstances, may easily be resurrected. The 'new' form of Empire that Hardt and Negri, for example, describe co-exists with very old forms of empire; the post-modern methods of control and management co-exist with nineteenth-century ideas of sovereignty, sixteenth-century notions of self-defence. It is as though the different layers of imperialism continue to co-exist within the discipline in the manner suggested by Freud – drawing on Darwin – when outlining his model of the mind in *Civilization and Its Discontents*:

> But have we a right to assume the survival of something that was originally there, alongside of what was later derived from it? Undoubtedly. There is nothing strange in such a phenomenon, whether in the mental field or elsewhere. In the animal kingdom we hold to the view that [as] the most highly developed species we have proceeded from the lowest; and yet we find all the simple forms still in existence today.[2]

Sovereignty may be likened not only to Freud's model of the mind, but to a domestic constitution which, while regulating everyday political and economic affairs, also contains within itself the special powers required to deal with states of emergency. International law is in a permanent state of emergency; it could not be otherwise, over the centuries, given that international law has endlessly reached out towards universality, expanding, confronting, including and suppressing the different societies and peoples it encountered. At the peripheries, then, sovereignty was continuously demarcating and policing these boundaries, applying and reinventing the emergency powers which incorporated, excluded and normalized the uncivilized, hence enabling conventional sovereignty to appear to operate unperturbed, stable and following its own course. International law can maintain its coherence and play its classic role of regulating state behaviour only by carefully defining the cultural sphere, the civilized world, in which it operates. Thus the colony, the primitive, is always and everywhere within sovereignty doctrine, if only because it must be excluded and managed.

The history of the relationship between the centre and periphery which is outlined here is particularly relevant to the peoples of the developing world; for it is a history which they have endured, of which they have been the victims. This is the history, these are the structures, which the peoples of the Third World must confront in attempting to

---

[2] Sigmund Freud, *Civilization and Its Discontents*, James Strachey ed. and trans. (New York, W. W. Norton, 1961), p. 15.

use international law to pursue their goals. But this is not merely the history of the Third World in international law because, in the final analysis, the First and the Third World, the colonizer and the colonized, are too intimately linked to permit the maintenance of such a distinction. International law, like sovereignty, like the colonial relationship itself, is indivisible. My attempt here, then, is not in any way to supplant completely the 'Westphalian model' of sovereignty, but rather in sketching a model of imperial sovereignty, to suggest the extraordinarily complex ways in which the two models relate to each other.

Principles of international law, like rules in general, inevitably have disparate and unpredictable effects on differently situated people. There is nothing in the least coincidental, however, about the debilitating impact of many of the classic doctrines of international law on Third World countries. My simple point is that these doctrines were created for the explicit purpose of excluding the colonial world, or else, are based on an exclusion which has already been effected – as when positivist jurists dismiss the state practice of the uncivilized Eastern states as irrelevant to the formulation of international law. This exclusion, and the imperialism which it furthers, constitute in part the primordial and essential identity of international law.

This point might be further suggested by two significant works on the history of international law, Richard Tuck's *Rights of War and Peace* and Martti Koskenniemi's *The Gentle Civilizer of Nations*. Each of these accounts of different aspects of the history of international law focuses on contrasts and transitions. Tuck's work, for example, focuses on the contrast between the 'scholastic' tradition represented by scholars such as Vitoria, and the 'humanist' tradition represented by scholars such as Grotius. Koskenniemi's work traces the transition from the formalist international law of the nineteenth century to the pragmatic, policy oriented jurisprudence, associated with American ascendancy, that emerged by the 1960s. The disturbing point for me is that, whatever the contrasts and transitions, *imperialism is a constant*. That is, both the scholastic (Vitoria) and the humanist (Grotius), both nineteenth-century formalism *and* late twentieth-century pragmatism, legitimized imperialism using entirely different vocabularies. Naturalism, positivism, pragmatism: these are the three major schools of jurisprudence in the history of international law, and they are seen as distinctive and radically different, the evolution of international law being understood as the transition – never entirely completed – from one to another. And yet, what I have concluded through my examination of these schools of jurisprudence – represented here for me by Vitoria, the nineteenth century and the League of Nations – is that each of them reproduces the basic structure of the 'dynamic of difference', the 'civilizing mission'.

My discussion has focused on the colonial origins of sovereignty doctrine, since sovereignty is, after all, the foundational concept of our discipline; but if my argument regarding the colonial origins of sovereignty doctrine, have any validity, then they may also illuminate the relationship between colonialism and all the other doctrines of international law in general that are based, in one manner or another, inevitably, on sovereignty. Here I have suggested the colonial dimensions of sovereignty, of international institutions, of international economic law, among other themes. And I sometimes speculate on what sort of histories would emerge from studies of particular doctrines and institutions in international law that began with the whimsical preface 'The colonial origins of'. The colonial origins of: international human rights law; investment law; law and development; international commercial arbitration; the World Bank, the International Monetary Fund (IMF) and the World Trade Organization (WTO); international humanitarian law; sources doctrine; good governance; contracts; intellectual property law; property law?

If this imperial structure of ideas is so pervasive within the doctrines and jurisprudence of international law, then a question that naturally arises is: why is this the case? This is only one of the many questions raised by the issues I have examined here to which I have no clear answer. Perhaps it has to do with the very character of sovereignty itself. Perhaps sovereignty, most simply associated with power, seeks to further itself in every way: by expanding its territory, its economic might, its particular culture and institutions. It is notable, for example, that whenever particular entities assume sovereign or quasi-sovereign powers, they generally seek to reproduce and extend these powers through an imperial narrative. An international institution such as the Mandate System (and its successor, the World Bank), unable to exercise any real sovereignty over the Western states, can nevertheless establish and expand itself by engaging in the 'civilizing mission', by formulating the standards and promoting the programmes that the backward must follow if they are to progress. The post-colonial state, once it emerges from the domination of colonialism, immediately asserts itself to be the 'universal' entity that all minorities, for example, must comply with, and it then reproduces the same divisions, between the 'modern' and the 'primitive', that animated the colonial enterprise. Sovereignty, then, is intimately connected with imperialism. The deep and enduring inequalities that afflict this planet might be attributed, simply, to inequalities in power: the strong dictate and the weak must comply. But power rarely presents itself simply as brute force, as shock and awe. Rather, it presents its violence in terms of an overarching narrative, and there are few more compelling stories that power can relate about itself when expanding than the great imperial narrative in which 'we' are civilized, peace-loving, democratic, humanitarian, virtuous, benevolent, and 'they' are uncivilized, violent, irrational, backward, dangerous, oppressed, and must therefore be sanctioned, rescued and transformed by a violence that is simultaneously, defensive, overwhelming, humanitarian and benevolent. The furtherance of justice, the promotion of humanitarianism; these are the great goals that imperialism has traditionally set itself.

The further important issue is the question of whether it is possible to create an international law that is not imperial; that can, in fact, further justice, increase the well being of humanity, without relapsing into the imperial project that I have attempted to sketch here. This is a large question, to which again I have no adequate answer. It is not my intention here to be deterministic, to relentlessly demonstrate that colonialism has always been reproduced by international law over the last five centuries of its existence and that this will therefore inevitably continue to be the case. Rather, I see this work as expressing certain historically based concerns which, if recognized, can surely be remedied. In making this argument regarding imperial sovereignty, I hope I have also demonstrated that there is no inherent logic to sovereignty doctrine; that imperialism has been continuously contested by jurists, peoples and individuals from both the First and the Third Worlds; and that it is possible to imagine and argue for very different understandings of the meaning of sovereignty – and, indeed, of international law. This is demonstrated, for example, by the arguments that were made by developing states in the context of the debate over permanent sovereignty over natural resources (PSNR). Sovereignty doctrine, then, is articulated, supported and developed through particular argumentative practices that are expressed through and underlie the decisions of jurists, the writings of scholars, and the resolutions of international institutions. It is possible to question these practices. To question, for example the strategic way that Vitoria characterizes the non-European peoples in a manner that brings them under the rule of international law without providing them with any of the benefits of that law, thus ensuring a particular outcome that appears inevitable and legally valid. Having identified these strategies, it may be possible to contest them, to deny whatever claims they make to being universal and logical interpretations of the doctrines in question. In other words, I hope that even as I have illustrated the constitutive persistence of colonialism, I have also shown the problems and weaknesses of the colonial doctrines and framework, the incoherence of the attempts of the nineteenth-century jurists to place and manage the uncivilized barbarian. The interrogation and undermining of these official narratives might enable the emergence of alternative histories, an aspect of a much larger project of struggle and contestation that has to take place at all levels.

I continue to hope, together with the many scholars who are working to reconstruct an international law precisely because of their awareness of the many ways in which it has operated to exclude and subordinate people on account of their gender, race and poverty, that international law can be transformed into a means by which the marginalized may be empowered. In short, that law can play its ideal role in limiting and resisting power. At the very least, I believe that the Third World cannot abandon international law because law now plays such a vital role in the public realm in the interpretation of virtually all international events. It is through the vocabulary of international law, concepts of 'self-defence', 'human rights' and 'humanitarian intervention' that issues of cause, responsibility and fault are being discussed and analysed, and interpretations of these doctrines which reproduce imperial relations must be contested. The construction of the 'other', I have argued, is crucial to the extension and universalization of international law. Complex issues arise as to whether it is possible to somehow imagine the 'other' and behave towards it in some different and non-imperial way.[3] The Peace of Westphalia, I have already suggested may be seen as one approach to precisely this problem.

Colonizer and colonized: this is the basic dichotomy that has structured the 'civilizing mission' which has been the focus of my analysis. This dichotomy, however, as I have argued in chapter 2 on the nineteenth century, was extraordinarily difficult to establish and police. Further, this dichotomy does not hold true, for the relationship between these two roles continuously shifts with history and circumstance. The United

---

[3] For an extended meditation on this issue, see Tzvetan Todorov, *The Conquest of America: The Question of the Other*, trans. from the French by Richard Howard (New York. HarperCollins, 1984).

States, now looming as an imperial power that surpasses Rome, the defining imperial power, was itself a colony – and, indeed, importantly defines
itself in terms of its revolution against colonialism. As I tried to suggest in chapter 6 on the war against terror (WAT), in the case of the
United States at least four different histories, each of them centring on
very different manifestations of imperialism, overlap and intersect in
extraordinarily complex ways: the history of slavery, the history of the
relationship between the Native Americans and the European settlers,
the history of America's war of independence and the history of earlier
instances of American expansion following the Spanish–American war of
1898. How do these histories contend with each other as America now
assumes an imperial role?. And which will prevail? Correspondingly,
many Third World states which have been the victims of colonialism
have themselves been imperial in their ambitions and practices, if not
in relation to other states then in relation to minorities and indigenous
peoples within their borders. Imperialism, is not by any means a purely
Western practice.

The experience of being both colonizer and colonized, then, is a
common one, and the question is how this duality might be used to
undermine the dichotomy between colonizer and colonized, self and
'other', on which the 'civilizing mission' is based. Unsurprisingly, the
United States denies any imperial ambitions even as it embarks upon
an imperial venture, precisely because an important aspect of its history, its identity as a nation that emerged through a war of independence against colonialism, provides a powerful resource of self-criticism
and questioning: the 'other' is not external to the self, but within. It
is surely significant, furthermore, that many Third World states and
leaders regarded the United States as an inspiration for their own anti-
colonial struggles.

As this suggests, further, there is no inherent virtue in the ideologies
or principles articulated by Third World states. As Onuma Yasuaki has
pointed out in his important work, hierarchy and inequality, the strict
maintenance of the division between the 'civilized' and the 'barbarian',
is far from peculiar to Western societies.[4] Rather, these concepts are
central to many of the major non-European civilizations such as those
of East Asia. What is required, then, is a jurisprudence that draws on

[4] Onuma Yasuaki, 'When Was the Law of International Society Born? – An Inquiry of the
History of International Law from an Intercivilizational Perspective', (2000) 2 *Journal of
the History of International Law* 1–66; see also Li Zhaojie, 'Traditional Chinese World
Order', (2002) 1 *Chinese Journal of International Law* 20–59.

all cultures, both Western and non-Western, to address the problems of imperialism. Further, as Edward Said has been at pains to point out, the search for purely 'Western' or 'non-Western' ideas is futile as cultures have continuously influenced each other over many centuries. It is for these reasons that it seems to me that the jurisprudence of Judge Weeramantry has been so important: it draws on a variety of legal systems and traditions in an attempt to create a truly universal international law that promotes a compelling vision of international justice. The point is not to condemn the ideals of 'the rule of law' 'good governance' and 'democracy' as being inherently imperial constructs, but rather, to question how it is that these ideals have become used as a means of furthering imperialism and why it is that international law and institutions seem so often to fail to make these ideals a reality. Such a jurisprudence, furthermore, might offer real possibilities of breaking the particular cycle that posits an imperial international law as being the only response to a hopelessly corrupt Third World; *either* Saddam Hussein with all his repression *or* shock and awe and the war to liberate Iraq.

As all this would suggest, there is no one agent (the 'Third World state') nor any one method ('positivism' or 'pragmatism') that will ensure the emergence of an anti-imperial international law. It appears to me that there is no substitute for continuously questioning developments in international law on the basis of a vision of international justice that is informed by an understanding of the colonial history of international law and its enduring effects. Lastly, and, perhaps, not entirely insignificantly, then, there is the international lawyer. Sovereignty doctrine, after all, does not exist independently of the scholars, the jurists and the practitioners who give it a particular content by arguing in particular modes and deciding what claims should be admitted and which rejected. 'Know thyself': this is surely one of the foundational principles of Western civilization (although it transpires that Buddhist teachings also assert the fundamental importance of self-knowledge). But if we do not understand the character of this discipline, then, of course, we cannot possibly bring about any change within it. This book attempts to clarify one aspect of the history of the discipline in the hope of illuminating its operations sufficiently to enable us to assess its results against our sense of justice; and in so doing, empower us to make, rather than simply replicate, history.

Bibliography

Abernethy, David B., *The Dynamics of Global Dominance: European Overseas Empires, 1415-1980* (New Haven: Yale University Press, 2000)

Abi-Saab, Georges M., 'International Law and the International Community: The Long Road to Universality', in Ronald St John Macdonald (ed.), *Essays in Honor of Wang Tieya* (Dordrecht: Martinus Nijhoff, 1994)

'The Newly Independent States and the Rules of International Law: An Outline', (1962) 8 *Howard Law Journal* 95-121

'The Newly Independent States and the Scope of Domestic Jurisdiction', (1960) 54 *American Society of International Law Proceedings* 84-90

'The Proper Role of International Law in Combating Terrorism', (2002) 1 *Chinese Journal of International Law* 305-314

Alexandrowicz, C. H., 'Doctrinal Aspects of the Universality of the Law of Nations', (1961) 37 *British Yearbook of International Law* 506-515

The European-African Confrontation: A Study in Treaty Making (Leiden: A. W. Sijthoff, 1973)

An Introduction to the History of the Law of Nations in the East Indies (Oxford: Clarendon Press, 1967)

'The Theory of Recognition *in Fieri*', (1958) 34 *British Yearbook of International Law* 176-198

Alford, William P., 'Exporting "The Pursuit of Happiness"', (2000) 113 *Harvard Law Review* 1677-1715

Ali, Syed Ameer, 'Islam in the League of Nations', (1919) 5 *Transactions of the Grotius Society* 126-144

Alvarez, Alejandro, 'Latin America and International Law', (1909) 3 *American Journal of International Law* 269-353

'The New International Law', (1930) 15 *Transactions of the Grotius Society* 35-51

Alvarez, Jose E., 'Crimes of States/Crimes of Hate: Lessons from Rwanda', (1999) 24 *Yale Journal of International Law* 365

'Do Liberal States Behave Better? A Critique of Slaughter's Liberal Theory', (2001) 12 *European Journal of International Law* 183-246

321

Amerasinghe, Chittharanjan Felix, *State Responsibility for Injuries to Aliens* (Oxford: Clarendon Press, 1967)

Amin, Samir, 'Imperialism and Globalization', (June 2001) *Monthly Review* 6–24 *Imperialism and Unequal Development* (New York: Monthly Review Press, 1977)

Anand, R. P., 'Attitude of the Asian–African States Toward Certain Problems of International Law', (1962), in F. Snyder and Surakiart Sathirathai (eds.), *Third World Attitudes Toward International Law: An Introduction* (Boston: Martinus Nijhoff, 1987), pp. 5–22

'Attitudes of the Asian–African States Toward Certain Problems of International Law', (1966) 15 *International and Comparative Law Quarterly* 55–75

New States and International Law (New Delhi: Vikas Publishing House, 1972)

'Role of the "New" Asian–African Countries in the Present International Legal Order', (1962) 56 *American Journal of International Law* 383–406.

Anderson, Benedict, *Imagined Communities: Reflections on the Origin and Spread of Nationalism* (2nd rev. edn., New York: Verso, 1991)

Anghie, Antony, 'Creating the Nation-State: Colonialism and the Making of International Law', unpublished SJD dissertation, Harvard Law School (1995) (on file with the author)

'Cultural Differences in International Law: The League of Nations and Two Visions of the Nation-State', (2002) 5 *International Center for Comparative Law and Politics Review* 4–13

'Finding the Peripheries: Sovereignty and Colonialism in Nineteenth Century International Law', (1999) 40(1) *Harvard International Law Journal* 1–80

'The Heart of My Home: Colonialism, Environmental Damage, and the Nauru Case', (1993) 34 *Harvard International Law Journal* 445–506

'Time Present and Time Past: Globalization, International Financial Institutions, and the Third World', (2000) 32 *New York University Journal of International Law and Policy* 243–290

Annan, Kofi, Speech to the United Nations General Assembly, 23 September 2003, Press Release SG/SM/8891

Ansah, Tawia, 'War: Rhetoric & Norm-Creation in Response to Terror', (2003) 43 *Virginia Journal of International Law* 797–860

Astorino, Samuel J., 'The Impact of Sociological Jurisprudence on International Law in the Inter-War Period: The American Experience', (1996) 34 *Duquesne Law Review* 277–298

Austin, John, *The Province of Jurisprudence Determined* (New York: Noonday Press, 1954)

Barker, Pat, *Regeneration* (New York: Plume, 1991)

Bartelson, Jens, *A Genealogy of Sovereignty* (New York: Cambridge University Press, 1995)

Baxi, Upendra, 'Voices of Suffering and the Future of Human Rights', (1998) 8 *Transnational Law and Contemporary Problems* 163–164, 125–169

Bayefsky, Anne F., (ed.), *Self Determination in International Law: Quebec and Lessons Learned: Legal Opinions* (The Hague: Kluwer Academic, 2000)

Becker, Elizabeth, 'A Nation Challenged: Renaming an Operation to Fit the Mood', *The New York Times*, September 26, 2001, 3

Bederman, David, 'The Souls of International Organizations: Legal Personality and the Lighthouse at Cape Spartel', (1996) 36 *Virginia Journal of International Law* 275–377

Bedjaoui, Mohammed, 'First Report on Succession of States in Respect of Rights and Duties Resulting From Sources Other Than Treaties', UN Doc. A/CN.4/204, in *Yearbook of the International Law Commission*, II, 1968, UN Doc. A/CN.4/SER.A./1968 Add 1

'General Introduction', in Mohammed Bedjaoui, *International Law: Achievements and Prospects* (Boston: Martinus Nijhoff, 1991)

Towards a New International Economic Order (New York: Holmes & Meier, 1979)

Beer, G. L., *African Questions at the Paris Peace Conference; With Papers on Egypt, Mesopotamia, and the Colonial Settlement* (New York: The Macmillan Co., 1923)

Benton, Laurel, *Law and Colonial Cultures: Legal Regimes in World History 1400–1900*, (Cambridge: Cambridge University Press, 2002).

Bentwich, Norman, *The Mandates System* (London: Longmans, Green, 1930)

Berger, Peter, 'Are Human Rights Universal?', in Barry M. Rubin and Elizabeth P. Spiro (eds.), *Human Rights and US Foreign Policy* (Boulder, CO: Westview Press, 1979), pp. 3–12

Berman, Nathaniel, '"But the Alternative is Despair": European Nationalism and the Modernist Renewal of International Law', (1993) 106 *Harvard Law Review* 1792–1903

'In the Wake of Empire', (1999) 14 *American University International Law Review* 1521–1554

'The Nationality Decrees Case, or, Of Intimacy and Consent', (2000) 13 *Leiden Journal of International Law* 265–295

'A Perilous Ambivalence: Nationalist Desire, Legal Autonomy and the Limits of the Interwar Framework', (1992) 33 *Harvard International Law Journal* 353–379

'Shadows: Du Bois and the Colonial Prospect, 1925', (2000) 45 *Villanova Law Review* 959–970

Bhabha, Homi, *The Location of Culture* (London: Routledge, 1994)

Boeke, J. H., *The Structure of Netherlands Indian Economy* (New York: International Secretariat, Institute of Pacific Relations, 1942)

Bowett, Derek, 'State Contracts With Aliens: Contemporary Developments on Compensation for Termination or Breach', (1988) 59 *The British Yearbook of International Law* 49–74

Boyle, Francis Anthony, *Foundations of World Order: The Legalist Approach to International Relations, 1898–1921* (Durham, NC: Duke University Press, 1999)

Bozeman, Adda B., *The Future of Law in a Multicultural World* (Princeton: Princeton University Press, 1971)

Bradley, Mark Philip, *Imagining Vietnam & America: The Making of Post-Colonial Vietnam, 1919–1950* (Chapel Hill, NC: University of North Carolina Press, 2000)

Brierly, J. L., *The Law of Nations: An Introduction to the International Law of Peace* (2nd edn., Oxford: Clarendon Press, 1936)

'The Shortcomings of International Law', (1924) 5 *British Yearbook of International Law* 4–16

Brolmann, Catherine, René Lefeber and Marjoleine Zieck (eds.), *Peoples and Minorities in International Law* (Dordrecht: Martinus Nijhoff, 1993)

Broms, Bengt, 'Natural Resources, Sovereignty Over', in R. Bernhardt (ed.), *Encyclopedia of Public International Law* (4 vols., New York: Elsevier, 1997), III, pp. 520–524

Brower, Charles, 'Notes and Comments: International Arbitration and the Islamic World: The Third Phase', (2003) 97 *American Journal of International Law* 643–656

Brownlie, Ian, 'The Expansion of International Society: The Consequences for the Law of Nations', in Hedley Bull and Adam Watson (eds.), *The Expansion of International Society* (New York: Oxford University Press, 1984) 357–369

'Legal Status of Natural Resources in International Law', (1979-I) 162 *Académie du Droit International, Recueil de Cours* 245–318

Legal Status of Natural Resources in International Law (Some Aspects) (Alphen aan den Rijn: Sijthoff & Noordhoff, 1980)

Bull, Hedley, 'The Emergence of a Universal International Society', in Hedley Bull and Adam Watson (eds.), *The Expansion of International Society* (New York: Oxford University Press, 1984), 118–141

Bull, Hedley and Adam Watson (eds.), *The Expansion of International Society* (New York: Oxford University Press, 1984)

Burley, Anne-Marie Slaughter, 'International Law and International Relations Theory: A Dual Agenda', (1993) 87 *American Journal of International Law* 205–239

Bush, George W., 'The National Security Strategy of the United States of America', September 17, 2002, Part V, http://www.whitehouse.gov/nsc/nssall.html

'Speech to the United Nations General Assembly, September 23, 2003', www.whitehouse.gov/news/releases/2003/09/20030923-4.html

'State of the Union Speech: The Axis of Evil', in Micah L. Sifry and Christopher Cerf (eds.), *The Iraq War Reader: History, Documents, Opinions* (New York: Touchstone Books, 2003)

Butler, Sir Geoffrey, 'Sovereignty and the League of Nations', (1920) 1 *British Yearbook of International Law* 35–44

Byers, Michael, 'Terrorism, the Use of Force and International Law after 11 September', (2002) 51 *International and Comparative Law Quarterly* 401–414

Byers, Michael and Georg Nolte (eds.), *United States Hegemony and the Foundations of International Law* (Cambridge: Cambridge University Press, 2003)

Capotorti, Francesco, *Study on the Rights of Persons Belonging to Ethnic, Religious and Linguistic Minorities*, Report to the UN Sub-Commission on the Prevention of Discrimination and Protection of Minorities, UN Doc. E/CN.4/Sub.2/384/Rev. 1 (1979)

Carty, Anthony, *The Decay of International Law?: A Reappraisal of the Limits of Legal Imagination in International Affairs* (Manchester: Manchester University Press, 1986)

'Law and the Postmodern Mind: Interwar German Theories of International Law: The Psychoanalytical and Phenomenological Perspectives of Hans Kelsen and Carl Schmitt', (1995) 16 *Cardozo Law Review* 1235–1292

'The Terrors of Freedom: The Sovereignty of States and the Freedom to Fear', in John Strawson (ed.), *Law After Ground Zero* (London: The Glass House Press, 2002), pp. 44–56

Cassese, Antonio, *Self-Determination of Peoples: A Legal Reappraisal* (New York: Cambridge University Press, 1995)

'Terrorism is Also Disrupting Some Crucial Legal Categories of International Law', (2001) 12 *European Journal of International Law* 993–1001

Castaneda, Jorge, 'The Underdeveloped Nations and the Development of International Law', (1961) 15 *International Organizations* 38–48

Cavallar, Georg, *The Rights of Strangers: Theories of International Hospitality, the Global Community and Political Justice Since Vitoria* (Aldershot: Ashgate, 2002)

Cerna, Christina M., 'Universal Democracy: An International Legal Right or the Pipe Dream of the West?', (1994–5) 27 *New York University Journal of International Law and Politics* 289–329

Chakrabarty, Dipesh, 'Postcoloniality and the Artifice of History: Who Speaks for "Indian" Pasts?', in Ranajit Guha (ed.), *A Subaltern Studies Reader, 1986–1995* (Minneapolis, MN, University of Minnesota Press, 1997), pp. 263–293

Chatterjee, Partha, *The Nation and Its Fragments: Colonial and Postcolonial Histories* (New York: Oxford University Press, 1994)

Chimni, B. S., *International Law and World Order: A Critique of Contemporary Approaches* (New Delhi, Newbury Park, CA: Sage, 1993)

Review Article, 'The Principle of Permanent Sovereignty Over Natural Resources: Toward A Radical Interpretation' (Review of Nico Schrijver, *Sovereignty Over Natural Resources: Balancing Rights and Duties*), (1998) 38(2) *Indian Journal of International Law* 208–217

'Third World Approaches to International Law: A Manifesto', in Antony Anghie, Bhupinder Chimni, Karin Mickelson and Obiora Chinedu Okafor (eds.), *The Third World and International Order: Law, Politics and Globalization* (Leiden: Brill Academic Publishers, Martinus Nijhoff, 2003)

Chossudovsky, Michel, 'Global Poverty in the Late 20th Century', (Fall 1998) 52 *Journal of International Affairs* No. 1, 293–311

The Globalization of Poverty: Impacts of IMF and World Bank Reforms (London: Zed Books, 1997)

Chowdhuri, R. N., *International Mandates and Trusteeship Systems: A Comparative Study* (The Hague: Martinus Nijhoff, 1955)

Clinton, Robert N., 'There is no Federal Supremacy Clause for Indian Tribes', (2002) 34(1) *Arizona State Law Journal* 113–260

Colby, Elbridge, 'How to Fight Savage Tribes', (1927) 21 *American Journal of International Law* 279–288

'Colloquium, International Law, Human Rights and LatCrit Theory', (1997) 28 *University of Miami Inter-American Law Review* 177–302

Columbus, Christopher, 'Letter of Columbus on the First Voyage', in Cecil Jane (ed. and trans.), *The Four Voyages of Columbus* (New York: Dover, 1988)

Commission on Global Governance, *Our Global Neighborhood: The Report of the Commission on Global Governance* (Oxford: Oxford University Press, 1995)

Conrad, Joseph, *Heart of Darkness* (Edinburgh: W. Blackwood & Sons, 1902)

'Heart of Darkness', in Morton Dauwen Zabel (ed.), *The Portable Conrad* (rev. edn., New York: Penguin Books, 1976)

Nostromo: A Tale of the Seaboard, Harmondsworth, Middlesex, Penguin Books, 1990 (first published 1904), p. 100

Cooper, Robert, 'The New Liberal Imperialism', *The Observer*, 7 April 2002, http://observer.guardian.co.uk/comment/story/0,6903,680093,00.html

Corbett, Percy, *The Growth of World Law* (Princeton: Princeton University Press, 1971)

'What is the League of Nations?', (1924) 5 *British Yearbook of International Law* 119–148

Cranston, Ruth, *The Story of Woodrow Wilson: Twenty-Eighth President of the United States, Pioneer of World Democracy* (New York: Simon & Schuster, 1945)

Crawford, James, *The Creation of States in International Law* (New York: Oxford University Press, 1979)

'The Right to Self-Determination in International Law: Its Development and Future', in Philip Alston (ed.), *Peoples' Rights* (New York: Oxford University Press, 2001), 7–67

Crawford, Robert M. A., *Idealism and Realism in International Relations: Beyond the Discipline* (London: Routledge, 2000)

Crenshaw, Kimberle (ed.), *Critical Race Theory: The Key Writings That Formed the Movement* (New York: New Press, 1995)

'Race Reform and Retrenchment: Transformation and Legitimation in Anti-Discrimination Law', (1988) 101 *Harvard Law Review* 1331–1387

Crowe, S. E., *The Berlin West African Conference 1884–1885* (Westport, CN: Negro Universities Press, 1970)

Damrosch, Lori Fisler and Bernard H. Oxman, 'Agora: Future Implications of the Iraq Conflict: Editors' Introduction', (July 2003) 97 *American Journal of International Law* 533–557

d'Andrade, M. Freire, 'Note, "The Interpretation of that Part of Article 22 of the Covenant Which Relates to the Well-Being and Development of the Peoples of Mandated Territories"', *Permanent Mandates Commission, Minutes of the Seventh Session*, League of Nations Doc. C.648 M.237 1925 VI (1925)

Dickinson, Edwin D., 'The New Law of Nations', (1925–26) 32 *West Virginia Law Quarterly* 4–32

Dirks, Nicholas B., 'From Little King to Landlord: Colonial Discourse and Colonial Rule', in Nicholas B. Dirks (ed.), *Colonialism and Culture* (Ann Arbor: University of Michigan Press, 1992), pp. 175–208

Donnelly, Jack, *Universal Human Rights in Theory and Practice* (Ithaca, NY: Cornell University Press, 1989)

Dore, Isaak I., *The International Mandate System and Namibia* (Boulder, CO: Westview Press, 1985)

Doyle, Michael W., *Empires* (Ithaca, NY: Cornell University Press, 1986)

'Draft Convention on Slavery', (1926) 11 *League of Nations Official Journal* 1542

Drumbl, Mark, 'Victimhood in Our Neighborhood: Terrorist Crime, Taliban Guilt, and the Asymmetries of the International Legal Order', (2002) 8 *North Carolina Law Review* 1–113

Dupuy, René-Jean (ed.), *The Future of International Law in a Multicultural World: Workshop, The Hague, 17–19 November 1983* (London: Martinus Nijhoff, 1984)

Edwards, Randle, 'The Old Canton System of Foreign Trade', in Victor H. Li (ed.) *Law and Politics in China's Foreign Trade* (Seattle: University of Washington Press, 1977), pp. 360–378

Eide, Asbjorn, *Possible Ways and Means of Facilitating the Peaceful and Conservative Solution of Problems Involving Minorities*, Report to the Sub-Commission on Prevention of Discrimination and Protection of Minorities, UN Doc.E/CN. 4/Sub.2/1993/34 (1993)

Elias, Taslim O., *Africa and the Development of International Law* (Leiden: A. W. Sijthoff, 1972)

Eliot, T. S., *The Waste Land* (New York: Boni & Liveright, 1922)

Engberg-Pedersen, Poul *et al.* (eds.), *Limits of Adjustment in Africa: The Effects of Economic Liberalization, 1986–94* (Copenhagen: Centre for Development Research in association with James Currey, 1996)

Engle, Karen, 'Culture and Human Rights: The Asian Values Debate in Context', (2000) 32 *New York University Journal of International Law* 291–333

Fain, Haskell, *Normative Politics and the Community of Nations* (Philadelphia, PA: Temple University Press, 1987)

Falk, Richard, 'The New States and International Legal Order', (1966-II) 118 *Académie du Droit International, Recueil de Cours* 1–102

  On Humane Governance: Toward A New Global Politics (Cambridge: Polity Press, 1995)

Fanon, Frantz, *Black Skin, White Masks* (Charles Lam Markham trans., New York: Grove Press, 1967)

  The Wretched of the Earth (Constance Farrington trans., New York: Grove Press, 1963)

Fatouros, A. A., 'International Law and the Third World', (1964) 50 *Virginia Law Review* 783–823

Fenwick, Charles G., *Wardship in International Law* (Washington, DC: Government Printing Office, 1919)

Ferguson, Niall, *Empire: The Rise and Demise of the British World Order and the Lessons for Global Power* (New York: Basic Books, 2003)

Fidler, David, '"A Kinder, Gentler System of Capitulations?" International Law, Structural Adjustment Policies, and the Standard of Liberal, Globalized Civilization', 35 *Texas International Law Journal* 387 (2000)

Fieldhouse, D. K., *The Colonial Empires: A Comparative Survey from the Eighteenth Century* (London: Weidenfeld & Nicolson, 1966)

Fisher, William W., III, Morton J. Horwitz and Thomas Reed (eds.), *American Legal Realism* (New York: Oxford University Press, 1993)

Fitzpatrick, Peter, *Modernism and the Grounds of Law* (Cambridge: Cambridge University Press, 2001)

Forbes, W. Cameron, *The Philippine Islands* (2 vols., Boston: Houghton Mifflin Co., 1928), II

Foucault, Michel, Alan Sheridan (trans.), *Discipline and Punish: The Birth of the Prison* (2nd edn., New York: Vintage Books, 1995, 1977)

   'Governmentality', in Graham Burchell, Colin Gordon and Peter Miller (eds.), *The Foucault Effect: Studies in Governmentality* (Chicago: University of Chicago Press, 1991), pp. 87–104

   'Two Lectures', in Michel Foucault, Colin Gordon (ed.), Colin Gordon *et al.* (trans.), *Power/Knowledge* (New York: Pantheon Books, 1980), pp. 78–108

Fox, Gregory H., 'The Right to Political Participation in International Law', (1992) 17 *Yale Journal of International Law* 539–607

Francioni, Francesco, 'Compensation for Nationalisation and Foreign Property: The Borderland Between Law and Equity', (1975) 24 *International and Comparative Law Quarterly* 255–283

Franck, Thomas M., 'The Emerging Right to Democratic Governance', (1992) 86 *American Journal of International Law* 46–91

   The Empowered Self: Law and Society in the Age of Individualism (New York: Oxford University Press, 1999)

   'The New Development: Can American Law and Legal Institutions Help Developing Countries?', (1972) *Wisconsin Law Review* 767–801

   Editorial Comment, 'The "Powers of Appreciation": Who is the Ultimate Guardian of UN Legality?', (1992) 86 *American Journal of International Law* 519–523

   Recourse to Force: State Action Against Threats and Armed Attacks (Cambridge: Cambridge University Press, 2002)

Frank, André Gunder, *The Underdevelopment of Development* (Stockholm: Bethany Books, 1991)

Freud, Sigmund, James Strachey (ed. and trans.), *Civilization and Its Discontents* (New York: W. W. Norton, 1961)

   James Strachey (ed. and trans.), *The Interpretation of Dreams* (New York: Avon, 1965)

Friedmann, Wolfgang, 'The Changing Dimensions of International Law', (1962) 62 *Columbia Law Review* 1147–1165

   'The Disintegration of European Civilisation and the Future of International Law', (1938) 2 *Modern Law Review* 194–214

   'The Position of Underdeveloped Countries and the Universality of International Law', (1963) 2 *Columbia Society of International Law Bulletin* 5–12

Fromkin, David, *A Peace to End All Peace* (New York: H. Holt, 1989)

Furedi, Frank, *The New Ideology of Imperialism: Renewing the Moral Imperative* (London: Pluto Press, 1994)

Furnivall, J. S., *Colonial Policy and Practice: A Comparative Study of Burma and Netherlands India* (Cambridge: Cambridge University Press, 1948)

Progress and Welfare in South-East Asia: A Comparison of Colonial Policy and Practice (New York: Secretariat, Institute of Pacific Relations, 1941)

Gallagher, John and Ronald Robinson, 'The Imperialism of Free Trade', (1953) 6 *The Economic History Review* 1–15

Gathii, James Thuo, 'Good Governance as a Counter Insurgency Agenda to Oppositional and Transformative Social Projects in International Law', (1999) 5 *Buffalo Human Rights Law Review* 107–174

'International Law and Eurocentricity', (1998) 9 *European Journal of International Law* 184–211

'The Limits of the New International Rule of Law on Good Governance', in Edward K. Quashigah and Obiora Okafor (eds.), *Legitimate Governance in Africa* (The Hague: Kluwer Law International, 1999)

'Neoliberalism, Colonialism and International Governance: Decentering the International Law of Governmental Legitimacy', (2000) 98 *Michigan Law Review* 1996–2054

'Retelling Good Governance Narratives on Africa's Economic and Political Predicaments: Continuities and Discontinuities in Legal Outcomes Between Markets and States', (2000) 45 *Villanova Law Review* 971–1035

Geertz, Clifford, *The Interpretation of Cultures* (New York: Basic Books, 1973)

Gellner, Ernest, *Nations and Nationalism* (Oxford: Blackwell, 1983)

Gess, Karol, 'Permanent Sovereignty Over Natural Resources', (1964) 13 *International and Comparative Law Quarterly* 398–449

Gilbert, G., 'The Legal Protection Accorded to Minorities in Europe', (1992) 23 *Netherlands Yearbook of International Law* 67–104

Gong, Gerrit, *The Standard of 'Civilization' in International Society* (New York: Oxford University Press, 1984)

Goodman, Ryan and Derek Jinks, 'Measuring the Effects of Human Rights Treaties', (2003) 14 *European Journal of International Law* 171–183

Gordon, Ruth, 'Saving Failed States: Sometimes a Neocolonialist Notion', (1997) 12 *American University Journal of International Law and Policy* 903–974

'Some Legal Problems with Trusteeship', (1995) 28 *Cornell International Law Journal* 301–347

Gray, Christine, *International Law and the Use of Force* (New York: Oxford University Press, 2000)

Greenblatt, Stephen, *Marvelous Possessions: The Wonder of the New World* (Chicago: University of Chicago Press, 1991)

Grotius, Hugo, *De Jure Belli ac Pacis Libri Tres*, Francis W. Kelsey, ed. (Oxford: Clarendon Press, 1925)

Grovogui, Siba N'Zatioula, *Sovereigns, Quasi Sovereigns, and Africans: Race and Self-Determination in International Law* (Minneapolis, MN: University of Minnesota Press, 1996)

Guha, Ranajit, 'Introduction', in Ranajit Guha (ed.), *A Subaltern Studies Reader, 1986–1995* (Minneapolis, MN: University of Minnesota Press, 1997), pp. ix–xxii

Guha-Roy, S. N., 'Is the Law of Responsibility of States for Injuries to Aliens a Part of Universal International Law?', (1961) 55 *American Journal of International Law* 863–891

Gunning, Isabelle R., 'Modernizing Customary International Law: The Challenge of Human Rights', (1991) 31 *Virginia Journal of International Law* 211–247

Hale, Robert L., 'Coercion and Distribution in a Supposedly Non-Coercive State', in William W. Fisher, III, Morton J. Horwitz, and Thomas Reed (eds.), *American Legal Realism* (New York: Oxford University Press, 1993), pp. 101–108

Hales, James C., 'The Reform and Extension of the Mandate System', (1940) 26 *Transactions of the Grotius Society* 153–210

Hall, H. Duncan, *Mandates, Dependencies and Trusteeship* (Washington, DC: Carnegie Endowment for International Peace, 1948)

Hall, W. E., *A Treatise on International Law* (2nd edn., Oxford: Clarendon Press, 1884)

Hardt, Michael and Antonio Negri, *Empire* (Cambridge, MA: Harvard University Press, 2000)

Hathaway, Oona, 'Testing Conventional Wisdom', (2003) 14 *European Journal of International Law* 185–200

Held, David and Anthony McGrew, 'The Great Globalization Debate: An Introduction', in David Held and Anthony McGrew (eds.), *The Global Transformations Reader: An Introduction to the Globalization Debate* (Cambridge: Polity Press, 2000), pp. 1–44

Henkin, Louis, Richard C. Pugh, Oscar Schachter and Hans Smit, *International Law* (3rd edn., St Paul, MN: West Publishing Co., 1993)

Hobsbawm, Eric, *The Age of Empire, 1875–1914* (New York: Pantheon Books, 1987)

Hobson, J. A., *Imperialism: A Study* (4th edn., London: George Allen & Unwin, 1948)

Hochschild, Adam, *King Leopold's Ghost: A Story of Greed, Terror, and Heroism in Colonial Africa* (Boston: Houghton, Mifflin, 1999)

Horowitz, Donald, *Ethnic Groups in Conflict* (Berkeley: University of California Press, 1985)

Horwitz, Morton J., *The Transformation of American Law 1870–1960: The Crisis of Legal Orthodoxy* (New York: Oxford University Press, 1992)

Hossain, Kamal and Subrata Roy Chowdhury (eds.), *Permanent Sovereignty Over Natural Resources* (New York: St Martin's Press, 1984)

Howard, Michael, 'What's in a Name? How to Fight Terrorism', (2002) 81 No. 1 *Foreign Affairs* 8–13

Hudson, Manley O., 'The Outlook for the Development of International Law', (1925) 11 *ABA Journal* 102–106

'The Prospect for International Law in the Twentieth Century', (1925) 10 *Cornell Law Quarterly* 419–459

Hughes, H. Stuart, *Consciousness and Society* (New York: Knopf, 1958)

Iglesias, Elizabeth M., 'Global Markets, Racial Spaces and the Role of Critical Race Theory in the Struggle for Community Control of Investments: An Institutional Class Analysis', (2000) 45 *Villanova Law Review* 1037–1073

Ignatieff, Michael, 'Nation-Building Lite', *New York Times Magazine*, July 28, 2002, p. 28

International Bank for Reconstruction and Development (World Bank), *Development and Human Rights: The Role of the World Bank* (Washington, DC: World Bank, 1998)

   World Development Report, 1998/99: Knowledge for Development (New York: Oxford University Press, 1998)

Jackson, Robert H., *Quasi-States: Sovereignty, International Relations, and the Third World* (Cambridge: Cambridge University Press, 1990)

James, Henry, *The Portrait of a Lady* (Boston: Houghton, Mifflin & Co., 1881)

James, Patrick, *International Relations and Scientific Progress: Structural Realism Reconsidered* (Columbus: Ohio State University Press, 2002)

Jenks, C. Wilfred, *The Common Law of Mankind* (London: Stevens & Sons, 1958)

Jessup, Philip C., *Elihu Root* (New York: Dodd, Mead & Co., 1938)

   A Modern Law of Nations (New York: Macmillan, 1948)

   Transnational Law (New Haven: Yale University Press, 1956)

Johnson, Chalmers A., *Blowback* (New York: Metropolitan Books, 2001)

Joyce, James, *Ulysses* (Paris: Shakespeare & Co., 1922)

Kant, Immanuel, 'Perpetual Peace', in Hans Reiss (ed.), *Kant: Political Writings* (Cambridge: Cambridge University Press, 1991), pp. 93–130

Kanya-Forstner, A. S., 'The War, Imperialism, and Decolonization', in Jay Winter, Geoffrey Parker and Mary R. Habeck (eds.), *The Great War and the Twentieth Century* (New Haven: Yale University Press, 2000), pp. 231–262

Karnow, Stanley, *In Our Image: America's Empire in the Philippines* (New York: Random House, 1989)

Kausikan, Bilhauri, 'Asia's Different Standard', (1993) 92 *Foreign Policy* 24–41

Kennedy, David, 'The Disciplines of International Law and Policy', (1999) 12 *Leiden Journal of International Law* 9–133

   'International Law and the Nineteenth Century: History of an Illusion', (1997) 17 *Quinnipiac Law Review* 99–138

   'The Move to Institutions', (1987) 8 *Cardozo Law Review* 841–988

   'Primitive Legal Scholarship', (1986) 27(1) *Harvard International Law Journal* 1–98

   'Some Reflections on the Role of Sovereignty in the New International Order', Presentation to the Canadian Society of International Law (October 17, 1992) (on file with the author)

   'When Renewal Repeats: Thinking Against the Box', (2000) 32 *New York University Journal of International Law and Politics* 335–500

Kennedy, Duncan, 'A Cultural Pluralist Case for Affirmative Action in Legal Academia', in Duncan Kennedy, *Sexy Dressing Etc.: Essays on the Power and Politics of Cultural Identity* (Cambridge, MA: Harvard University Press, 1993), pp. 34–82

Sexy Dressing Etc.: Essays on the Power and Politics of Cultural Identity (Cambridge, MA: Harvard University Press, 1993)

Kiernan, V. G., *From Conquest to Collapse: European Empires from 1815 to 1960* (New York: Pantheon Books, 1982)

Kingsbury, Benedict, 'Sovereignty and Inequality', (1998) 9 *European Journal of International Law* 599–625

Klabbers, J. and R. Lefeber, 'Africa: Lost Between Self-Determination and *Uti Possidetis*', in Catherine Brolmann, René Lefeber and Marjoleine Zieck (eds.), *Peoples and Minorities in International Law* (Dordrecht: Martinus Nijhoff, 1993), pp. 37–76

Knop, Karen, *Diversity and Self-Determination in International Law* (New York: Cambridge University Press, 2002)

Kooijmans, Pieter Hendrik, *The Doctrine of the Legal Equality of States: An Inquiry into the Foundations of International Law* (Leiden: Sijthoff, 1964)

Korman, Sharon, *The Right of Conquest: The Acquisition of Territory by Force in International Law and Practice* (New York: Oxford University Press, 1996)

Koskenniemi, Martti, 'Carl Schmitt, Hans Morgenthau and the Image of Law in International Relations', in Michael Byers (ed.), *The Role of Law in International Politics* (Oxford: Oxford University Press, 2000), pp. 17–34

From Apology to Utopia: The Structure of International Legal Argument (Helsinki: Finnish Lawyers' Publishing Co., 1989)

The Gentle Civilizer of Nations: The Rise and Fall of International Law 1870–1960 (Cambridge: Cambridge University Press, 2002)

'"The Lady Doth Protest Too Much", Kosovo, and the Turn to Ethics in International Law', (2002) 65 No. 2 *Modern Law Review* 159–175

'Lauterpacht: The Victorian Tradition in International Law', (1997) 2 *European Journal of International Law* 215–263

Kreijen, Gerard, 'The Transformation of Sovereignty and African Independence: No Shortcuts to Statehood', in Gerard Kreijen (ed.), *State, Sovereignty, and International Governance* (Oxford: Oxford University Press, 2002), pp. 45–107

Kunz, Josef L., 'On the Theoretical Basis of the Law of Nations', (1924) 10 *Transactions of the Grotius Society* 115–141

Landauer, Carl, 'From Status to Treaty: Henry Sumner Maine's International Law', (2002) XV(2) *Canadian Journal of Law and Jurisprudence* 219–254

'J. L. Brierly and the Modernization of International Law', (1993) 25 *Vanderbilt Journal of Transnational Law* 881–917

Langenhove, Fernand van, *The Question of Aborigines Before the United Nations: The Belgian Thesis* (Brussels: Royal Colonial Institute of Belgium, 1954)

Lansing, Robert, *Notes on Sovereignty: From the Standpoint of the State and of the World* (Washington, DC: The Carnegie Endowment, 1921)

Lauterpacht, Hersch, *The Function of Law in the International Community* (Oxford: Clarendon Press, 1933)

'The Mandate Under International Law in the Covenant of the League of Nations', in Hersch Lauterpacht, Elihu Lauterpacht (ed.), *International Law* (4 vols., Cambridge: Cambridge University Press, 1970), III, pp. 29–84

Lawrence, Thomas, *The Principles of International Law* (Boston: D. C. Heath, 1895)

Lee-Warner, William, *The Protected Princes of India* (London: Macmillan & Co., 1894)

Lenin, V. I., *Imperialism: The Highest Stage of Capitalism* (New York: International Publishers, 1939)

'Let's All Go to the Yard Sale', *The Economist*, 27 September 2003, 44

Lewis, David Levering, *The Race to Fashoda: European Colonialism and African Resistance in the Scramble for Africa* (New York: Weidenfeld & Nicolson, 1987)

Li Zhaojie, 'Traditional Chinese World Order', 1 *Chinese Journal of International Law* 20–59 (2002)

Lillich, Richard B. (ed.), *The Valuation of Nationalized Property in International Law* (Charlottesville, VA: University Press of Virginia, 1975)

Lindley, M. F., *The Acquisition and Government of Backward Territory in International Law* (London: Longmans, Green & Co., 1926)

  The Acquisition and Government of Backward Territory in International Law: Being A Treatise on the Law and Practice Relating to Colonial Expansion (New York: Negro Universities Press, 1969)

'List of Questions which the Permanent Mandates Commission Desires Should be Dealt with in the Annual Report of the Mandatory Powers', (1926) 10 *League of Nations Official Journal* 1322–1328

Lorimer, James, *The Institutes of the Law of Nations: A Treatise of the Jural Relations of Separate Political Communities* (Edinburgh: Blackwood & Sons, 1883)

Lowe, Vaughan, 'The Iraq Crisis: What Now?', (2003) 52 *International and Comparative Law Quarterly* 859–871

Lugard, Lord Frederick, *The Dual Mandate in British Tropical Africa* (Hamden, CT: Archon Books 1965)

Maine, Sir Henry Sumner, *Ancient Law: Its Connection with the Early History of Society and Its Relation to Modern Ideas* (1st American edn., New York: C. Scribner, 1864)

  International Law: A Series of Lectures Delivered Before the University of Cambridge, 1887 (London: John Murray, 1888)

Marks, Susan, *The Riddle of All Constitutions: International Law, Democracy and the Critique of Ideology* (Oxford: Oxford University Press, 2000)

Mason, Anthony, 'The Rights of Indigenous Peoples in Lands Once Part of the Old Dominions of the Crown', (1997) 46 *International and Comparative Law Quarterly* 812–830

May, Ernest R., *Imperial Democracy* (New York: Harcourt, Brace & World, 1961)

Mayall, James (ed.), *The Community of States* (London: Allen & Unwin, 1982)

McNair, Lord Arnold, 'The General Principles of Law Recognized by Civilized Nations', (1957) 33 *British Yearbook of International Law* 1–19

McNair, Lord Arnold (ed.), *Oppenheim's International Law* (4th edn., 2 vols., London: Longmans, Green & Co., 1928), I

Megret, Frederic, 'War? Legal Semantics and the Move to Violence', (2002) 13 *European Journal of International Law* 361–399

Mehta, Uday Singh, *Liberalism and Empire: A Study in Nineteenth Century British Liberal Thought* (Chicago: University of Chicago Press, 1999)
  Liberalism and Empire: A Study in Nineteenth Century British Liberal Thought (Chicago: University of Chicago Press, 1999)
Mickelson, Karin, 'Rhetoric and Rage: Third World Voices in International Legal Discourse', (1998) 16(2) *Wisconsin International Law Journal* 353–419
Moore-Gilbert, Bart, *Postcolonial Theory: Contexts, Practices, Politics* (New York: Verso, 1997)
Morgenthau, Hans J., 'Positivism, Functionalism and International Law', (1940) 34 *American Journal of International Law* 260–284
Murphy, Sean, 'Terrorism and the Concept of "Armed Attack" in Article 51 of the UN Charter', (2002) 43 *Harvard International Law Journal* 41–51
Mutua, Makau wa, 'Why Redraw the Map of Africa?: A Moral and Legal Inquiry', (1995) 16 *Michigan Journal of International Law* 1113–1176
Naipaul, V. S., *The Mimic Men* (Harmondsworth: Penguin Books, 1980)
Nehru, Jawaharlal, *The Discovery of India* (New York: The John Day Co., 1946)
Norton, Patrick M., 'Law of the Future or Law of the Past? Modern Tribunals and the International Law of Expropriation', (1991) 85 *American Journal of International Law* 474–505
Nussbaum, Arthur, *A Concise History of the Law of Nations* (rev. edn., New York: Macmillan, 1954)
Nyamu, Celestine, 'How Should Human Rights and Development Respond to Cultural Legitimization of Gender Hierarchy in Developing Countries?', (2000) 41(2) *Harvard International Law Journal* 383–418
O'Brien, W. V. O. (ed.), *The New Nations in International Law and Diplomacy* (New York: Praeger, 1965)
O'Connell, Daniel P., 'Independence and Problems of State Succession', in W. V. O. O'Brien (ed.), *The New Nations in International Law and Diplomacy* (New York: Praeger, 1965), pp. 7–41
  The Law of State Succession (Cambridge: Cambridge University Press, 1956)
Ofuatey-Kodjoe, W., *The Principle of Self-Determination in International Law* (New York: Nellen Publishing Co., 1977)
Okafor, Obiora Chinedu, *Re-Defining Legitimate Statehood: International Law and State Fragmentation in Africa* (Boston: Martinus Nijhoff Publishers, 2000)
Oloka-Onyango, J., 'Beyond the Rhetoric: Reinvigorating the Struggle for Economic and Social Rights in Africa', (1995) 26 *California Western International Law Journal* 1–71
Onuma, Yasuaki *A Normative Approach to War: Peace, War, and Justice in Hugo Grotius* (Oxford, Clarendon Press, 1993)
  'When Was the Law of International Society Born? – An Inquiry of the History of International Law from an Intercivilizational Perspective', 2 *Journal of the History of International Law* (2000) 1–66
Oppenheim, Lassa, *International Law: A Treatise* (2nd edn., London: Longmans, Green & Co., 1912)

'The Science of International Law. Its Task and Method', (1908) 2 *American Journal of International Law*, 313–56

Orford, Anne, 'Globalization and the Right to Development', in Philip Alston (ed.), *People's Rights* (New York: Oxford University Press, 2001), pp. 127–184

Reading Humanitarian Intervention: Human Rights and the Use of Force in International Law (Cambridge: Cambridge University Press, 2003)

Ormsby-Gore, W., *The League of Nations Starts, An Outline by Its Organizers* (London: Macmillan & Co. Ltd., 1920)

Orwell, George, 'Rudyard Kipling', in *Dickens, Dali & Others* (New York: Reynal & Hitchcock, 1946), pp. 140–160

Pagden, Anthony, *Lords of All the World: Ideologies of Empire in Spain, Britain and France c.1500–c.1800* (New Haven: Yale University Press, 1995)

Paulsson, Jan, 'Arbitration Unbound: Award Detached from the Law of Its Country of Origin', (1981) 30 *International & Comparative Law Quarterly* 358–387

'Delocalisation of International Commercial Arbitration: When and Why it Matters', (1983) 32 *International & Comparative Law Quarterly* 53–61

'Third World Participation in International Investment Arbitration', (1987) 2 ICSID Rev. 19–65

Pellet, Alain, 'No, This is Not War!', http://www.ejil.org/forum_WTC/ny-pellet.html

Pendleton, Michael D., 'A New Human Right – The Right to Globalization', (1999) 22 *Fordham International Law Journal* 2052–2095

Perham, Margery, 'Introduction', in Lord Frederick Lugard, *The Dual Mandate in British Tropical Africa* (5th edn., London: Frank Cass, 1965)

Permanent Mandates Commission, Minutes of the Third Session, League of Nations Doc. A. 19 1923 VI at 283 (1923)

Minutes of the Sixth Session, League of Nations Doc. C.386M.132 1925 VI at 47 (1925)

Minutes of the Twenty-Seventh Session, League of Nations Doc. C.251.M.123 1935 VI at 26–29 (1935)

Minutes of the Twenty-Eighth Session, League of Nations Doc. C.439 M.228 1935 VI at 15–21 (1935)

Peters, Karl, *New Light of Dark Africa* (London: Ward, Lock & Co., 1890), pp. 192–193, 213–215, 520–531; reprinted in Philip D. Curtin (ed.), *Imperialism* (New York: Harper & Row, 1971), pp. 74–84

Petry, Carl F. and M. W. Daly (eds.), *The Cambridge History of Egypt* (Cambridge: Cambridge University Press, 1998)

Pieper, Ute and Lance Taylor, 'The Revival of the Liberal Creed: The IMF, The World Bank, and Inequality in a Globalized Economy', in Dean Baker, Gerald Epstein and Robert Pollin (eds.), *Globalization and Progressive Economic Policy* (Cambridge: Cambridge University Press, 1998), pp. 37–63

Pinto, Moragodage C. W., '"Common Heritage of Mankind": From Metaphor to Myth and the Consequences of Constructive Ambiguity', in Jerzy Makarczyk (ed.), *Theory of International Law at the Threshold of the 21st Century:*

Essays in Honour of Krysztof Skubiszewski (The Hague: Kluwer Law International, 1996), pp. 249–268

Pomerance, Michla, *Self-Determination in Law and Practice* (The Hague: Martinus Nijhoff, 1982)

Porras, Ileana, 'On Terrorism: Reflections on Violence and the Outlaw', in Dan Danielsen and Karen Engle (eds.), *After Identity: A Reader in Law and Culture* (New York: Routledge, 1995), pp. 294–313

Potter, Pitman B., 'Political Science in the International Field', (1923) 17 *American Political Science Review* 381–391

Pound, Roscoe, 'Philosophical Theory and International Law', (1923) 1 *Biblioteca Visseriana Dissertationum Ius Internationale Illustrantium* 71–90

Prunier, Gérard, *The Rwanda Crisis: History of a Genocide* (New York: Columbia University Press, 1995)

Pye, Lucian W. and Sidney Verba (eds.), *Political Culture and Political Development* (Princeton: Princeton University Press, 1965)

Quashigah, Edward Kofi and Obiora Chinedu Okafor (eds.), *Legitimate Governance in Africa: International and Domestic Legal Perspectives* (The Hague: Kluwer Law International, 1999)

Rajagopal, Balakrishnan, 'From Modernization to Democratization: The Political Economy of the "New" International Law', in Richard Falk, Lester Edwin J. Ruiz and R. B. J. Walker (eds.), *Reframing the International: Law, Culture, Politics* (New York: Routledge, 2002), pp. 136–162

'From Resistance to Renewal: The Third World, Social Movements, and the Expansion of International Institutions', (2000) 41 *Harvard International Law Journal* 529 578

'International Law and the Development Encounter: Violence and Resistance at the Margins', (1999) 93 *American Society of International Law Proceedings* 16–27

'International Law and Third World Resistance: A Theoretical Inquiry', in Antony Anghie, Bhupinder Chimni, Karin Mickelson and Obiora Okafor (eds.), *The Third World and International Order: Law, Politics and Globalization* (Leiden: Brill Academic Publishers, Martinus Nijhoff, 2003), pp. 145–172

Ram, K. V., 'The Survival of Ethiopian Independence', in Gregory Maddux (ed.), *Conquest and Resistance to Colonialism in Africa* (New York: Garland, 1993)

Ramos, Efren Rivera, 'The Legal Construction of American Colonialism: The Insular Cases', (1996) 65 *Revista Juridica Universidad de Puerto Rico* 225–328

Ransom, David and Margaret Bald, 'The Dictatorship of Debt', (1999) 46:10 *World Press Review* 6–8

Ratner, Steven R., 'Corporations and Human Rights: A Theory of Legal Responsibility', (2001) 111 *Yale Law Journal* 443–545

Reif, Linda C., 'Building Democratic Institutions: The Role of National Human Rights Institutions in Good Governance and Human Rights Protection', (2000) 13 *Harvard Human Rights Journal* 1–69

Reiss, Hans (ed.), *Kant: Political Writings* (Cambridge: Cambridge University Press, 1991)

Richardson, III, Henry J., 'Gulf Crisis and African–American Interests Under
    International Law', (1993) 87 *American Journal of International Law* 42–82
    'US Hegemony, Race and Oil in Deciding United Nations Security Council
    Resolution 1441 on Iraq', (2003) 17(1) *Temple International and Comparative
    Law Journal* 101–157
Riles, Annelise, 'Aspiration and Control: International Legal Rhetoric and the
    Essentialization of Culture', (1993) 106 *Harvard Law Review* 723–740
Rittich, Kerry, *Recharacterizing Restructuring: Law, Distribution and Gender in Market
    Reform* (The Hague: Kluwer Law International, 2002)
Rivers, W. H. R., 'The Psychological Factor', in W. H. R. Rivers (ed.), *Essays on the
    Depopulation of Melanesia* (Cambridge: Cambridge University Press, 1922),
    pp. 84–113
Roberts, J. M., *A History of Europe* (Oxford: Helicon, 1996)
Rodney, Walter, *How Europe Underdeveloped Africa* (London: Bogle-L'Ouverture
    Publications, 1972)
Roling, B. V. A., *International Law in an Expanded World* (Amsterdam: Djambatan,
    1960)
Root, Elihu, 'President McKinley's Instructions to the Commission to the
    Philippine Islands', in W. Cameron Forbes, *The Philippine Islands* (Boston:
    Houghton Mifflin Co., 1928), II, appendix VII
Rostow, Walt W., *The Stages of Economic Growth: A Non-Communist Manifesto*
    (Cambridge: Cambridge University Press, 1960)
Rubin, Alfred P., 'International Law in the Age of Columbus', (1992) XXXIX
    Netherlands International Law Review 5–35
Rumble, Wilfrid E., 'Introduction', in John Austin, *The Province of Jurisprudence
    Determined* (Wilfrid E. Rumble, ed., New York: Cambridge University Press,
    1995), pp. vii–xxiv
Said, Edward, *Culture and Imperialism* (New York: Knopf, 1993)
    Orientalism (New York: Pantheon Books, 1978)
Saito, Natsu T., 'Crossing the Border: The Interdependence of Foreign Policy
    and Racial Justice in the United States', (1998) 1 *Yale Human Rights and
    Development Law Journal* 53–84
Sauvant, Karl P., *The Group of 77: Evolution, Structure, Organization* (New York:
    Oceana Publications, 1981)
Schrijver, Nico, *Sovereignty Over Natural Resources: Balancing Rights and Duties*
    (Cambridge: Cambridge University Press, 1997)
Schwebel, Stephen M., 'The Story of the UN's Declaration on Permanent
    Sovereignty Over Natural Resources', (1963) 49 *American Bar Association
    Journal* 463–469
Scott, David, *Refashioning Futures: Criticism After Postcoloniality* (Princeton:
    Princeton University Press, 1999)
Scott, James Brown, *The Spanish Origin of International Law* (Oxford: Clarendon
    Press, 1934)
Seed, Patricia, *Ceremonies of Possession in Europe's Conquest of the New World,
    1492–1640* (New York: Cambridge University Press, 1995)

Shalakany, Amr A., 'Arbitration and the Third World: A Plea for Reassessing Bias Under the Specter of Neoliberalism', (2000) 41 *Harvard International Law Journal* 419–468

Shen, Jianming, 'National Sovereignty and Human Rights in a Positive Law Context', (2000) 26 *Brooklyn Journal of International Law* 417–446

Shihata, Ibrahim F. I., 'Democracy and Development', (1997) 46 *International and Comparative Law Quarterly* 635–643

Shotwell, James T., (ed.), *The Origins of the International Labor Organization* (2 vols., New York: Columbia University Press, 1934), I

'Sick Patient, Warring Doctors', *The Economist*, 18 September 1999, 81

Simpson, A. W. Brian, *Human Rights and the End of Empire: Britain and the Genesis of the European Convention* (New York: Oxford University Press, 2001)

Sinha, S. Prakash, 'Perspective of the Newly Independent States on the Binding Quality of International Law', (1965) 14 *International and Comparative Law Quarterly* 121–131

Skogly, Sigrun I., 'Structural Adjustment and Development: Human Rights – An Agenda for Change', (1993) 15:4 *Human Rights Quarterly* 751–778

Slaughter, Anne-Marie, 'International Law in a World of Liberal States', (1995) 6 *European Journal of International Law* 503–538

Smuts, J. C., 'The League of Nations: A Practical Suggestion', reprinted in David Hunter Miller, *The Drafting of the Covenant* (2 vols., New York: G. P. Putnam's Sons, 1971, 1928), II, pp. 23–60

Snow, Alpheus H., *The Question of Aborigines in the Law and Practice of Nations* (New York: Putnam, 1921)

Sornarajah, M. S., 'The Climate of International Arbitration', (June 1991) 8 *Journal of International Arbitration* 47–86

'Economic Neo-Liberalism and the International Law on Foreign Investment', in Antony Anghie, Bhupinder Chimni, Karin Mickelson and Obiora Okafor (eds.), *The Third World and International Order: Law, Politics and Globalization* (Leiden: Martinus Nijhoff, 2003), pp. 173–191

The International Law on Foreign Investment (Cambridge: Cambridge University Press, 1994)

The Settlement of Foreign Investment Disputes (The Hague: Kluwer Law International, 2000)

Spence, Jonathan D., *The Search for Modern China* (New York: Norton, 1991)

Spivak, Gayatri Chakravorty, *A Critique of Postcolonial Reason: Toward a History of the Vanishing Present* (Cambridge, MA: Harvard University Press, 1999)

Steiner, Henry J., 'Ideals and Counter-Ideals in the Struggle Over Autonomy Regimes for Minorities', (1991) 66 *Notre Dame Law Review* 1539–1568

'Political Participation as a Human Right', (1988) 1 *Harvard Human Rights Yearbook* 77–134

Stone, Julius, 'A Common Law for Mankind?', (1960) 1 *International Studies*, 414–442

The Quest for Survival: The Role of Law and Foreign Policy (Cambridge, MA: Harvard University Press, 1961)

Strang, David, 'Contested Sovereignty: The Social Construction of Colonial Imperialism', in Thomas J. Biersteker and Cynthia Weber (eds.), *State Sovereignty as Social Construct* (Cambridge: Cambridge University Press, 1996), pp. 22–50

Stuart, Peter C., *Isles of Empire: The United States and its Overseas Possessions* (Boston: University Press of America, 1999)

Sugarman, David, 'A "Hatred of Disorder": Legal Science, Liberalism and Imperialism', in Peter Fitzpatrick (ed.), *Dangerous Supplements* (Durham, NC: Duke University Press, 1991), pp. 34–67

'Symposium, Critical Race Theory and International Law: Convergence and Divergence', (2000) 45 *Villanova Law Review* 827–970

Taft, IV, William H., Legal Adviser, Department of State, 'The Legal Basis for Preemption', November 18, 2002, http://www.cfr.org/publications

Taft, IV, William H. and Todd F. Buchwald, 'Preemption, Iraq, and International Law', (2003) 97 *American Journal of International Law* 557–563

Tambiah, Stanley, 'Ethnic Conflict in the World Today', (1989) 16 *American Ethnologist* 335–349

Tennant, Chris, 'Indigenous Peoples, International Institutions, and the International Legal Literature from 1945–1993', (1994) 16 *Human Rights Quarterly* 1–57

'They Say We're Getting a Democracy', *The Economist*, 15 November 2003, 9

Thomas, Chantal, 'Critical Race Theory and Postcolonial Development Theory: Observations on Methodology', (2000) 45 *Villanova Law Review* 1195–1220

Thomas, Jeremy, 'History and International Law in Asia: A Time for Review?', in Ronald St John Macdonald (ed.), *Essays in Honor of Wing Tieya* (Dordrecht: Martinus Nijhoff, 1994)

Thornberry, Patrick, *International Law and the Rights of Minorities* (New York: Oxford University Press, 1994)

'Self-Determination, Minorities, Human Rights: A Review of International Instruments', (1989) 38 *International and Comparative Law Quarterly* 867–889

Tieya, Wang, 'International Law in China: Historical and Contemporary Perspectives', (1990-II) 221 *Académie du Droit International, Recueil De Cours* 195, 232–237

Tiruchelvam, Neelan, 'Federalism and Diversity in Sri Lanka', in Yash Ghai (ed.), *Autonomy and Ethnicity: Negotiating Competing Claims in Multi-Ethnic States* (Cambridge: Cambridge University Press, 2000), pp. 197–218

Todorov, Tzvetan, *The Conquest of America: The Question of the Other*, trans. from the French by Richard Howard (New York: HarperCollins, 1984)

Tomlinson, B. R., 'Economics and Empire: The Periphery and the Imperial Economy', in Andrew Porter (ed.), *The Oxford History of the British Empire: The Nineteenth Century* (Oxford: Oxford University Press, 1999), pp. 53–75

Tomuschat, Christian (ed.), *The Modern Law of Self-Determination* (Dordrecht: Martinus Nijhoff, 1993)

'Status of Minorities Under Article 27 of the UN Covenant on Civil and Political Rights', in Satish Chandra (ed.), *Minorities in National and International Laws* (New Delhi: Deep & Deep Publications, 1985), pp. 31–68

Trubek, David M., 'Towards a Social Theory of Law: An Essay of the Study of Law and Development', (1972) 82 *Yale Law Journal* 1–50

Trubek, David and Marc Galanter, 'Scholars in Self-Estrangement: Some Reflections on the Crisis in Law and Development Studies in the United States', 1974 *Wisconsin Law Review* 1062–1102

Tuck, Richard, *The Rights of War and Peace: Political Thought and the International Order From Grotius to Kant* (New York: Oxford University Press, 1999)

Udokang, Okon, *Succession of New States to International Treaties* (New York: Oceana Publications, 1972), pp. 462–464

Umozurike, U. O., *International Law and Colonialism in Africa* (Enugu: Nwamife Publishers, 1979)

Self-Determination in International Law (Hamden, CT: Archon Books, 1972)

Vagts, Detlev F., 'Hegemonic International Law', (2001) 95 *American Journal of International Law* 843–848

Vattel, Emer de, *The Law of Nations or Principles of Natural Law Applied to the Conduct and to the Affairs of Nations and of Sovereigns* (Charles G. Fenwick trans., Washington, DC: Carnegie Institution of Washington, 1916)

Verzijl, J. H. W., *International Law in Historical Perspective* (Leiden: A. W. Sijthoff, 1968), I

Victoria, Franciscus de, *De Indis et de Ivre Belli Relectiones* (Ernest Nys ed., John Pawley Bate trans., Washington, DC: Carnegie Institution of Washington, 1917)

Wade, Robert Hunter, 'The Invisible Hand of American Empire', (2003) 17(2) *Ethics and International Affairs* 77–88

'Japan, the World Bank, and the Art of Paradigm Maintenance: The East Asian Miracle in Political Perspective', (May 1996) 217 *New Left Review* 3–36

Walker, Thomas Alfred, *A History of the Law of Nations: From the Earliest Times to the Peace of Westphalia* (Cambridge: Cambridge University Press, 1899)

Watson, Adam, *The Evolution of International Society: A Comparative Approach* (London: Routledge, 1992)

Webster, Daniel, US Secretary of State, Letter to Henry Fox, British Minister in Washington (April 24, 1841), 29 *British and Foreign State Papers* 1840–1841 (London: HM Stationery Office, 1857), p. 1138

Wedgwood, Ruth, 'The Fall of Saddam Hussein: Security Council Mandates and Preemptive Self-Defense', (2003), 97 *American Journal of International Law* 576–585

Weeramantry, Christopher G., *Nauru: Environmental Damage Under International Trusteeship* (New York: Oxford University Press, 1992)

Wendt, Alexander, *Social Theory of International Politics* (Cambridge: Cambridge University Press, 1999)

Westlake, John, *Chapters on the Principles of International Law* (Cambridge: Cambridge University Press, 1894)

Wheaton, Henry, *Elements of International Law* (Boston: Little, Brown and Co., 1866)

Wickremasinghe, Nira, 'From Human Rights to Good Governance: The Aid Regime in the 1990s', in Mortimer Sellers (ed.), *The New World Order: Sovereignty, Human Rights and Self-Determination of Peoples* (Oxford: Berg Publishers, 1996), pp. 305–326

Wilde, Ralph, 'From Danzig to East Timor and Beyond: The Role of International Territorial Administration', (2001) 95 *American Journal of International Law* 583–606

Williams, Patricia, *The Alchemy of Race and Rights* (Cambridge, MA: Harvard University Press, 1991)

Williams, Jr., Robert A., *The American Indian in Western Legal Thought: The Discourses of Conquest* (New York: Oxford University Press, 1990)

Willoughby, W. W. and C. G. Fenwick, *Types of Restricted Sovereignty and of Colonial Autonomy* (Washington, DC: Government Printing Office, 1919)

Wilson, Woodrow, 'The Fourteen Points' (January 8, 1918), reprinted in Ruth Cranston, *The Story of Woodrow Wilson: Twenty-Eighth President of the United States, Pioneer of World Democracy* (New York: Simon & Schuster, 1945), pp. 461–463

Wing, Adrien Katherine, 'A Critical Race Feminist Conceptualization of Violence: South African and Palestinian Women', (1997) 60 *Albany Law Review* 943–976

Woolf, Leonard, *Empire and Commerce in Africa: A Study in Economic Imperialism* (London: Allen & Unwin, 1920)

  The Village in the Jungle (London: Arnold, 1913)

Woolf, Virginia, *Mrs. Dalloway* (New York: Harcourt, Brace & Co., 1925)

'Work of the Permanent Mandates Commission', (1926) 10 *League of Nations Official Journal* 1306 at 1310

Wright, Quincy, *Mandates Under the League of Nations* (Chicago: University of Chicago Press, 1930, New York: Greenwood Press, 1968)

Yanaghita, M., Note, 'The Welfare and Development of the Natives in Mandated Territories', *Permanent Mandates Commission, Annexes to the Minutes of the Third Session*, League of Nations Doc. A.19 (Annexes) 1923 VI at 282 (1923)

Yee, Sienho, 'The Potential Impact of the Possible US Response to the 9–11 Atrocities on the Law Regarding the Use of Force and Self-Defence', (2002) 1 *Chinese Journal of International Law* 280–287

Yoo, John, 'International Law and the War in Iraq', (2003) 97 *American Journal of International Law* 563–576

Young, Robert J. C., *Postcolonialism: An Historical Introduction* (Oxford: Blackwell, 2001)

Zimmern, Alfred, 'International Law and Social Consciousness', (1935) 20 *Transactions of the Grotius Society* 25–44

Index

Abernethy, David, 174
Abi-Saab, Georges, 198, 202, 237
Abu Dhabi, 226, 227, 242
acquired rights, 213, 214–216, 220, 239, 242, 243
Afghanistan, 278, 279, 299–301, 306
Africa
  Berlin Conference *see* Berlin Africa Conference 1884–5
  mandate territories, 116, 121
  nineteenth-century sovereign states, 58
  post-colonial boundaries, 205–207
  structural adjustment programmes, 260
  terra nullius, 91
  treaties with chiefs, 71
aggression, 30, 135
Al Qaeda, 278
alcohol, sale, 122
Alexander VI, Pope, 17
Alexandrowicz, C. H., 36, 38, 58, 70
Alford, William, 284
Algeria, 139
alienation, 105, 108
Alvarez, Alejandro, 109, 130, 136, 154, 155
Alvarez, Jose, 194, 296
ambassadors, 23, 43
Amerindians *see* Indians (Amerindians)
Amin, Samir, 182, 246
AMINOIL, 242–243
Anand, R. P., 7, 108, 198, 200–201, 202, 208
Annan, Kofi, 292, 299
Ansah, Tawia, 275
anthropology, 63, 66, 265
anti-colonial movements, 72, 137, 138–139
arbitral decisions
  complicity with colonialism, 241, 242
  post-colonial foreign investment disputes, 223, 225–226

sources of law for international contracts, 226–235, 237–238
Asia
  1997 crisis, 256
  Asian Values, 255–256, 271
  capitulations, 85, 87–90
  colonial period, 108
  degree of civilisation, 61
  economic development, 255–256
  legal systems, 228, 229
  and rule of law, 200
  sovereign states, 58
Asquith of Bishopstone, Lord, 227, 228, 229, 238, 242, 243
assimilation
  by colonisation, 82–84
  by compliance with civilisation standards, 67, 84–87
  by protectorates, 87–90
  by treaty, 67–82
  mandate control techniques, 186–187
  positivist project, 66
  and sovereignty, 66
  techniques, 66, 67–90
Atlantic Charter 1941, 212
Austin, John
  customary law, 46
  definition of law, 45, 62, 99
  definition of sovereignty, 58, 88, 99
  influence, 44–46, 57, 63
  and international law, 5, 34, 41, 44–46, 50, 64
Australia
  Aborigines, 83, 112
  mandate power, 121
  and Nauru, 1, 144, 175, 187, 218
  terra nullius, 33, 111
Austria, 92, 181
Austro-Hungarian Empire, 119
Axis of Evil, 277–278, 306

native cultures
  chiefs, 168, 170–171
  and Mandate System, 161–168, 175
  and modernity, 168–171
  and political institutions, 168–171
  preservation, 168–170
  and scientific assessments, 185
  transformation through economics,
    162–168
natural law
  dynamic of difference, 315–316
  exclusion from sovereignty, 26–28
  and human law, 41–42
  international law, 35
  positivist departure from, 40–48, 54–55
  revival, 125
  sovereigns, 41
  universalism, 52, 54
  Vitoria, 11, 16, 17–21, 23
natural resources *see* permanent
  sovereignty over natural resources
Nauru, 1–2, 123, 175, 176, 178, 187, 191,
  194, 218
Negri, Antonio, 245, 314
Nehru, Jawaharlal, 172, 192
neo-colonialism, 11, 118, 192
neo-conservatism, 245
neo-liberalism, 236, 240, 245, 256, 260,
  262, 271
Netherlands, 12, 92, 215, 216
new imperialism
  as self-defence, 291–298, 304
  defensive imperialism, 292, 294–298
  generally, 273–274
  and old forms, 314
  United States, 273, 279–291, 318–319
  war on terror, 274–279, 302–303
New International Economic Order, 10–11,
  199, 211–220, 235, 236, 245, 313
New Zealand, 1, 121, 144, 175
Nicaragua Case, 303–304
Niger river, 74, 92
Nigeria, 74, 158, 164
nineteenth-century imperialism
  complicity of international law with, 109
  economic imperialism, 141
  expansion, 32–33, 65, 67
  and formalism, 195
  intellectual imperialism, 63
  and science, 48
  and trade, 67–69
nineteenth-century jurists *see also* specific
    writers
  legacy, 107–114
  positivism *see* positivism
  prominent names, 39
  scientific international law, 101

Nkrumah, Kwame, 118
Non-Aligned Movement, 306
non-European–non-civilised societies
  alienation, 105, 108
  anthropological classification, 61, 78
  assimilation, 40, 66, 67–90
  characteristics, 63, 311–312
  compliance with civilisation standards,
    67, 84–87
  contracts, 226–235, 240
  control techniques, 186–190, 192,
    264–266
  disempowerment by international law,
    312
  governance, 247–254
  guardianship, 76
  imposition of international law on, 54
  Islamic states, 277
  legal personality, 77–78, 82, 95–96, 105,
    219, 220
  legal system replacement, 146
  and Mandate System, 149–156
  native welfare in mandates, 158–162
  neo-colonial attitudes, 193–194
  outside law, 66
  peripherality, 35
  and positivism, 37
  positivist characterisation, 66
  and positivist definition of sovereignty,
    56–65
  positivist distinction, 52–56, 62–63, 70,
    112, 252
  positivist exclusion from sovereignty, 35,
    52–63, 65, 102–107
  recognition *see* recognition
  and rules of international law, 242–244
  sale of alcohol to, 122
  scientific data on, 186
  and self-defence, 304–309
Non-Proliferation Treaty, 305
North Korea, 277
Northrop, F. S., 200
Norway, 92
nuclear weapons, 304–305
Nuclear Weapons Case, 293, 294, 304–305
Nyamu, Celestine, 272
Nyasaland, 73–74

occupation
  Berlin Conference, 93–94
  and sovereignty, 82–84
oil resources, 144, 163
Oppenheim, Lassa
  and Austin, 45
  and natural law, 43
  nature of law, 48
  positivist, 39, 40

pragmatism
  basis of jurisprudence, 188–189
  challenge to positivism, 118, 127–131
  and colonialism, 195
  dynamic of difference, 315–316
  from formalism to, 127–131
  inter-war period, 10, 11, 118
  and Mandate System, 180–181
  and native labour, 164–166
pre-emptive self-defence, 275–277, 279,
    293–298, 300
primitive societies, 4, 9
proper law, international contracts,
    226–235
property rights, non-Christians, 18
protectorates
  assimilation technique, 67, 87–90
  flexibility, 89–90
  internal and external sovereignty, 85,
    87–90
  purpose, 88–90
  and sovereignty, 85, 87–90, 105–106
psychology, 134, 187, 265
Puerto Rico, 288–289
Pufendorf, Samuel, 43–44, 295

Qatar, 226
quasi-sovereignty, 76–78
quasi-treaties, 232, 233, 234–235

race
  basis of international law, 103
  centrality of colonial discrimination, 7
  critical race theory, 8, 289–291
  and League of Nations, 146
  positivism, 40
  positivist racialisation of law, 55, 56
  positivist racialisation of sovereignty,
    99–107
  US racism, 288
  vocabulary, 101
railroads, 159, 163
Rajagopal, Balakrishnan, 267
recognition
  doctrine, 75–76, 79
  non-European states, 53, 242
  and positivism, 98–100
  principles, 78–80
  purposes, 76
Rees, M. Van, 150, 151, 161
Renaissance, 29
Richardson, Henry, 290
right to education, 260
right to health, 260
Rivers, W. H. R., 175
rogue states, 270, 277–278, 279, 291, 297,
    304

Roling, B. V. A., 198
Roman Empire, 96
Roosevelt, Theodore, 138
Root, Elihu, 145, 281–285, 288
Ruanda-Urundi, 171, 172–173, 190
rule of law
  Asian societies, 200
  civil states, 296
  colonial function, 193, 267
  imperial version, 272
  international order, 124
  Mandate System, 267–268
  universalism, 320
Russia, 92, 119, 137, 139
Rwanda, 171, 194

Said, Edward, 38, 320
Samoa, 286
Saracens, 17, 26, 27
Sarraut, Albert, 143
science
  and Bretton Woods Institutions, 193
  and colonial project, 66, 185–186
  economic development, 264–265
  international law as, 48–52
  and native cultures, 185
  nineteenth-century status, 48
  and positivism, 101, 128
  social sciences, 128–131, 136
self-defence
  Grotius, 292–293
  history, 291–298
  new imperialism, 291–298, 304
  pre-emptive self-defence, 275–277, 279,
    293–298, 300
  and terrorism, 291–298, 303–309
  Third World, 303–309
  Vitoria, 22, 292, 294–295
self-determination
  debate, 99
  and international law, 35
  and PSNR, 211, 212, 219
  UN adoption of doctrine, 196
  and Woodrow Wilson, 139
self-government
  Iraq, 280
  and League of Nations, 118
  mandates, 119, 121, 140, 180, 192, 266
  US policy in Philippines and Iraq,
    282–287
self-knowledge, 320
September 11 events, 274, 275, 291–292,
    299–301, 306
Siam, 58, 67, 84, 138
Sierra Leone, 139
Sinha, Prakash, 200, 202
Slaughter, Anne-Marie, 296, 297

CAMBRIDGE STUDIES IN INTERNATIONAL AND COMPARATIVE LAW

Transboundary Damage in International Law
Hanqin Xue

European Criminal Procedures
Edited by Mireille Delmas-Marty and John Spencer

The Accountability of Armed Opposition Groups in International Law
Liesbeth Zegveld

Sharing Transboundary Resources
International Law and Optimal Resource Use
Eyal Benvenisti

International Human Rights and Humanitarian Law
René Provost

Remedies Against International Organisations
Basic Issues
Karel Wellens

Diversity and Self-Determination in International Law
Karen Knop

The Law of Internal Armed Conflict
Lindsay Moir

International Commercial Arbitration and African States
Amazu A. Asouzu

The Enforceability of Promises in European Contract Law
James Gordley

International Law in Antiquity
David J. Bederman

Money-Laundering
Guy Stessens

Good Faith in European Contract Law
Reinhard Zimmerman and Simon Whittaker

On Civil Procedure
J. A. Jolowicz

Trusts
A Comparative Study
Maurizio Lupoi

The Right to Property in Commonwealth Constitutions
Tom Allen

International Organizations Before National Courts
August Reinisch

The Changing International Law of High Seas Fisheries
Francisco Orrego Vicuña

Trade and the Environment
Damien Geradin

Unjust Enrichment
Hanoch Dagan

Religious Liberty and International Law in Europe
Malcolm D. Evans

Ethics and Authority in International Law
Alfred P. Rubin

Sovereignty Over Natural Resources
Nico Schrijver

The Polar Regions and the Development of International Law
Donald R. Rothwell

Fragmentation and the International Relations of Micro-States
Jorri Duursma

Principles of the Institutional Law of International Organizations
C. F. Amerasinghe